CONTENTS

MID-ATLANTIC AND ONTARIO

UPPER SOUTH

Country Inns
and
Back Roads

NORTH AMERICA

1993–1994

Jerry Levitin

HarperPerennial

A Division of *HarperCollins*Publishers

Other books by Jerry Levitin

Country Inns and Back Roads, New England
Country Inns and Back Roads, California
Country Inns and Back Roads, Britain and Ireland

FIRST EDITION

Designed by Joan Greenfield

ISSN: 70-615664
ISBN: 0-06-273194-7

93 94 95 96 97 ◆/RRD 6 5 4 3 2 1

PREFACE

When I became responsible for revising the late Norman Simpson's Berkshire Traveller series in February 1989, I was surprised to learn that most books on inns and bed and breakfast establishments are written by authors who do not visit the inns they write about. In fact, many reviews are simply paid advertisements, written by the innkeepers, and the publisher receives a payment for the inclusion.

You can feel assured that the inns and B&B's in *Country Inns and Back Roads: North America* are visited on a regular basis and the reviews are updated each year. And since there is no cost for inclusion, you can be doubly sure that each inn listed is based on its own merits.

I have also noticed that few guidebooks take into account the personalities of the innkeepers. Guidebooks will list facts regarding the inns' settings, locations, and interior decoration, but as Norman Simpson believed, the key to a successful inn is the traveler's feeling of being welcomed. An efficiently run, beautifully decorated inn situated on a lovely site will not be listed between the covers of any of the *Country Inns and Back Roads* books if it is missing that intangible human warmth. Of course, to determine that extra ingredient, the inn and its innkeepers need to be visited.

In past years, I have distinguished between full-service inns that serve lunch and dinner and bed & breakfast inns, which serve only the morning meal. These were reviewed in two different books, *Country Inns and Back Roads: North America* and *Bed & Breakfast American Style*, respectively. However, In 1992 I decided to combine the two to list the best of both worlds, plus a few select small hotels that never quite fit into either of the old books. You'll find this new format to continue in the future for *Country Inns and Back Roads: North America* and in my two new regional guides, *Country Inns and Back Roads: New England* and *Country Inns and Back Roads: California*.

The change is based on our nation's traveling habits. Many states and areas within states do not offer many traditional inns, but may have plenty of B&Bs. For example, the West tends to have inns that spread out with cottages or single-story lodges. Classic inns, with the restaurant on the ground floor and the rooms above, are generally found in the East. Why not, then, let you select from one book only?

In addition, many readers told me that going from inn to inn made them crave a respite from the full-course dinners that they were being served each night. For a change, they welcome a B&B or a hotel where many meal options are available.

But all the books in the series still share that *Country Inns and Back Roads* feeling—a hospitality, a warmth that makes you want to return again and again.

Although there are exceptions to every rule, this book generally lists lodgings that have five or more rooms to rent, but no more than 40; a common area where guests can congregate away from the public; private baths; high standards of cleanliness; and innkeeper involvement. The meals are freshly prepared and served in a relaxing atmosphere.

I look for a place that caters to the overnight guest first, rather than the dining guest. This preference eliminates some very fine restaurants with guest rooms above. My ideal is the inn that only serves houseguests. However, financial considerations often require the innkeeper to open the dining room to the general public.

HOW THE BOOK IS ORGANIZED

This book is divided into geographical sections. Each of these sections has its own keyed map showing the approximate location of every accommodation. Of further assistance is the Index, which lists the establishments alphabetically and another index that lists the towns alphabetically and the Inn's rates. We have also compiled some new indexes that can help you locate inns offering special activities or amenities.

The paragraphs following the narrative accounts of my visits contain essential information about the amenities offered and nearby recreational and cultural attractions. Reasonably explicit driving directions are also included here.

If you are displeased with one of my selections, or if you feel that a wonderful inn has inadvertently been overlooked, please let me hear from you by using the form printed in the back of the book.

MEAL PLANS

You'll notice references to the following "plans" throughout the text and also in the index of rates. Here are some thumbnail definitions of the terms.

"European plan" means that rates for rooms and meals are separate. "American plan" means that all meals are included in the cost of the room. "Modified American plan" means that breakfast and dinner are included in the cost of the room. The rates at certain inns-commonly known as "bed and breakfasts" include a continental or full breakfast with the lodging.

RATES

I include a listing of rates in the Index. Space limitations preclude any more than a general range of rates for each inn, and these should not be considered firm quotations. Please check with the inns for their various rates and special packages. It should be noted that many small inns do not have night staffs, and innkeepers will appreciate it if calls are made before 8:00 P.M.

RESERVATIONS & CANCELLATIONS

At most of the inns listed in this book, a deposit is required for a confirmed reservation. Guests are requested to please note arrival and departure dates carefully. The deposit will be forfeited if the guest arrives after the date specified or departs before the final date of the reservation. Refunds will generally be made only if the reservation is canceled 7 to 14 days in advance of the arrival date, depending upon the policy of the individual inn, and a service charge will be deducted from the deposit.

It must be understood that a deposit ensures that your accommodations will be available as confirmed and also assures the inn that the accommodations are sold as confirmed. Therefore, when situations arise necessitating your cancellation on short notice, your deposit will not be refunded.

FOR FOREIGN TRAVELLERS

Welcome to North America! Many of you are making your first visit, and we're delighted that you'll be experiencing some of the *real* United States and Canada by visiting these country inns. Incidentally, all of them will be very happy to help you make arrangements and reservations at other inns listed in the book.

AUTHOR'S BACKGROUND

Most writers of inn guidebooks have never had the experience of actually owning and operating an inn. I presently own the award winning Inn at Sunrise Point near Camden, Maine, a three-room, four-cottage B&B that is on the ocean's edge. In addition, I owned and operated an urban inn in San Francisco for five years, and I've run a consulting business for innkeepers. In the summer you will find me either visiting Inns for the books or at my Inn in Camden, Maine.

Northern New England and

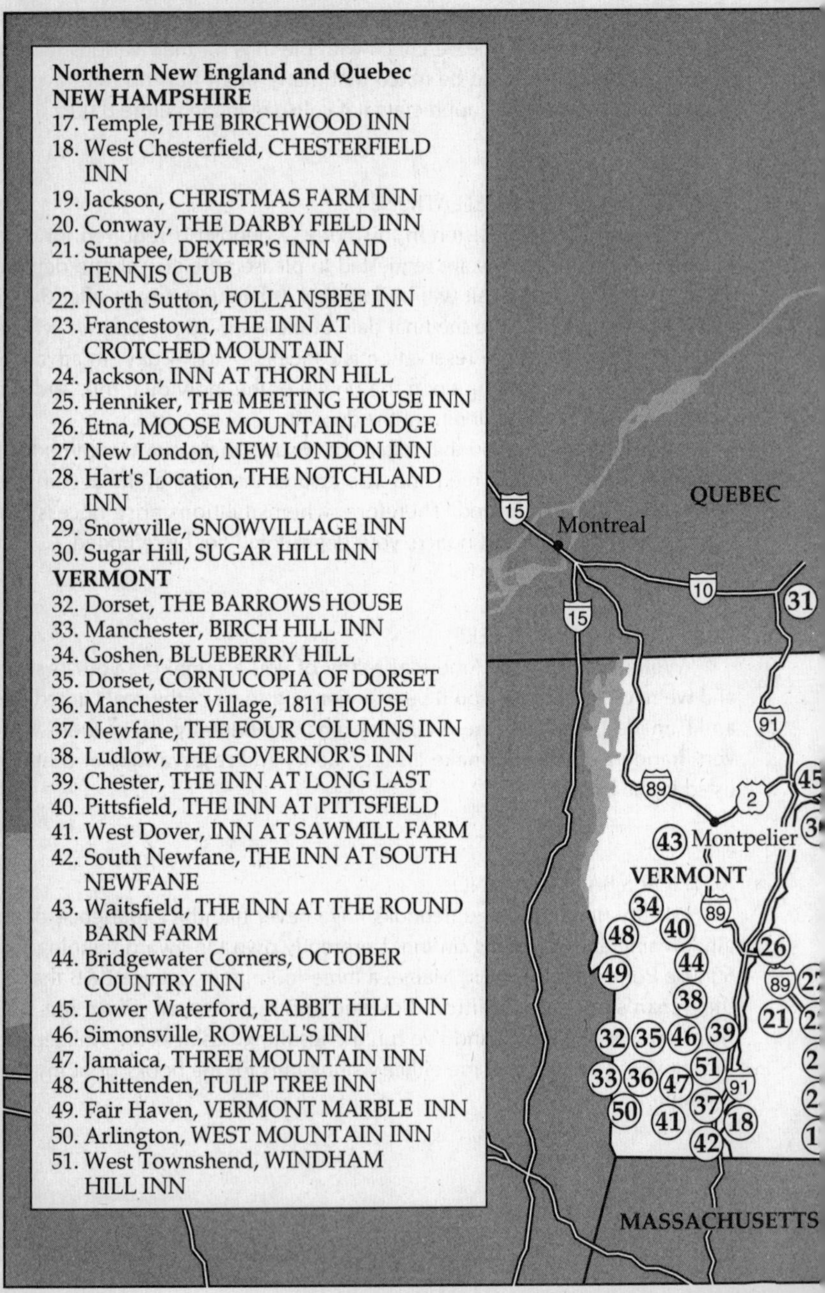

QUEBEC

15 Montreal

15

10

31

91

89

2

45

43 Montpelier

VERMONT

34

40

89

26

48

44

89

2

49

38

21

2

32 35 46 39

2

51

33 36 47

91

2

50 41

37 18

2

42

1

MASSACHUSETTS

Quebec

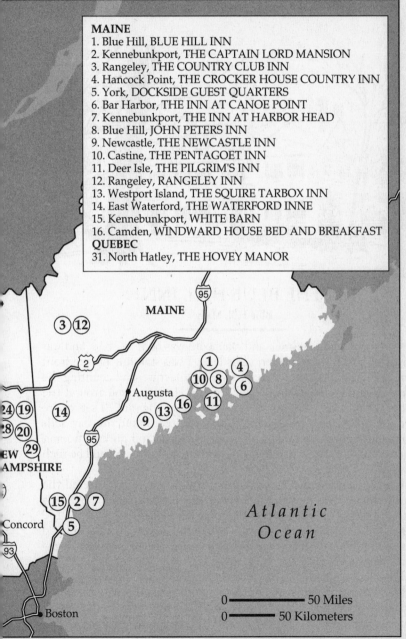

MAINE
1. Blue Hill, BLUE HILL INN
2. Kennebunkport, THE CAPTAIN LORD MANSION
3. Rangeley, THE COUNTRY CLUB INN
4. Hancock Point, THE CROCKER HOUSE COUNTRY INN
5. York, DOCKSIDE GUEST QUARTERS
6. Bar Harbor, THE INN AT CANOE POINT
7. Kennebunkport, THE INN AT HARBOR HEAD
8. Blue Hill, JOHN PETERS INN
9. Newcastle, THE NEWCASTLE INN
10. Castine, THE PENTAGOET INN
11. Deer Isle, THE PILGRIM'S INN
12. Rangeley, RANGELEY INN
13. Westport Island, THE SQUIRE TARBOX INN
14. East Waterford, THE WATERFORD INNE
15. Kennebunkport, WHITE BARN
16. Camden, WINDWARD HOUSE BED AND BREAKFAST
QUEBEC
31. North Hatley, THE HOVEY MANOR

MAINE

95

③ ⑫

2

Augusta

①

⑩ ⑧ ④
⑥

㉔ ⑲

⑭

⑯ ⑪

⑨ ⑬

㉘ ⑳

㉙

95

EW
AMPSHIRE

⑮ ② ⑦

Concord ⑤

93

*Atlantic
Ocean*

0 ———— 50 Miles
0 ——— 50 Kilometers

● Boston

Maine

THE BLUE HILL INN
Blue Hill, Maine

This home of dignified brick and clapboard was built in 1830, and was converted to a village inn ten years later. I was standing on the front lawn, admiring the lovely Federal-style architecture, and counting the many chimneys, when innkeeper Donald Hartley came around the corner with a load of wood. "Good afternoon!" he said. "I see you're here for our sailing excursion." I was excited about the day sails arranged for guests aboard the 50-foot New England pinky schooner *Summertime*, but didn't realize my new white deck shoes would be such a giveaway.

Donald told me more about the inn's history as we entered the front hallway. "We've celebrated its sesquicentennial in 1990, as a matter of fact. The inn has been in continuous operation now for 150 years." I also learned that the inn's wonderful granite foundation had been quarried locally, and that the inn is listed on the National Register of Historic Places.

Mary and Donald Hartley prior to their careers as innkeepers, were both active in the management of community-based programs for the developmentally and mentally disabled. "The inn offers us the opportunity to meet and enjoy people, and to broaden our span of skills," Mary explained, as she readied the tray of scrumptious-looking hors d'oeuvres for the nightly innkeepers' reception. The reception is held in the two cozy parlors, or the perennial garden where cocktails, wine, and soft drinks are available.

The inn's common rooms, dining room, and eleven guest rooms are decorated with 19th-century furnishings. The parlors offer comfortable easy chairs and couches grouped around attractive, working fireplaces. Oriental carpets accent polished wood floors, and colorful print wall-papers contrast with crisp, white trims. Many of the guest rooms have fireplaces, and all have private baths, some with old-fashioned tubs.

New to the Inn is a 1850 pump melodian, hammock for the garden and packages with a pinky schooner for a day of sailing and overnight aboard.

When Mary and Don took over the inn, they made it a priority to provide the most wonderful food possible and hired a new chef de cuisine who specializes in contemporary foods prepared with classical French techniques.

When I returned, feeling like an old salt with an enormous appetite, the aromas were even more tantalizing. Dinner is served by candlelight and includes six courses, beginning with homemade soup. I was served a subtle chicken and lentil finished with chive broth. My entrée of sea scallops and spinach and mushrooms with tomato-basil coulis was melt-in-the-mouth tender. A sorbet was offered to clear the palate before a crisp, colorful salad of watercress and tomatoes dressed with walnut vinaigrette was served. A slice of rich flourless chocolate torte with a dollop of coffee cream made me wish I had room for seconds, but I knew morning would bring a full breakfast.

The Blue Hill Inn is in the center of the village, so galleries, antique shops, and fine stores are within walking distance. A weekly concert series takes place all summer at Kneisel Hall, and the famous Haystack School of Crafts is only a short drive away. In the winter, Blue Hill Mountain has cross-country skiing and snowshoeing. But I think I'll stick to the water, and keep my deck shoes handy. Maybe I'll even add a captain's hat next year!

THE BLUE HILL INN, P.O. Box 403, Blue Hill, ME 04614; 207-374-2844. An 11-gue-stroom (private baths) historic inn located in the center of the village of Blue Hill. All-size beds. Open year-round. Modified American plan, and B&B rates. Wonderful food. Water sports, music festivals, and Acadia National Park nearby. No pets. Smoking not permitted. Mary and Donald Hartley, owners/hosts.

DIRECTIONS: From Augusta, take Exit 95. Take Rte. 3 south of Belfast, through Bucksport; 2 mi. east of Bucksport, take Rte. 15 south to Blue Hill. From Bangor, take Rte. 5 south. From Ellsworth, take Rte. 172 west.

THE CAPTAIN LORD MANSION
Kennebunkport, Maine

I remember it very well: in fact, it was only last summer. It was a Wednesday morning in mid-July and I joined the Captain Lord breakfast group at nine-thirty. (There had been an earlier breakfast group at eight-thirty.) Many of the guests were seated in a large but somewhat formal dining room enjoying coffee and planning the day's activities. A large jigsaw puzzle was on the dining room table and a couple of guests were playing Chinese checkers in one corner. The Chippendale chairs, beautiful cabinets, and crystal chandelier were indications that this was indeed an important room during the many years of the mansion's existence.

Meanwhile, the morning breakfast chimes were rung, and almost as one, the waiting guests rose, crossed the hallway, and walked into the ample Captain Lord kitchen, where breakfast is served.

I took advantage of the moment to walk around and admire the handsome woodwork and lovely period wallpapers of this mansion, built during the War of 1812.

I walked to the front of the house where a beautiful curving banister led up a rather formal staircase to the third floor. Throughout the mansion, Rick and Bev have displayed antiques, Oriental rugs, and other tasteful *objets d'art*. One parlor has been set aside as a gift shop offering attractive mementos of the area, as well as smaller items such as cups, saucers, plates and the like.

Ample use has been made of the generously-sized hallways on the second and third floors, which contain handsome cabinets, antique children's sleighs, duck decoys, quilts, prints of sailing ships, a spinning wheel, and even a basket of washed wool.

I peeked into a few of the spotless guest rooms whose doors were open, and there fluffy comforters, handmade quilts or 100% wool blankets, and Posturepedic mattresses reigned supreme. There are additional rooms in Phoebe's Fantasy, a beautiful Federal house next door, named for Captain Lord's wife. Furnished in much the same manner, it has king- and queen-sized four-posters and canopied beds, antiques, and working fireplaces.

I returned to the kitchen where the guests were all seated around the lovely harvest table, listening to Rick tell his tales and wonderful jokes. There was lots of laughter and appreciative comments about the breakfast of orange juice, fresh homemade breads, muffins, toast, and coffee, and, if desired, a soft-boiled egg.

Being in the hospitality business as long as I have, I begin to appreciate those innkeepers that not only are successful, but give something back to the industry without always looking for a handout. Rick and Bev are always ready and willing to give advice on the telephone to fledgling newcomers or packing a bag to speak at seminars or conferences throughout the U.S. I'm also grateful to them for their advice in my task of updating this book.

THE CAPTAIN LORD MANSION, Box 800, Kennebunkport, ME 04046; 207-967-3141. A 16-guestroom (private baths) mansion-inn in a seacoast village. All-sized beds available. Lodgings include breakfast. No other meals served. Open year-round. Near the Rachel Carson Wildlife Refuge, the Seashore Trolley Museum, the Brick Store Museum, and lobster boat tours. Bicycles, hiking, xc skiing, deep-sea fishing, golf, indoor swimming, and tennis nearby. No pets. One house cat in residence. Bev Davis and Rick Litchfield, owners/hosts.

DIRECTIONS: Take Exit 3 (Kennebunk) from the Maine Tpke. Take left on Rte. 35 and follow signs through Kennebunk to Kennebunkport. Take left at traffic light at Sunoco station. Go over drawbridge and take first right onto Ocean Ave., then take fifth left off Ocean Ave. (3/10 mi.). The mansion is in the second block on left. Park behind building and take brick walk to office.

THE COUNTRY CLUB INN
Rangeley, Maine

Rangeley, Maine, is one of those places in the world that has a special kind of charisma. There are few locations that offer such beauty and grandeur in all seasons. The combination of wide skies, vast stretches of mountain woodland, and the placid aspect of Rangeley Lake have been drawing people to this part of western Maine since long before the roads were as passable and numerous as they are today.

Innkeeper Sue Crory of the Country Club Inn says, "The dramatic lake and mountain scenery surrounding us will tranquilize even the most jangled nerves." At an elevation of nearly 2,000 feet, the Country Club Inn offers a magnificent view. Each of the guest rooms has a picture window, and the dining room and lounge both offer a scenic view of the lake, which reminds me of similar stretches of lake and mountains in certain sections of Scotland—Loch Ness being one. The cathedral-ceilinged living room has heavy beams, wood paneling, and many, many different comfortable sofas, armchairs, and rocking chairs. There are jigsaw puzzles in various states of completion, huge shelves of books, and a great moosehead over one of the fieldstone fireplaces.

Sue elaborated on how they are enjoying being a year-round operation and mentioned the many activities during the summer season—excellent fishing (landlocked salmon and square-tailed trout), hiking the many trails (including the Appalachian Trail, which goes through this area), boating, canoe trips, a swimming pool, and a variety of lawn games. For those who love golf there's a challenging 18-hole public golf course adjacent to the inn. Tennis courts are nearby.

The inn is located in the heart of the northwestern mountains of Maine's ski country, surrounded by Saddleback and Sugarloaf mountains, which offer downhill and cross-country skiing.

THE COUNTRY CLUB INN, P.O. Box 680C, Rangeley, ME 04970; 207-864-3831. A 19-guestroom (private baths) resort-inn overlooking Rangeley Lake in western Maine, 45 mi. from Farmington. All-sized beds. Modified American plan. Breakfast and dinner served to travelers by reservation. Open mid-May to mid-October and late

December to late March. Near many cultural, historic, scenic, and recreational attractions. Swimming pool, horseshoes, bocci, volleyball, and croquet. A public 18-hole golf course adjacent to the inn. Tennis and lake swimming nearby. Fishing, hiking, and canoeing. Snowmobiling and xc skiing at doorstep. Downhill and xc skiing at Saddleback and Sugarloaf Mts. Two dogs in residence. CCs: Visa, MC, AE. Sue Crory and family, owners/hosts.

DIRECTIONS: From Maine Tpke., take Auburn Exit 12 and follow Rte. 4 to Rangeley. From VT and NH, take I-91 to St. Johnsbury; east on Rte. 2 to Gorham and Rte. 16 north to Rangeley. From Bar Harbor, Rte. 1A to Rte. 2 to Rte. 4. From Montreal, Rte. 10 to Rte. 112 to Rte. 147 to Rte. 114; then Rte. 26 to Rte. 16 to Rte. 4.

THE CROCKER HOUSE COUNTRY INN

Hancock Point, Maine

Finding a beguiling, secluded place for an overnight stay on a trip to Canada via U.S. I would delight many a weary traveler. And it could be the perfect solution for those who enjoy the activity and excitement of Bar Harbor, Acadia National Park, and Blue Hill, but also want a quiet hideaway nearby. On Hancock Point, three minutes from the ocean, the Crocker House Country Inn is all of the above.

The entrance leads into a living room that is electric, to say the least, with good comfortable old wicker furniture, a big window seat, some rather striking modern primitive paintings, a very handsome rug of Indian design, a backgammon set, and lots of growing plants. At the very moment I walked in I was greeted with a flute concerto by Jean Pierre Rampal wafting from the stereo. It all seemed quite casual and quite natural.

The guest rooms are bright and cheerful. Almost all of them have been redecorated and some have stenciling on the upper walls. They are large enough to accommodate two people very comfortably.

Innkeeper Richard Malaby told me a little bit about the past history of this part of Maine. "Hancock was once a thriving shipbuilding community and also the terminus of the Washington, D.C., to Bar Harbor express train. It was the port from which the famed Sullivan Quarry shipped its cobblestones to pave the streets of Boston, New York, and Philadelphia. I'm afraid that the Crocker House is a lone survivor of those days of the past."

One might expect the dinner menu to consist of good hearty upcountry Maine food; therefore, I was quite surprised to find some international dishes such as poached salmon Florentine, gray sole meuniére, and veal Monterey, which I ordered. It was very thinly sliced veal, sautéed in Madeira with avocado and tomato and topped with Monterey jack cheese. The menu also had filet au poivre, scallops in sorrel and cream, broiled swordfish, broiled halibut Dijon, and other treasures from the sea.

THE CROCKER HOUSE COUNTRY INN, Hancock Point, ME 04640; 207-422-6806. A 10-guestroom (private baths) secluded country inn about 8 mi. north of Ellsworth, ME. Queen, double, amd twin beds. Breakfast and dinner served daily. Open from May 1 to Thanksgiving. Bicycles and dock moorings available for guests. Tennis, swimming, and walking nearby. Just 30 min. from Mount Desert Island, Acadia National Park, and Bar Harbor. Blue Hill and the east Penobscot peninsula easily accessible. Richard Malaby, owner/host.

DIRECTIONS: Follow Rte. 1 approx. 8 mi. north from Ellsworth. Turn right at sign for Hancock Point and continue approx. 5 mi.

DOCKSIDE GUEST QUARTERS

York, Maine

Harriette Lusty and I were having a light luncheon on the porch of the restaurant at Dockside Guest Quarters. It was a day such as I have experienced here many times in the past, watching the wonderful harbor traffic as all kinds of craft make their way through the harbor to the ocean. Even though it had been a very hot day out on I-95, here on this lovely porch there was a wonderful breeze that made even sitting in the sun a joy.

"Oh, we do some very wonderful things here on the Fourth of July," Harriette exclaimed. "We have a thirty-five-foot-long flag with only thirty-seven stars that is brought out, and placed on the lawn, because

it is much too large for any flagpole. At noontime we set off our cannon, and all of our staff and their families and friends, as well as our neighbors, come over and stand by. It's really quite a ceremony and we leave one of our postcards at each door, inviting all the guests to come up to the shoot. It takes place right over there by the flagpole. We use that brass one-pounder saluting cannon usually kept in the hallway near the front door. Everybody gets into a wonderful Independence Day mood."

The Dockside Guest Quarters is composed of the original New England homestead of the 1880s, called the Maine House, and four multi-unit cottage buildings of contemporary design, with guest rooms that have their own porches and water views. The three-level restaurant is also separate and overlooks the harbor and marina docks.

The innkeepers are the David Lusty family. David is a real "State of Maine" man, complete with a wonderful Down East accent. The Lustys have raised four sons at Dockside, and now their second son, Eric, and his wife Carol have returned to take a hand in the running of the inn. Third son Philip and his wife Anne have also joined the family business. Philip is the new manager of The Restaurant.

There's always a great deal of Colonial history to share in the York area; the center of town is a National Historic District. This is within a pleasant walking distance of Dockside. Tours are conducted by the York Historical Society. "Our statue of a Civil War Confederate soldier instead of a 'Yankee in Blue' is always an object of curiosity," David told me. "Our Union soldier statue has been located in a small town in South Carolina."

DOCKSIDE GUEST QUARTERS, P.O. Box 205, Harris Island Rd., York, ME 03909; 207-363-2868. A 21-guestroom (19 private baths; some studio suites with kitchenettes) waterside country inn 10 mi. from Portsmouth, N.H. American plan available. All-sized beds available. Continental-plus breakfast served to houseguests only. Restaurant serves lunch and dinner to travelers daily except Monday In May, open Friday and Saturday only; daily from Memorial Day weekend thru end of October. York Village is a National Historic District. Wheelchair access. Lawn games, shuffleboard, badminton, fishing, and whale-watching from premises. Golf, tennis, and ocean swimming nearby; safe and picturesque paths and roadways for walks, bicycling, and jogging. Clipper is their cat in residence. CCs: Visa, MC. Eric, Carol, David, and Harriette Lusty, owners/hosts.

DIRECTIONS: From I-95 (northbound) take exit 4 (last exit before the northbound toll gate at York) to U.S. 1, then south on Rte. 1 to first light. Left at light onto Rte. 1A. Follow 1A thru center of Old York Village, take Rte. 103 (a side street off Rte. 1A leading to the harbor) across York River bridge. First left after crossing bridge and watch for signs to the inn.

THE INN AT CANOE POINT
Bar Harbor, Maine

Perched at the edge of Frenchman's Bay, the Inn at Canoe Point offers tranquility on two wooded, secluded acres surrounded by water. The English Tudor-style inn was built as a family summer cottage in the late 1800s and still retains a relaxed air. It was, in fact, a private residence until 1986 and has since been modernized. I found it difficult to remember that Bar Harbor, with its tourists and crowds, was only two miles away, so quiet and restful is the atmosphere.

Even though the mood is relaxed, the inn's interior is an elegant mixture of antiques and traditional furnishings. The main entry hall/living room has a fireplace and a baby grand piano that is always in need of exercise. In the Ocean Room, a magnificent fieldstone fireplace anchors one side, and an equally magnificent 180° view of the ocean and mountains dominates the other. A full breakfast, which can include blueberry French toast, pancakes, or a cheese-and-spinach quiche, is served here, or on the adjacent deck in sunny weather. One morning I made an attempt to finally read Hemingway's *The Old Man and the Sea* while I curled up in front of the fire, but the ever-churning sea itself continually drew my gaze, so I just gave up and enjoyed the thrill of the show.

The five guest rooms mirror the rest of the inn's warm, casual style and overlook either the water or the rocky shoreline and dark pines. All the rooms have spotless modern bathrooms. The Garret Suite, the inn's largest, takes up the third floor and includes a sleeping room with

French windows that open to the ocean, and a sitting room with a small balcony. The room can comfortably sleep four.

Innkeeper Donald Johnson had been coming to Bar Harbor for almost twenty years before buying the inn. Therefore, he is quite familiar with the surrounding area and makes an excellent tour guide.

THE INN AT CANOE POINT, Box 216, Bar Harbor, ME 04644; 207-288-9511. An elegant 5-guestroom (private baths) secluded summer cottage on Maine's coast. King, queen and twin beds. Full breakfast. Open all year. Near Bar Harbor, Acadia National Park, and the Bluenose Ferry Terminal. Not appropriate for young children. No pets. Donald Johnson and Esther Cavagnaro, owners/hosts.

DIRECTIONS: The inn is 15 mi. from Ellsworth, ME off Rte. 3; 2 mi. from Bar Harbor.

THE INN AT HARBOR HEAD
Kennebunkport, Maine

"... surrounded by sea roses, an ocean view and the tang of salt air," said the brochure describing the Inn at Harbor Head. When this sensual description materialized before my mind's eye, I leaned back in my office chair and knew it was time to head for the seaside.

The inn sits on a knoll overlooking Kennebunkport's Cape Porpoise Harbor. The weathered gray of the shingled, rambling old farm house mirrors the soft hues of the rocky, sheltered shoreline. If I were a painter, I would find unlimited material here.

Interestingly enough, I discovered that innkeeper Joan Sutter is an artist who has gone from sculpture to what she calls "wall painting." Her artistic touch can be seen throughout the inn: in the spectacular guest rooms' highly expressive murals; in her refined choice of furnishings; in the subtlety of color.

The inn's seaside cottage ambience encourages a sandals-and-soft-cotton freedom outdoors, yet the interior is sophisticated and elegant. The formal sitting room is appointed with lovely Oriental rugs, a Chinese screen, and a twinkling crystal chandelier. But don't feel restrained by this elegance; just snuggle into a wingback chair and relax.

The five romantic guest rooms have luxurious tiled baths; two have whirlpools. Each is tastefully decorated in a highly individual fashion. I was given the Garden Room, a study in Zen tranquillity. Here Joan has created a serene environment, from the "little river of rocks" that crosses the path to the canopy bed, to her drawings of plum and peach blossoms that seem to float on the wall. Even the spare lines of a twisted pine outside the French doors that open onto a private sundeck enhance the mood.

Guests have full use of the grounds, the waterfront dock, and the sun-warmed floats. Just ask for a beach permit, grab a fluffy towel and beach chair—and off you go! But before heading out with your suntan lotion and a romance novel under your arm, linger over breakfast. Mine began with with tender poached pears and continued with eggs baked in puff pastry with a perfect, lemony hollandaise sauce.

THE INN AT HARBOR HEAD, Pier Rd., Cape Porpoise, RR2 Box 1180, Kennebunkport, ME 04046; 207-967-5564. A beautifully decorated 5-guestroom (private baths) home overlooking Cape Porpoise Harbor. King and queen beds. Full breakfast. Closed Thanksgiving and Christmas weeks. No smoking or pets. CCs: Visa, MC, AE. Joan and David Sutter, owner/hosts.

DIRECTIONS: Take Rte. 9 thru Kennebunkport for 2-1/2 mi. to the village of Cape Porpoise. At Wayfarer Restaurant, leave Rte. 9E. Proceed on Pier Rd. 3/10 mi. to inn.

JOHN PETERS INN

Blue Hill, Maine

Driving down a country road in Maine, I was more than surprised to come upon an impressive, formal structure positioned on top of a grassy knoll: the John Peters Inn. Built in 1815, this historic Greek Revival mansion, with its columns and brick facade, is surrounded by twenty-five beautiful acres on the tidal waters of Blue Hill Bay.

Hosts Rick and Barbara Seeger recently renovated the inn and added a new carriage house. As Rick took me on a tour of the carriage house, he detailed the six units: small kitchens, queen-sized beds, fireplaces, and decks for lounging.

The Seegers' bouncy Welsh terrier welcomed us as we strolled into the inn's common room. A baby grand piano, beautiful antiques, and two large fireplaces create an elegant, yet comfortable, atmosphere. The guest rooms, with views of Blue Hill Bay and the countryside, reflect tasteful charm. Each is artfully decorated in a different color and has antique country furniture and Oriental rugs. Five rooms have cozy fireplaces.

Breakfast is served on the lovely enclosed porch overlooking the harbor, where you can view yachts and Maine's famous schooners. Amid crystal, silver, and linens, you will idle over Barbara's eggs Benedict, muffins, fresh-squeezed orange juice, pecan waffles, special-blend coffee, seasonal fruits, and a most marvelous treat, lobster omelets with fresh asparagus or artichoke hearts.

JOHN PETERS INN, Peters Point, Box 916, Blue Hill, ME 04614; 207-374-2116. A 14-guestroom (private baths) Greek Revival mansion and a 6-room (private baths) newly built guest house, beautifully situated on Blue Hill Bay. All-sized beds. Open all year. Walk to village of Blue Hill; 40-minute drive to Bar Harbor. Canoeing and sailing; biking and hiking on Blue Hill or in nearby Acadia National Park. Breakfast included. No pets. One dog in residence. CCs; Visa, MC. Barbara and Rick Seeger, owners/hosts.

DIRECTIONS: From the south, take coastal Rte. 1 from Camden or Rte. 3 from Augusta to Bucksport. Turn right after crossing Bucksport Bridge. Follow combined Rtes. 1 and 3 for 6 mi. to Rte. 15; take Rte 15 south to Blue Hill. Inn just 1/2 mi. north of village, just off Rte. 176 east.

THE NEWCASTLE INN
Newcastle, Maine

A bright green awning accents the entrance to this beautiful white clapboard Federal-style Colonial. Built in the 1800s as a Cape carriage house, the structure began its life as an inn during the 1930s. It is a classic New England country inn, just what Ted and Chris Sprague were looking for when they began their search in 1985.

"I'd become a bit disenchanted with teaching," Ted confided to me, "yet I still wanted a career where I could have a positive influence on others. Innkeeping offers that opportunity." After two years and many hours spent in research, on seminars, consultants, and visits to over one hundred inns, they ended up on Newcastle's stoop.

Ted and I were relaxing in lawn chairs under a towering backyard shade tree. The yard edges up to the banks of the Damariscotta River, a tidal river met by the sea, and the pristine sands of Pemaquid Beach. "Chris is a natural at this (innkeeping)," he continued, with obvious pride. "She grew up working in her father's gourmet grocery and knows good food."

Chris' award winning recipes may be sampled at breakfast and dinner, both of which are included in your room rate. In the morning, the sunlight illuminates the tones of the dining room's quarter-sawn yellow pine floors and the room just seems to glow. Breakfast includes a special homebaked bread, juice, fresh fruit and entrée. Just imagine the heady aroma of spicy gingerbread still warm from the oven! Entrées may include an egg dish, Grand Marnier French toast, fluffy lemon zest pancakes, or bread and butter pudding. Ham or country sausage accompanies your entrée.

Complimentary hors d'oeuvres are served prior to dinner. The inn has a full liquor license and offers beers, imported ales, and a variety of wines. The five-course dinner is elegant yet simple, and a real delight. Served on lovely botanical-patterned china, the menu changes with Chris' whim, and the seasons. When I visited, George's Greek lamb with kaseri cheese was the evening's special.

After dinner I took my hefty slice of apple almond-cream pie into the common room. This room's unique stenciled floor is a sample of Chris' artistry, as are the pieces of intricate crewelwork and needlepoint displayed throughout the inn.

There are two other comfortable areas for relaxation: the more formal fireplace-warmed living room, and the wicker furnished glassed and screened-in porch, a popular gathering spot during the spring and summer.

The inn's spacious hallways and staircases give way to the fifteen intimate second and third floor guest rooms. Traditional Colonial colors appear in wallpapers, borders, and bed coverings. Some rooms have canopied beds and all have private, modern bathrooms. My room, as do many of the others, had windows facing the river.

The Newcastle Inn offers seclusion, an unhurried schedule, excellent food, and charming innkeepers in Ted and Chris. They certainly made the right career change.

THE NEWCASTLE INN, River Road, Newcastle, ME 04553; 207-563-5685. A 16-guestroom (private baths) traditional New England country inn on the Damariscotta River. Open year-round. All sized beds. Modified American plan. Swimming, fishing, boating, bird watching, antiquing nearby. No smoking. No pets. CCs: Visa, MC. Chris and Ted Sprague, owners/hosts.

DIRECTIONS: In Maine take Rte. 95 north to Rte. 1 Exit (Bath/Brunswick). Go 7 mi. north of Wiscasset. Watch for Inn sign on right; go right on River Rd.

THE PENTAGOET INN
Castine, Maine

For many years I regarded Castine as one of the best-kept secrets in the world. I also discovered that when I ran into other people who knew

about Castine, we felt as if we belonged to an exclusive club—something akin to people who have climbed Mount Everest.

I'm sure that many people do stumble on Castine, but it's not on the road to anywhere. Its principal claim to fame is the fact that originally it was settled by British Loyalists, who, after the American Revolution, decided they preferred to remain under King George and so moved from Boston up to this lovely out-of-the-way location. There are many markers in the town reminding us that such an exodus did take place.

One of the first things that Lindsey and Virginia Miller and I found that we have in common was a love of porches. I've spent many a happy hour rocking on porches of country inns all over North America. "That's just the way we feel," said Virginia. "As a matter of fact, that's why we have extended the porch all the way to the back of the main building. You'll notice that we've put window boxes and standing flowerpots in as many places as possible, and our new green awning has been a real blessing."

Well, the talk went on from porches to breakfast. "I must step in here," Lindsey declared. "This morning, besides a cup of fresh tropical fruit, we had a fresh herb omelet. Our French toast is filled with cream cheese and fresh orange, and topped with blueberry sauce. In addition to that there are sausage links or grilled rib eye steak and we continue with our famous Pentagoet muffins."

In the ensuing conversation we talked about many other interesting changes the Millers had made. "When we first arrived in the fall of

1985 we became aware that the inn needed more dining space and more common areas for the guests," Virginia recalled. "We spent the first winter correcting this by creating a very inviting library with an upright Bosendorfer piano and most of our personal collection of books." I agreed that it provides a good place for guests to relax with a book, play the piano, or listen to some classical music.

"The addition of the back dining room was an inspiration," Virginia said, "and I'm happy to say we are well known for our dinners. Part of this is because we have an excellent chef and we offer a variety of main dishes including Maine lobsters, lobster pie, grilled fresh salmon steak with dilled hollandaise, a peppered rib eye steak, and a roast leg of lamb. It's part of a five-course meal which includes soup and dessert."

Some exciting things have happened above the first floor of the Pentagoet, too. For example, by redesigning the second- and third-floor guest rooms, the Pentagoet now has twelve guest rooms with private baths and two with half-baths. In addition, the annex next door, 10 Perkins Street, also has very attractive guest rooms.

THE PENTAGOET INN, Main St., P.O. Box 4, Castine, ME 04221; 207-326-8616. A 17-guestroom (private baths) inn in a seacoast village on the Penobscot Peninsula, 36 mi. from Bangor. King and queen beds available. Modified American plan includes breakfast and dinner. Dinner available to outside guests by reservation. Open May to October Tennis, swimming, backroading, village strolling, craft shops, chamber music concerts, Maine Maritime Academy, Acadia National Park, and Blue Hill nearby. No pets. One orange tabby cat in residence. Smoking on porches only. Lindsey and Virginia Miller, owners/hosts.

DIRECTIONS: From the south, follow I-95 toward Augusta and use Rte. 3 exit to Belfast. Follow Rte. 1 to a point 3 mi. past Bucksport. Turn right on Rte. 175 to Rte. 166 to Castine. Look for Maine Maritime Academy sign; turn left onto Main St.

THE PILGRIM'S INN
Deer Isle, Maine

Originally a rambling Colonial-style home, today you can enjoy a unique inn here. Travelers really have to be looking for Deer Isle and the Pilgrim's Inn. It's a good hour's drive from U.S. 1, east of Bucksport, to the Blue Hill Penninsula. Deer Isle sits just off the southern flank of the mainland, and no matter how you arrive, it's necessary to cross over the suspension bridge at Eggemoggin Reach.

A four-story, gambrel-roofed red house, this building has overlooked the long harbor on the front and the millpond in the rear since 1793. Jean and Dud Hendrick moved here a few years ago after acquir-

ing the Pilgrim's Inn. Much of the original building has remained almost completely unchanged, with the original Colonial feature of two large rooms and a kitchen on the ground floor still intact. One of these rooms is the Common Room of the present-day inn.

Most of the guest rooms are quite large and feature richly hued pine floorboards, wood stoves, country furniture, and a selection of books and magazines. They are enhanced by coordinated Laura Ashley fabrics, used for curtains, lampshades, quilts, and cushions.

Number 15 is an enchanting house in the village. It sits over the harbor, affording the occupants unparalleled sunset views from its back deck. It is completely furnished and equipped so that guests may choose to prepare their own meals if they are so foolish as to pass up Jean's fabulous cuisine. It is the quintessential honeymoon cottage or retreat for four friends (it has a hide-a-bed in front of the fireplace in the living room in addition to the upstairs bedroom).

Turning one of the first-floor parlors of the main inn into a warm reading room and library has also worked well allowing guests to quietly read.

The mail boat run to Isle au Haute is a most romantic day trip, and the sailing here is terrific.

THE PILGRIM'S INN, Deer Isle, ME 04627; 207-348-6615. A 13-guestroom (8 private baths) inn in a remote island village on the Blue Hill Peninsula on the Maine coast. Queen, double, and twin beds available. Modified American plan, May 15 to November 1, includes a hearty breakfast and a creative dinner. In season, outside dinner reservations are accepted. A 4-day minimum reservation is requested in Aug. Bicycles, badminton, table tennis, regulation horseshoes, croquet, and a rowboat for the millpond on the grounds. All types of cultural and recreational advantages, including golf, fishing, sailing, hiking, and browsing nearby. No pets. One English Springer Spaniel in residence. Dud and Jean Hendrick, owners/hosts.

DIRECTIONS: From Boston, take I-95 to Brunswick exit. Take coastal Rte. 1 north past Bucksport. Turn right on Rte. 15, which travels to Deer Isle down the Blue Hill Peninsula. At the village, turn right on Main St. (Sunset Rd.) and proceed one block to the inn on the left side of the street, opposite the harbor.

RANGELEY INN
Rangeley, Maine

Coming into the town of Rangeley, perched on scenic Rangeley Lake, I thought the big blue clapboard building with the long veranda across the front had the look of one of those grand old summer hotels.

Meeting Fay and Ed Carpenter in the roomy lobby with its country-print wallpaper and comfortable wing chairs and sofas, I had an immediate feeling of warmth and friendliness. I was not surprised to discover they had earned an Innkeeper of the Year award. "We've found innkeeping to be a very rewarding career," Ed told me. "We really enjoy getting to know our guests with all their varied backgrounds and interests."

Looking through some of the comments and letters from their guests, I realized that their cuisine played an important part in the overall picture. "Our daughter Sue is responsible for making our kitchen one of the finest in Maine," Fay said. "She's self-taught, and there just isn't anything she can't do." "That's absolutely true," Ed broke in, "I never cease to be amazed by how creative she is with her seasonings, garnishes, textures, and taste."

I had the opportunity to sample Sue's cooking, and it was indeed a pleasure. I tried the sole Victoria, which was stuffed with crabmeat, shrimp, cream cheese, finely chopped vegetables, and wrapped in phyllo dough. Some other interesting entrées with blueberry chicken,

sautéed in fresh blueberries, blueberry schnapps, and spices, and lemon grass shrimp, prepared with garlic, ginger, sliced carrots, scallions, snow peas, peppers, water chestnuts, and lemon grass.

The dining room, with its high ceiling and many windows, has an elegant but informal atmosphere. The dining tables were carefully laid with china and stemware on double rose tablecloths. The fresh flowers and candlelight added a note of romance.

"That's a beautiful antique ceiling," I exclaimed, looking up at the peach-colored, ornate pressed tin admiringly.

"I'll tell you a secret, I put that ceiling up myself," Ed replied, with refreshing candor.

I think refreshing candor may be the keynote of this inn. Ed and Fay and their two daughters, Sue, who is the chef, and Janet, who served me breakfast with a most infectious smile, have a straightforward, friendly manner that puts everyone at ease.

The guest rooms are simply furnished with country-print wallpapers and various-sized beds. Fay told me that some of the rooms still have the old clawfooted, cast-iron "soakers." "We've started to add the old-fashioned shower heads and duck curtains." There are additional motel-style rooms in a separate building, which looked very clean and comfortable.

Ed showed me around the several acres of lawn and garden bordering on Haley Pond, a bird sanctuary. Not only are there ducks, Canada geese, and herons, but at the moment, Ed tells me, they have two pairs of loons.

RANGELEY INN, P.O. Box 398, Main St., Rangeley, ME 04970; 207-864-3341 or 5641. A 51-guestroom (private baths) village inn and motor lodge on the eastern shore of Rangeley Lake in western Maine. Breakfast and dinner served daily; limited dining in early December and late spring. Wheelchair access. Summer events such as Blueberry Festival and Fiddlers' Contest and evening entertainment, also pool table and board games on premises. Guided canoe trips, dogsled races, and all the summer and winter activities of lake and mountain areas. No pets. One cat in residence. Limited smoking. Fay and Ed Carpenter, owners/hosts.

DIRECTIONS: From Maine Tpke. take Auburn Exit 12 and follow Rte. 4 to Rangeley. From NH Rte. 2, take Rte. 16 north to Rangeley. Inn is at southern end of village on Rte. 4 (Main St.).

THE SQUIRE TARBOX INN
Westport Island, Maine

Karen Mitman and I were walking through the woods behind the Squire Tarbox Inn toward Squam Creek. We were two people being

escorted by seven lively, handsome Nubian goats in various shades of brown and beige. It being June, we passed through patches of butter-cups and lupine, and our group occasionally paused while one of the goats decided to nibble.

"Come on, Garbo," Karen called. "We call her Garbo because she thinks she's kind of dramatic. We arrived at the serene saltwater inlet that has a little dock and a screened-in shed for just sitting and looking through the binoculars provided. A rowboat waits patiently for the energetic guest.

"Most of our guests are from the city, and it's just nice for them to come here and sit. The combination of the water, the sky, the clouds, the little marshy island, and the trees offers a special quiet privacy."

The Squire Tarbox is in a section of Maine that is sufficiently off the beaten track to be unspoiled and natural. The main house has both the wainscoting of the early 1800s and the rustic wide-board construc-tion of the 1700s. It is quite small—eleven guest rooms have a cozy "up country" feeling with Colonial prints and colors and some working fireplaces. A large hearth with the original bake oven, pumpkin pine floors, and hand-hewn beams set the tone for this rambling Colonial farmhouse.

There are several choices for sitting around in front of fireplaces to enjoy reading or conversation, especially in a captivating three-story barn with large doors that open out on a screened-in sundeck. There is a player piano, an antique music box, Colonial wooden toys, and English wooden puzzles for further amusement.

Karen and her husband, Bill, are very friendly, conversational peo-ple, who make innkeeping seem almost deceptively simple. Their back-ground at the Copley Plaza in Boston must have much to do with this.

Karen and I sat in the little shed and continued our conversation while the goats cavorted on the pine needles. "I know you remember when we brought in our first goats," she said. "We were a little hesitant, but they have been a most rewarding experience for our guests. Now we have a new cheesemaking room and have packaged some goat cheese for sale to our guests. The cheese is served every night before dinner as well. Dinner is at seven o'clock in an intimate Colonial dining room and usually begins with a soup that could be made with fresh fruit or vegetables. The second course is a salad, and the main course is usually local fish or chicken or an occasional roast, always served with three vegetables that reflect some creative thinking, such as mint-glazed carrots, cranberries with red cabbage, or spinach with cheese and pasta. One of the most popular desserts is a chocolate concoction known as the Squire's 'Sin Pie.'"

THE SQUIRE TARBOX INN, Westport Island, R.D. 2, Box 620, Wiscasset, ME 04578; 207-882-7693. An 11-guestroom (private baths) restored Colonial farm midway between Boston and Bar Harbor on Rte. 144 in Westport, 10 mi. from Wiscasset. All-sized beds available. Modified American plan—includes continental breakfast and full leisurely dinner. Open late May to late October Within a 30-min. drive of L.L. Bean, beaches, harbors, shops, and museums of midcoast Maine. Eleven animal pets outside. CCs: Visa, MC, AE, Dis. Bill and Karen Mitman, owners/hosts.

DIRECTIONS: From Maine Tpke., take Exit 9 and follow Rte. 95 to Exit 22 (Brunswick, ME). Take Rte. 1 to Rte. 144, 7 mi. north of Bath. Follow Rte. 144 for 8-1/2 mi. to inn.

THE WATERFORD INNE

Waterford, Maine

"There is no textbook definition of a country inn," Barbara Vanderzanden exclaimed. "We are in the country—not located in a town; we are historic—built in 1825; and we are small—ten rooms, and a mother-daughter team does it all. I believe our guests really love us because our inn is small and intimate, since it is a converted family home. When they say they feel like an honored guest in our home we know we've succeeded."

Rosalie, Barbara's mother, added, "We frequently have guests comment on how clean everything is." We were sitting on the porch enjoying the view.

What they failed to mention was their constant attention to detail and their guests' comfort.

My eye happened to travel to what was one of the most sumptuous-looking vegetable gardens I have ever seen, and it prompted a ques-

tion: "What are some of the things that you grow in your own garden for your kitchen?"

"Well, we grow practically all our own herbs," explained Rosalie, who is the cook. "We like fresh herbs in the salad dressing. We also have tomatoes, brussels sprouts, broccoli, peppers, squash, and pumpkins."

'We serve tenderloin of beef with béarnaise, shrimp Pernod, and various veal and pork dishes as entrées. Dinner is fixed-price every evening for both houseguests and visitors. We do all our own baking, and our guests seem to enjoy it very much."

At the Waterford Inne, located in the little-known Oxford Hills area of western Maine, "small and tidy" is beautiful. Merely an hour northwest of of Portland, it's a region of rolling countryside, pristine lakes, active streams and rivers, farms and forests. To city-dwellers looking for an escape from congestion, noise and bustle, it's a paradise. The pace is slower, with no freeways and very few traffic lights. There are no shopping malls here, although the shopping havens of Freeport and North Conway, just across the New Hampshire border, are less then an hour's drive away.

All of the bedrooms have been carefully decorated, usually with some theme in mind. For example, the Chesapeake Room has a fireplace stove and a private porch. The decorations are in the Eastern Shore theme, with duck decoys and waterfowl. Even the sheets and towels have colorful waterfowl on them. The Nantucket room, complete with whaling prints and harpoon; the Strawberry room, bright with red accessories; the Safari room with...well I'll let you wait and see—all of the rooms have either antiques or attractive country furniture.

THE WATERFORD INNE, Box 149, Waterford, ME 04233; 207-583-4037. A 10-gue-stroom (7 private baths) farmhouse-inn in the Oxford Hills section of southwest Maine, 8 mi. from Norway and South Paris. All-sized beds available. Closed March, April, and Thanksgiving week. Breakfast and dinner served to travelers by reservation. European plan. Within a short distance of many recreational, scenic, and cultural attractions in Maine and the White Mountains of New Hampshire. Cross-country skiing and badminton on grounds. Lake swimming, golf, rock hunting, downhill skiing, hiking, canoeing nearby. Alcoholic beverages not served. Well-behaved pets welcome; however, advance notification is required and a fee is charged. Two cats in residence. CCs: AE. Rosalie and Barbara Vanderzanden, owners/hosts.

DIRECTIONS: From Maine Tpke.: use Exit 11, follow Rte. 26 north approx. 28 mi. into Norway, then on Rte. 118 west for 8 mi. to Rte. 37 south (left turn). Go 1/2 mi., turn right at Springer's General Store, up the hill 1/2 mi. From Conway, NH: Rte 16 to Rte. 302 east to Fryeburg, ME. Take Rte. 5 out of Fryeburg to Rte. 35 south, thence to Rte. 118, which is a left fork (with Rte. 35 going right). Continue on Rte. 118 east, past Papoose Pond camping area, then watch for right turn onto Rte. 37. Go 1/2 mi. to Springer's General Store. Take immediate right turn, 1/2 mi. up hill.

THE WHITE BARN
Kennebunkport, Maine

A welcome and an "excellent table" have greeted the guests at The White Barn Inn since 1880 when it operated as a popular Boothby boardinghouse. Settled in a residential area, the luxurious inn and renowned restaurant are just a short stroll from the beach and charming township of Kennebunkport.

Kennebunkport is a post-card Maine village. Rustic fishing boats, with barnacled hulls, lobster pots, gliding seagulls, and Victorian, shingled cottages settle compatibly with art galleries and fashionable boutiques.

In 1988, Laurie Bongiorno and Laurie Cameron purchased the property, completely renovating and restoring the old inn. Both Lauries, husband and wife, embraced the project well prepared from outstanding careers in the hospitality industry.

The original industry was erected in the 1840s. As farming became secondary to housing guests, annexes and wings were added. The gatehouses and cottage were built in the early 1900s.

"We really were adamant about preserving the character sensitive to the inn," the male Laurie told me. "We wanted to meet the expectations of our guests with decor in keeping with the period of the furnishings, unique art work, and little touches that create individual, personable service."

Those little touches, like fresh flowers from the inn's floral cutting gardens, and homemade sweets on the pillow, appear throughout the guest rooms.

The rooms within the main inn are cozy and quaint with coordinated fabrics and wall coverings, accenting the New England period furnishings. All rooms have private baths stocked with fluffy bathrobes and scented toiletries.

Queen Anne furnishings highlight the elegant gatehouse suites. Plump overstuffed chairs, fireplaces, king-sized, four-poster beds, and roomy, marble bathrooms with whirlpools and separate showers, offer the ultimate in pampering and comfort.

Besides the expansive, open air front porch, where afternoon tea is served in the summer, the inn has four living rooms. Guests can read, sample complimentary brandy and port or, in the chilly months, sidle up to a roaring fire for tea and conversation.

The inn's exceptional New England cooking can be enjoyed in the main dining room contained within two restored barns or in the more traditional dining room of the main house.

Featuring exposed wood walls, a soaring three story ceiling, views to the woods, and a lively piano bar, the barns beckoned to me. Candles played soft shadows on the polished, plank pine floors as I studied the menu, which changes weekly, to provide guests with the freshest seasonal produce and fish.

I started with an appetizer of bacon-wrapped sea scallops in an unusual maple mustard cream. The scallops, melt-in-the-mouth juicy; the mustard, tart yet maple sweet, was just the right accompaniment to my entrée, Lightly Grilled Native Salmon. Perfectly grilled it was, with a dollop of salmon roe, morel sauce and crisp-steamed asparagus tips. A glass of California Chardonnay completed my enjoyment. All dinners include a lovely, composed salad or delicately flavored sorbet. A variety of desserts are available.

Included in the room rate, a hearty continental breakfast is served in the breakfast room. Lots of chintz and lace curtains create a cheerful morning environment.

Miles of wooded trails can be explored pedalling bicycles complimentary from the inn, or hike the extensive nature preserve of the Kennebunks. I spent one whole afternoon wandering the gardens of the sixty-acre monastery directly across the street from the inn.

The White Barn is romantic, relaxing, and a gastronomic pleasure

---

THE WHITE BARN INN, PO Box 560C, Beach Street, Kennebunkport, ME, 04046; 207-967-2321. A 24-room New England country inn & restaurant on the rugged Maine coast. Private bath, all- sized beds. Suites with fireplaces and whirlpool baths. Hearty continental breakfast included. Dinners available, dinner jackets requested for gentlemen guests. Two night minimum weekend and holiday stays. Smoking restricted. Not suitable for children under 12. Walk to beach, galleries, boutiques and antique shops. Bicycle and hiking trails & gardens. No pets allowed. CCs: AE, MC, V. Laurie Bongiorno & Laurie Cameron, owners/hosts.

DIRECTIONS: From northbound I-95, take Exit 2, Ogunquit/Wells. Follow Rte. 9 east to Rte. 35. Turn right on Beach St. Inn located 1/4 mi. on the right. From south I-95, take Exit 3, to Kennebunk. Follow Rte. 35 south 5 mi. to Rte. 9 intersection. Continue straight onto Beach St. Watch for inn on right.

WINDWARD HOUSE BED AND BREAKFAST

Camden, Maine

I'll always remember Jon and Mary Davis. Not only are they a warm couple who own the Windward House B&B, but they actually *almost* got me, a confirmed landlubber, onto a windjammer. Just when I thought I had an excuse—not remembering my wind breaker—Mary thoughtfully offered to get one for me. That thoughtfulness continued throughout my visit.

Jon spent thirty years as a corporate director with AT&T before moving to Camden in 1986. During those years, Mary spent her time as a registered nurse and the owner of a gourmet catering business. They both loved Camden, "where the mountains meet the sea," as Jon says, and decided Windward House would meld their talents into a wonderful way of life.

The home is located in the heart of Camden in the delightful High Street Historic District that overlooks the harbor. Fine restaurants, shops, and performing arts venues are all within walking distance, and just by stepping off the back deck hikers can tread some great trails.

A light blue-gray, the stately clapboard Greek Revival has harmo-

nious cream trim and burgundy windows and doors. Colorful flower beds frame the front porch and deck. The beautifully renovated home was placed on the National Historic Register in 1989.

The first floor is suited to the comfort of Windward's guests. All the rooms are attractive and furnished with antiques and local art. Whether you choose the large living room with its soapstone fireplace crackling on cool days, or the comfortable library filled with books, magazines, stereo and television, you'll find much to do during a stay-at-home evening. Refreshments, including port and sherry, are an appreciated extra.

Quilts, fresh flowers, period furnishings (including wonderful antique beds), and soft colors create a quiet, restful atmosphere in the guest rooms. All rooms have private, modern baths.

I know you'll enjoy Mary's super breakfasts, served by—who else?— Jon. Her peaches and cream French toast is exceptional. Sitting on the back deck with my fourth cup of coffee, I was amused by the youthful antics of Muffins, the inn's senior citizens cat, as she fearlessly stalked wild birds on a tree limb some fifteen feet above the ground. With her example in mind, I thought again about sailing the windjammer...then had another cup of coffee.

WINDWARD HOUSE BED AND BREAKFAST, 6 High St., Camden, ME 04843; 207-236-9656. A 6-guestroom (private baths) inn overlooking Camden Harbor. Queen, double and twin beds. Full breakfast. Open all year. Children over 10. Smoking restricted. No pets; boarding arrangements available. One dog in residence. CCs: Visa, MC. Mary and Jon Davis, owners/hosts.

DIRECTIONS: Once in Camden, inn is just one blk. north of Camden Harbor.

New Hampshire

THE BIRCHWOOD INN
Temple, New Hampshire

Judy and Bill Wolfe and I were enjoying a quiet moment in the back parlor of the Birchwood Inn, and I could see by the light in his eye that Bill was most enthusiastic about being an innkeeper.

The Birchwood Inn, sitting on one corner of the village green, is listed on the National Register of Historic Places and is believed to have been in operation since 1775. The present Federal-style brick building, along with the adjacent barn, was probably built about 1800, and the records document a history of changing uses that mirror the evolution of the small town tavern in New England.

The small, tucked-away village of Temple has no telegraph wires in the center of the town, and it's pretty much the same as it's been for two hundred years, with the Grange Hall, Congregational Church, village store, Revolutionary cemetery, and old blacksmith shop.

In 1965, probably the most interesting and prized feature of the inn was discovered when some early wall murals were uncovered under layers of old wallpaper. The paintings proved to be the work of the well-known muralist Rufus Porter, painted between 1825 and 1833. Fortunately, they were restored and are now being carefully preserved by Bill and Judy.

Today, the inn is characterized by comfortable furniture, a Steinway square grand piano, wide floorboards, checked tablecloths of yellow, red, brown, and blue, music in the background, and many tiny little areas where guests can enjoy a tête-à-tête. On the other hand, there is much opportunity for sociability. Judy said, "We have developed countless friendships with lovely people from all over the world without ever leaving the comforts of our little inn. The opportunity to reach out to people of all interests is a rare privilege afforded to both innkeepers and their children alike." The Wolfes find that their three children enjoy being involved with inn activities.

The guest rooms are decorated according to different themes—there is the Music Room, the Seashore Room, and the Train Room, among others. Homemade quilts add a real country touch. Five rooms have private baths, while two rooms share two hall baths.

The kitchen is handled in an interesting way because Bill does the cooking. Judy bakes breads and desserts, including blueberry-lemon bread, blueberry cobbler, chocolate cake, and various pies and tortes. The evening menu is on a slate blackboard, and on the night of my visit included crab soup, baked stuffed lobster, and chicken piccata. They have a new cookbook, titled *The Birchwood Sampler*, with 255 of their most requested recipes.

THE BIRCHWOOD INN, Rte. 45, Temple, NH 03084; 603-878-3285. A 7-guestroom (5 private baths) village inn in southern New Hampshire. Double and twin beds available. Open year-round. Breakfast included in room rate. Dinner not served on Sunday or Monday Wheelchair access. Hiking, horseshoes, xc skiing, hayrides, summer theater, ice skating, superb backroading, and numerous historic houses nearby; also the Cathedral in the Pines. One cat in residence. No credit cards. Judy and Bill Wolfe, owners/hosts.

DIRECTIONS: Take Rte. 3 north to Nashua. At Exit 7W follow Rte. 101 west through Milford to Rte. 45. Turn left 1-1/2 mi. to Temple. From I-91 at Brattleboro take Rte. 9 east to Keene to Rte. 101 through Peterborough, over Temple Mtn. to Rte. 45. Turn right, 1-1/2 mi. to the inn.

CHESTERFIELD INN
West Chesterfield, New Hampshire

I've always had a soft spot in my heart for country inns that have histories as farmhouses. The Chesterfield Inn is one of these. The traditional New England center-hall Colonial, with its two attached barns, is more than 200 years old. Built in the 1780s, the building first functioned as a tavern and then as a private farmhouse. The clapboard structure was renovated in 1984. Sitting on a hill above the Connecti-

cut River, the panoramic views are to the lovely Vermont Green Mountains to the west.

After looking at more than eighty country inns, Phil and Judy Hueber hiked the Chesterfield Inn's 10 acres and knew it was "the one." Phil had been a marketing director for Dun & Bradstreet and Judy a manager for Mutual of New York prior to the move to their "dream inn" and a much less stressful way of life.

One of the most attractive aspects of the inn comes from its unusual construction. In order to reach the three intimate dining rooms, one must walk through the kitchen. The candlelit dining room tables are set with crisp white linens, Dudson floral china, and crystal water glasses. The rooms are softened by Oriental carpets.

Dinner is leisurely. My first course was a colorful salad of roasted red peppers with fresh basil. An exotic main course of Brazilian fish and shrimp, stewed in a sauce of coconut, tomatoes, peanuts, and ginger, was exceptional. A crisp garden salad, using tender bibb lettuce from the inn's garden, was tossed with a tangy, homemade house dressing. Along with my after-dinner espresso, I ordered pumpkin cheesecake, one of Carl's specialties. I made a mental note to ask him how he makes it so creamy.

Cathedral ceilings, weathered barn boards, and exposed beams highlight the nine spacious guest rooms. Many of the walls are handstenciled, and period antiques and handmade quilts—a hobby of Judy's—decorate the comfortable rooms. As an avid reader, I particularly appreciated the rooms' cozy sitting areas and three-way reading lamps. All rooms have full baths, two with Jacuzzis, and thick, large towels. Some have fireplaces and two have balconies. My room had a lovely view onto the inn's pond.

The Huebers have stocked the rooms' small refrigerators with chardonnay, champagne, mineral water, and imported beers. Air-conditioning is quiet, and telephones and television are available.

A beehive fireplace dominates the sitting room. Colonial furnishings, a brass chandelier, a 20-foot-high ceiling, and lots of windows make this room a wonderful place for relaxing.

Judy whips up a super breakfast that might include fruit-filled crepes or summer vegetable custard and is served on the cheery remodeled sun porch or outside on the terrace.

CHESTERFIELD INN, Rte. 9, West Chesterfield, NH 03466; 603-256-3211. A 9-guestroom (private baths) country inn plus a guest house with 4 garden patio fireplace rooms on a hill above the Connecticut River Valley. Open all year. King and double beds. Breakfast included. Gourmet dinners Wednesday to Sunday Close to outdoor activities and cultural offerings. Two cats in residence. Judy and Phil Hueber, owners/hosts.

DIRECTIONS: Traveling north on Rte. 9, take Exit 3 and follow to lights. Go straight, across river, 2 mi. Inn is on the left. From Keene, NH, travel west on Rte. 9 for 20 min. Inn is on the right.

CHRISTMAS FARM INN

Jackson, New Hampshire

Christmas Farm was given its name many years ago, and Sydna and Bill found it inspirational. Using subtle variations of red and green in the decor, naming their guest rooms after Santa's reindeer and elves, sending out semiannual newsletters from the North Pole, and having a big Christmas celebration in the middle of July, they keep the feeling and spirit of Christmas alive all year.

As I drove up the country road my first view of the inn, with its white clapboards and green shutters, was very inviting. The main house, built in the 1770s, is set back on a little knoll, across a green lawn with huge maple trees and masses of flowers. The green rocking chairs on the long front porch with its overhanging roof, hanging plants, and flowers seemed to beckon me to "come and set a spell." The screen door is the kind I expected to slam when it closed.

Bill obligingly took me on a tour up the little road that wound around the hill and through the woods. There are several cottages with names like the Sugar House, the Smoke House, and the Livery Stable,

in a lovely, woodsy setting, with little yards and porches where you can sit out and enjoy the birds and the flowers. They are all different, with attractive and comfortable furnishings. Some have fireplaces, and all have beautiful mountain views. The 1777 Saltbox and the Barn are closer to the main house and have several guest rooms and suites. The ground floor of the huge Barn is also a leisure center with table tennis, a piano, and a TV.

Guest rooms in the main house are decorated in Laura Ashley fabrics and antique reproductions. Two rooms have Jacuzzis. Cheerful plaids cover the settees and chairs in the two cozy sitting rooms; one room has a corner fireplace with a raised hearth, and the other has a TV and VCR. There's an old-fashioned phone booth in the entry.

My dinner in the pleasant dining room with its many windows overlooking the flower gardens was delightful. Everything was excellent, from my appetizer of ravioli of crab with saffron and chives, to the entrée of grilled tuna with spinach, garlic, herbs, and diced tomatoes, to the ambrosial finale of an amaretto-soaked sponge cake served in a raspberry sauce and topped with chocolate. All of the breads and rolls are freshly baked. I gently awakened the next morning to that wonderful aroma wafting in my bedroom window.

CHRISTMAS FARM INN, Jackson, NH 03846; 603-383-4313. A 37-guestroom (36 private baths) comfortable farmhouse inn with cottages and suites on 14 acres on a country road in the rolling farmlands and forests of the White Mountains. Modified American plan. Breakfast and dinner served to travelers by reservation. Open year-round; various packages available. Swimming pool, sauna, putting green, horseshoes, shuffleboard, volleyball, table tennis on grounds. Golf, tennis, fishing, hiking, all summer/winter sports, and cultural and sports events nearby. No pets. No smoking in dining room. Sydna and Bill Zeliff, owners/hosts.

DIRECTIONS: From Rte. 16, go through village. Follow Rte. 6B up the hill 1/2 mi. to the inn.

THE DARBY FIELD INN

Conway, New Hampshire

There's a real sense of adventure involved in just making the last stage of the journey to reach Darby Field Inn. I turned off Route 16 and followed the Darby Field sign, plunging into the forest on a wonderful dirt road that seemed to climb ever upward. Following this road through the forest, again I had the great feeling of expectation that something would emerge at the top of the mountain that was going to be grand, and grand it is.

The Darby Field Inn has a most impressive panoramic view from its terrace dining room and many of the bedrooms. On this particular day Marc and Maria Donaldson, the innkeepers, took turns making sure that I saw all of the redecorating that had been accomplished in the inn, and we also had a chance to talk about the great view of the mountains.

"Over there is South Moat Mountain," Marc explained, "and that's Mount Washington just to the right. We can also see Adams and Madison and White Horse Ledge in the center."

The Darby Field Inn sits on the edge of the White Mountain National Forest, where guests can cross-country ski, snowshoe, and hike to nearby rivers, waterfalls, lakes, and open peaks. Fortunately, there's a very pleasant swimming pool on the terrace, providing guests

with not only a cooling dip in the hot days of summer, but still another view of the mountains.

Maria and I did a short tour of the rooms. "Each room has its own country personality," she observed. "Some have four-poster beds, patchwork quilts, and braided rugs. Most of them have private baths and, as I'm sure you've noticed, many face our special view of the valley."

There is a cozy little pub where both guests and Marc and Maria's friends can come together. This is adjacent to the living room, which has as impressive a stone fireplace as I have ever seen.

I was curious about the origins of Darby Field Inn. "Samuel and Polly Chase Littlefield first came up here in 1826, when it was hard work farming through all those generations of hard winters and long distances," Maria recounted. "Later on, the home took in summer guests, and it was then that the innkeeping tradition began. In the 1940s, a man from Boston and his family came here, and the original farmhouse became the living room section of what was to be known as the Bald Hill Lodge. The barn and blacksmith shop came down and in its place the dining room and kitchen section was built. The swimming pool was added and even a small ski lift for guests."

As one might expect, the menu is a bit on the hearty side with lamb chops, filet mignon, veal piccata, and roast duckling satisfying outdoor-oriented appetites.

Marc and Maria met in Venezuela, Maria's homeland, and came to Darby Field in 1979. They saw it as a country home for their children and an opportunity to meet guests from all parts of the world.

As Marc and Maria walked me out to the car, she said, "We can't let you go without pointing out our garden where we get so many of the good things we serve at the inn, including snow peas, peppers, cabbage, corn, lettuce, and brussels sprouts."

THE DARBY FIELD INN, Bald Hill, Conway, NH 03818; 800-426-4147 (NH: 603-447-2181). A 16-guestroom (14 private baths) White Mountain country inn, 3 mi. from Conway. All-sized beds available. Modified American plan. Closed April Bed and breakfast offered at various times, so I would suggest checking with the inn in advance. Within convenient driving distance of all of the Mt. Washington Valley cultural, natural, and historic attractions, as well as several internationally known ski areas. Swimming pool and carefully groomed xc skiing trails on grounds. Tennis and other sports nearby. One dog in residence. CCs: Visa, MC, AE. Marc and Maria Donaldson, owners/hosts.

DIRECTIONS: From Rte. 16: Traveling north turn left at sign for the inn (1 mi. before the town of Conway) onto Bald Hill Rd., and proceed up the hill 1 mi. to the next sign for the inn and turn right. The inn is 1 mi. down the dirt road on the left.

DEXTER'S INN AND TENNIS CLUB

Sunapee, New Hampshire

What a day! The sky was the bluest of skies, the sun was the sunniest of suns, and New Hampshire during the last week in June was really showing off for the rest of the world. I crested the hill and found Dexter's Inn basking in all of this glory, its bright yellow paint and black shutters blending well with the black-eyed Susans, Queen Anne's lace, and other summertime flowers and the green trees in the background.

As I looked east from the summit of the hill a magnificent scene of green foliage and Sunapee Lake came into view. I strolled up the granite steps of the inn, and stepped into the entrance, over which was the date 1804. Here again was the comfortable library-living room with some appropriate paintings of New Hampshire mountains and countryside. The furniture had been brightly slipcovered, and the room was wonderfully cool after the midday heat. I took a moment and stepped out to a screened-in porch with white wicker furniture and a ceiling painted to look like a canopy. It looked like a wonderful place to spend an evening.

Now I opened the door to the side terrace with its round tables and bright yellow umbrellas, remembering that I first sat here perhaps ten years earlier. There were tennis courts on both sides of the broad lawn and some tennis players were having a lively game. I could hear guests splashing in the swimming pool.

I went to see some of the guest rooms in the main house, which are reached by funny little hallways that zigzag around various wings, and also the guest rooms in the barn across the street. Everything looked tiptop. Extra towels awaited me in my room—someone knew I planned to play tennis. The Holly House cottage is a real plus. Because it is fully equipped with a kitchen, washer/dryer, living room with fireplace and two bedrooms with king and twin sized beds along with their own private baths, it is well suited for families, two couples traveling together or small seminars.

In the fall you will find apples in your room. You can eat one and take the others to the field to feed Alvin, Annie and Carolyn, the Scottish Highland cattle who roam the pastures. They are fascinating to watch.

At mealtime expect to find homemade soups and breads, fresh poached salmon, thick lamb chops, brandied chicken, rosemary haddock, or exceptional filet mignon. A sampling of desserts includes lemon mouse, chocolate walnut torte, and butterscotch pecan pie.

DEXTER'S INN AND TENNIS CLUB, Box 703R, Stagecoach Rd., Sunapee, NH 03782; 603-763-5571, 800-232-5571. A 19-guestroom (private baths) resort-inn in the western New Hampshire mountain and lake district. All-size beds. Modified American plan; European plan available in late June and Sept. Breakfast, lunch, and dinner served to travelers by advance reservation; closed for lunch and dinner on Tuesday during July and Aug. Lunches served only in July and Aug. Open from early May to mid-November Three tennis courts and teaching pro, pool, croquet, and shuffleboard on grounds. Lakes, hiking, backroading, and championship golf courses nearby. Pets allowed in Annex only. CCs: Visa, MC. Michael and Holly Simpson-Durfor, owners/hosts.

DIRECTIONS: From north and east: use Exit 12 or 12A, I-89. Continue west on Rte. 11 for 6 mi.—just 1/2 mi. past Sunapee to a sign at Winn Hill Rd. Turn left up hill and after 1 mi., bear right on Stagecoach Rd. From west: use Exit 8, I-91, follow Rte. 103 east into NH—through Newport 1/2 mi. past junction with Rte. 11. Look for sign at Young Hill Rd. and go 1-1/2 mi. to Stagecoach Rd.

FOLLANSBEE INN
North Sutton, New Hampshire

When the Reileins purchased Follansbee Inn in 1985, they were already in love with the area surrounding the small country village of North Sutton. Dick left a career in computer sales and Sandy gave up her position as a hospice worker to realize their dream of having an inn. "We wanted an inn since staying in many in England on our honeymoon," Sandy told me. "And since we've had one, we have no regrets!"

The Follansbee Inn is nestled near lovely, peaceful Kezar Lake, four miles from, as Sandy says, "the nifty New England town of New London." The Follansbee family built the rambling, distinctive farmhouse in 1840, and it was expanded in the 1920s. Crisp and clean, the white clapboard and green-trimmed house has a traditional old fashioned front porch for evening "dawdling."

"We don't have any television here," Dick told me as he ushered me into the cozy sitting room, "just great conversation." I was pleased to practice this rather rare art as we sat in overstuffed chairs next to the wood-burning stove. The room is paneled with weathered barn wood, which lends an air of timelessness. Another meeting room has comfortable sofas, a fireplace, and a small service bar.

In the winter months, hot kir and cider are served around the fire: a welcome treat after an afternoon of cross-country skiing. Summers bring Follansbee slush, served as guests relax on the front porch. The inn also has a nice selection of wines and beer. Several local brews are offered. By the way, Follansbee is a nonsmoking inn. "We want our guests to enjoy this clean New Hampshire air, inside and outside," Dick said.

The twenty-three guest rooms are each decorated differently. Carpeting, new mattresses, and lovely antiques create a comfortable atmosphere. Shared baths are large, with claw tubs and showers, and private baths have either tub showers or shower stalls. The bayberry soap waiting in my soap dish was an aromatic surprise.

One of the most wonderful things about Follansbee Inn is Kezar Lake. First of all, the view to the lake is spectacular. There's something about the sight of a peaceful lake the first thing in the morning that just starts the day off on the right note. Dick and Sandy invited me to the inn's private lakefront and pier to show me their new handmade wooden rowboat one afternoon. "Isn't she great!" Sandy proudly said. "We have quite an armada now: a sail board, rowboat, canoe, and paddleboat." For an afternoon of lazing, take one of the boats to the small island in the middle of the lake and enjoy one of Sandy's picnic lunches as you soak up some sun.

Breakfast begins in the dining room, with homemade granola, juices, coffee, and tea. Guests are then invited into the cozy kitchen to feast on lots of fresh fruit, muffins, and either an egg casserole, pancakes, or French toast. Evening dining is leisurely. Dick can suggest just the perfect wine to accompany your meal.

FOLLANSBEE INN, P.O. Box 92, North Sutton, NH 03260; 603-927-4221. A 23-guestroom (11 private baths) authentic New England country inn on Lake Kezar. King, double, and twin beds. Closed portions of November and April. Hearty breakfast included; picnic lunch and dinner available. Boating, fishing, hiking, biking, picnicking, golf, tennis, xc skiing from doorstep, summer playhouse, and musical concerts. Downhill skiing 4 miles away. No pets. One dog in residence. No smoking. Dick and Sandy Reilein, owners/hosts.

DIRECTIONS: Take I-89 to Exit 10. Follow signs to North Sutton, about 2 miles. The inn is behind the big white church.

THE INN AT CROTCHED MOUNTAIN
Francestown, New Hampshire

Once again I turned off Route 202 at Bennington, New Hampshire, and followed Route 47 toward Francestown. I noticed that an unusual number of beaver dams had been built by our industrious friends. Admiring the farms on both sides of the road, I wound my way ever upward through the grove of trees, coming once again to the Crotched Mountain Inn, just a few paces from the base of a ski area.

The inn was originally built as a farmhouse in 1822. The first owner constructed a secret tunnel from his cellar to the Boston Post Road, incorporating his home as a way station to shelter runaway slaves on the Underground Railroad. During the late 1920s, it was to become one of the most spectacular farms in New England, boasting an internationally recognized breed of sheep, champion horses, and Angora goats.

Unfortunately, the house was destroyed by fire in the mid-30s, rebuilt, and John and Rose came on the scene in 1976.

Rose is an attractive Indonesian woman. She is in complete charge of the kitchen, doing a great deal of the cooking. The menu includes roast duck with plum sauce, sautéed bay scallops, and Indonesian-style scallops with sautéed tomatoes, onions, pepper, and ginger. There is a low ceiling pub with a roaring fire for after dinner guests to enjoy their night cap.

As I was leaving, Rose walked out to the car and said, "Do tell your readers that we love children to come here, and we have many things for them to do and see, and they always seem to have a good time."

THE INN AT CROTCHED MOUNTAIN, Mountain Rd., Francestown, NH 03043; 603-588-6840. A 13-guestroom (8 baths) mountain inn in southern New Hampshire, 15 mi. from Peterborough. Double and twin beds. European plan. Open from mid-May to the end of October, and from Thanksgiving thru the ski season. During winter and holiday periods, dinner is served on Friday and Saturday Dinner is served from Tuesday thru Saturday during the remainder of the year. Within a short distance of the Sharon Arts Center, American Stage Festival, Peterborough Players, Crotched Mt. ski areas. Swimming pool, tennis courts, xc skiing, volleyball on grounds. Golf, skiing, hill walking, and backroading in the gorgeous Monadnock region nearby. No credit cards. Two dogs in residence. Rose and John Perry, owners/hosts.

DIRECTIONS: From Boston, follow Rte. 3 north to 101A to Milford. Then Rte. 13 to New Boston and Rte. 136 to Francestown. Follow Rte. 47 for 2-1/2 mi. and turn left on Mountain Road. Inn is 1 mi. on right. From New York/Hartford, take I-91 north to Rte. 10 at Northfield to Keene, NH. Follow 101 east to Peterborough, Rte. 202 north to Bennington, Rte. 47 to Mountain Rd. (approx. 4-1/2 mi.); turn right on Mountain Rd. Inn is 1 mi. on right.

INN AT THORN HILL

Jackson, New Hampshire

What a transformation! When I last saw Mount Washington from my guest room, it had been at sundown the previous day. The mountain's eminence had caught and reflected the last rays of the sun, until it finally disappeared in the ever-deepening hues of blue that marked a mid-September evening in northern New Hampshire. This morning the top of the mountain was completely white. A 6-inch snowfall had

powdered several peaks of the Presidential Range, and Jack Frost had brushed some streaks of red, orange, yellow, and russet through the greenery. When I went down for breakfast there was an electricity in the air that comes with the arrival of a change in season.

Innkeepers Jim & Ibby Cooper moved to village of Jackson in 1992. During their lifetime, they had been accustomed to a much more cosmopolitan environment than the village of Jackson (population 650) provided. But the Coopers had no trouble adapting, and quickly left any attachment to their previous careers in hotel management and teaching, where Ibby taught in a one school house for the homeless.

The Inn at Thorn Hill Inn was designed by noted architect Stanford White, who also designed the Washington Square Arch in New York City. Gossip holds that White was shot to death by a jealous husband. Built originally as a private mansion for Katherine Prescott Wormeley, a distinguished translator of the works of Balzac, the property with its gambrel-roofed main house on 7.5 quiet country acres became her winter abode. The quintessential grand country residence was completed in 1891.

Three different types of accommodations are available at the inn: the main inn, the carriage house, and the cottages. Each room has a private bath and is individually decorated with Victorian antiques. The inn is by no means rustic, catering to a clientele who appreciate a genteel atmosphere. The first floor, with its forty-two-seat dining room, has a Victorian flavor. The parlor offers the inn's only television and a baby grand piano, and the spacious drawing room with its soapstone wood stove, lace curtains, and antique furnishings provides a comfortable ambience that is hospitable and welcoming. The inn's long living room has been divided into three separate areas where guests can gather for conversation or for games at the gaming tables.

Views to the surrounding mountains, and unique Victorian accents, highlight the guest rooms. The Carriage House next door offers a 20-by 40-foot great room with a fireplace, seven comfortable guest rooms and a Jacuzzi. Decor is country-inspired and the environment perfect for group get-togethers. The other three cottages offer the ultimate in privacy with the option to participate in the group environment. All rooms and cottages have modern baths with either showers or shower/tub combos. The inn's dining room is reserved for the public by reservations. In addition to individual tables for those who desire romantic privacy, there is a common table that seats eight, for the adventurous who love to swap travel stories and good conversation. Besides the scrumptious, full breakfast, a varied dinner menu is prepared to order, offering appetizers like a country pâté of veal, pork, and chicken livers flavored with brandy, and entrées of lobster pie and roast breast of duck with montmorency sauce. All entrées are served with fresh vegetables. The inn's built-in pool and winter sports, including the Jackson Ski Touring cross-country trail network, provide enjoyable exercise for any season. Plays, dance troupes, and concerts take place at various times during the year. Art and quilt workshops are conducted various weeks thoughout Spring and Fall.

INN AT THORN HILL, Thorn Hill Rd., Box A, Jackson, NH 03846; 603-383-4242. A 20-guestroom (private baths) inn within sight of Mount Washington. Various packages available, including European, Modified American, and B&B plans. Breakfast and dinner served daily. All-size beds. Closed April. Many cultural and recreational activities nearby. No Smoking. Kennel nearby. Jim and Ibby Cooper, owners/hosts.

DIRECTIONS: Take I-95 to the Spaulding Turnpike and follow Rte. 16 north to Jackson. Once in the village, take Rte. 16A through the covered bridge to Thorn Hill Rd. and turn right; go up the hill.

THE MEETING HOUSE INN

Henniker, New Hampshire

Located in the beautiful Contoocook Valley, nestled at the base of Pat's Peak Ski Area, The Meeting House waits for those who love and appreciate a small rural environment. Henniker is home to New England College and takes its name from the original meeting house, built more than 200 years ago, at the base of Craney Hill.

Located on a quiet, secondary country road, the refurbished farmstead is bordered by two meandering mountain-fed streams. Its 5 acres of wooded land provide wonderfully peaceful hiking trails. As innkeeper Cheryl Bakke stated, "The inn is a quiet jewel awaiting your discovery."

And a jewel it is. Bill and June Davis, and Cheryl Davis Bakke and her husband, Peter, have owned and operated The Meeting House Inn and Restaurant for many years. They were charmed by the quaint town of Henniker, and chose it as an ideal location to begin "hands-on" innkeeping. For them, the "hands-on" part started immediately. They purchased the buildings, which previously had not been used as an inn, and began renovating. "We literally started from scratch," Bill, the former owner of an executive search firm, told me. "We wanted the inn to have our own signature."

That unique family signature is apparent throughout The Meeting House. The style is eclectic, with personal family antiques and treasures in all the rooms. Even the intricate needlepoint pieces have been stitched by family members.

Each guest room has its own personality. "Rooms are *chosen* by our guests rather than *assigned*," Cheryl told me as she showed me to my romantic suite. "We want people to relax in the comforts of their own personalities and thoughts."

Wide pine floors, canopy brass beds, comfortable furnishings, designer sheets, and fluffy extra pillows are just part of what encourage total relaxation. All rooms have private baths. I really luxuriated as I soaked in a deep, hot bath, made fragrant by a few drops of complimentary homemade Henniker wild rosewater cologne.

The common room has a phone, television, VCR, and some interesting mystery puzzles that can be taken back to your room for an evening of *who-dunit*. A solar recreation area, comprised of a hot tub and sauna, is also available for guest use. Tiny twinkling Christmas tree lights peep from the plants surrounding the tub, creating a magical atmosphere.

Breakfast is always a surprise. Delivered in a charming country basket, each morning's unwrapping brings a delightful selection, including a home-baked goody. The menu is changed seasonally. Accompanied by Grensil, the inn's affectionate Maine coon cat, I took my treasure basket to breakfast on the sunny deck where I could appreciate the rock gardens and flowers that surround the inn.

In the evening, hearty New England cookery can be enjoyed in The Meeting House restaurant, housed in the inn's authentic, carefully preserved barn. Open to the public, dinner is available Wednesday through Sunday. The recently added solar greenhouse bar is just the spot to have one of Bill's famous fourteen-ingredient Bloody Marys. The bar is full-service, and includes nonalcoholic selections. An extensive wine list is also available.

A unique display of small plastic bags, filled with sand from around the world, hang from the restaurant walls: "The Sands of Time." What began as one guest's way of sharing a vacation experience has grown into a nostalgic collection that former guests send from such exotic locations as Mt. Everest and the floor of the Atlantic Ocean. Such "sharing" is an indication of just how much warmth and friendliness is found, and remembered, at the Meeting House. As the inn's brochure states, it is "A place in time to return to again and again."

THE MEETING HOUSE INN, 35 Flanders Rd., Henniker, NH 03242; 603-428-3228. A 6-guestroom (private baths) country inn located in the Contoocook Valley. All-size beds. Open all year. Breakfast included, dinners available Wednesday through Sunday, Sunday brunch. Gift and antique shops, downhill and xc skiing, water sports, theaters nearby. No smoking or pets. Maine coon cat in residence. June and Bill Davis, and Cheryl and Peter Bakke, Owners-hosts.

DIRECTIONS: From Henniker, take Rte. 114 south about 2 mi. to Pat's Peak Sign. Turn right (Flanders Rd.); the inn is about 1/2 mi. on the right.

MOOSE MOUNTAIN LODGE

Etna, New Hampshire

Up the hill I drove to the lodge and its fabulous view.

Moose Mountain Lodge is a rustic building high on the western side of Moose Mountain, built in 1938, mostly of logs and stones gathered from the surrounding forests and fields. The broad porch extends across the entire rear of the lodge, and has foreground views of the rolling New Hampshire countryside and, in the distance, of famed Vermont peaks as far away as Rutland. Peter Shumway the owner is fond of saying there is a 99-mile view.

I passed through the new entryway and walked into the kitchen, as

almost everyone does, joining Peter and Kay Shumway around the big table for a wonderful breakfast visit.

The kitchen is one of the centers of activity at Moose Mountain Lodge. "We run an open kitchen here," Kay said. "I like it when guests wander in and ask 'What's for lunch?' Incidentally, most of the time it's soup and salad." This is Kay's domain and it reveals her many interests besides cuisine, including flowers and plants. In the middle of the big butcher-block table was a copy of *Webster's New Collegiate Dictionary*. How can you go wrong in a kitchen that is also a haven for the intellectually curious!

There are twelve lodge-type, rustic bedrooms with colorful quilts, lots of books and magazines, bunk beds and conventional single and double beds, and a rustic air that I seldom find these days.

"Many things are different here in the summer, including the menus," Kay remarked. "Summer meals have lots of fish and some meats with light sauces; all of the vegetables from the garden and all the fresh fruits that I can pick (right next to the front door); sometimes cold soups. We have salads and homemade breads and generally fruit desserts.

"However, in the wintertime we serve stuffed squash, lots of potatoes and big roasts, and always a huge salad and all kinds of desserts. Everything is put out on the buffet table so guests can have whatever they want and they can sit wherever they wish."

In winter there are extensive cross-country ski trails everywhere, and the winter scenery is spectacular. It's great to come in after skiing and grab a cookie from the seemingly bottomless cookie jar.

Hanover and Dartmouth College are seven miles down the road. It's easy to attend a concert or sporting event or browse through the Dartmouth bookstore, the largest and most complete in New England. The Shumways are involved in several Biking, Canoeing and Hiking Inn to Inn programs.

MOOSE MOUNTAIN LODGE, Etna, NH 03750; 603-643-3529. A 12-guestroom (5 shared baths) rustic lodge a few miles from Hanover, NH. Queen, double, and twin beds available. Open from December 26th-March 20th and late May until October 20th. Breakfast, lunch, and dinner served to houseguests only. Xc skiing for all abilities on grounds or nearby. Ski equipment available. Hiking, biking, walking, canoeing, backroading, and many recreational and cultural attractions nearby, including Dartmouth College. No pets. One dog in residence. Peter and Kay Shumway, owners/hosts.

DIRECTIONS: If arriving for the first time, stop in Etna at Landers Restaurant or the Etna Store and telephone the lodge for directions. The last mile up the mountain is steep, and when the road is icy, guests are met at the bottom parking lot with a 4-wheel-drive vehicle. Etna is on the map, a few miles east of Hanover.

NEW LONDON INN

New London, New Hampshire

On three lovely landscaped acres, the New London Inn overlooks the town green of the village of New London. Located on the main street of what will soon be a designated historic area, the three-story white clapboard, green-shuttered, Federal-style building has been operated as an inn for more than 150 years. Innkeepers Maureen and John Follansbee informed me that they would soon be applying for inclusion in the National Historic Register.

Extensive renovation of the inn began three years ago. The thirty guest rooms, decorated in subtle shades of green, yellow, lavender, blue, and pink, are furnished with antiques and wicker. The result is a fresh, airy atmosphere. Telephones were recently installed in each room. The private baths were modernized, but some still offer the old-fashioned charm of claw-foot tubs.

After busy careers in New York, Maureen and John made the decision to pool their talents and open an inn. Maureen had spent seventeen years in human resources, and John had worked for twenty-five years in international insurance, prior to their search for an inn. When they finally found what they wanted, the cart rather came before the horse. "First, we fell in love with the town and the area," Maureen told me. "Then we decided we really wanted the challenge of restoring this beautiful inn."

Maureen is an avid gardener, and eager to give you a guided tour of her prize-winning horticultural masterpieces. John can direct you to the nearby cross-country ski areas. A golf course and the Mount Sunapee lake region are less than two miles away. And, for those who love the thrill of uncovering that long-sought-after, one-of-a-kind hat pin, antique shops are in the immediate area.

A cozy mixture of antique and contemporary furnishings assure comfort in the common rooms. Television is available in the living room and bar. The inn has a full liquor license, and serves beer, wine, and spirits.

Breakfast is included with the room tariff and is served in the lovely dining room. Surrounded by Federal-period wallpaper, raised paneling, and new Windsor chairs, you will be treated to fresh fruit, juice, and a choice of entrée and side dish. On chilly mornings, the 200-year-old fireplace warms the room.

Dinners offer wonderful appetizers, such as pepper pasta with Italian bacon and fresh vegetables. Soup usually follows, and could be something like chilled tomato lime and scallop. I had an entrée of spiced beef medallions with lime-cilantro butter and avocado sauce. What a combination of flavors!

NEW LONDON INN, Main St., P.O. Box 8, New London, NH 03257; 603-526-2791. A 30-guestroom (private baths) Federal-style inn on 3 acres overlooking the New London village green. Open all year. All-sized beds. Breakfast included, dinner available. Skiing, golf, public beaches, antique shops, and theater nearby. No pets. Maureen and John Follansbee, owners/hosts.

DIRECTIONS: From I-89, inn is approximately 3 mi. off Exit 11 from the south, or Exit 12, from the north. Follow signs to New London.

THE NOTCHLAND INN

Hart's Location, New Hampshire

New Hampshire has the highest mountains in the Northeast, including the majestic Mount Washington. The air is almost crystalline, and the granite, evergreen forests, and icy snow-fed streams offer an invigorating atmosphere for body and soul.

Only 10 miles from Mount Washington, at the entrance to Crawford Notch, The Notchland Inn sits on a picturesque knoll with a commanding view of the Saco River valley. The Inn's 400 acres spread to touch the bases of four different mountains.

Off a major highway, the inn has served travelers for more than a century, and played an active role in the history of New Hampshire's White Mountains. Dr. Samuel Bemis, a successful dentist and inventor, completed the English-style manor house in 1862. Using native granite and timber, the handsome mansion was constructed by methods Dr. Bemis had studied in Europe. To achieve the clean cuts so obvious in the stone even today, the granite was drilled by hand at intervals. The holes were plugged with wooden dowels, which, when wet, split the granite with amazing precision.

John and Pat Bernardin purchased Notchland in 1983. The inn had been abandoned for some time, so the Bernardins began the work-intensive process of restoring the inn to its former Victorian grandeur. The huge brick chimneys, embossed metal ceilings, tiled fireplaces, and hardwood interior have been carefully and lovingly refurbished. Modern updating, like private tiled baths, has been done to complement the Victorian design. The atmosphere is delightfully casual and comfortable.

All eleven guest rooms have their own fireplaces and private baths. The rooms are bright and airy and are furnished with local and English

antiques and decorated with designer wall coverings and fabrics. The placement of beds and chairs takes advantage of the incredible views to the mountains beyond.

Pat and John are a couple with varied interests and an unending flow of energy. Believing in the tradition of the country inn, where the family runs the business, they have no staff, choosing rather to do everything themselves. And they do *everything*. When I asked John, a former nuclear engineer, what he did for fun, he laughed and said, "I like bicycling, skiing, and fixing up the place, and fixing up the place, and ..."

One of the Bernardins' hobbies is their sanctuary for endangered species of domestic animals. I had never heard of endangered domestics, but Pat immediately educated me. "They're rare, almost extinct, breeds of goats and sheep." You can visit their collection of llamas, minauture horses, and their famous golden retriever, Ruggs, who has rescued many a misdirected hiker. Wild critters also wander in now and then: deer, moose, and that masked bandit, the raccoon. Recently a large barn complex was completed to house the animals. A team of Belgian draft horses has been added to the menagerie to take the guests for hay/sleigh rides through the woods.

It's difficult to imagine Pat having much time to spend whipping up gourmet breakfasts and dinners, but she does. A former chief chef, she focuses her culinary expertise on preparation of fabulous five-course dinners that include hearty homemade soups, crisp salads, a choice of three of four entrées, like beef Wellington, and luscious desserts. Breakfast is equally wonderful. Both meals are served in the inn's intimate dining room by the fire.

Notchland has a wealth of outdoor sports. John just recently cleared five miles of cross-country ski trails to add to the 12 already in use. After a nippy day in the snow, you can return for a soak in the hot tub by the pond, and then relax in the library with a video. Or read in one of the other three sitting rooms, where you'll find comfortable chairs and warming fires.

THE NOTCHLAND INN, Hart's Location, NH 03812; 603-374-6131, 800-866-6131. An 11-guestroom (private baths) Victorian manor house nestled in the mountains near Crawford Notch. King, queen and double size beds. Modified American plan. Open all year. Excellent winter sports, hiking, and boating. Antique shops, outlet centers, and theaters nearby. No pets. Ruggs, a golden retriever, in residence. CCs: Visa, MC, AE. Pat and John Bernardin, owners/hosts.

DIRECTIONS: From North Conway, follow Rte. 302 north for 20 min. into the White Mt. National Forest. The inn is very noticeable on a knoll above the highway.

SNOWVILLAGE INN

Snowville, New Hampshire

Frank, Trudy, and Peter Cutrone are a family after my own heart, and Snowvillage Inn is one of my favorite inns. Not only is it unusual to have a father-mother-son team pool their diverse skills to operate an inn, but Trudy also shares my interest in writing. The trio purchased the 1900s inn in May 1986. "When we do 'business', I call my parents partners," Peter informed me, smiling. "When we talk 'family', it's Mom and Dad."

Originally a retreat for historical writer, Frank Simonds, the country inn is located 1,000 feet up Foss Mountain in the New Hampshire rural village of Snowville. Mr. Simonds valued the peace and solitude, the absolutely spectacular view of the White Mountains, and the property's 10 acres of forest and lawns that keep neighbors and traffic at bay. The Cutrones chose Snowvillage Inn after first deciding to adopt a new life-style, then agreed on their approach to innkeeping: "country casual." Snowvillage was to be a place where guests could relax and put up their feet. And it is.

Coming up the graceful, flower-edged drive, three attractive buildings meet your gaze: the many-gabled main house with attached chalet, the converted 150-year-old red barn, and the quaint chimney house. Though separated by a lush center lawn and old stone walls, the three buildings are closely connected by driveways. The New England architecture is enhanced with colorful window boxes of flowers.

The living room and lounge are elegant, adorned with Oriental rugs, a huge brick fireplace, and well-stacked bookcases. Games like chess and Tak-a-Radi are available in a beautiful, hand-carved Swiss cupboard. Peter's expertise as a wood craftsman is apparent in his handsome oak grandmother clock in the comfortable living room. Paintings of Trudy's Austrian ancestors smile down from the walls, and sprays of fresh flowers appear everywhere.

In keeping with the inn's literary heritage, each of the eighteen guest rooms is dedicated to a writer and displays a selection of the author's work. The rooms are romantic and cozy with a blend of New England and Alpine Provincial furnishings ranging from period antiques to quality reproductions. Colors of dusty rose, blue, mint, and fiery poppy red accent country cottons and natural muslin linens. I found the welcome basket in my room a particularly friendly gesture, especially when I uncovered the buttery chocolate chip cookies. A new room has been recently added by combining two rooms and having twelve windows for a breathtaking view from your pillow of Mt. Washington the the White Mountains.

Dining at Snowvillage Inn is exquisite. My dinner began with a warm loaf of walnut beer bread, accompanied by a salad course of greens topped with an unusual bourbon dressing. This was followed by creamy tomato soup and an entrée of Viennese beef tenderloin in a delicious sauce, rice pilaf, and a colorful sauté of squash with yellow and red peppers. Trudy's luscious French silk pie, slathered in whipped cream and shaved chocolate curls, completed the meal. Breakfast is also included with the room fee.

I was treated to an exceptional final evening at Snowvillage Inn when I attended Trudy's Americanized version of her native Austria's traditional Solstice Festival, a celebration of the return of light to the land. Tiki torches stood in for more traditional ones, but the spirit brought on by song, wine, and good food created an evening truly worthy of this ancient ritual.

_____

SNOWVILLAGE INN, Snowville, NH 03849; 603-447-2818. A 18-guestroom (private baths) mountain inn retreat. Closed April. All-size beds available. Modified American plan; breakfast with B&B rates. Clay tennis courts, sauna, fitness course in woods, volleyball, horseshoes, and a wide, restful screened porch on premises. Llama hikes with gourmet lunch during summer. No pets. Two dogs and three cats in residence. CCs: Visa, MC, AE. Frank, Trudy, and Peter Cutrone, owners/hosts.

DIRECTIONS: 120 miles from Boston and 55 miles from Portland, ME. From Boston take I-95 N to Spaulding Turnpike North in Portsmouth, NH (Exit 4). When the turnpike ends after Exit 18 it becomes Rte. 16 North. (Do not get off turnpike prematurely.) Follow Rte. 16 North to Rte. 25; take a right and go east for 5 miles. Take a left on Rte. 153 North. (Do not take Rte. 153 before this point.) Go 10 miles on 153 North; pick up Inn sign and turn right at Crystal Lake Beach to Snowville (1 mile). Turn right at Inn sign and come up the mountain 3/4 mile. Congratulate yourself.

SUGAR HILL INN

Sugar Hill, New Hampshire

Stepping onto the wide veranda of Sugar Hill Inn, with its flowers and white wicker furnishings, I was reminded of the gracious old homes I've visited in the South. The 17th-century farmhouse is set on a natural rock foundation, and is stretched along a spacious lawn dominated by an old horse-drawn surrey. A powerful telescope on the veranda invites night-time star searching.

Sugar Hill Inn was built as a home for one of the hardy early-American families who came to the White Mountain area in search of a better way of life. The home was built in the traditional way, using post and beam construction, and relied on handsome rock fireplaces in the principal rooms for heat. Wide pumpkin pine boards were used for woodwork and flooring. Over the years, three cottages were added in a cluster to the west of the original inn. In 1972, improvements were made to the total facility and the inn was renamed Sugar Hill Inn.

Jim and Barbara Quinn, Rhode Island residents who had been in the grocery business, purchased the inn in 1986 and made substantial efforts to infuse the inn with their own personal warmth and, in Jim's words, "their desire to develop first-time guests into longtime friends."

The two charming common rooms have original fireplaces, mantels, and stone hearths. Decorated in a Colonial style, with beautiful sugar-maple flooring accented by Oriental rugs, the rooms are quite lovely and comfortable. The living room has an antique 1906 player piano with a large assortment of piano rolls. I had particular fun with the rousing rendition of "Alexander's Ragtime Band" that we played during an after-dinner sing-along. A television is available, and board games and a variety of reading materials and puzzles are set out for entertainment.

I stayed in one of the country cottages adjacent to the main inn and found it spacious and homey. Each cottage has its own covered front porch for enjoying the evening twilight. All the guest rooms are individually decorated with handmade quilts on antique beds and hand-braided rugs on the floors. Barb has used her artistic flair to design and paint wall stencils modeled after original patterns found during renovation. As an inveterate late-night reader, I was happy to find good lighting for reading in bed. All rooms have immaculate private baths with mostly tub/shower combinations.

The inn's light, airy dining room is a perfect spot for enjoying a breakfast of such specialties as walnut pancakes, along with fresh fruits and home-baked muffins served on country crockery. In the evening, the ambience is changed with candlelight for a dinner that features two entrées and the finest of fresh and locally grown fruits, vegetables, poultry, and meats. Jim prepares all of the meals and has some wonderful specialties like his chicken Washington, a tender chicken breast stuffed with rich crabmeat and sauce. I recommend the excellent pecan bourbon pie for dessert. The inn has a fine selection of wines, beer, and full spirits to accompany your dinner.

SUGAR HILL INN, Rte. 117, Sugar Hill NH 03580; 603-823-5621. A 14-guestroom (private baths) traditional New England inn and cottages 5 mi. from Franconia. Open May thru mid-November, and December 26 thru March. All-size beds. Full breakfast included; dinner available on premises. B&B rates not available during fall seasons or holidays. All seasonal sports. Antique and outlet shopping, museums, theater, and chamber concerts nearby. No pets. No smoking. CCs: Visa, MC. Jim and Barbara Quinn, owners/hosts.

DIRECTIONS: From Boston, take Exit 38 from I-93. Turn right on Rte. 18 through Franconia. Turn left on Rte. 117. The inn is 1/2 mile up the hill on the right. From New York, take Exit 17 from I-91. Go east on Rte. 302 and turn right onto Rte. 117. The inn is on the left 1/2 mile before Rte. 18.

Quebec

THE HOVEY MANOR
North Hatley, Quebec, Canada

We were winding up a tour of 10-mile-long Lake Massawippi ("deep waters" in Algonkian). Steve Stafford slowed down the motor launch as we approached the inn's docks. I had a wonderful view of Hovey Manor's secluded twenty-five acres sprawled across the hillside with its lovely English gardens leading down to two beaches.

In 1899, Henry Atkinson, a wealthy industrialist from Atlanta, purchased this prime site. The antebellum-style home he built was inspired by George Washington's Mount Vernon. Henry's books still predominate in the Manor's beautiful library lounge. In 1950 Robert F. Brown, the first innkeeper, ingeniously transformed the estate into a country inn which became renowned for its quality and charm. The present innkeepers, Steve and Kathy Stafford, purchased Hovey Manor in 1979 and have continued the tradition.

Kathy's flair for decorating is evident throughout the property. All the guest rooms and lovely public rooms have been thoroughly upgraded and individually decorated. Each of the 35 rooms has a private bath; most face the lake and many feature some combination of a wood-burning fireplace, a canopy bed, a whirlpool bath, or a private balcony. Turn-down service was added last year, and the fireplaces are laid and ready to light every day.

Several years ago, the cuisine at Hovey Manor underwent a dramatic transformation. A contemporary French cuisine is served and guests enjoy choosing from the varied, imaginative dishes enhanced by produce from the Manor's own herb and edible flower gardens. On many evenings there is also live classical piano music. Steve says, "We've been delighted with the results of our improvements. Quebec's Ministry of Tourism has given us the highest rating for both cuisine (four forks) and accommodations (five fleurs-de-lis), which is rare for a country inn. The response from our guests has allowed us to remain open all year so that we've been able to develop a really good team. Turnover is low, and it makes Kathy and me happy to receive so many compliments regarding the friendliness and professionalism of our staff."

Although a traditional inn, Hovey Manor has all the resort facilities for a complete vacation experience. In summer there's an activities program, and the canoes, paddleboats, windsurfers and lighted tennis courts are free. Steve is an avid tennis player and happy to accept challenges from like-minded guests. In 1990, a new heated pool was built, nestled into the hillside above the beach; poolside lunches and sundown coctails now beckon. Sailboats, water-skiing, and cruises that take you to the picturesque village of North Hatley are available at reasonable rates right on site. Golfers can be challenged by playing any of the 10 golf courses within an half-hour's drive and there's English summer stock at the Piggery Theatre two minutes away.

Remember, this is the land of the maple leaf; the fall foliage is wonderful. In winter, Hovey has fifty kilometers of groomed cross-country trails right at its door. There's even a ski package offering inn-to-inn skiing—the inns transfer the cars and the baggage. For downhill skiers, there's a convenient interchangeable ticket, valid at four big mountains in the area, all with extensive snow-making equipment. In Hovey's historic Coach House bar you'll enjoy the unique après-ski atmosphere, and on selected evenings the chefs broil steaks and fresh salmon over the live charcoal hearth.

Yet another recent innovation "au Manoir" are the unique "fishing lunches." The Staffords have constructed a deluxe winter fishing cabin for the ice in front of the manor. A fisherman-chef provides all the gear and know-how and then cooks up the guests' catch in the cabin, along with a Quebecois-style lunch. This makes for a memorable outing.

Whatever the season, I think that Hovey Manor provides a happy vacation experience. It's worthwhile as a destination in itself.

HOVEY MANOR, North Hatley, Quebec, Canada J0B 2C0; 819-842-2421. A 35-guestroom (private baths) resort-inn (12 with wood-burning fireplaces) on Lake Massawippi, 1/2 hr. from U.S./Canada border. Queen, double, and twin beds. Modified American and European plans. Breakfast, lunch, dinner served every day. Open all year. Wheelchair access. Lighted tennis court, two beaches, sailing, canoeing, paddle-boats, water skiing, windsurfing, fishing, xc skiing, and sleigh rides on grounds. Downhill skiing, horseback riding, racquet sports, and golf (10 courses) nearby; also many scenic and cultural attractions nearby. Sorry, no pets. Stephen and Kathryn Stafford, owners/hosts.

DIRECTIONS: Take Vermont I-91 to Vermont/Quebec border and follow Rte. 55 to No. Hatley Exit 29. Follow Rte. 108E for 5 mi. to T-junction at Lake Massawippi in North Hatley. Turn right for 3/4 mi. to Hovey Manor sign and private drive on left.

Vermont

THE BARROWS HOUSE

Dorset, Vermont

Sally and Tim Brown have been operating this 18th-century inn since 1986, and love the small Vermont town of Dorset. "We thought that the Barrows House was really a unique property," Sally said. "Its got such a lovely parklike setting, and the multiple buildings offer privacy for guests." The main house was built around 1804, two of the other seven were built in the 19th century, and the remaining five buildings were finished in the mid-20th century. To provide continuity, the Browns have painted all the buildings in the Colonial style: a crisp white with black shutters.

Only a two-minute walk from town, the inn is spread over 11 acres that include two tennis courts and a swimming pool. Neighboring homes are nearby, creating a pleasant rural village atmosphere.

The Barrows House is ideal for family visits. The Browns are only the fourth family to have owned the inn since 1900, and their children often help out during the summer months. Their son Thatcher enjoyed cooking in the inn's kitchen so much during past summers that he has now graduated from Cornell School of Hotel Administration. The only "kid" left at home now are their keeshonds, Katrina, who, according to Sally, "has become a special hostess in the tavern and on our new cocktail terrace," and Beluga.

All of the eight buildings have been completely renovated, and with new rugs, fabrics, curtains, and paint. The common areas are comfortably furnished and, in keeping with the inn's Colonial origins, are decorated with stenciling and many antique period pieces.

The bedrooms are individually furnished in a variety of country styles using combinations of floral and print fabrics interspersed with period and antique furnishings. Television, air-conditioning, and refrigerators are in all the suites, and some of the other rooms. All rooms but two have private baths.

Enhancing the inn's dining reputation was one of the interesting challenges that drew the Browns away from careers in finance. The Barrows House is a full-service inn, where a country breakfast and dinner are served daily. Dinner is a four-course gourmet treat, with six to ten choices of appetizers, a main course, and dessert. A crisp green salad with three dressings comes paired with fresh hot bread.

Breakfast begins with juice, fruit, and cold cereals followed by a pancake special and an egg dish, served with bacon, sausage and great home fries.

Although lunch is not available regularly, a brown-bag picnic can be arranged.

THE BARROWS HOUSE, Rte. 30, Dorset, VT 05251; 802-867-4455. A 28-guestroom (private baths) 200-year-old colonial country inn on 12 acres in the heart of the picturesque Vermont village. All-sized beds. Open year-round. Modified American plan or B&B available. Close to historic Manchester and shopping. Swimming pool and tennis courts on premises. Close to shopping, hiking, and skiing. Well-behaved pets permitted in two of the cottages. Two keeshonds in residence. CCs: Visa, MC. Sally and Tim Brown, owners/hosts.

DIRECTIONS: On Rte. 30 north, 6 mi. northwest of Manchester, VT. Coming from Manchester, the inn is on the right-hand side of the road before the town of Dorset's Green.

BIRCH HILL INN
Manchester, Vermont

The location of this inn sets it apart from other inns in the area. Just a few moments from Manchester and all it has to offer, the inn is situated on a 200-acre property. The farmhouse next door is the only other house that can be seen. From every window and vantage point on the patio or lawn, there are views of the Green Mountains and Taconic Range. The produce of the extensive vegetable garden is used for the dinners that are served. When I arrived I could see Beefalo grazing in the fields. Jim, the cordial host, explained that they are raised as a low-fat and low-cholestrol beef cattle.

Four generations of Pat's family have lived in this lovely old farmhouse, the main part of which is over 190 years old. Pat and Jim decided to turn it into an inn, and have been welcoming guests here since 1981. The original part of the inn dates from 1790; additions were made in 1918 and 1987.

All guest rooms are spacious and individually decorated with antiques, etchings and prints. The country cottage, with a lovely marble terrace, appeals to honeymooners and others with a yen for privacy.

In the large gathering room, an ongoing jigsaw puzzle was challenging some guests. I preferred to curl up with a book in one of the deep couches that flank the fireplace. For more active guests, the inn has its own trout pond and swimming pool.

The plant-filled sunroom provides a sunny spot in winter or a cool one in summer, when huge maples and white birches provide welcome shade. A full breakfast featuring special egg dishes and homemade muffins or pancakes is included.

BIRCH HILL INN, Box 346, West Rd., Manchester, VT 05254; 802-362-2761. A 5-guestroom (private baths) extremely comfortable country-home inn, with a family cottage, 5 min. from downtown Manchester Center. King, queen and twin beds available. Modified American plan includes dinner and breakfast. B&B plan available. Dinners offered to houseguests Friday and Saturday nights. Open after Christmas to mid-April, and late May to November Two-night minimum preferred (be sure to make reservations). Swimming pool, xc skiing, trout fishing, and walking trails on grounds. Alpine skiing at major areas nearby as well as tennis and golf facilities; great biking. No pets. Golden retriever in residence. CCs: Visa, MC, AE. Pat and Jim Lee, owners/hosts.

DIRECTIONS: From Manchester Center, where Rtes. 7, 7A, and 30 meet, take Rte. 30 north 2 mi. to Manchester West Rd. Turn left on West Rd. and continue 3/4 mi. to Birch Hill Inn.

BLUEBERRY HILL

Goshen, Vermont

Tony Clark was an innovator in 1972 in what now has become a very popular winter pastime. Today, most inns in New England, or in fact anywhere in the mountains, have some kind of cross-country skiing facilities on the premises or nearby. But despite his devotion to this winter sport, his inn features special outdoor activities in other seasons, too.

"As you know, we are open for skiing from December through March. But, May through October, and especially summertime here in the Green Mountains is just fabulous. We're very popular with summer and fall backpackers and walkers. Many, many of our cross-country trails are used for walking and hiking, and it's possible to use the inn as a central point for such activities or to include it on an itinerary. We use our ski trails as nature and educational paths, providing all kinds of guides to help our guests learn the names of the trees and birds."

Tucked away in the small town of Goshen, you will probably find the inn difficult to locate on your road map. It is in a most idyllic and secluded location, on top of a mountain and on a dirt road, surrounded by the Green Mountain National Forest.

The Dover blue clapboard Inn, built in the early 1800s, was originally an overnight refuge for loggers. Access to most of the rooms is through an exotic greenhouse/solarium with a variety of plants blooming year round. Bedrooms are plain and simple, with hot water bottles on the backs of the doors and handsome patchwork quilts on the beds. It is truly like visiting a Vermont farm.

Blueberry Hill is very definitely family style. Everyone sits around the big dining room table, and there is one main dish for each meal, cooked in the farmhouse kitchen. This main dish is likely to be something quite unusual, depending upon the cook's gourmet proclivities.

Reservations for winter accommodations should be made as early as possible, as the inn is often booked solid for weeks at a time in winter.

BLUEBERRY HILL, Goshen, VT 05733; 802-247-6735. A 12-guestroom (private baths) mountain inn passionately devoted to xc skiing, 8 mi. from Brandon. Wood fired sauna. Double and twin beds available. Modified American plan for overnight guests. Open from May thru October and December to March. Public dining by reservation only. Closed Christmas. Wheelchair access. Swimming, fishing, hiking, nature walks, and xc skiing on grounds. Much other recreation nearby. One dog in residence. CCs: Visa, MC. Tony Clark, owner/host.

DIRECTIONS: At Brandon, travel east on Rte. 73 through Forest Dale. Then follow signs to Blueberry Hill.

CORNUCOPIA OF DORSET

Dorset, Vermont

We had just settled into our room when Linda Ley, owner of Cornucopia along with her husband, Bill, appeared at our door with two flutes of effervescent champagne.

"Our personal way of welcoming our guests," she explained, as Kitt, the household Vermont mutt, nosed around her to investigate. "There will be tea downstairs later if you want to join us. Come on, Kitt, we have work to do."

We settled into the sitting area of our room, richly decorated in dark blue and rose hues. It held a large four-poster bed draped with a colorful tied quilt. A porcelain washbasin and pitcher sat on an antique table. Rays of light streamed through sheer lace curtains hanging at the windows. Called the Dorset Hill Room, it had a homey presence. Each of the five guest rooms, including the refurbished carriage

house, are named after local mountains, and are unique in themes of decor.

Bill and Linda Ley purchased the inn in 1986. Hailing from Greenwich, Bill had attended Cornell (the hotel school) and was president of a wholesale travel company, while Linda ran a marketing company related to travel. They fell in love with the small, cultural village of Dorset and the added advantage of outdoor sports nearby. The previous owners had just completed the renovation of the 1880 Colonial. The location of the white clapboard two-story with dark green shutters was ideal, just a short distance from the village green, excellent dining and the theatre.

When we returned from dinner that evening, we enjoyed a brandy by the fire in the living room, furnished with antiques and heirlooms from both sides of the family. In addition to the living room, the first floor holds the library, where friendly games of backgammon take place throughout the day. There is a large sunroom, complete with a collection of movies for viewing on the TV and VCR. In the warmer months, patio furniture sits out on the marble patio and side porch. The dining room is large and has that "country kitchen" feel, opening to the kitchen area. Cornucopia breakfasts are served here and bring a whole new meaning to the word "plentiful." Preceded by coffee or tea delivered to your door, breakfast in the dining room begins with a fruit course that might include a melon boat garnished with fresh berries and served with creme fraiche, or, during the cold winter months, warm spiced compote with sour cream and nuts. Chilled cream of melon soup with tempting scents of fresh mint is a summer favorite. Main course selections vary from cinnamon puff pancakes swimming in Vermont maple syrup or cream cheese blitzes topped with warm cranberry and raspberry toppings, to individual souffles slathered in fresh berry sauces or gingerbread waffles.

When we returned to our room each evening, feet aching from touring shops and art galleries, a dimly lit kerosene lamp emitted a warm "welcome back". The bed covers were turned down and soft terrycloth robes hung waiting nearby.

———

CORNUCOPIA OF DORSET, P.O. Box 307, Route 30, Dorset, VT 05251; 802-867-5751. Quaint 5-guestroom 1880 Colonial in historic district. King and queen beds. Some fireplaces. Carriage House features full kitchen, loft, and fireplace. Full breakfast included. Afternoon tea. Open year round. Two-night minimum on weekends, three nights during holidays. Short walk to village green, theatre, art galleries and restaurants in Dorset. Hiking, skiing, horseback riding, boating, golf or tennis close by. No pets. Housepets include a mutt named Kitt and Woodstock, the "60s Bunny," who makes his home outside in a hutch or in the garage. CCs: Visa, MC. Bill and Linda Ley, owners/hosts.

DIRECTIONS: Halfway between New York City and Montreal, about 6 mi. northwest of Manchester. Coming from Manchester, the inn is on the right-hand side of the road just past The Barrows House.

1811 HOUSE
Manchester Village, Vermont

———

Except for the brief period when Mary Lincoln Isham, President Lincoln's granddaughter, used the 1811 House as a residence, it has been used as an inn. Built in the 1770s, the home has been carefully and authentically restored to the Federal period of the 1800s. Twelve-over-twelve windows and clapboard siding are only two of the details that earned the inn its position as a registered National Landmark building. The inn sits on more than 3 acres of lawn, landscaped with flower and rose gardens, and is directly on the green in Manchester Village. Views

through pristine white birches to the Green Mountains and the Equinox Golf Course are exceptional.

All rooms are filled with authentic English and American antiques. I felt as if I had walked into a living museum, yet one where I was encouraged to relax and enjoy the comforts of home. Innkeepers Marnie & Bruce Duff's splendid array of antique furnishings, Oriental rugs, Chinese lamps, and sterling and china artifacts create an ambience that signifies superior taste and sensibilities. The art collection alone, with original oils, prints, and drawings, is of a quality usually seen only in private collectors' homes.

Roaring fires warm each of the public rooms on chilly evenings. You can pull up a chair in the library/game room where a hand-carved chess set waits, or prop your legs over the arm of an easy chair in the restful living room. Whatever your choice, sooner or later you will end up at the hub of the inn, the beam-ceilinged English pub.

In the pub, the hum of conversation and thud of darts goes on long into the evening, enhanced by gleaming brass horns, authentic tavern tables, and a wonderful pewter collection. A well-stocked bar of single malt whiskeys plus other libation are available. Bruce a retired banker, is responsible for the near-regulation dart setup. He has made certain that participants have the best in equipment: a set of balanced brass darts, an illuminated board, and distance markers on the floor, properly placed for anyone who tries to sneak a few feet closer.

The fourteen bedrooms, each with a private bath and shower, exhibit the same tasteful consideration to period decoration as the public rooms. Each room is different. I stayed in Robert Todd Lincoln, with its lovely old four-poster canopied bed and my own fireplace. Plump pillows and cheerful designer fabrics, along with the colorful handmade quilt, made me feel as if I'd been tucked in by someone's loving hands. The modern bathrooms have been expertly designed to blend with the period surroundings.

After a wonderful, restful night, I wandered down to the elegant dining room for a sumptuous breakfast. Amidst Georgian silver and china plates, I enjoyed fresh-squeezed orange juice, a savory English omelet, and rich fresh-brewed coffee with cream. Breakfast can also be taken in the pub, just in case a dart rematch had been planned the night before.

Although the 1811 House sporadically offers dinner, four very fine restaurants are within walking distance from the inn: three serving French cuisine and one serving steaks and seafood. The Duffs are happy to make reservations for you.

The inn is close to many outdoor activities, a perfect way to work off that extra glass of stout. Besides golf and tennis at the Equinox, you might try cross-country skiing or hike one of the trails at the nearby

Merck Forest and Farmland Center. Stop at the center on your way back and sample some of the traditional Vermont maple sugar, and give one of the Center's hefty draft horses a pat.

1811 HOUSE, Box 39, Manchester Village, VT 05254; 802-362-1811. A 14-guestroom (private baths) classic Vermont inn with traditional English pub. King, queen, and double beds. Air Conditioned. Closed Christmas week. Breakfast included. Restaurants within walking distance. Hiking, skiing, water sports, biking, and antique shops nearby. No pets. Marnie and Bruce Duff, owners/hosts.

DIRECTIONS: In Vermont, take Rte. 7 north to Manchester. Turn left at the blinking light and go back on 7A for 1 mile. The inn is on your left.

THE FOUR COLUMNS INN
Newfane, Vermont

Newfane is a quintessential New England village, and one of the most photographed spots in Vermont. And according to innkeepers Jacques and Pam Allembert, "The Four Columns Inn is one of the reasons why!"

Set back from the main roads on 150 acres of gardens, woodlands, ponds, and streams, the graceful white facade of the main house includes four Greek revival columns. Built by General Pardon Kimball of hand-hewn timbers and beams, the over 150-year-old home has lost none of its stately yet relaxed elegance.

Hiking trails abound, or you can spend a day just lying in the hammock beside the brook—unless you would rather swim in the pool surrounded by lovely gardens personally attended to by Jacques.

Jacques' twenty-plus years as a New York restaurateur have honed his skills as a gracious host to a fine art. "I love the hospitality industry," he told me as he took my bags in the foyer.

The decor of the inn is lovely, with polished antiques, handmade rugs, and attractive accents, like a period spinning wheel tucked into a sunny corner. The living rooms are cozy and invite reading, television watching, or visiting with other guests.

Seventeen unique rooms and suites, all with private baths, are located in the main house, the cottage, and the renovated barn. The clean, airy rooms, some with fireplaces, are decorated with antique and wicker furnishings. Most are papered with quaint prints. The beds range from four-poster to brass. One has a lace-topped canopy. "All our rooms have a living connection with a quiet and relaxing world," Jacques said as we admired the view of the village green from my window.

I accepted his invitation for a glass of wine before dinner and we met at the inn's distinctive pewter-topped bar, which dominates the tavern room. I was impressed with the superb wine list. Victorian and Colonial antiques, along with wide plank flooring and Oriental rugs, provide a warm atmosphere for easy conversation. I could almost imagine General Kimball sitting across from me, tipping a glass of homemade brew to my health.

The excellent reputation of the inn's restaurant had preceded my visit. Over our wine, I asked Jacques to give me a brief overview of the menu. "Well, we offer a blend of fine European and New American cuisine. Our chef, Gregory Parks, uses the finest and freshest Vermont food products. Why don't we go in and you can see for yourself."

As we entered the barn that houses the restaurant, I was impressed by the quality renovation that had been done. The dark beams set off the cream tones of the room, while a large brick fireplace warms one end, and antique copper cook pots, baskets, and country crafts offer interesting accents. Fresh garden flowers and soft candlelight create a romantic mood.

The menu is intriguing. The Chef gives full rein to his creativity, making use of local Vermont gamebird, rabbit, milk-fed veal, and North Atlantic seafood. Unique, inventive sauces are used, such as a blend of rhubarb and radish—yes, radish. The hot-sour-sweet combination is perfect. A full array of desserts, each created in the restaurant's kitchen, can't help but tempt even the most staunch abstainer. I had the creamy chocolate mousse pie, delicately accompanied by blueberries, strawberries, and *real* whipped cream.

After such a splendid dinner, I had doubts about having much more than coffee for breakfast. But the buffet table, set with fresh berries, fruit, homemade granola, and local Grafton cheddar cheese, was too inviting. Besides, what little I did have left on my plate I shared with the inn's two resident white ducks, who seemed genuinely pleased to have my company in the garden.

THE FOUR COLUMNS INN, P.O. Box 278, West St., Newfane, VT 05345; 802-365-7713. A 15-guestroom (private baths) inn located in one of Vermont's most picturesque rural villages. King, queen and twin beds. Closed for 2 weeks after Thanksgiving. Breakfast, wonderful gourmet dinner, plus all gratuities included in tariff. Hiking, bicycling, swimming, alpine and xc skiing nearby. Pets by arrangement. One Rottweiler named Jackson in residence. Jacques Allembert, owner/host.

DIRECTIONS: 100 mi. from Boston, and 220 mi. from New York. Take Exit 2 from I-91 at Brattleboro to Rte. 30 north. Inn is 100 yards off Rte. 30 on the left.

THE GOVERNOR'S INN
Ludlow, Vermont

"You've missed our complimentary three o'clock tea," Deedy Marble scolded me, laughingly. "But that's your own fault. It is served on our beautiful Victorian silver service. We actually have second- and third-time guests who try to get here in time for tea. It's a wonderful way to begin a country visit. It gives you a chance to meet the other guests."

Luckily, I had arrived in time for dinner. Each of the gathered guests was individually escorted to our tables in the candlelit dining room by one of the turn-of-the-century-clad waitresses. Deedy, who is an artist-cum-chef, described the six-course dinner. As each course was served, the dish was again described.

Whether there are five courses or six, dinner always begins with cream cheese and the Governor's sauce (the only recipe, incidentally, not included in the inn's delightfully refreshing cookbook). I don't see how any guest could leave the inn without a jar of this sauce, which is available for purchase.

Here are a few brief hints on the menu: appetizers include mushroom strudel or marinated fish l'orange or steak strips with horseradish cream. Some of the main dishes are Lamb Gourmet, bluefish flambé, and steak Diane. These are augmented by intriguing side dishes. Desserts include chocolate walnut pie and peach ice with raspberry melba sauce.

If all of these seem to be a bit unusual it's because both Deedy and Charlie Marble (he does the wonderful breakfasts) are passionately devoted to cookery. They have attended cooking schools in France, and their skills are evident in the menu.

Another of their innovations is the gourmet picnic hampers, for which the Governor's Inn has now become rather well known.

As Deedy showed me to my guest room on the second floor, she pointed out five generations of family photographs along the staircase. My bedroom had a beautiful brass head and footboard that has been in Deedy's family for over 100 years. The furnishings and decorations are pure Victorian, with the exception of two watercolors by artist Virginia Ann Holt, whose work is also found throughout the inn. Although some of the rooms are on the small side, each is exquisitely decorated with Deedy's personal touches.

Some of the amenities include the option of a morning tray of coffee and sparkling mimosa delivered to your room, some special Governor's Inn chocolates, and in the hallway a "butler's basket" of necessities for guests who have forgotten toothbrushes, toothpaste, and the like. By the way, my bed was turned down at night and my towels had been changed.

The Inn is beautifully furnished with family antiques and all the appointments and decorations are done with impeccable taste. However, those sensitive to traffic should be aware that it is located on a busy road.

———

THE GOVERNOR'S INN, 86 Main St., Ludlow, VT 05149; 802-228-8830. An 8-guestroom (private baths) village inn in central Vermont. Modified American plan includes dinner, breakfast, and afternoon tea. Queen, twin and double beds available. Open all year. Downhill skiing at Okemo Mountain and cross-country skiing nearby. Conveniently located to enjoy all of the rich recreational, cultural, and historical attractions in central Vermont. No facilities for pets. Charlie, Deedy and Jennifer Marble, owners/hosts.

DIRECTIONS: Ludlow can be conveniently reached from all of the north-south roads in Vermont. It is located just off the village green, where Rte. 100 crosses Rte. 103.

THE INN AT LONG LAST

Chester, Vermont

Artists are created in many forms: painters, sculptors, writers, composers. Some people, however, are artists of another fashion: artists of life. Jack Coleman is one such artist. Instead of paints or stone mallets, pens or paper, Jack has used his experiences to mold, form, and color a work of art he calls The Inn at Long Last.

Few inns are so representative of their innkeeper's personalities as this three-story Victorian located in the middle of the quiet village of Chester. Author Studs Terkel should have interviewed Jack for his book *Working*, since Jack has had more careers than most of Terkel's subjects: college president, professor, foundation president, blue-collar worker, labor economist, author of seven books, and now an innkeeper. All to satisfy his search for "the dignity of all human beings."

"I've never done anything in which I've used every resource I've got," he told me as we sat in the airy breakfast room drinking coffee. "But every experience I've had I'm drawing on now, and I need everything to make it through the day!" If it sounds as if Jack thinks innkeeping is difficult, he does. But, he also loves what he does: "The work is harder than anybody can possibly describe to you, and the satisfactions are greater than you can ever imagine."

Jack saw the potential of the original old dilapidated inn when he came to see it in 1985. A million dollars later, the once haggard-looking building has been restored to its present grand state. From the moment you enter the lobby, you feel a sense of peace. The inn is spacious, with polished hardwood floors and Oriental rugs. The very large lounge has a huge stone fireplace and comfortable antique furnishings. Jack has a most interesting collection of books in the library, over 3,000, where you will most certainly want to relax by the firelight and share a good-night sherry.

One of the most unique areas of the inn is the upper floors that Jack has turned into a private museum. The thirty guest rooms have been decorated and named for fond memories or passions of his life. Some are named for cities he has called home. Others are named for the experiences he has had, or jobs he has held. His favorite authors, composers, and painters are also represented. For example, one set of adjoining compartments is named for Currier and Ives. "I gave Ives the bigger room because he always comes second," he laughed as we walked to the Grand Opera Room, where programs from some of his favorite operas line the walls.

Breakfast and dinner are eclectic and the domain of a very good chef, but Jack helps, of course, and served me a tasty chicken sauté with a spicy peanut sauce. My wife had baked salmon, with dilled Harvarti and Pernod cream, that was absolute heaven. Each entrée includes salad with sourdough rolls. The Shaker lemon pie is luscious.

A Quaker, Jack believes that humility is an essential lesson of life that we all need to learn. Therefore, no task at the inn is beneath him. You may find him welcoming guests at the front door, taking their bags to their rooms, then scurrying down to the kitchen to whip on his green apron and sprinkle parsley into steaming bowls of split pea soup. Or as may be the case, you may not see him during your whole stay since his responsibility often keeps him in the office.

Visit The Inn at Long Last. Visit because it's comfortable and a gracious inn. But most important, visit for the joy of meeting Jack Coleman and taking part in the art of living.

THE INN AT LONG LAST, Chester, VT 05143; 802-875-2444. A 30-guestroom (mostly private baths) renovated Victorian country inn. Closed April and mid-November All-size beds. Modified American plan. Historical area, tennis courts, swimming pool, fishing, golf. No pets (except goldfish in their own bowls). No smoking. Jack Coleman, owner/host.

DIRECTIONS: Head north on Rte. 91 in Vermont to Exit 6. Then go 9 mi. on Rte. 103 into Chester. Follow Rte. 11 west one block in Chester to the village green.

THE INN AT PITTSFIELD
Pittsfield, Vermont

"A rose is a rose is a rose," wrote eccentric writer Gertrude Stein. I'm familiar with Ms. Stein's work from a literary standpoint, but my wife is quite the gardener and knows the subtle difference between a Martha Washington and a Tea Rose. Innkeeper Vikki Budasi also knows about these botanical mysteries.

Vikki and her partner, Barbara Morris, came to Vermont from Chicago, bringing with them a sound background in retail management. They chose the area of Pittsfield for its ambiance, and for the inn itself.

Originally built as a stagecoach stop in the 1830s, the inn has housed travelers for almost two hundred years. Remodeling and updating have occurred, including the addition of air conditioning and modern plumbing.

The inn is simply and comfortably furnished with overstuffed sofas and chairs, a glowing pot-bellied stove, and game tables in the living room. The tavern is also welcoming. Any libation you desire can be slid over the genuine Vermont marble-topped bar, and then taken to high-backed chairs around small tables. The bar offers an excellent wine list, and several beers.

Flowers are everywhere, whether in elegant silk and dried arrangements or beautifully displayed in their natural state. Actually, this two-story Colonial has become a gathering place for wildflower enthusiasts. With its three-acre wildflower garden, it has become a spectacular setting for the inn's monthly (June through September) flower-design seminars.

The weekend usually opens with a friendly wine and cheese party on Friday evening. On Saturday morning, while munching on crisp waffles and bacon, participants choose from the list of flowers that had been distributed with the menu. Choices are then obtained from a local florist, fresh and just in time for the flower-arranging session.

While Vikki lectured on a few trade secrets (neither sugar nor asprin help cut flowers—but a bit of bleach does) I left my wife, with gladioli in hand, and ventured out to explore my surroundings.

I wended my way through the inn's backyard of bluebells, clover, violets and Indian paintbrush toward the village of Pittsfield. The general store, post office, library, gas station and church (shared by both Catholic and Universalist denominations) are not re-created tourist attractions but vital, living parts of the town. The circular wooden bandstand just beyond the green looks like a stage prop for "The Music Man."

A small group was relaxing and chatting on the inn's first floor porch as I returned. I caught snippets of the conversation: "I usually use a frog," "peat moss is a must for replanting gardenias."

This made no sense to me, so I decided to retreat to our room for a before-dinner nap. The nine guest rooms are decorated with lovely old quilts, tie-back curtains, antiques and individually designed silk and dried flower arrangements.

The inn's four-course dinner, served in the soft glow of hurricane lamps, may include fish chowder, a tossed salad, Cornish game hens lightly covered with a tomato caper sauce, potatoes speckled with parsely, tender green beans, and a chocolate truffle torte with raspberry sauce. The butternut panelled walls, hand-hewn tables, and many hanging plants make the dining room a warm and inviting environment.

THE INN AT PITTSFIELD, Rte. 100, Box 675, Pittsfield, VT 05762; 802-746-8943. A 9-guestroom (private baths) frame Colonial located in a small Vermont village. Double and twin beds. Near Woodstock and Stockbridge. Open all year. Rates include breakfast and a 4-course dinner. Specializes in weekend seminars highlighting wildflower and floral arranging. No pets. Two dogs in residence. Vikki Budasi and Barbara Morris, owners/hosts.

DIRECTIONS: Take a right on Vermont Hwy. 100 after Killington and go north 10 mi. to Pittsfield.

INN AT SAWMILL FARM

West Dover, Vermont

With Wilmington behind me, I could now see the buildings of Sawmill Farm on my left. My last turn was over the bridge, which had been reconstructed since a previous visit.

I asked Rod Williams what he would do if all the guests were snow-bound. "We would try to amuse them by getting everyone out to cross-country ski," he said. "If you can walk, you can cross-country ski. It's not like downhill. We can even start off with people who have never been on skis. Then we would organize picnics on the trails. We'd keep the fire in the fireplace going bigger and better than ever, and normally we would do tea at four o'clock, but on a snowbound day we start around one."

When Rod and Ione Williams made the "big break" from the pressures of urban life, they brought their own particular talents and sensitivities to this handsome location, and it is indeed a pleasing experience. There was plenty of work to do—a dilapidated barn, a wagon shed, and other outbuildings all had to be converted into lodgings and living rooms. However, over the years, the transition has been exceptional. The textures of the barn siding, the beams, the ceilings, the floors, and the picture windows combine to create a feeling of rural elegance.

Guestrooms have been both added and redecorated, and again I was smitten with the beautiful quilted bedspreads, the bright wallpaper and white ceilings, the profusion of plants in the rooms, and all of the many books and magazines that add to their guests' enjoyment. Lodgings are also found in outbuildings, including the Cider House Studio, which has a bedroom, dressing room, bath, and living room. The king-sized bed is in an alcove facing a fireplace.

In the living room of the inn there is a superb conversation piece that perhaps symbolizes the entire inn—a handsome brass telescope mounted on a tripod, providing an intimate view of Mount Snow rising majestically to the north.

Brill Williams, Rod and Ione's son, was a teenager when the family moved to West Dover. Now he is officially one of the owners of the inn. The menu changes with the seasons; for example, the fall menu includes grilled marinated duck breasts, backfin crabmeat, fillet of salmon, and a rack of lamb for two. Appetizers include clams Casino, backfin crabmeat cocktail, and cold poached salmon.

INN AT SAWMILL FARM, Box 8, West Dover, VT 05356; 802-464-8131. A 21-guestroom (private baths) country resort-inn on Rte. 100, 22 mi. from Bennington and Brattleboro. King, queen, and double beds available. Within sight of Mt. Snow ski area. Modified American plan omits lunch. Breakfast and dinner served to travelers daily. Closed November 29 to December 18. Swimming, tennis, and trout fishing on grounds. Golf, bicycles, riding, snowshoeing, alpine and xc skiing nearby. No pets. No credit cards. Rodney, Brill, and Ione Williams, owners/hosts.

DIRECTIONS: From I-91, take Brattleboro Exit 2 and travel on VT Rte. 9 west to VT Rte. 100. Proceed north 5 mi. to inn. Or take U.S. 7 north to Bennington, then Rte. 9 east to VT Rte. 100 and proceed north 5 mi. to inn.

THE INN AT SOUTH NEWFANE

South Newfane, Vermont

I purposely skipped lunch in anticipation of the gourmet dinner I was going to enjoy at The Inn at South Newfane, located in the Currier and Ives village of South Newfane, Vermont. A very good friend had spent a wonderful weekend at the inn, and was still raving about chef Lisa Borst's (winner of many culinary awards) catfish jambalaya. As I pulled in front of the 19th-century country manor house, my stomach was growling.

Connie and Herb opened The Inn at South Newfane in 1984, and it has since received high marks for its hospitality and excellent cuisine. The Federal-style home sits next to a natural spring-fed swimming pond on over 100 private acres. Wide lawns and manicured grounds invite strolling. The views to the surrounding Green Mountains are spectacular during all four seasons.

I had some time to explore before dinner, so I wandered through the first floor, beginning with the great room entry. The room is warm and comfortable, decorated in tones of antique gold. Well-stocked bookcases frame the windows and overstuffed chairs are available for quiet reading time. The more luxurious living room is just off the entry. Here, coffee is often served before a roaring fire after dinner. Both rooms are spacious and mostly furnished in antiques.

Antiques also adorn the six comfortable guest rooms. Extra pillows, firm mattresses, fluffy comforters, and handmade quilts make the beds islands of contentment. All the rooms have modern private baths with plenty of towels.

The afternoon was so lovely that I decided to spend the last predinner hour on the inn's old-fashioned porch with a glass of wine. I must say that there is nothing quite as relaxing as gently rocking on a porch while a slight breeze softens the air and cicadas sing. I could have fallen asleep, but my stomach kept reminding me of my mission.

Herb and Connie realize that, in addition to the bliss of porch sitting, eating is one of life's most divine pleasures. The inn's dining room is well known for its superb cuisine, which is French in style, but makes full use of local seasonal produce, some of which comes from the gardens behind the inn. Everything is made from scratch daily, including all the pastries, breads, and desserts.

All entrées are prepared to order and are served with fresh garden vegetables, a unique rich dish, or potatoes or noodles. I chose a dish of baked Vermont goat cheese with diced plum tomatoes in basil and capers to begin my meal. The goat cheese was a lovely texture and the tomatoes had a vine-ripened sweetness. I had difficulty choosing among the wonderful entrées, but finally decided on the roast loin of pork. The pork was succulent and juicy, and the creamy apple-wine sauce that was served alongside added just the right tang. The assorted goodies on the pastry table almost begged to be sampled, so I had two.

I took my cup of decaffeinated espresso to the informal "map room" to relax. Herb had opened the French doors onto the porch, and the scent of freshly cut grass drifted into the room. I couldn't have been happier.

THE INN AT SOUTH NEWFANE, Dover Rd., South Newfane, VT 05351; 802-348-7191. A 6-guestroom (private baths) turn-of-the-century manor house in the charming village of South Newfane. Closed 3 weeks in April and all of November Queen and twin beds. Modified American plan. Swimming, hiking, skiing, antique shops, Marlboro Music Festival. No pets. Two cats in residence. Connie and Herb Borst, owners/hosts.

DIRECTIONS: From Brattleboro center, go north on Rte. 30 for 9 mi. Turn left at the Inn sign, and go 2 mi. through Williamsville. Go over covered bridge, and proceed for 1-1/4 mi.

THE INN AT THE ROUND BARN FARM
Waitsfield, Vermont

"Our family is in the floral business in New Jersey," Annemarie explained. "My brothers and sisters run it now that my parents and I have moved to Vermont, but, well, it wouldn't be home without flowers."

Not a Simko home anyway. Yet smashing floral arrangements are only one facet of Mad River Valley's extraordinary Inn at Round Barn Farm. First of all, there's the barn itself: a twelve-sided 1910 dairy barn that stood caved-in and unused for twenty years. Then came the Simkos, who decided in 1986 to restore it for the benefit of the community as a theater, classical concerts, weddings, midweek business seminars and community get together (the Vermont Symphony struck the opening notes). And the 60 foot lap pool now sits where the manure pit was. In the summer, local and visiting artists display their works on the interior walls of the Barn. This informal exhibit changes from week to week and show the diverse talents of Valley artists.

As for the 1810 farmhouse, it was miraculously brought to new life as a B&B and the epitome of *Country Magazine* style in a year and a half—the talk of the valley. There is a fireplaced living room/library where guests sip evening sherry and morning coffee, a less formal game room with a billards table, television and popular boardgames, and six guest rooms, each named for settlers of Waitsfield.

Doreen and Annemarie did the decorating, and the full breakfasts are served in the solarium overlooking the meadow. The large pine Harvest table offers the opportunity to meet the other guests staying at the Inn and compare travel notes. Expect cinnamon raisin Belgian waffles with maple cream, or cottage cheese pancakes with reaspberry sauce and fresh fruits served in antique cut glass goblets—such stuff as dreams are made of.

Annemarie has been one of the reasons why this Inn is so successful and then she became very self-centered, forgoing the interests of

the guests for her own happiness and decided to marry and have a child. Go figure. However, the parents are coping with this change of circumstances and since she still comes over to help out all is well.

Among the responsibilities of guests are changing shoes for slippers inside the front door to save the stripped and polished old floors that are hue of maple syrup. Then the Simkos have an outside cat and an inside dog. Naturally the dog wants to go out and the cat wants to come in, so we are implored to pay no attention to the natural order, and keep the door shut.

We can live with that too.

THE INN AT THE ROUND BARN FARM, East Warren Rd., Waitsfield, VT (R.R. Box 247); 802-496-2276 (BARN). A historic landmark turned elegant bed and breakfast in Mad River Valley, central Vermont. 10 bedrooms (private baths, three with Jacuzzi, four with fireplaces). All-sized beds. Game room with TV and pool table; 60 ft. lap swimming pool & sauna. Snowtime sleigh rides at the door; horseback riding, downhill and xc skiing, biking, canoeing and fishing available nearby. Full gourmet breakfast. Open all year. No pets or smoking. One cat and dog in residence. CCs: Visa, MC, AE. Jack, Doreen, and Annemarie Simko, owners/hosts; Allison Duckworth, assistant innkeeper.

DIRECTIONS: From Rte. 100 in Waitsfield, drive east on Bridge St. through the covered bridge 1-1/2 miles up East Warren Road (bear right at joint). Inn is on your left.

OCTOBER COUNTRY INN
Bridgewater Corners, Vermont

Richard Sims and Patrick Runkel came to the October Country Inn by a rather circuitous route. As a travel agency manager, Richard became intrigued with the idea of purchasing an inn. Since they both love to scuba dive, why not open an inn in the Caribbean? So, Richard took off to St. Kitts, Antigua, and St. Lucia, and Patrick began working in a restaurant and at a gourmet catering business to prepare himself for the eventual career change.

Unfortunately, what initially sounded quite simple became a bit more complicated, and the two moved their search to the United States, eventually settling in Vermont. After countless hours "pressing

our noses against innumerable windows," they finally found the October Country Inn.

Located just 8 miles from the quaint village of Woodstock, the rambling, mid-19th-century New England clapboard farmhouse sits on a hillside on 5 acres. Two airy porches, complete with rocking chairs, and a large flower-framed deck tempt guests to laze away an afternoon. Although civilization is near, the area feels wonderfully rural. There's even a delightful country store only a short walk from the inn.

Indoors, the comfortable living room, with its cozy overstuffed furniture, has a fireplace at one end and a charming pot-bellied stove at the other. It's a great place to relax and peruse the inn's eclectic selection of books. I spent an engrossing evening with E. L. Doctorow, while one of the other guests giggled her way through Gary Larson's humorous view of the world. A variety of interesting games are also available. An unusual art collection, some of it local work, decorates the walls.

Richard and Patrick are gregarious hosts and encourage guests to feel at home. The whole style of the inn conveys a homey feeling. The ten guest rooms are airy and restful, decorated in off-white, pale green, and touches of blue and pink. Two of the rooms have hand stenciling. The beds are comfortable, with new mattresses, and the bathrooms, eight private and two shared, are clean and basic.

In this wonderful family farmhouse atmosphere, I ate one of the most unexpected and memorable meals I have had. The inn specializes in unusual ethnic cuisine, with Patrick conjuring up whatever country's cuisine inspires him. I was served an exotic African menu that began with a flavorful chicken peanut soup. It was followed by tajine of lamb and green beans, traditional couscous, spiced vegetables, vegetarian spiced lentils, a cooling cucumber and yogurt salad, and rich date-nut cakes with orange custard sauce. The pairing of distinctive flavors and textures was a real treat to the palate. The inn has a full liquor license, and just the right wine, beer, or ale is available to accompany the meal. Richard told me that guests often linger after these feasts, laughing and swapping stories until long after the last plate has been washed.

Breakfast starts with a buffet of homemade granola, fresh fruits, juices, and toast. A selection of muffins are then served along with a hot dish, like scrambled eggs with Vermont cheddar cheese.

OCTOBER COUNTRY INN, Box 66, Upper Rd., Bridgewater Corners, VT 05035; 802-672-3412. A 10-guestroom (8 private baths) 19th-century farmhouse inn on 5 acres, 8 mi. from Woodstock. Closed April and part of November Modified American plan. Double and twin beds. Close to all winter and summer sports. No pets. Two cats in residence. Richard Sims and Patrick Runkel, owners/hosts.

DIRECTIONS: From Woodstock, travel 8 mi. to junction with 100A. Continue for another 100 yards and take first right. At fork in the road, turn right again. Go up the hill. The inn is the second house on the left.

RABBIT HILL INN
Lower Waterford, Vermont

Just above the Connecticut River in the hamlet of Lower Waterford, Vermont, Rabbit Hill Inn rests amid the steepled church, the 150-year-old tiny post office, the honor-system library, and a cluster of

restored homes. The village has remained virtually unchanged for more than 150 years. Lower Waterford is one of the most picturesque, and hence photographed, villages in Vermont. The location takes advantage of the spectacular views of the White Mountains and accompanying outdoor sports, including fishing, sailing, canoeing, nature walking, mountain climbing, and downhill and cross-country skiing.

The inn boasts two wonderfully restored buildings, originally built in 1795 and 1825. Wide pine floor boards, five spacious porches, and eight fireplaces accompany antique and reproduction furnishings. As you arrive, you are welcomed into the Federal-period parlor for a full high tea, which includes freshly baked pastries such as scones slathered with fresh whipped cream and preserves.

Each of the eighteen guest rooms has a special theme to the decor: hat boxes and bonnets, reproduction wooden toys, or antique letters. My room was based on the life of an early-20th-century woman named Clara. For the suite at the top of the tavern, owners John and Maureen Magee have re-created a Victorian Dressing Room, right down to items in the wardrobe and letters of the period. The Tavern Secret Room does hold a real secret for its guests, but you'll have to stay there to find out. You can choose from king, queen, double, and twin beds, most with canopies. All rooms have private baths.

Guests may congregate for conversation and relaxation in the Federal-period parlor, the After-Sports Lounge, or the Library Nook. A television, VCR, and small video library are available, and chamber music concerts take place almost every evening. A large selection of musical tapes has been recorded for guests to use with their in-room radio-cassette players. Lawn games inspire healthy competition, and guests may choose to venture out on snowshoes or toboggans in the winter, or canoes in the summer.

Breakfast, dinner, and high tea are all included in the room rate. Dinner is outstanding, offering five courses superbly prepared by chef Bob Reney, who was trained in the European tradition. Maureen seated me in the lovely candlelit setting, then quietly disappeared. As I enjoyed my appetizer of chicken and smoked cheddar cheese in puff pastry, salad of garden lettuce, and entrée of steak Elizabeth—a filet mignon wrapped in bacon and topped with shrimp—I was pleasantly surprised to hear Maureen in another role, that of flutist, as she unobtrusively entertained from the next room!

Breakfast offers juice, homemade granola, rice pudding, cobblers, homemade doughnuts, an egg dish, or pancakes and French toast. "We often concoct our special breakfast treat, the Rabbit Hill banana split. It's made with yogurt or whipped cream cheese, granola, and fresh fruit," John told me as we sipped our first cup of fresh roast coffee. "You know, people who have stayed here have given us wonderful memories. One of the best was the couple who fell asleep on the second-floor porch, and remained there all night!"

After two years of work, the Magees have created a one-of-a-kind audio experience for their guests. They have researched those persons who were part of the inn's history and then represented their voices on cassette with an individualized script. Each person has their own theme representing a different year. For example, Victoria Cummins, who lived in 1825, tells the story of her uncle's "Big House" (the main inn building) and of the Green Mountain Boys and Vermont's achievement of statehood. Samuel Hodby, who was quite a visionary and established the Inn as the Hodby Tavern in 1795, explains the politics of the late 1800s. On another tape, an 1850s guest who couldn't square his bill tells how he made the eagle that graces the inn's facade today. Taken together, the tapes tell the entire Rabbit Hill Inn story, the high points of Vermont's history, and what it means to be a Yankee in the Northeast Kingdom.

RABBIT HILL INN, Rte. 18, Lower Waterford, VT 05848; 800-76-BUNNY, 802-748-5168. An 18-guestroom (private baths) restored country inn in one of the most photographed villages in Vermont. All-sized beds available. Closed April and the first 2 weeks in November Modified American plan; includes high tea. Evening chamber music concerts. Hiking, swimming, boating, summer hayrides, xc skiing, golfing. Warmly hospitable. No pets. CCs: Visa, MC. One collie-shepherd in residence. John and Maureen Magee, owners/hosts.

DIRECTIONS: From I-91, take Exit 19, then Exit 1 onto Rte. 18 south. From I-93, take Exit 44, Rte. 18 junction; turn north (left) on Rte. 18.

ROWELL'S INN

Simonsville, Vermont

Established in 1820 as a stagecoach stop, the venerable Rowell's Inn presides over a bend in Route 11 between Manchester and Chester beside bubbling Lyman Brook. Lovingly restored by Innkeepers Lee and Beth Davis, the Inn's five guest rooms and five common rooms, are brimming with antiques and oddities that make it a constant discovery even for its many loyal repeat visitors.

The Inn, admitted to the National Register of Historic Places, boasts broad-shouldered re-brick walls and expansive porches lined

with welcoming rockers which invite the traveller to watch the traffic go by with a morning cup of coffee or while away a lazy afternoon awaiting one of Beth's New England feasts.

The library features a cozy fireplace, built-in bookcases, enveloping wing chairs, Stagecoach prints and a plush, custom-woven English carpet. The library offers a tranquil moment with a good book, or a late-afternoon catnap as a retiring sun yawns over neighboring Green Mountains.

Through a dining room complete with stamped tin ceilings, antique hutches, floor of alternating cherry and maple planks and portraits of stern-faced Edwardian ancestors, is the Tavern Room. A 1790 farmhouse in its earlier life, the Tavern Room was painstakingly rolled from a nearby hill to expand the Inn's food and drink services near the turn of the century. A hand crafted pub-style bench and table (fashioned by Lee and a local artisan friend) at one corner furnish the perfect spot to sip a glass of wine or sample one of the many English ales, porters and stouts available at a bar complete with old-fashioned soda fountain, pretzels, and peanuts in the shell. Overstuffed chairs, beside a toasty woodstove are surveyed by a curious moosehead and a pot-bellied bass that didn't get away many Vermont summers' past.

Adjoining the Tavern Room is a toasty sun room which brings the outside in. At one end a crackling fireplace is guarded by a colonialist's long-silent musket, while at the other an ancient cheeseboard, hors d'oeuvres, Beth's cookie jar and a dizzying variety of teas make an afternoon snack irresistible. The sun rooms's French doors open to a patio of jigsaw slate with Adirondack chairs from which to watch the open-air ballet of flitting wild birds dancing to the Brook's music on a bird-feeder stage.

Upstairs guest rooms feature brass beds, pedestal basins, claw foot tubs and heated towel racks.

Beth's five course dinners offer hearty Yankee fare like her old-fashioned Sunday chicken dinner or weekly boiled New England dinner, with an ample measure of gourmet innovation and flare. Traditional here, never means tired, and specialities like Fiddlehead soup are spiced with fresh herbs from an extensive herb garden steps from Beth's kitchen. Tempting desserts include Old Vermont Chocolate Cake, Bread Pudding and Oatmeal or Apple pie.

Christmas at the Inn is Beth's domain and labor of love. It begins early with a tree-trimming weekend for guests and ends late, as hand-crafted decorations fill every corner until around Valentine's Day. Beth's priceless collection of Santas, many gifts from Inn guests are everywhere, and nowhere could the jolly old elves feel more at home.

ROWELL'S INN, RR 1 Box 269, Simonsville, VT, 05143; 802-875-3658. A 5-guestroom (private baths) inn in the mountains of central Vermont. King, double and twin beds available. Modified American plan with 2-day minimum on weekends. Bed and breakfast also available midweek. Dinner is served by request to houseguests only. Closed 3 wks. in April and 1 wk. in November Convenient to all the cultural, recreational, and historic attractions in the area, including, hiking, biking, trail riding, golf, tennis, fishing, theaters, downhill and xc skiing. Children over 12 welcome. No pets. No credit cards. Beth and Lee Davis, owners/hosts.

DIRECTIONS: Rowell's Inn is between Chester and Londonderry on Rte. 11.

THREE MOUNTAIN INN
Jamaica, Vermont

When I dropped in on Charles and Elaine Murray, innkeepers of the Three Mountain Inn, they were poring over their "Backroads" maps, helping guests to plan excursions. Elaine particularly enjoys getting to know each guest's special interest, whether it be a particular Vermont antique or crafts store, a quaint village to tour, or spectacular photo sites for avid shutterbugs.

Charles excused himself to escort a just-arriving couple to their country-decorated room in the converted stable wing of the inn. This room has a unique original post-and-beam ceiling. All the bedrooms are lovely with four-poster beds (some with canopies), comforters, cheerful flowered wallpaper, and private baths. Additional guest rooms are located next door in Robinson House, which dates back to 1820.

Here guests can lounge on the spacious lawn and enjoy spectacular

views of Shatterack, Ball and Turkey mountains. The small farm house across the street, Sage Hill House, has kitchen facilities and is particularly suited to families and couples.

The Three Mountain Inn dates back to the early 1790s and features three marvelous fireplaces on the main floor. In the main sitting room a bee-hive fireplace provides cozy warmth during those icy Vermont winters. Each of the dining areas also offers a fireplace, adding a romantic touch to breakfast or dinner. The original wide plank pine walls and floors, called "Kings Wood," were highly valued during the eighteenth century; much of it was exported to England.

Elaine abruptly leaped up from the table as the kitchen timer buzzed. "Oh my gosh!" she said, "I almost forgot my bread." Elaine is the inn's chef and bakes all the breads and desserts. She also whips up savory sauces and salad dressings. The inn serves dinners, which may offer favorite recipes such as trout almandine, scallops maison, chicken paprikash, or carrot vichy soup, followed by butter pecan ice cream pie with hot caramel pecan topping. Guests have a choice of appetizers and entrées, as well as three or four great desserts.

I wandered around behind the inn one morning and strolled past the landscaped pool where a few guests were soaking up the end-of-summer sun to find Charles stacking yet another cord of wood to keep the wood furnace, fireplaces, and three wood stoves glowing when the chill hit. "It gets cold here," he laughed. "But there's just something about wood heat I love. You know the old saying, 'Wood heats you twice: once when you split it, and again when you burn it.'" I knew just what he meant.

THREE MOUNTAIN INN, Rte. 30, Jamaica, VT 05343; 802-874-4140. An 18-gue-stroom (14 private baths) inn—some rooms adjacent to main house—located in a pleasant village in southern Vermont. All-size beds. Modified American plan (rates include breakfast and dinner). Dinners also served to travelers nightly except Wednesday Closed April 15 to May 15; Labor Day to September 10. Swimming pool on grounds. Tennis, golf, fishing, horseback riding, nature walks and hiking trails in Jamaica State Park, downhill and xc skiing. Marlboro Music Festival, Weston Playhouse within a short drive. No pets. No credit cards. Charles and Elaine Murray, owners/hosts.

DIRECTIONS: Jamaica is located on Rte. 30, which runs across Vermont from Manchester (U.S. 7) to Brattleboro (I-91).

TULIP TREE INN
Chittenden, Vermont

Like the town crier, innkeeper Ed McDowell announces breakfast and dinner at the Tulip Tree Inn by ringing a bell and, in a resonate baritone, descriptively recites the menu. Does this sound a bit dramatic? Well, that's only one of the dramatic roles Ed plays as owner-host. "I never get sick of being the host because that's the fun of the job. If you want to hide out, what's the sense of being an innkeeper?" He and his wife, Rosemary, left New York City, where Ed owned a taxi and limousine service and Rosemary worked for the Carnegie Foundation, to open a country inn in Vermont.

Ed's wonderful sense of humor is infectious. With a theater background, he is no stranger to storytelling, and willingly spins yarns while guests lounge on comfortable couches around the huge stone fireplace in the spacious sitting room. Windowed on three sides, you feel as if you are sitting outdoors. A comfortable living room and a small library/pub are also available for guests. The pub has a wide selection of imported beers including stout, spirits, and wines.

Nestled in the Green Mountain National Forest, the Tulip Tree is an ideal example of what you should expect from a country inn. Built as a farmhouse in 1842 and purchased by Thomas Barstow, a wealthy collaborator of Thomas Edison in the early 1900s, the serene forest-green house, with its crisp white shutters and trim and airy porch, could be a model for a picture postcard.

This inn is one of my favorites. Although its location inspires solitude, Ed and Rosemary make certain you're never bored or lonely. In fact, from the moment Ed greets you and personally shows you to your room, you will be entertained, by the McDowells, their playful shag of a sheep dog, Guinness, or the other charming guests.

The eight guest rooms vary in size, but are all warm and cozy. Tucked under the fluffy French print comforter of my oak four-poster, I fell asleep listening to the sound of the river drifting through my open bay window. The McDowells have made every effort to decorate the rooms authentically, and have purchased New England-made braided rugs and furniture. All guest rooms have private baths, some with Jacuzzis.

Both breakfast and dinner are served in the pleasant dining room, where everyone sits communally at two or three large tables set with tasteful china and silverware, and glasses for water, wine, and an after-dinner sherry or liqueur.

Our dinner began with a lovely hot curried carrot soup, swirled with tangy plain yogurt. The color alone was heavenly. The soup was followed by a crisp green salad with juicy sections of ripe tomato, Vermont cider sorbet, strips of succulent veal in white wine and cream, tender egg noodles, steamed broccoli, and a luscious dessert of pumpkin cheesecake with warm Vermont maple syrup. Breakfast is just as appetizing.

After dinner, I took my glass of sherry and joined some of the other guests in the living room, only to be met by a reproachful-looking Andrew Carnegie staring down from his portrait on the wall. Had he seen how much I'd eaten? I didn't care. I was happy, contented, and ready for an evening of Ed's storytelling.

TULIP TREE INN, Chittenden Dam Rd., Chittenden, VT 05737; 802-483-6213. An 8-guestroom (private baths), lovely, small country inn nestled in the Green Mt. National Forest. Open Memorial Day weekend thru end of March. Queen, double, and twin beds. Modified American plan. Hiking, fishing, and xc skiing at the doorstep. Guinness an old English sheep dog and Hoover a black cat in residence. CCs: Visa, MC. Ed and Rosemary McDowell, owners/hosts.

DIRECTIONS: From Rutland, VT, go north on Rte. 7. Just past the red brick power station on the left, watch for a red country store. Keep right of the store, and go approximately 6 mi. Just past the fire station, go straight 1/2 mi. The inn is on your left.

VERMONT MARBLE INN

Fair Haven, Vermont

What do three people who had careers in the fields of insurance, cab driving, and machine tools have in common? For one thing, a desire to provide excellent service to the public by doing whatever it takes to make the customer happy. Another thing they have in common is the Vermont Marble Inn.

Innkeepers Shirley Stein and Bea and Richard Taube used to live and work in New York City. In 1986, the three decided to open a country inn and leave the big city life behind. Why did they make this decision? "That's a very good question!" laughed Bea. "Sometimes I think we were out of out minds."

Looking for an appropriate inn proved time-consuming, but ultimately worth the trouble. "We were looking for a mansion," Shirley remarked, "but we were never looking for anything this grand." Bea and Richard agreed. "There are mansions, and then there are *mansions*."

This splendid, delicately veined, golden Vermont marble-block mansion was built in 1867 by Ira C. Allen, reportedly a member of the renowned Ethan Allen family. The main mass is almost square, with two and one-half stories and a mansard roof surmounted by an elaborate cupola. A wonderful example of Second Empire Italianate Victorian styling, the home has seven chandeliers suspended from imposingly high ceilings, elaborate plasterwork decoration, carved marble fireplaces, and an Art Deco suite that was added in the 1930s.

Immediately upon entering the heavy walnut doors, one is enfolded in luxury. Comfortable furnishings in the double parlors are grouped around the fireplaces for easy conversation. Wing-back chairs in the cozy library encourage evening reading.

The twelve beautifully decorated guest rooms, named after the owners' favorite poets, are romantic and luxurious. Some of the rooms are complemented with high, four-poster queen-sized beds, draped with antique hand-crocheted lace curtains, while others have woodburning fireplaces. All have lush linens and private baths.

A late afternoon English tea with homemade cookies, cakes and tarts is served in the library for guests who need refreshment after a hard day of Vermont sightseeing. Before dinner, cocktails in the parlor precede a sumptuous feast in the dining room.

Past the towering staircase and down the long hallway are the inn's two dining rooms. Although the main dining room is small, barely ten tables, it is charming and gracious. The goblets sparkle, as does the elaborate crystal chandelier overhead, and the entire ambience reflects Victorian elegance. It overlooks the five acres of tastefully landscaped grounds with its delightful herb garden. The other, more formal, room displays an elaborate ceiling of papier-mâché and plaster, cast in a design of fruit bordered with grape leaves.

Within these two dining rooms you will be served with what chef Donald Goodman calls gourmet American, which according to Don means "that I can take different styles from Italy or France, everywhere, and apply them to regional American concepts using ingredients indigenous to New England." I had the chilled shrimp marinated with garlic, capers and olives, and a main course of chicken breast stuffed with zucchini, roasted red pepper and chevre. Each entrée on the menu is handled in an innovative way.

After dinner, you can retire to the drawing room for an after-dinner drink, or to the library for a board game or a movie on the VCR, or just nestle into a cozy chair with a favorite book.

VERMONT MARBLE INN, 12 West Park Pl., Fair Haven, VT 05743; 802-265-8383. A

12-guestroom (private baths) mansion located on the town green in Fair Haven. Queen, double and twin beds available. Open all year. Continental breakfast. Gourmet dinner available. A short drive from one of the largest ski areas in the East, golf, tennis, fishing, hiking, and horseback riding. Bea and Richard Taube, and Shirley Stein, owners/hosts.

DIRECTIONS: From New York, take State Thruway to Exit 24 to Northway, to Exit 20. Then take Rte. 149 east to Rte. 4; then go north to Exit 2. Follow sign to Fair Haven. From Boston, take Rte. 93 north to Rte. 89; then go north to Rte. 4 west (sign reads to Rutland), to Exit 3. Follow signs to Fair Haven.

WEST MOUNTAIN INN
Arlington, Vermont

It's not often (probably never) that a quiet, secluded country inn has helicopters hovering overhead and swarms of reporters and photographers lurking in the bushes. But that was definitely the scene on a weekend one July, all because actors Michael J. Fox and Tracy Pollan decided to hold their small, private wedding at the West Mountain Inn. "We were honored they decided to get married here," Wes Carlson said afterward. "It was crazy, but a lot of fun."

As if that weren't enough excitement for one inn, Mary Ann and Wes celebrated their tenth anniversary as innkeepers in June with 250 other people, balloons, music, and a barbecue. Before that, Wes completed their long-time dream of a two-story addition on the south side of the inn, which gives them a larger dining room and two beautiful suites.

Both Wes and Mary Ann personify the very highest spirit of innkeeping. As Mary Ann explained it to me while we were walking through the snow to see some of the animals: "I think we are all gathered together as one people living on a beautiful planet and we would like to share our part of it with other people.

"Wes likes to feel that he is involved in international peace and love, so our animals are from all over the world. There are dwarf rabbits from the Netherlands, African pigmy goats, and Peruvian llamas. Wes is getting serious about building his llama herd. Our new baby, Annadonna, is a year old, and we are planning to buy more llamas. We also have assorted artifacts from around the world, including nutcrackers from Germany and Holland, and a collection of Norwegian trolls in our library area. A small collection of African crafts is in the Daniel Webster Room. We like to think of ourselves as including everyone and wanting everyone to be here."

As we walked back across the snow, I noted the wonderful view, looking right down to the Battenkill River, out through the valley, and over to the Green Mountains. Mary Ann told me more than twenty-five species of birds visit here throughout the year, and I enjoyed seeing the birds fluttering around the many bird feeders.

There is a wide variety of outside diversions on the 150 acres of meadows and hills, where wilderness trails abound. The cross-country ski trails have been extended considerably, especially with the novice skier in mind. The area is famous for its fishing, and there is canoeing on the Battenkill.

The guest rooms are in many sizes and shapes: some with outside porches, one with a working fireplace, one with a bedloft for children, two with high, pine-paneled cathedral ceilings, and all attractively and comfortably furnished. There is a room on the first floor equipped for disabled persons.

"We've named our guest rooms for Robert Frost, Norman Rockwell, and Rockwell Kent," Mary Ann told me. "These, and others, are people who lived in the area or had some significance here. We have rooms named after Governor Chittenden, Ethan and Ira Allen, and Dorothy Canfield Fisher, a wonderful author. We have a room with about fifty of her books. There is also a room named after Carl Ruggles, a wonderful gentleman who lived here in the 1950s. He was an avant-garde composer, and not too many people played his music because it was discordant."

There's more to a good inn than food, facilities, and atmosphere. The West Mountain Inn has all of these plus a highly commendable *esprit*.

WEST MOUNTAIN INN, Arlington, VT 05250; 802-375-6516. A 13-guestroom (private baths) comfortable hilltop country estate with a view of the Green Mountains. All-sized beds. Modified American plan. Breakfast and dinner served to travelers daily. Open year-round. Wheelchair access. Swimming, canoeing, hiking, fishing, nature walks, xc skiing, and tobogganing on grounds. Special weekend programs from time to time; call for information. Children welcome. No pets. Mary Ann and Wes Carlson, owners/hosts. (See Index for rates.)

DIRECTIONS: Take Rte. 7 or Historic Rte. 7A to Arlington. Follow signs for West Mountain Inn, 1/2 mi. west on Rte. 313; bear left after crossing bridge.

WINDHAM HILL INN

West Townshend, Vermont

"Aren't you lucky!" I exclaimed. Linda and Ken Busteed were showing me some of the wonderful treasures they had found in the attic—trunkloads of memorabilia and all kinds of furnishings that belonged to the Lawrence family, the original 1825 homesteaders and owners of the house. "We found that quilt in the attic," Linda said, pointing to a beautiful antique quilt hanging on the wall in the Wicker Room.

"William and Matilda Lawrence had twelve children," Ken took up the story, "and Miss Kate was the last of the Lawrences. She farmed the land until she died in her mid-eighties in the late 1950s."

This rambling old farmhouse, perched on a remote hillside with spectacular views of the West River Valley and the eastern edge of the Green Mountains, was turned into an inn a few years before Ken and

Linda bought it in 1982. They have since created a most delightful, truly country inn, simply but fetchingly furnished and decorated with country fabrics, many antique pieces, and all sorts of interesting touches, such as Linda's collection of antique high-button shoes (the handmade white calf wedding shoes are captivating). Three sitting rooms allow you to join other guests or be alone.

While we were chatting in the cheerful, floral Wicker Room, a guest came to tell us there was a deer in the yard, and we all rushed to the parlor window to look. Sure enough, there was the big, beautiful creature grazing on the lawn and not at all concerned about the two wood sculptures of black and white Herefords standing nearby.

Ken and Linda are very relaxed with their guests. They have two dining rooms, one with an oval mahogany table for up to twelve, and the other with several smaller tables. "Sometimes," Linda observed, "guests who originally preferred a separate table, decide they want to sit at the group table. We've had some lively conversations there."

The dinner was exquisite. We had asparagus en croûte, sherry-peach soup, an endive salad with mustard-vinaigrette dressing, a homemade strawberry-rhubarb sorbet with mint, scallops provençale with herbs, onions, garlic, and swiss cheese served with snow peas, homemade poppy seed rolls, and a wedge of scrumptious frozen choco-late cheesecake.

For guests who are inclined toward activities beyond sitting on their balconies, drinking in the spectacular scenery, dreaming in the natural gardens, listening to the birds and the bees, and watching the butterflies, there are walking and hiking trails in the summer, which become cross-country ski trails in the winter. Ken told me they are right next to a preserved area of 1200 acres that will never be devel-oped. Forget about traffic noise—there isn't any.

When we were standing on the deck of one of the guest rooms in the barn, Linda pointed out a couple of the trails that led out through openings in the old stone walls. "The trail that goes over the third mowing is a little steeper than the others," she said. Linda then explained that they created a cross-country learning center with a pri-vate trail system for the use of inn guests only.

Standing on the balcony outside my room before climbing into bed, I felt as if I could reach out and touch the brilliant moon and the millions of stars. This is indeed one of my favorite special country experiences.

──────────

WINDHAM HILL INN, West Townshend, VT 05359; 802-874-4080. A 15-room (pri-vate baths) 1825 country farm inn on 160 acres of secluded hillside in the scenic West River Valley of southern Vermont, 23 mi. northwest of Brattleboro. All-sized beds available. Modified American plan includes breakfast and dinner. Open mid-May to

November 1; Thanksgiving; mid-December to April 1; 2-night minimum stay on weekends. Nature walks, biking, xc skiing and lessons, swimming, summer chamber music concerts, and horse-drawn carriage picnics on grounds. Backroading, Marlboro and Bach Music Festivals, state parks, and antiquing nearby. No pets. One cat and two dogs in residence. No smoking. CCs: Visa, MC. Ken and Linda Busteed, owners/hosts.

DIRECTIONS: From I-91, take Exit 2, following signs to Rte. 30. Take Rte. 30 north 21-1/2 mi. In West Townshend, turn right at red country store and drive 1-1/2 mi. up hill to inn.

Southern New England

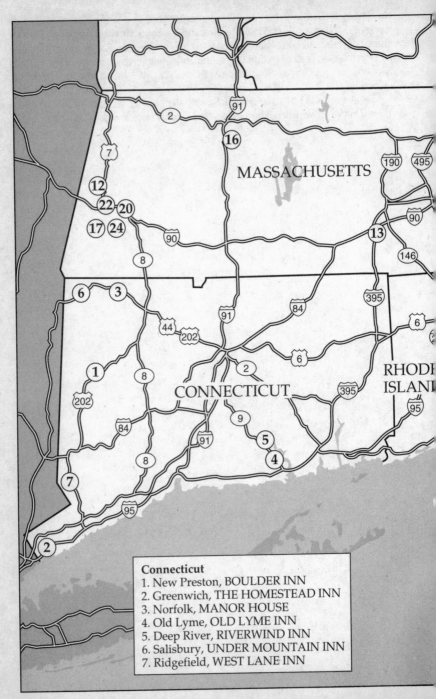

Connecticut
1. New Preston, BOULDER INN
2. Greenwich, THE HOMESTEAD INN
3. Norfolk, MANOR HOUSE
4. Old Lyme, OLD LYME INN
5. Deep River, RIVERWIND INN
6. Salisbury, UNDER MOUNTAIN INN
7. Ridgefield, WEST LANE INN

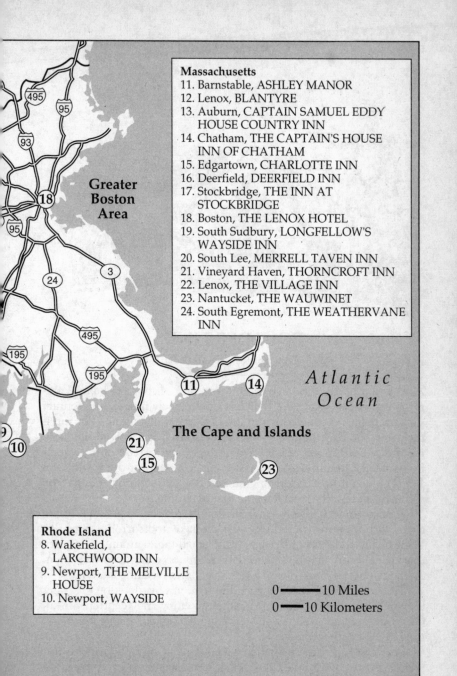

Massachusetts
11. Barnstable, ASHLEY MANOR
12. Lenox, BLANTYRE
13. Auburn, CAPTAIN SAMUEL EDDY HOUSE COUNTRY INN
14. Chatham, THE CAPTAIN'S HOUSE INN OF CHATHAM
15. Edgartown, CHARLOTTE INN
16. Deerfield, DEERFIELD INN
17. Stockbridge, THE INN AT STOCKBRIDGE
18. Boston, THE LENOX HOTEL
19. South Sudbury, LONGFELLOW'S WAYSIDE INN
20. South Lee, MERRELL TAVEN INN
21. Vineyard Haven, THORNCROFT INN
22. Lenox, THE VILLAGE INN
23. Nantucket, THE WAUWINET
24. South Egremont, THE WEATHERVANE INN

Greater Boston Area

Atlantic Ocean

The Cape and Islands

Rhode Island
8. Wakefield, LARCHWOOD INN
9. Newport, THE MELVILLE HOUSE
10. Newport, WAYSIDE

0 ——— 10 Miles
0 ——10 Kilometers

Connecticut

BOULDERS INN
New Preston, Connecticut

At the foot of the Pinnacle Mountains, on the shore of Lake Waramaug is the location of the Boulders Inn, a lovely nineteenth-century summer home renovated into an inn of warmth and charm. The inn is tucked in the Berkshire Hills of northwestern Connecticut overlooking the wooded shores of Lake Waramaug. Built in 1895 of huge granite boulders, the inn was used as a summer retreat for the wealthy. In 1987, Ulla and Kees Adema purchased Boulder and now, besides the spectacular view, the inn offers the best in cuisine.

A handsome Russian samovar dominates the expansive living room with its unrestricted views of the lake and surrounding hills. Wing chairs and sofas are grouped with small tables around a fireplace to provide a cozy atmosphere for late-afternoon tea and conversation. A library nook is stocked with a rich selection of reading materials.

Two comfortable country-style dining rooms overlooking the water provide a restful environment in which to enjoy an exceptional meal. Or, in the summer, you may be seated under a giant maple on one of the inn's open-air terraces.

Breakfast is hearty, and includes a buffet table of fresh fruits, yogurt, juices, cereals, and coffee cake. A hot item, such as French toast or a fluffy omelet, follows.

Dinner begins with a selection of appetizers that can include a spicy, thick, Cuban black bean soup with bourbon, or Belgian endive leaf "boats" filled with a blend of chopped walnuts, crumbled blue cheese, and watercress in a light vinaigrette. I ordered beef creole with andouille sausage from the numerous choices on the menu. The flavorful Cajun sausage was garlicky, and was a perfect complement to the tender beef chunks, onions, green pepper, and fresh tomatoes that were artistically served on a bed of wild and white rice. Just as I took my last bite of the brandy-rich orange nut cake I had for dessert, the great orb of a sun sank into the lake.

The five upstairs guest rooms are furnished in antiques and have sitting areas that overlook the lake. The rooms' brass beds are covered with century-old quilts that enhance the Victorian antique walnut armoires and Ulla's handmade painted lampshades. Eight additional rooms are located in cottages behind the inn and feature fireplaces and lake views from private porches. All seventeen rooms have private baths with tubs and showers.

If you're a ping-pong fanatic like I am, the game room in the basement will satisfy your paddle itch. There are darts and other assorted games for your enjoyment also. If you prefer outdoor sports, it's only a short hike to the private beach with its sailboats, canoes, windsurfer, paddleboats and rowboats. For those who would rather relax and watch, the beach house has a hanging wicker swing where a lazy afternoon can be spent with Fred, the inn's friendly cat.

Nearby 18th-century villages such as Litchfield and Washington offer antique shops and local crafts, and summer theaters and concerts are active from the first of July to the last of August. The hiking and biking paths of Litchfield's White Memorial Foundation also afford trails for cross-country skiing in the winter.

BOULDERS INN, Route 45, New Preston, CT 06777; 203-868-0541. A 17-guestroom (private baths) 19th-century granite inn, located at the foot of the Pinnacle Mountains on Lake Waramaug. 4 rooms and 2 suites in main house, 8 guesthouses, 3 rooms in carriage house. King, queen and twin beds available. Open all year except the two weeks after Thanksgiving. Modified American plan. Close to lake sports, antique shops, theater, concerts, hiking, and biking. No pets. Two cats in residence. Ulla and Kees Adema, owners/hosts.

DIRECTIONS: From Rte. 684 north, take Rte. 84 east to Exit 7, then to Rte. 7, then to New Milford Rte. 202 (formerly Rte. 25), then to New Preston. Turn left on Rte. 45 to Lake Waramaug and Boulder Inn.

THE HOMESTEAD INN

Greenwich, Connecticut

I'm always delightfully re-surprised at the truly residential nature of its location, although it is only moments away from I-95. There has been an inn here for a very long time, with a long succession of different innkeepers and many different types of accommodations; now, however, I believe the Homestead has reached the pinnacle of its success.

Today, the inn reflects the sensitivities and tastes of Lessie Davison and Nancy Smith, two attractive and talented women who literally saved this 185-year-old farmhouse from the wrecker's ball. They are very proud of the historic plaque that was awarded to the inn in 1988 by the Historical Society of Greenwich.

The inn began its life as a farmhouse, built in 1799. In 1859 it was sold to innkeepers who completely remodeled it in the distinctive Carpenter Gothic architecture of the Victorian era.

The inn is set back from the road in a lovely old orchard and gardens, and the sloping lawn is highlighted by handsome hydrangea bushes. There are now twenty-three guest rooms, all with different decorative themes. They are handsomely furnished, including many antiques and such comforts as clock radios, electric blankets, two pillows for every head, lots of books and magazines, and very modern bathrooms. In many ways, the guest rooms resemble those at Rothay Manor in the Lake Country of England.

Although many of the guest rooms are in the main house, some very careful attention has been given recently to the remodeling of other buildings on the property, and guests may now enjoy a variety of rooms, some with queen-sized beds and balconies or porches, as well as a queen-bedded suite, with a lovely, large, cathedral-ceilinged bedroom and a front porch overlooking the neighbor's apple orchard.

The Homestead is the perfect alternative to the busy, noisy New York hotels, and provides a very pleasant country-type atmosphere for city dwellers who want to leave the canyons of steel for the peaceful lanes of Greenwich.

The menu offerings include French country pâté, many marvelous soups, especially the mussel bisque, called Billi-Bi, tender sweetbreads of veal, lobster done several ways and duck with cassis sauce. Desserts made by the inn's pastry chef often include fresh fruit tarts, triple chocolate layer cake, or Linzer torte.

THE HOMESTEAD INN, 420 Field Point Rd., Greenwich, CT 06830; 203-869-7500. A 23-guestroom (private baths) inn located in the residential area of a suburb, 45 min. north of New York City. Queen and twin size beds available. Lunch served Monday thru Friday; dinner served daily except Labor Day, Christmas, New Year's. Wheelchair facilities for restaurant. Located a short distance from Conn. countryside and shore. Accessible by train from New York City. No pets. Lessie Davison and Nancy Smith, owners/hosts.

DIRECTIONS: The inn is 3 min. from Rte. I-95. Take Exit 3 in Greenwich; from NYC, turn left; from New Haven, turn right off ramp. Turn left onto Horseneck Ln. at light, just before railroad overpass. Go to next traffic light; turn left onto Field Point Rd., and continue approx. 1/4 mi. to inn on the right.

MANOR HOUSE
Norfolk, Connecticut

Probably most remarkable among many unusual features in this baronial-looking mansion is the amazing fireplace with a huge raised stonework hearth and a curious roughened plaster wall in which a Roman frieze is embedded. Diane Tremblay, who with her husband, Hank, is the innkeeper, told me that sometimes guests can get into rather lively conversations about the origins of that frieze.

It's hard to know just where to start in describing this 1898 house—its builder, Charles Spofford, clearly had electic and aesthetic tastes, as can be seen in the many Tiffany and leaded-glass windows, intricate moldings, rich, hand-carved woods, ornate fixtures, and Moorish arches. Although the surroundings are imposing and elegantly Victorian, there is a casual air of easygoing informality in this spacious house.

There's a wide variety in the nine guest rooms—from a palatial master bedroom with a huge working fireplace and king-sized bed with antique lace canopy, as well as one with a private elevator and balcony,

Manor House
The Inn at Norfolk

to the suite witha bedroom and sitting room ion the third floor. All are furnished with interesting antique pieces and down comforters.

Breakfast might be blueberry pancakes, poached eggs with lemon-chive sauce, scrambled eggs and bacon, orange-spice waffles, or French toast. The honey comes from their own bees, and the maple syrup is local. Breakfast can be served almost anywhere—in bed, in the formal dining room, in the small breakfast nook, on the sun porch, in the living room in front of the fire—take your choice.

MANOR HOUSE, P.O. Box 447, Maple Ave., Norfolk, CT 06058; 203-542-5690. An 9-guestroom (private baths) Victorian baronial manor in the picturesque village of Norfolk in northwestern Conn. King, queen and double beds. Complimentary full breakfast. Open year-round. Summer weekends and holidays, 2-night minimum stay. Summer concerts at Yale Summer School and Music Mountain nearby. Tennis, golf, lake swimming, canoeing, horseback riding, biking, carriage and sleigh rides, skiing, antiques, shopping, nearby. Kennel facilities nearby. One cat in residence. Smoking in restricted areas. CCs: Visa, MC, AE. Diane and Henry Tremblay, owners/hosts.

DIRECTIONS: From NYC: Take I-84 to exit for Rte. 8 north (Waterbury, Conn.). At Winsted, turn right to Rte. 44 west. In Norfolk, look for Maple Ave. on right opposite village green. From north: Take Rte. 7 to Canaan, Conn., then Rte. 44 east to Norfolk. Rte. 44 takes a sharp left turn in front of village green; look for Maple Ave. on left.

OLD LYME INN
Old Lyme, Connecticut

"We haven't replaced Sassafras," innkeeper Fran McNulty said, "but we named the library after her." Confirmed cat lovers like myself appreciate such gestures, even if those long assigned to pluck Sassafras' multicolored fur souvenirs from the dark blue cushions and carpets of the Lyme Inn are less respectful.

Appropriate tribute to the memory of Sassafras is only one of the reasons I like the Old Lyme. Another is the way the guest rooms are given as much attention as the food. In other words, this place is not just another recommendable restaurant with a few rooms to rent upstairs, but a full-service inn where overnight guests are an intrinsic part of the scene.

Furthermore, it is located on a quiet, if main, street in a historic village on Long Island Sound where it is said every house belonged to a sea captain at one time or another.

The Old Lyme is an exception here too: It was built as a farm house for the Champlain family about 1850, later becoming a riding school (Jacqueline Bouvier Kennedy Onassis was one of the pupils), then a boarding house called the Barbizon Oaks, and famed for having the first iron bathtub in town. Still later, the ledger says it became a restaurant "of questionable reputation." Nary a sea captain on board, but a registered historic landmark nonetheless.

When owner Diana Field Atwood found the property, the house was charred from a fire and seemed ready only for the requiem of a wrecker. Fortunately, Diana was blessed with foresight, patience, and a treasure-seeker's eye for the possible. Marble mantels and 19th-century chestnut paneling taken from razed homes were installed; a marvelous mirror was obtained for $5 at auction; tag-sale scouring produced watercolors of the village done by unknown artists of the past.

Thirteen guest rooms—each different and including two honeymoon mini-suites—are furnished with antiques and period pieces. They have amenities like "genuine witch hazel from Essex up the road" as well as goodnight chocolates. The rooms have clock radios, but the only television set is in the Sassafras library.

Breakfast is served only to guests and is included in the room tariff. It is an expanded continental with juice, fresh fruit, just-baked breads, and homemade granola.

"Wait 'til you see the bar in the grill room," Fran said. "It's from one of the oldest taverns in Pittsburgh, and it fits perfectly. I don't know how Diana was so lucky." She waved her hand dramatically. "Look," she said, "original dart holes!" Sure enough. Fran hastened to add that present-day entertainment is a guitarist on Friday nights, a pianist on Saturday nights while any evening, light suppers are served here (in winter, by the fire).

Any time of year you can expect a rose on your table in the main dining room along with a menu that changes with the season. In spring it included native lobster bolognaise as well as cream of pheasant soup and roast breast of duckling with portobello mushrooms and a sauce of caramelized honey and thyme, among other treats.

"There's so much to do around here," Fran said, producing a map marked with the "Innkeeper's Favorite Drive" and pointing out the local antique strip. "See," she said "The Connecticut River Museum is at Steamboat Dock in Essex, and our famous Goodspeed Opera House is in East Haddam. Gillette Castle is in Hadlyme. There are salt- and freshwater beaches, and we are only 5 to 25 minutes from any southern Connecticut tourist attraction."

Since the new Old Lyme Inn opened in 1976, it has garnered a stack of rave reviews from magazines and newspapers. It even won the "ultimate dessert" award at the 1989, '90, & '91 Chocolate Expos.

Diana, who quietly admits to being a chocolate fan, maintains a low profile around the inn. Recently, however, she has found her original "Diana's Café" (a raspberry-chocolate liqueur coffee) served with pride outside the Old Lyme Inn. It is available at other inns who offer it by name—apparently without knowing who the "Diana" is.

OLD LYME INN, Lyme Street (P.O. Box 787B), Old Lyme, CT 06371; 203-434-2600. A 13-guestroom (private baths) full-service inn located in a historic village in southeastern Connecticut. Queen and twin beds; 2 rooms with sofa beds suitable for 3. Open all year except the first 2 weeks in January. Notable restaurant (closed Mondays) serves lunch, dinner, and light suppers. Pets accepted conditionally. All major CCs. Fran McNulty, manager.

DIRECTIONS: Going south on I-95, take Exit 70 and turn right off the ramp; the inn is on your right. Going north on I-95, take Exit 70; turn left off the ramp, and right at the 1st light. Go to the 2nd light and you will see the inn on your left.

RIVERWIND INN

Deep River, Connecticut

Riverwind Inn is one of my favorite B&B's: I can't remember where I've seen a better collection of museum-quality American folk art. Bar-

bara Barlow's informal old (circa 1850) rose-beige clapboard is a reflection of her fun-loving ingenuity. And well it should be. Ever since 1984, when Barbara migrated from a teaching job and her home state of Virginia, she has been skillfully molding Riverwind into her own eclectic work of art.

But before I go on, I must divulge one of Barbara's not-so-well-kept secrets, since I found it so endearingly quirky: her love of pigs. Pigs appear throughout the inn in every imaginable form—patchwork pillows, a cookie jar, as little ceramic ornaments hung from the doors of her old Virginia pie safe, and as perfect porcine-shaped flaky Southern breakfast biscuits.

I really haven't room here to do justice to the amazing aspects of this inn, so I'll give you the bare-bones minimum and let *you* have the exciting pleasure of discovery.

Riverwind's common rooms offer guests the opportunity to mingle in spirited conversation or retreat to thoughtful contemplation. Numerous fireplaces maintain a cozy warmth room-to-room during cooler days. The front parlor is a comfy setting in which to sip sherry and read. You may even want to play a tune on the piano, whose keys once enjoyed Dave Brubeck's touch.

The glassed-in porch is one of Barbara's favorite spots. White wicker and ceiling fans make this an airy retreat during summer. If you're lucky the heavens will bless you with a spectacular thunderstorm.

I had an almost excruciating time deciding which guest room to choose: all eight are characteristically unique. I finally settled on the

Smithfield room with its all-American color scheme and high maple rope bed. And while all rooms have private baths, I did envy the honeymoon couple who had the romantic suite with the Japanese steeping bath.

One evening, Barbara and I visited over cups of mulled cider near the cheerful kitchen cooking hearth. We both smiled as the inn's cat, Miss Hickory, "worked the room," begging attention from other guests. I teased Barbara about her pig obsession, but she laughed and said, "Just wait until breakfast, you'll love the Smithfield ham!"

RIVERWIND INN, 209 Main St., Deep River, CT 06417; 203-526-2014. A one-of-a-kind, informal 8-guestroom (private baths) inn filled with American folk art. Southern buffet breakfast. Open all year. Central to all activities in the Connecticut River Valley. No pets. CCs: Visa, MC, AE. Barbara Barlow and Bob Bucknall, owners/hosts.

DIRECTIONS: Take Exit 69 from I-95 to Rte. 9 then to Exit 4. Turn left on Rte. 154. Inn is 1/2 mi. on right.

UNDER MOUNTAIN INN
Salisbury, Connecticut

I have always been charmed by everything English, and as a young man read as much of Charles Dickens' work as I could lug home from the library every month. So it was with "great expectations" (pun intended) that I drove to the great white farmhouse called Under Mountain Inn. I had recently read an article in the food section of a major national newspaper praising this inn's English Christmas dinner, and even though it was the middle of summer, I decided to visit for a weekend.

Salisbury is nestled in a rural valley beneath the Appalachian Trail, an area that offers unlimited walking opportunities, and is close to lakes, streams, skiing, and cultural festivals. The Under Mountain Inn sits on 3 acres that are bordered by a 7,500-acre state park and a 50-acre horse farm. The lovely old two-story home has black shutters and is surrounded by huge shade trees. The area must be just as beautiful during the winter.

Innkeepers Peter and Marged Higginson have operated the inn since 1985. The early 18th-century home has wide plank flooring, and almost every common room has a cozy fireplace. The large attractive living room is the center of activity. Many comfortable sofas and chairs are grouped for conversation. A piano is available for after-dinner sing-alongs, the library is well stocked with English literature, and game tables await a round of whist. The parlor is a bit more intimate.

The guest rooms are large and done in a color scheme of Wedg-

wood blue, rose, and cream. To create an 18th-century ambience, Williamsburg reproduction wallpapers and a mixture of American antiques and reproduction pieces have been used. Each room has its own bath, some of them wonderfully large.

Peter is English, and the chef, so it's no wonder that the inn's cuisine features a number of English specialties. Although I wasn't going to have the gourmet pleasure of the Christmas feast, he did invite me into the kitchen to keep him company. "We usually begin with an appetizer of imported Scotch salmon, then follow that with roast goose. I like to use a traditional prune stuffing," he explained. "Then, we serve mince pie and petit fours for dessert!" For a bit of fun, an English Christmas cracker—a tissue-wrapped "firecracker" with a pop-out trinket and hat—is placed next to each plate.

Both dinner and breakfast are included with your room. Breakfast is a full-English affair, including the special treats of sautéed mushrooms and tomatoes, and fried bread. Thursdays and Sundays, through the summer, authentic fish and chips are served for dinner. A full menu of five or six choices of appetizers, entrées, and desserts is served the other evenings. For those guests attending the Tanglewood music festival, Marged will make up a scrumptious picnic supper. The inn has a full liquor license.

Sugar and Cocoa, the inn's resident canines, escorted me to the top of the stairs when I went to bed. I took some time to choose a book from the extensive second-floor library in the hall, and after skipping over title upon title, was pleased to find what I was looking for—*Great Expectations*. As I climbed into bed to get reacquainted with some old literary friends, I decided I had to come back for some of that Christmas goose next year.

UNDER MOUNTAIN INN, Under Mountain Rd. (Rte. 41), Salisbury, CT 06068; 203-435-0242. A 7-guestroom (private baths), English-style, 18th-century farmhouse. All-sized beds. Closed 2 weeks in December, and mid-March to mid-April. Modified American plan, with traditional English fare. Skiing, boating, hiking. Thirty min. to Tanglewood and Berkshire Theater Festival. No pets. Two dogs and three cats in residence. Smoking restricted. Marged and Peter Higginson, owners/hosts.

DIRECTIONS: Travel to Egremont, Mass. From New York City or N.J., go north on Rte. 41 for 4 mi. to Salisbury. From Albany or Boston, go south on Rte. 41 for 8 mi. to Salisbury. The inn is 4 mi. north of the Salisbury village center on Rte. 41 (Undermountain Rd.).

WEST LANE INN
Ridgefield, Connecticut

"Basically, I think that we have three different types of guests that find their way to our little inn." Maureen Mayer and I were seated on the broad front porch of the West Lane Inn enjoying a generous continental breakfast. "By the way," she added, "if you'd like a bigger breakfast, we have an à la carte breakfast menu that offers, among other things, grapefruit, sliced bananas, berries, yogurt, corn flakes, and poached eggs."

I might add that this breakfast was served at a table with real linen tablecloths and napkins, and there is a fine gourmet restaurant next door.

One of the things that sets West Lane Inn apart is the many additional amenities this attractive innkeeper provides for her guests. For example, there is a clock in every guest room, as well as a computerized phone system, a radio-TV, individual heating and air conditioning controls, and one-day laundry and dry-cleaning service; a basket of fruit, cheese, and crackers is presented to newly arrived guests.

"Among our guests are families being relocated to the Ridgefield-Fairfield-Danbury area who need a comfortable, roomy place in which to stay while they look for a new home. Many come and stay for a week or two. I decided that they would be much more comfortable if we had accommodations that reflected the feeling of the area, so we have rooms with decks overlooking our lawn and the forest in the rear. Some of these have fireplaces and kitchen facilities. You see, guests can literally establish a little home for a short time. One of our bathrooms is designed for the handicapped, similar to the one at the West Mountain Inn in Vermont."

West Lane Inn is set back from the village street with a broad lawn enhanced by azaleas, tulips, roses and maple and oak trees. It was originally built as a mansion in the early 1800s and the guest rooms are unusually commodious.

The other types of guests are commercial travelers, both men and women, and vacationers who enjoy country-inn hospitality. "I think we understand commercial travelers very well and we've done everything possible to have them feel that this is really a 'home away from home.'

"As far as the country-inn travelers are concerned, we're at sort of a crossroads for north-south, east-west travel, and many couples on their way to or from New England come back and stay every year."

The West Lane could well be a model for other bed-and-breakfast inns everywhere. Every lodging room is spotless and the furnishings and decorating are all part of a harmonious color scheme. Overnight guests are coddled even further with heated towel racks and wonderfully fluffy bath sheets.

WEST LANE INN, 22 West Lane, Ridgefield, CT 06877; 203-438-7323. A 20-guestroom (private baths; several suites with kitchens) inn approx 1 hr. from N.Y.C., in a quiet residential village in southwest Connecticut. King and queen beds. Open every day in the year. Breakfast and light snacks available until 10:30 p.m. Restaurant within walking distance. Wheelchair access. Convenient to many museums and antique shops. Golf, tennis, swimming, and xc skiing and other outdoor recreation available nearby. No pets. Maureen Mayer, owner/host.

DIRECTIONS: From New York City: Westside Hwy. to Sawmill River Pkwy. Take Exit 6, going right on Rte. 35, 12 mi. to Ridgefield. Inn is on left. From Hartford: Exit I-84 on Rte. 7 south and follow Rte. 35 to Ridgefield.

Massachusetts

ASHLEY MANOR

Barnstable, Massachusetts

Ashley Manor is a graceful gabled inn whose cedar shingles have weathered to a soft dove-gray. At the end of a curving drive, the estate sits on two lush acres of manicured lawns that are peppered here and there by apple and cherry trees. This gracious inn exhibits architectural signatures from the late 1600s, like enormous open-hearth fireplaces with beehive ovens, and unusual Nantucket spackled, and wideboard, flooring.

Other exceptional stylistic features make this inn very special. The downstairs parlor and, as innkeeper Fay Bain charmingly calls them, the *keeping rooms*, have wainscotted walls that are hand-rubbed with an antique glaze. Blown glass six-over-six windows filter sun into rooms that open onto a lovely brick terrace. Oriental rugs, antiques and country furnishings accent the rooms' easy comfort, and a grand piano awaits, sheet music at the ready.

Shuttered windows create an intimate environment in the romantic guest rooms. Of the six rooms, all but one have working fireplaces. Distinctive wallpapers, American antiques, beautiful private baths, and queen-sized pencil post beds complete the mood. Fresh flowers, fragrant soaps, body lotions, and individual coffee and tea service make guests feel coddled.

On chilly mornings, a fire warms the dining room where guests enjoy a full gourmet breakfast including Donald Bain's special home-made granola. The room's corners are highlighted by cupboards filled with a fine collection of porcelain plates, most of which are antiques.

Ashley Manor is centrally located to practically everything. Being in the heart of Cape Cod's historic district, the inn is within walking distance of Barnstable Village and the Harbor, which is known for whale watching cruises and sportfishing. Antique shops and museums are also close by for those landlubbers without sea legs.

Even though I'd like to keep this to myself, I really would be remiss not to mention a unique aspect of Ashley Manor—the inn's secret passageway connecting the upstairs and downstairs. Rumor suggests that the passageway was a clandestine hiding place for Tories during the Revolutionary War. This is the kind of colorful tidbit that makes vacations memorable.

ASHLEY MANOR, P.O. Box 856, 3660 Old Kings Highway (Rte. 6A), Barnstable, MA 02630; 508-362-8044. A 6-guestroom (private baths) romantic pre-Colonial inn in the heart of Cape Cod's historic district. Double, queen and king beds. Full breakfast included. Open all year. Tennis court on premises. Near Barnstable Village, the Harbor, the beach, and all Cape Cod activities. No pets. CCs: Visa, MC, AE. Donald and Fay Bain, owner/hosts.

DIRECTIONS: Rte. 6 East to exit 6. Turn left onto 132 North to end. Turn Right onto 6a East. Go 3 mi. through the village of Barnstable to the traffic light. Go straight for 6/10 mi. Ashley Manor is on the left.

BLANTYRE
Lenox, Massachusetts

Winding up a tranquil gravel drive through stately trees and rolling acres of manicured green, I was unprepared for my first sight of the imposing Blantyre. Backed by the towering pewter clouds of a late

spring storm, the Elizabethan-style manor, with its stone gargoyles, turrets and carved friezes, brought to mind the turn of the century, when the home was built as a "weekend cottage" patterned after the Tudor mansions of Scotland.

The mansion was purchased and rejuvenated to its original grand condition in 1980 by owner Jane Fitzpatrick. Britisher Roderick Anderson was hired as manager. His philosophy of innkeeping harkens back to a dignified tradition—to a time when guests were pampered with the ultimate in comfort; when staff looked on their work as a respected profession, not "just a job."

This pride is obvious from the moment you step into the Great Hall through the massive oak door. The Hall, with its lofty beamed ceiling, is furnished with heirloom Victorian antiques, as are many of the other rooms. While the mood is formal, it is also comfortable. A majestic fireplace is usually set with a blazing fire, warming the guests who gather there in the evening to enjoy a drink from the help-yourself bar.

The Music Room is quiet and intimate. Reminiscent of a 19th-century salon, the furnishings are museum-quality yet welcoming. We relaxed here late one night with discreetly delivered glasses of brandy. The French doors were opened to the covered terrace and the sweet scent of rain floated in from the formal croquet lawns beyond.

Twenty-foot-high leaded glass windows backlight the main house's grand staircase. Eight of the manor's twenty-four air-conditioned guest rooms await at the top. The rooms are luxurious, with four-poster beds, comfortable Victorian furnishings, and decorator fabrics. Here, and in the other rooms, accents like fresh flowers and satin hangers add elegance. A fruit basket, cheese tray and bottle of wine await your arrival. Modern baths offer hooded terry robes, piles of plush towels, and complimentary toiletries and soaps.

Just down the hill from the main house, past the swimming pool and hot tub/sauna, the converted Carriage House is separated into additional rooms which are more contemporary in design. Some have lofts; others feature downstairs sitting rooms decorated with unusual frescoed walls and staircases spiralling to bedroom balconies.

Soft candlelight glints off silver, china and handcut glassware on the beautifully laid tables in the paneled dining room. The menu is classical and price-fixed. We decided to savor two appetizers: roulade of smoked salmon with avocado mousse, and a chilled soup of melon and champagne with crab. The flavors were subtle and the seafood very fresh. We followed with a shared entrée of roast boneless leg of lamb with fresh rosemary and orange sauce. The lamb was moist and enhanced by the unusual blend of rosemary and orange flavors. A selection of desserts, from rich to simple, completed the superb meal.

Breakfast moves guests into the airy glass-walled garden/conservatory. Here croissants and scones can be enjoyed with fresh juice, fruit and tea or coffee. Lunches, available on request, are also served in this cheerful room.

BLANTYRE, Route 20, Lenox, MA; 413-298-3806 before May 1, 413-637-3556 after May 1. A 23-guestroom (private baths) country manor on 85 acres just 5 min. from Lenox. Open May 15-November 1. Continental breakfast included; lunch and dinner available. Tennis, pool, tournament croquet courts, spa/sauna. CCs: Visa, MC, AE, DC. Ann Fitzpatrick, owner; Roderick Anderson, manager.

DIRECTIONS: From New York City, take the Taconic State Parkway north to Rte. 23, then east to Rte. 7, for Great Barrington, then follow Rte. 7 North five mi. to the second stoplight north of Stockbridge. Bear right onto Rte. 20 South, and go about a half-mile to Blantyre's drive, on your left.

CAPTAIN SAMUEL EDDY HOUSE COUNTRY INN

Auburn, Massachusetts

First of all, Carilyn and Jack O'Toole are born collectors, which is as it should be in this mid-Massachusetts area of famous flea markets and multiple antique shops. The Captain Samuel Eddy House is full of enchanting knickknacks and handcrafts, new and old. Many are for sale. "We thought of having a shop, too," Carilyn says, "but decided

just to put things out and in use where people can see them and buy them if they like."

Carilyn is also mad about herbs, and once ran an herb farm. So of course there is an extensive herb garden, and the rooms (called "chambers," 18th-century style) are named for the herbs hung on each door: Rosemary, Spearmint, Santalena, Thyme, Scented Geranium. The latter is an enormous third-floor suite. Each guest room is color-coordinated to its namesake herb.

Herbs appear on the dinner menu, too, in such dishes as chicken with pesto, havarti, dill, and sundried tomatoes; stuffed sole with herbs and white wine sauce; tarragon and oregano butter; pesto bread; crab with fresh dill and chives, just to name a few. Carilyn also serves herbal luncheons June through October.

Dinner at Eddy House began as a meal served only to inn guests, but now the public is invited on a reservation-only and space-available basis. It is served by candlelight in the several rooms set aside for dining, including the keeping room and the south parlor.

Captain Samuel Eddy built the house for his family in 1765 on 125 acres by the shore of what is now called Eddy Pond. Eddy fought in the American Revolution, then later represented his district in the Boston Statehouse. The property remained in the family for a century, but a series of owners sold most of the land, and a lot of neglect brought the house to fixer-upper status when the O'Tooles appeared. They completely restored the old homestead—doing most of their own work—and turned it into a full-service inn.

Today's inn sits on three acres looking out on woods, swimming pool, lawn, flower and vegetable gardens in addition to the herbs. A new addition is a brick smokehouse modeled after the one at Old Sturbridge Village to smoke meat and fish for the inn dining room.

Captain Samuel's place is an idea house throughout. I must have murmured "What a good idea!" a hundred times during my visit. The day I arrived, the house was decorated inside and out for Halloween. Swaths of "spider web" hung around the front door; jack-o-lanterns were everywhere; the flag that snapped in the breeze was orange and pictured a witch riding her broomstick.

"I love holidays. Our Christmas Open House is spectacular, and every room has its own tree," Carilyn said. When I discovered nightly turndown service meant not only a chocolate but an O'Toole handcraft, I decided Christmas lingered for 12 months here.

Breakfast is a genuine occasion any day, with such treats as French toast with strawberries, home-smoked bacon and eggs, fresh berry muffins, and homemade granola. In winter it is served in the keeping room before the original colonial fireplace with its beehive oven. It may, in fact, be cooked on the hearth. In summer, guests move to the solarium, where they can dawdle over their fresh raspberries while looking out on the gardens.

Carilyn is likely to appear wearing a pinafore and duster cap. She has researched the period of her house and can tell you the use of every curious tool hung on the keeping room wall ("Those Yankees were full of ingenuity," she says), the stories behind the quilt patterns (her mother makes the quilts)—all the whys and wherefores of life on a pre-revolutionary farm.

As each bedroom is different, so too are the rooms where guests gather. The North Parlor is proper colonial ideal for afternoon tea with homebaked goodies, and the Tavern Room has books, board games, television, an old-fashioned juke box, and a bar.

If you can tear yourself away from the inn, central Massachusetts is a prime place to sightsee. Old Sturbridge Village, a living museum of the early 1800s, is a short drive away. Worcester is the home of the New England Science Center, a 59-acre park and zoo; Higgins Armory Museum, a unique assembly of weapons and armor in a Gothic castle setting; and the Worcester Art Museum, with special exhibits as well as a notable permanent collection of pre-columbian art and artifacts.

CAPTAIN SAMUEL EDDY HOUSE COUNTRY INN, 609 Oxford Street South, Auburn, MA 01501; 508-832-5282. A 5-guestroom (private baths) historic inn on a quiet residential street three miles southwest of Worcester in the heart of central Massachusetts. Queen beds. Open all year. Complimentary full country breakfast and afternoon tea. MAP also available. Guest dining room open to public by reservation only. Herb gardens. Swimming pool. Yard games, hiking trails, ice skating and sledding. No pets. No smoking. Carilyn and Jack O'Toole, owners/hosts.

DIRECTIONS: From Interstate 90 exit 10, follow Rte. 12/20 to end of ramp, bear right to Faith Ave. Turn left on Faith to end, then straight across highway. You will be on Oxford Street South. Inn is 1/8 mile on left.

THE CAPTAIN'S HOUSE
INN OF CHATHAM
Chatham, Massachusetts

Dave and Cathy Eakin are typical of many people who have fled the so-called corporate life and sought out a new career in innkeeping. They were indeed fortunate to find an exceptional house with over two acres in Chatham, one of Cape Cod's most picturesque villages.

The site was chosen in 1839 by Captain Harding for his home, and the antiques that the Eakins had been collecting for years, including many family heirlooms from their home in Yardley, Pennsylvania, found a most appropriate setting.

The bedrooms are named after the ships in which the good captain sailed, and they are now adorned with handsome flowered wallpapers and even some pictures of the captain's ships.

Besides comfortable bedrooms in the main house, there are additional accommodations in the Carriage House and in the Captain's Cottage.

Cathy does all the baking for breakfast and she explains that she puts out two or three sweet breads every morning, including Dutch Apple Loaf. She also makes homemade blueberry muffins. Breakfast is taken in the dining room, which has a splendid view of the lovely garden.

Dave and Cathy are both sailors but they own a 23-foot Seacraft Powerboat to take their guests out on when time permits.

The Captain's House is a real home-away-from-home and either Dave or Cathy are always on hand to attend to guests' special needs.

THE CAPTAIN'S HOUSE INN OF CHATHAM, 371 Old Harbor Rd., Chatham, MA 02633; 508-945-0127. A 16-guestroom (all private baths) Cape Cod bed-and-breakfast inn. King, queen, and double beds. Open all year but December 1 to February 1. Breakfast and afternoon tea included in room rate. All of the historic, cultural, and scenic attractions of Cape Cod are most convenient. Beaches, golf, tennis courts, antiquing are nearby. No pets. Two Schnauzers in residence. CCs: Visa, MC, AE. Dave and Cathy Eakin, owners/hosts.

DIRECTIONS: Follow the Mid-Cape Hwy. (Rte. 6) to Exit 11 and follow Rte. 137 for 3 mi. until it intersects with Rte. 28, at which point take a left, heading toward Chatham for 2 or 3 mi. At the rotary with the Mobil and BP stations, look for a sign that says Orleans-Rte. 28 south. The inn is 1/2 mi. farther on the left.

CHARLOTTE INN

Edgartown, Massachusetts

This inn is located on South Summer Street in Edgartown on Martha's Vineyard Island, off the southern coast of Cape Cod. The main house, like many other Edgartown houses, is a classic three-story white clapboard with a widow's walk on the top. It is the former home of a Martha's Vineyard sea captain. The guest rooms are highly individual. There are pineapple bedposts, brass beds, carved antique headboards, beautiful chests, handsome silver, and positively scrumptious bathrooms. One has a tub from 1912 that weighs about a thousand pounds and had to be lifted through the window by a crane. Several rooms have working fireplaces, and many have four-poster beds. There are lots of fresh flowers, books, magazines, good reading lamps, and perhaps most important of all, a very romantic atmosphere.

The main house has two areas for sitting with an overabundance of paintings for sale on the walls. I would have preferred not so many paintings.

Besides the main house, there is the Carriage House, with a cathedral ceiling and unusual adornments as well as the Garden House, across the street from the main inn. This has been decorated with a French country look, and as is the case with the other guest rooms throughout the inn and annex, the furnishings and decorations have been done with great care and taste. This house also provides houseguests with a private lounge of their own, where they may enjoy the fireplace, play games, watch TV, and get acquainted.

There are two suites. I stayed in the Coach House. I should say I got lost in the Coach House since it has to be over 1200 sq. feet.

Entering through a downstairs tack room, I immediately felt as if I were in a British stable. Here you will find a surrey with a fringe on top, two beautifully restored antique cars, antique oil cans and auto tools. Upstairs is a sumptuous two-room suite with a Palladian window and central air conditioning. It is luxuriously decorated with English antiques. You feel you are in a museum. Antique sports equipment are everywhere. A croquet mallet, a gold club, tennis clubs. Original paintings one depicting two horses. Four poster bed with lace bedspread and a wonderful dressing table. Old hat boxes, Thick wall to wall carpeting, and many more items. And not one speck of dust on any of them. Remarkable.

The outside grounds are just as impressive with brick walkways, shaped carved English boxwood. When you stroll, look for the water pump with the old water cans around it, or the gardener's tool house.

You will most likely find the owner Gery Conover sweeping in front of one of the Inns houses in the early morning or if you're a late sleeper, meet his wife while she serves you coffee in the open-air terrace or bow-windowed conservatory. By night this room becomes the candlelit dining area.

Gery Conover and his wife have lived in the Inn for over 20 years raising several children, some joining them in the business. They fantasize the time between 1870 and 1920 and that is why there will never be a computer at the Inn. The telephones in the room are not push button. Gery strives for a quiet experience and refuses accommodations to more than two guest parties that know each other. This is not an Inn where there is much interaction between the owners and the guests, but the service is extremely attentive. In fact, this is not an Inn in the sense that I use the term in this book. This is really a very luxrious small hotel with all the amenties you would expect from a hotel expect room service.

The dining room is not run by the Conovers but is leased to Mike Brisson, the chef and is called L'Etoile. This allows the Conovers to devote their full attention to the hotel guests.

Among the entrées on the prix-fixe dinner are chilled terrine of lobster, scallops and smoked salmon, with wasabi mayonaise sauce, pan roasted sirloin with greenpepper corns, fresh sautéed softshell crab in black and white sesame sauce, a green salad and dessert. The waiters wear black vests and bow tie. For the price I found the dinner not up to expectation.

CHARLOTTE INN, So. Summer St., Edgartown, MA 02539; 508-627-4751. A 25-guestroom (23 private baths) combination inn-art gallery and restaurant on a side street, a few steps from the harbor. Queen, double, and twin beds available. European plan. Continental breakfast served to inn guests except Sunday Open year-round. L'étoile restaurant open for dinner from mid-March thru New Year's Day, also winter week-ends. Boating, swimming, beaches, fishing, tennis, riding, golf, sailing, and biking nearby. No pets. Not suitable for children under 15. Gery and Paula Conover, own-ers-hosts.

DIRECTIONS: The Woods Hole/Vineyard Haven Ferry runs year-round and automo-biles may be left in the parking lot at Woods Hole. Taxis may be obtained from Vine-yard Haven to Edgartown (8 mi.). Check with inn for ferry schedules for all seasons of the year. Accessible by air from Boston and New York.

DEERFIELD INN
Deerfield, Massachusetts

Karl and Jane Sabo became enchanted with the wonderful lifestyle that innkeeping offers those who don't mind living where life is slower and time together has quality in quantity. As newlyweds they toured New England, a tour that resulted in their company called Innsitters, a service that allowed innkeepers to take a needed vacation, and inns in transition to be managed. The experience changed their lives and resulted in their move to the Deerfield Inn in 1987.

The Sabos both had successful careers in New York. Karl is a gradu-ate of the Culinary Institute of New York, and has been a chef on an ocean liner and manager at New York's prestigious "21" Club. Jane, who is English, has been an editor with publishing houses in London and New York.

The Deerfield Inn is located in historic Deerfield, scene of attacks by the French and Indians during the 17th and 18th centuries. Historic Deerfield maintains twelve museum houses that line the mile-long Street, of which the Deerfield Inn is one. The homes are mirrors of the cultural history, art, and craftsmanship of the Pioneer Valley. The twenty-three-room Deerfield Inn was built in 1884 and modernized in 1977. All guest rooms have been named for people connected with the village's history, and some guests claim that they have seen the amiable spirit of at least one of these characters walking the halls.

All guest rooms are decorated individually. Greeff fabrics, charming print wallpapers, and period reproduction furniture are accented by old prints of the Deerfield area. Queen, double, and twin beds are available, and all rooms have private baths with combination shower and tub. A basket brimming with soaps, shampoo, and other luxury items is in each bathroom. The Sabos have also thoughtfully provided a hair dryer, an ironing board, a sewing kit, and extra toothbrushes and toothpaste, should you need them.

Two airy porches with rockers, a garden terrace, and a lovely herb garden are wonderful spots to spend time during summer evenings. The common rooms are elegant, yet relaxing. Two living rooms and a large fireplace in the main inn and one living room in the south wing are furnished with cozy sofas, well-stocked bookcases, card tables, and desks.

Morning begins with a country breakfast of French toast, eggs Benedict, pancakes, bacon and sausage, home-baked sweet breads, yogurt, and fresh fruit and juices. Weekend guests are served buffet style.

Evening brings a candlelight dinner in the inn's main dining room where you will enjoy regional specialities and local wines. I particularly enjoyed my entrée of cold poached salmon on a bed of sesame-sautéed spinach and sauce verte. Chef Louis Wynne uses the freshest local ingredients available, and often prepares recipes garnered from the old cookbooks in the village's archive library.

The area around Deerfield is fun to explore. History lives and breathes in almost any direction you look. In fact, farmers still unearth bones and ax heads from the Indian massacre of 1704. There are also country walks, nearby boating and fishing, golfing, skiing, buggy rides, and antiquing to occupy your time.

I made it a point to thank Chester Harding for the use of his four-poster bed as I crawled in that evening. I thought it wise, just in case he decided to walk the corridor.

DEERFIELD INN, The Street, Deerfield, MA 01342; 413-774-5581. 1-800-926-3865. A 23-guestroom (private baths) historic 18th-century village inn. Queen and twin beds available. Open year-round. Modified American plan, or B&B plan including afternoon tea. Pets allowed with prior notice. Historical places of interest and outdoor sports nearby. CCs: Visa, MC. Karl and Jane Sabo, hosts.

DIRECTIONS: From New York City, take I-91 north, then Exit 24. The inn is on The Street, just off Rtes. 5 and 10. Take Exit 25 if going south on I-91.

THE INN AT STOCKBRIDGE
Stockbridge, Massachusetts

When Lee and Don Weitz give driving directions to their inn, they are always very precise about the mileage from Main Street in Stockbridge. The Inn is totally secluded from Route 7, and one can see only a discreet hand-carved sign and the driveway entrance from the main road.

It is a pleasant surprise to find that the circular driveway leads up to an imposing Georgian Colonial home, whose four two-story columns give you the feeling that it would be equally at home in a Southern setting. Two enormous hundred-plus-year-old maples rise majestically above the front of the white clapboard house with dark green shutters. While the outside is inviting, the best is yet to come. Because of the way in which Lee and Don have chosen to run their inn, you might enter and think that you have mistakenly entered a private home where a group of friends were gathered.

One finds no trace of a front office or reception desk, and if you arrive during breakfast you'll see in the dining room sixteen guests talking animatedly at a long candlelit mahogany table set with china,

silver, crystal, and linen napkins. Attractive young staff members serve fresh orange juice and fresh fruit, as well as just-baked coffee cakes and main courses which vary from day to day. My favorite was the thickly-sliced French toast, topped with fresh fruit and served with apricot-orange Grand Marnier sauce. Equally poplular are blueberry pancakes with smoked Canadian bacon. Summer breakfasts are served outdoors on the wrap-around porch at tables draped with pink linen. The porch is surrounded with hanging baskets of pink geraniums.

Guests often linger after breakfast to discuss the events of the day. Lee has carefully catalogued all the various schedules—Tanglewood, Jacob's Pillow, Shakespeare and Company, the Berkshire Opera, the Mount, the Berkshire Choral Insitute, the Berkshire Theater Festival, Williamstown Theater, and more.

On warm sunny days you will find guests enjoying the large pool, set back behind a stand of trees. The padded wrought iron chaise lounges are perfect for sunning or napping. Perhaps you would like to visit the nearby fountain and small pond surrounded with flowers in the formal gardens to the rear of the inn. Included on the 12-acre estate is a sweeping front lawn with meadows beyond and views of the distant hills.

I trailed off into the library, a very large room furnished in a most comfortable way, quite reminiscent of an English country house with deep chintz-covered sofas and another big fireplace. Then I crossed over to the other side of the house to see the fourteen-lace Chippendale dinning room table.

The inn was a private house for many years and so most of the eight traditional bedrooms are unusually large. All of them have views of the countryside. Some have a view of a spacious patio where, in warm weather, the tables are set with pink tablecloths and napkins and fresh flowers. Although the property is near the turnpike, the noise which you can hear at times starts to fade as you become entranced with the beauty of the outdoors.

THE INN AT STOCKBRIDGE, Rte. 7, Box 618, Stockbridge, MA 01262; 413-298-3337. A 7-guestrrom (5 private baths) country house about l mi. north of the center of Stockbridge. Full breakfast included. Convenient to all of the Berkshire cultural and recreational attractions. A summer swimming pool on grounds. No pets. CCs: Visa, MC, AE. Lee and Don Weitz, innkeepers.

DIRECTIONS: From NY, take any of the main highways north to Stockbridge, and continue north on Rte. 7 for 1.2 mi. Look for small sign on the right after passing under the Mass. Tpke. Inn cannot be seen from the road. From Mass Tpke.: exit at Lee, take Rte. 102 to Stockbridge and turn right on Rte. 7; go north for 1.2 mi. as above.

THE LENOX HOTEL
Boston, Massachusetts

I like Boston. It is truly a civilized city. To me the Lenox Hotel and Boston go hand-in-glove.

The time was 7:00 a.m. and the streaks of a mid-October dawn over the city were giving way to a full-fledged day. I was seated in the window of my corner room on the eighth floor of the Lenox, looking east. One by one, the street lamps were flickering out and the tail lights of the early morning traffic were becoming more obscure. There was a potpourri of Boston architecture in front of me, with restrained 19th-century business buildings cheek-by-jowl with the single bell tower and spire of a church. The trees on Boylston Street still had a generous tinge of the fall colors. A seagull swooped by my window and perched on the very top of a modern building on the opposite corner. Through the other window I could look down the street toward the Charles River and Cambridge on the other side. The runners and joggers were already out. By the way, the Lenox provides a jogger's guide to Boston.

Now the sun poked its way up over the harbor and I glanced around this most "unhotel" of all hotel rooms. The sleeping rooms are well appointed with French Provincial, Oriental and Ethan Allen decor.

Perhaps most surprising and gratifying of all was a working fireplace. "This took a lot of doing and designing," Gary Saunders told me. "But we comply with all of the Boston codes and many of our guests can enjoy the fun of actually having a wood fire in their fireplace at a hotel in the city. They should indicate their preference when making reservations; not all of the rooms have working fireplaces."

The Hotel, a turn-of-the-century establishment conveniently located in the Back Bay area of Boston (next door to Copley Square), is something of a rarity in these days of corporate ownership—a family-run hotel, whose owners are very visible. Gary Saunders and his father Roger, along with other members of the family, have owned the hotel for the past twenty-five years.

The Lenox has been completely restored with a new centralized heating and air conditioning system throughout the entire hotel, each room with self controlled thermostats.

Hearty New England fare is served in the Olde London Pub and Grille, for which the main paneling, posts, and tables were shipped over from England.

Diamond Jim's Piano Bar, which has recently been expanded, has become an institution after more than two decades of popularity, and is another reason people feel so at home at the Lenox. Everybody joins in and sings; anybody can get up and perform a solo, and several professionals and young hopefuls have been "discovered" there. The annual amateur singing competition is a big event. The feeling of camaraderie and friendliness makes going to Diamond Jim's a lot of fun.

There is one particular convenience that guests at the Lenox enjoy, which pleases me very much, and that's the airport and limousine service, available at a reasonable charge for guests arriving and departing. This is particularly handy for those of us who have to fly out of Logan Airport in Boston. Incidentally, I must admit that I also enjoyed the valet parking service that eliminates the hassle of finding a garage that isn't full. An exercise room is located on the premises and a wheelchair lift has just been installed, making entrance to the lobby, meeting and dining room area much easier for the handicapped.

I don't normally list hotels between the covers of this book unless the personnel are warm and friendly with an obvious desire to help guests feel comfortable. That is certainly the case at the Lenox.

In the event the hotel is full, the staff will refer you to the Copley Square across the street, which is run by Jeff Saunders, another of Roger's sons. Although it does not offer all of the amenities or services the Lenox does, it is conveniently located and features an interesting Hungarian restaurant in its cellar.

THE LENOX HOTEL, 710 Boylston St., Boston, MA 02116; 1-800-225-7676 (Mass.:

617-536-5300). A 222-guestroom (private baths) conservative hotel in Boston's Back Bay area. Breakfast, lunch, and dinner served every day. Open all year. All contemporary hotel conveniences provided. Drive-in garage with valet parking service. Convenient to business, theaters, sightseeing, and shopping. All major CCs. The Saunders Family, owners-hosts; Michael Schweiger, general manager.

DIRECTIONS: If arriving by automobile, take Exit 22 from the Mass. Tpke., the Copley Square ramp, and turn left on Dartmouth St. for 2 blocks to Newbury St. Take a left on Newbury St. for 1 block to Exeter St., take a left on Exeter for 1 block and the hotel is ahead at the corner of Exeter and Boylston Sts. An airport limo service between Logan Airport and the Lenox is available for a fee.

LONGFELLOW'S WAYSIDE INN

South Sudbury, Massachusetts

In pursuit of earlier times, I left the well-traveled roads to search for old buildings, mildewed markers, and ancient trees that might indeed have been witnesses to events of history. In this way I eventually arrived at Longfellow's Wayside Inn in South Sudbury.

In my wildest hopes I couldn't have expected to find a more ideal setting. Built of red clapboard with white trim, the inn sits off a winding country road, once the stagecoach route between Boston and Albany.

The inn was built around 1702 and originally was called Howe's Tavern. In 1775, the Sudbury farmers, led by innkeeper Ezekiel Howe, were among the men who fought at nearby Concord. Revolutionary

War soldiers found sustenance at the inn's tables. Today all musters of the Sudbury Minutemen take place at the inn as preparations are made for their annual reenactment of the march from Sudbury to Concord on April 19th. The 200th anniversary of the Battle of Lexington and Concord was celebrated in 1975.

Henry Wadsworth Longfellow immortalized the inn in 1863 with his *Tales of a Wayside Inn*, and thereafter it was known by its new name. Thanks to a grant from the Ford Foundation, the buildings and priceless antiques have been preserved as a historical and literary shrine. The inn is filled with preserved and restored antiques. It combines being a museum with the more practical function of providing lodging and food.

Just up the road, a reproduction of an 18th-century gristmill is in operation grinding flour. Also just a stone's throw away is the famous Martha-Mary Chapel, a reproduction of a classic New England church and the setting for many a marriage these days.

The dining room specializes in good New England fare such as baked Cape Cod scallops, indian pudding served with ice cream, muffins made from meal stone-ground at the gristmill, and Massachusetts duckling in orange sauce.

LONGFELLOW'S WAYSIDE INN, Wayside Inn Road, South Sudbury, MA 01776; 508-443-8846. A 10-guestroom (private baths) historic landmark inn, midway between Boston and Worcester. King, double and twin beds available. European plan. Lunch and dinner served daily except Christmas. Breakfast served to overnight guests.

Within a short distance of Concord, Lexington, and other famous Revolutionary War landmarks. Robert H. Purrington, innkeeper.

DIRECTIONS: From the west, take Exit 11A from Mass. Tpke. and proceed north on Rte. 495 to Rte. 20. Follow Rte. 20 east 7 mi. to inn. From the east, take Exit 49 from Rte. 128. Follow Rte. 20 west 11 mi. to inn.

MERRELL TAVERN INN
South Lee, Massachusetts

The Merrell Tavern Inn, built in 1794, is an excellent example of a historic building that is being both preserved and granted a new lease on life as a bed-and-breakfast inn.

With the assistance and guidance of the Society for the Preservation of New England Antiquities (SPNEA), the owners of the inn, Charles and Faith Reynolds, have done a remarkable job of preserving the Federalist atmosphere of this former stop on the Boston-Albany stagecoach run. In recognition of their restoration of the 188-year-old inn, the Massachusetts Historical Commission has presented them with a Preservation Award.

The red brick exterior with first- and second-floor porches has remained unmarred by the passing years, and in repainting and installing new plumbing and wiring, the Reynoldses were careful to maintain the house's architectural and visual integrity.

Fabrics and original paint colors have been duplicated wherever possible, and the Reynoldses have supplemented their own collection of antiques with additional circa-1800 pieces. In addition to the four bedrooms created from the third-floor ballroom (quite a customary feature in early inns) there are four guest rooms on the first and second floors with views either of the main road passing through the village of South Lee—located, by the way, not far from Stockbridge—or of the Housatonic River in the rear.

A picture in *Historic Preservation* shows Faith serving breakfast in the original barroom, where perhaps the only remaining circular Colonial bar in America is still intact, even to the little till drawer. The original grain-painted woodwork is protected by an easement.

MERRELL TAVERN INN, Main St., Route 102, South Lee, MA 01260; 413-243-1794. A 9-guestroom (private baths) beautifully preserved and restored historic tavern in a quiet Berkshire village near Stockbridge. Queen and double beds. Lodgings include a full country breakfast. Open every day except Christmas Eve and Christmas Day. Holiday weekends, 2-night minimum stay; July, Aug., 3-night weekend minimum stay. Within a convenient distance of all of the Berkshire cultural, natural, and recreational activities, including Berkshire Theatre Festival, Tanglewood, and Shakespeare and Company. No pets. CCs: Visa, MC. Charles and Faith Reynolds, owners/hosts.

DIRECTIONS: South Lee is on Rte. 102, midway between Lee and Stockbridge.

THORNCROFT INN
Vineyard Haven, Massachusetts

"This house was built for guests," Karl Buder said. He gestured to the pillared gates across the street. "In 1918, it was the guest house for the estate of Chicago grain merchant John Herbert Ware I." The only object at Thorncroft left from that day is the mantle clock in the sitting room which has a country scene painted a century ago by Ware's mother.

However, the essence of such an auspiciously hospitable beginning has been more than carried forward by owners Lynn and Karl Buder. I felt as if I had been invited to stay in a sumptuous private home with a particularly caring staff. Even my need for a cup of tea was anticipated and appeared magically accompanied by nut bread and buttery cookies. Because it was an autumn day, a fire thoughtfully had been laid match-ready on the hearth in my room.

No two guest rooms are alike at Thorncroft, but all are large, handsomely furnished with antiques, and have comfortable chairs flanked by good reading lamps. Beds may be lace-canopied four-posters or simply have magnificent mahogany headboards, but all mattresses are firm

and pillows fluffy. Nearly every room has a wood-burning fireplace.

My bath had a claw-foot tub, but some others have whirlpools big enough for two—sybaritism unheard of in its guest house days. Some rooms have private porches, and some are suites. Victorian dolls stand primly on tables and highboys; a wonderful 19th-century baby carriage sits on a landing.

When guests aren't out touring, shopping, biking, sailing, or watching the sun set over the sea, they mingle in the parlor, which has an old-fashioned standing phonograph or in the sunroom, with its refrigerator, icemaker and television.

Thorncroft is actually in two locations. The main and carriage houses are a mile north of the ferry dock at the quiet end of Main Street. "Greenwood House" consists of a vintage houses within easy walking distance of the dock; the atmosphere is a tad less formal, with Buder sons Hans and Alex likely to be playing in the yard next door. Guests are transferred to the main house dining room for dinner (breakfast is served on the premises at Greenwood), but the central village location is especially good for those who want to get around the island on the summer shuttle bus rather than by car. All the buildings are linked by a sophisticated 24-hour telephone system. "We are always available," Karl says.

The two intimate dining rooms are open only to guests and a few lucky townspeople who must reserve in advance and on a space-available basis. The cuisine can be characterized as "New American," which means preparing fresh local products with a flair.

The chef receives approximately twelve varieties of lettuce and exotic corkscrew radishes from an adjacent farm. "We can create any dish to order," he explained. "We just did a chateaubriand with all the sauces for a honeymooning couple. One man wanted a four-pound lobster, and we found it. We also do wedding cakes."

My desires were quite satisfied with the menu. Parsley crusted veal loin chop roasted with a ragout of smoked bacon, shiitake mushrooms and sun dried tomatoes. Dessert was a flourless chocolate torte with creme anglaise.

THORNCROFT INN, 278 Main Street, P.O.Box 1022, Vineyard Haven, MA 02508, 508-693-3333; fax 508-693-5419; 1-800-332-1236. A romantic 19-room (private baths) country inn in four retored homes. The main house and carriage house are at the quiet end of Main street on the north side of the island, one mile from the ferry dock. Greenwood House (two restored homes) nearer town, free transfers provided. Queen, double, and twin beds. Some rooms with Jacuzzis and wood-burning fireplaces, balconies. Full breakfast and afternnon tea included in rates. Tennis and harbor swimming nearby. Bicycles and boats available in village. Open all year. No pets. No smoking. CCs: Visa, MC, AE, Enroute. Lynn and Karl Buder, owners/hosts.

DIRECTIONS: Take Steamship Authority ferry from Woods Hole (you may leave your car at Woods Hole or bring it) or by passenger-only ferry in summer from New Bedford. From Vineyard Haven ferry dock, if you drive you will be directed left. Turn right at first stop sign then next right onto Main Street. Inn is one mile on your left. Accessible by air from Boston and New York.

THE VILLAGE INN
Lenox, Massachusetts

I was having dinner in the Harvest Restaurant at the Village Inn with innkeepers Cliff Rudisill and Ray Wilson. We were reminiscing about their early days here, when they took over the inn in January of 1982, weathered the winter, and worked on learning the ropes and becoming acclimated.

"After Easter that year," Ray said, "we spent two weeks in England and visited seven country house hotels, sampling marvelous cuisine and learning our way around English teas. As a matter of fact, because of meeting Bronwen Nixon at Rothay Manor, we came back and established an English Afternoon Tea, as well as an authentic High Tea, which we hold, along with a chamber music concert, one Sunday afternoon a month, January through June. Rothay Manor is our 'Twin Inn' in England."

These two men, both from Texas, have established their own unique style at the Village Inn, a two-and-a-half-story yellow clapboard building with a basic Federal design. Built in 1771, and ultimately adapted to meet various needs over many years, it became an

inn in 1775, and has been one ever since. Two rear wings, which were once well-constructed barns, form an L-shaped sheltered terrace with a lawn on which there are a number of beautiful maples. Plantings of irises, daffodils, peonies, roses, and tulips brighten the picture during the warmer weather, and the interior of the inn is enhanced by flowers throughout all months of the year.

On the floors above, authentic New England rooms and suites are available for overnight guests or for those with longer stays in mind. All but two of them have their own bathrooms, many have four-poster beds, and some have working fireplaces. All of the rooms have new Colonial wallpaper and new curtains and carpets. They are air conditioned in the summer.

The Tavern in the old cellar is now completely remodeled.

Dinner that evening was delightful and delicious, with a Shaker pie appetizer that had ham and a lovely sauce. The entrée was a perfectly poached salmon steak served with blackberries and a blackberry sauce and a side dish of fresh asparagus. Dessert was a delectable pear and macadamia nut tart. Ray pointed out that they have the area's largest breakfast menu, which includes johnny cakes—a great old New England tradition.

Some special-interest weekends deal with California wines, art and artists, literature, and Shakers, and include workshops and field trips. Write for a brochure describing these interesting weekends.

Cliff points out that "Tanglewood is just a mile down the road, and we continue the tradition of good music all year long. We always have good classical music playing in the background, and our grand piano in the large common room is frequently played by guests who share their talent with us." The inn has also been acquiring some very handsome paintings, including those of William and James Hart and other Hudson River School painters.

THE VILLAGE INN, Church St., Lenox, MA 01240; 413-637-0020. 1-800-253-0917; Fax: 413-637-9756. A 29-guestroom inn (all but 2 with private baths) in a historic Berkshire town, 4 mi. from Stockbridge, 8 mi. from Pittsfield, and 1 mi. from Tanglewood. All sizes of beds available. Breakfast and afternoon tea served daily to travelers. Dinner served Tuesday thru Sunday Open every day of the year. Lenox is located in the heart of the Berkshires with many historical, cultural, and recreational features. Swimming in pleasant nearby lakes. All seasonal sports, including xc and downhill skiing, available nearby. No pets. Personal checks accepted. CCs: all major cards. Cliff Rudisill and Ray Wilson, owners-hosts.

DIRECTIONS: After approaching Lenox on Rte. 7, one of the principal north-south routes in New England, exit onto Rte. 7A to reach the village center and Church St. When approaching from the Mass. Tpke. (Exit 2), use Rte. 20W about 4 mi. and turn left onto Rte. 183 to center of town.

THE WAUWINET
Nantucket, Massachusetts

The only thing left from the inside of the old Wauwinet is the fireplace mantel in the dining room, yet so true has been the striving towards keeping the spirit of this 19th century Nantucket landmark, I felt immediately in tune with both past and present country inns by the sea.

Actually, two seas—three if you count the Sound, which is visible beyond the sand bar that embraces Nantucket Harbor. The Wauwinet is situated on a neck of land between the Atlantic and Nantucket

waters, the only inn on the island with such strategic placement. You are on twenty-six miles of beaches.

Bostonians Jill and Steve Karp loved the old place when they summered in the neighborhood, and when they heard the closed-down Wauwinet House was for sale, they bought it. Under their caring and personal supervision, the gray shingle exterior was restored, and the interior completely rebuilt.

This was a labor of love, and it shows. Jill selected the one-of-a-kind country antiques and worked with the decorators every step of the way. Steve, a builder of shopping malls rather than inns, says he was able to do something "just for us this time." Both the restuarant, Topper's, and the inn boat, Topper's II, are named for the Karp family terrier, whose portrait hangs in the main dinning room.

Though they live off-island, Jill and Steve are often at their inn. They bring it presents—like "Woody," the 1936 Ford station wagon that serves as a unique runabout and represents the inn at the annual Daffodil Weekend parade of vintage automobiles every April.

Each guest room is different, so let me tell you about mine, a standard double and one of the few with twin beds. The walls, ceiling and chintz are the same blue on cream flower pattern; the beds are white iron with brass trim; the tables and armoire, antique pine. A bouquet of fresh garden flowers sits beside two books about Nantucket. Nice extras include a basket of excellent toiletries, eyelet-trimmed cotton sheets, two big fluffy bed pillows per bed, good reading lights, a hair dryer, and a TV-VCR combination stowed out of sight until wanted.

There are larger, more country-elegant rooms with grander views in the inn, but none have more charm.

In the library/sitting room downstairs I found a wide selection of board games and books ranging from current best sellers to those popular when the Wauwinet advertised "Shore Dinners for 25 Cents." You can identify with your choice of decade. I was glad to see books and games for children as well.

The selection of videos also includes films for youngsters. This is another thing I like about the Wauwinet; the guests are a natural mix of ages. The cottages are expecially nice for families—the largest, "The Anchorage," has three bedrooms and is in great demand.

Outside there is croquet, and a wonderful creative 600 sq. ft. chess board with chess players that come to your waist to move around. Or you can walk the 26 miles of beaches. A 4-wheel drive will take you over the sand dunes and between mid-june and labor day an old sea captain will boat you to a distance shore with your prepared picnic from the Hotel and pick you up later that day. There is a 14 foot Capri sailboat, row boats, tennis and bicycles for your use.

The general manager has had quiet a glorious past. He first managed the well known Salishan Lodge in Oregon, then the Inn at Williamsburg and now is happy pampering the guests at Wauwinet. He often takes guests on a history and nature walk. His wife can be found sitting you at dinner. (She's actually the food and beverage director). They met at Salishan.

Topper's presents the New American Cuisine, which places great emphasis on just-picked locally grown vegetables, top quality meats, pastas, and such delicacies as Nantucket Bay scallops with Asian vetetables and ginger-garlic vinaigrette. I had the smoked blue fish pate and a scotch malt that even with my research on my book on Britain and Ireland hadn't come across it. It is called Michel Couvreur and is very smooth. Next came Baby field greens with goat cheese. Grilled Arctic Char was wonderful. My partner had Grilled Medal-lions of beef with sweet and sour chutney. Make sure you take the Santa Fe Thunder Cloud for dessert. It consists of chantilly cream, baked cocoa meringue, a scoop of chocolate moose and carmelized sugar.

A full breakfast of your choice is served as part of the room rate. Try the turkey hash. I know it sounds awful but it was wonderful.

Although the Wauwinet is a peaceful eight miles from the village of Nantucket, there is no need to rent a car or bring your own the 30 miles across from the mainland. Complimentary jitney service from inn to town and back every hour is not only convenient but a delight-ful ride along the moors and cranberry bogs.

THE WAUWINET, P.O. Box 2580, Nantucket, MA 02584; 508-228-0145, fax 508-228-0712, toll free except Canada and MA 800-426-8718. A full-service 40-gue-stroom (private baths) country inn with 5 cottages. King, queen and twin beds avail-able. Private beach, Har-tru tennis courts, bicycles, sailboats and watersports. Free transfers to town 8 miles away. Open late April-October No pets. Jill and Steve Karp, owners; Russell Cleveland, manger/host.

DIRECTIONS: From ferry, take Main St. to Orange, left to rotary circle, then Milestone Rd. to Polpis Rd; left to Wauwinet Rd., follow to inn. Without car, take taxi from air-port to Wauwinet; from ferry, taxi or walk to information center on Federal St. where you can pick up the Inn jitney on one of its scheduled trips.

THE WEATHERVANE INN
South Egremont, Massachusetts

"Good evening, folks, how are you? I'm the innkeeper, Vince Mur-phy." While I was having a welcome cup of tea in front of the very cozy fireplace at the Weathervane Inn on a midwinter afternoon, Vincent Murphy excused himself at least four times to welcome new guests.

Vince is a man who has the knack for making people feel welcome immediately.

Among the things that I look for in an inn are qualities of memorability. Besides innkeeper Murphy, who is, as he says, "a private investigator from the streets of New York," there are many other memorable features here.

The Weathervane Inn, listed in the National Register of Historic Places, is a small cluster of buildings set off the highway, with sections dating back to 1785. It is located in the lovely little village of South Egremont in the Berkshires, where there are many pre-1800 houses and a graceful church. Replete with wide-board floors, beautiful moldings, and an original fireplace that served as a heating and cooking unit with a beehive oven, the inn has a comfortable, warm atmosphere.

There are eleven very attractively furnished country inn guest rooms, with private baths, enhanced by Anne's eye for design and her needlework. Antique maple high double beds and some king-sized beds, all with coordinated linens, along with Anne's handmade pierced lampshades, all combine to make each room distinctive. There are many dried flower arrangements, ball fringe curtains, books and magazines, and good reading lamps.

I talked to Anne about the menu at the Weathervane. "Well," she said, "the kitchen is my domain and I'm very proud of the response that our guests have had to our entrées. Our specialties have been Cornish hens with kiwi sauce, veal Dijonnaise, pork tenderloin Normandy, duckling with black cherries seafood Mornay, and soups like split pea, New England chowders, and a hearty borscht. We've had to print our recipe for celery seed dressing because so many of our diners requested it."

Vince came cruising by and decided to make his contribution: "Let me tell you about our desserts—Trish is the pastry chef par excellence! The best homemade pies with the best crust. All kinds of fresh fruit combinations—blueberry-peach, strawberry-blueberry, peach-nectarine, and pear blueberry. And her cheesecake and chocolate chip walnut pie get nothing but raves!"

There are two dining areas, including a new dining room overlooking the garden and the swimming pool, with a glimpse of the antique shop in a barn that has a feeling somewhat akin to the Sturbridge Village buildings. The shop specializes in early quilts and folk furniture and inn guests often wander back there to browse.

Eventually, we all sat down in front of the fireplace, next to a sort of little pub corner, and for an hour and a half I was beguiled by the various members of the Murphy family. Vince really is a private investigator, but he takes all of the Mike Hammer jokes with exceptionally good grace and even adds a few of his own. "I did that for many years in the city," he said, "and I still go in about one day a week, but all of us have taken up this new life here in the country. As a matter of fact, I'm even a member of the South Egremont Volunteer Fire Department!"

———————

THE WEATHERVANE INN, Rte. 23, South Egremont, MA 01258; 413-528-9580. An 11-guestroom (private baths) village inn in the Berkshire foothills. All-sized beds available. Modified American plan in summer; in winter, modified American plan, Thursday through Sunday. Breakfast served to houseguests. Dinner served to travelers Friday and Saturday. Closed Thanksgiving to December 26. Limited wheelchair access. Swimming pool on grounds. Golf, tennis, bicycling, backroading, hiking, horseback riding, fishing. downhill and xc skiing nearby. Tanglewood, Jacob's Pillow, Berkshire Playhouse, Norman Rockwell Museum, and great antique shops all nearby. No pets. One dog in residence. Vincent, Anne, and Patricia Murphy, innkeepers.

DIRECTIONS: From New York City follow Sawmill River Pkwy. to Taconic Pkwy. to Rte. 23 east. South Egremont and the inn are about 2 mi. past the Catamount ski area on Rte. 23.

Rhode Island

LARCHWOOD INN
Wakefield, Rhode Island

Frank Browning and I were talking about lobsters, a subject that is near and dear to the hearts of those who are fortunate enough to live near New England's coastal waters. The Larchwood Inn certainly qualifies in this respect, since it's just a few minutes from the great beaches of southern Rhode Island.

"We buy from one source, and we know we're getting the best," he told me. "On Monday, we have special dinners of either twin lobsters or prime rib, and it is one of our most popular nights in the week. We always have a full-sized lobster every night and twin lobsters on Monday. I hope your readers will reserve ahead for lobsters because there's always a great demand. By the way, on Mondays in the summertime we have a cabaret performer and a piano player. It really livens things up."

I wandered into one of the dining rooms, where there is a mural depicting the southern Rhode Island beaches. The tables were very attractively set for the next meal with green tablecloths. I noticed the living room had been redecorated since my last visit. It was very pleasant, with comfortable chairs and a fireplace with a very impressive ship's model on the mantel. There was also an exotic bird in a cage.

At this point, Frank returned, and I asked him about the ship's model. "That is a three-masted schooner, called *L'Astrolabe*, and everything was built to scale by a friend of mine. See the little boys on the deck—he thought of everything."

The Larchwood is a large mansion, dating back to 1831, in the village of Wakefield, set in the middle of a large parklike milieu with copper, beech, ginkgo, pin oak, spruce, mountain ash, maple, Japanese cherry trees, evergreens, dogwoods, and a very old mulberry tree. In all, there are three acres of trees and lawn.

The interior has many Scottish touches, including quotations from Robert Burns and Sir Walter Scott, and photographs and prints of Scottish historical and literary figures.

The conversation naturally turned once again to menu items, since Frank was the chef here for many years and is now carefully supervising the kitchen and dining room.

"We're in the process right now of working with the South County Hospital. They are coming out with low-cholesterol items, and they came to us to ask if we could cooperate with them. We're working on seven or eight items in our restaurant for their program. There will be lighter things, including different ways to serve chicken and fish."

I asked him about breakfasts, and I'm very glad I did. "We make the French toast with our own bread and offer it with either sour cream or whipped cream and warm strawberries. The strawberries make it absolutely fantastic. It's something that our guests really appreciate, along with our selection of different omelets."

Besides guest rooms in the main inn, there are additional attractively furnished guest rooms in the Holly House, a 150-year-old building across the street from the inn. Guests at the Holly House can enjoy breakfast, lunch, and dinner at the Larchwood Inn dining room.

My eye caught a card on the table that had a Catholic, Jewish, and Protestant grace, and also one from Robert Burns.

———

LARCHWOOD INN, 176 Main St., Wakefield, RI 02879; 401-783-5454. A 19-guestroom (13 private baths) village inn just 3 mi. from the famous southern RI beaches. Queen, double, and twin beds. European plan. Breakfast, lunch, dinner served every day of the year. Swimming, boating, surfing, fishing, xc skiing, and bicycles nearby. One cat in residence. Francis Browning, owner/host.

DIRECTIONS: From Rte. 1, take Pond St. exit and proceed 1/2 mi. directly to inn.

THE MELVILLE HOUSE
Newport, Rhode Island

———

The Melville House is a lovely old Colonial with a fascinating past. The French general Rochambeau quartered some of his troops at the

39 Clarke Street address when they fought in the Revolutionary War under President George Washington. The Melvilles purchased the property during the 1800s and tore down the original home, moving the Frank Street house to the site. Because of alterations, the current structure is more of an 18th-century design.

Located in a quiet part of Newport's Historic District, the home is within walking distance of the Brick Market boutiques, the wharf, and excellent restaurants. Innkeepers Rita and Sam Rogers have been true to their motto, "Where the past is present," by decorating with Colonial and early American furnishings, yet modernizing where updating was needed.

The inn's interior is charming. While the sitting room is small, comfortable wing chairs frame the fireplace, inviting intimate conversation over complimentary afternoon sherry. It is here, also, that Sam's collection of old appliances is displayed. Formerly a small appliance designer, Sam will enthusiastically demonstrate cherry pitters, dough makers, coffee grinders, and mincers. In the adjacent sunny breakfast room, guests are encouraged to help themselves to a homemade breakfast served buffet-style at polished pub tables.

The corridor leading to the guest rooms is stocked with games and books for rainy days. Braided rugs, Colonial pineapple-post beds, handmade afghans, and bureaus restored by Sam decorate the guest rooms. The original low ceilings, which might be uncomfortable in another environment, create a secluded, homey feeling here.

THE MELVILLE HOUSE, 39 Clarke St., Newport, RI 02840; 401-847-0640. A 7-gue-stroom (5 private baths) Colonial located in Newport's Historic District. Breakfast included. Double & twin beds. Open March 1 to January 1. Within walking distance to boutiques, restaurants and the wharf. Newport Jazz Festival and other special events throughout the year. No pets. Off-street parking. CCs: Visa, MC, AE. Rita and Sam Rogers, owners/hosts.

DIRECTIONS: A 1-1/2 hour drive from Boston, and a 3-1/2 hour drive from New York. From the south, make a U turn around the square after exiting Rte. 114. Take a right on Clarke St. From NY, turn right when you come off the Newport Bridge. Go through first light, bear left at second light, then left at third light. Turn right on Clarke St.

WAYSIDE

Newport, Rhode Island

Part of the fun in visiting the "cottages" of the very rich is imagining how it would be to spend the night in such opulence. Now, if you have made reservations well in advance, you can turn into the circular driveway almost opposite the Elms and play houseguest for a night or more at the Wayside.

Among your neighbors: The Elms is across the street; down the block is Chateau-sur-Mer, Rosecliff (where *The Great Gatsby* was filmed), Mrs. Astor's Beechwood, Marble House, and Belcourt Castle. Tour guides will tell you all about the scandals as well as the costs of living it up in the Gilded Age.

This Georgian-style, 1890s mansion has several bedrooms so large that they are sitting rooms as well, and each is individually decorated. Alas, the retinue of servants is gone, and you must serve yourself a simple continental breakfast from a buffet in the lobby before starting out on foot to pay calls at the museum palaces of the neighbors.

After a day's walking, it's especially nice to be able to take a dip in the house swimming pool before heading out for dinner in one of the fine restaurants of Newport.

Oh yes, the servants' quarters are also available.

WAYSIDE, Bellevue Ave., Newport, RI 02840; 401-847-0302. A 10-guestroom (private baths) guest house on famous and fabulous Bellevue Avenue. Black and white television in every room. All-sized beds. Open year-round. Swimming pool, ocean beach, mansions, restaurants, shops nearby. No pets. No credit cards. Off-street parking. Reservations should be made well in advance. Al and Dorothy Post, owners/hosts.

DIRECTIONS: Bellevue Avenue is probably Newport's most famous street. As you drive toward Ocean Avenue, the Elms will be on your right. Watch for driveway on left marked Wayside (nothing so crass as house numbers in this neighborhood) and turn in.

Mid-Atlantic and Ontario

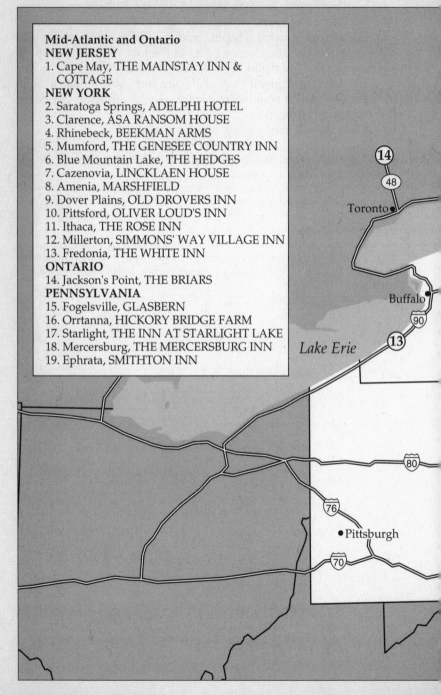

(14)
(48)
Toronto

Buffalo
(90)

Lake Erie   (13)

(80)

(76)

● Pittsburgh

(70)

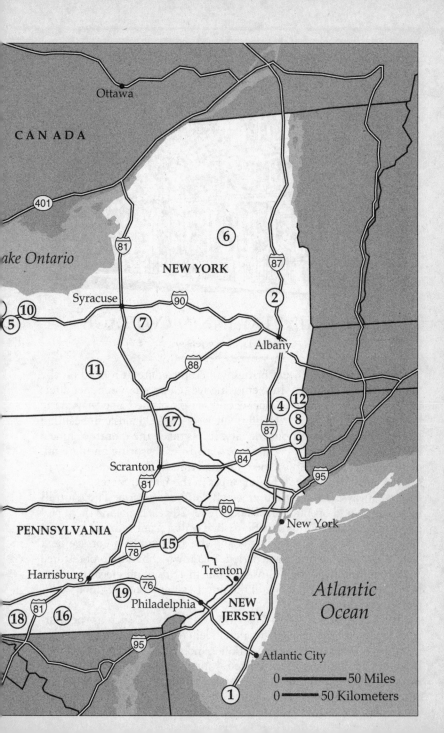

New Jersey

THE MAINSTAY INN & COTTAGE
Cape May, New Jersey

Tom and Sue Carroll were bringing me up to date as rocked on the veranda of the Mainstay Inn, enjoying ice tea on a lazy summer afternoon. "We just completed our second season of the Cape May music festival, a fantastic series of performances of classical music in beautiful historic settings throughout the city. It has made the month of June a really exciting time to be in Cape May. In early spring and late fall many guests come to enjoy the bird migrations. Cape May is now considered one of the ten best birding areas in the United States."

I've always admired their creativity and dedication. The Carrolls have owned and operated the Mainstay for 20 years, making them pioneers in an industry that has flourished only recently in our country. They have restored the Mainstay and the 1870 summer cottage next door with great fidelity to the period. In a town of hundreds of restored Victorian buildings, the Mainstay, built in 1872 as an elegant gentleman's club, is considered one of the finest examples of Victorian architecture and decoration.

To the original features that survived the years, such as the fourteen-foot ceilings with eight-foot chandeliers and many important furnishings, they added beautiful antiques and special touches. They used Bradbury & Bradbury silk-screened wallpapers; they had ceilings and walls decorated by an expert in stenciling; and they assiduously tracked down authentic fittings and fixtures.

The three parlors and huge guest rooms are almost all furnished in what is called Renaissance Revival. "It flows to the eye with graceful curves," Sue explained. "Walnut was used extensively during the 1870s, and there are very tall mirrors, tall headboards, and wardrobes. They're a shock compared to things today. Under some of the beds are chamber pots that roll out on wooden trays, and other beds have the original mosquito nets attached to small pulleys in the ceilings. I think the fun of staying here is that you are seeing furniture that would never go in your house, and it can be very exciting."

While we were chatting, I noticed an occasional horse and carriage clip-clopping by the inn. "Oh, yes," Sue said, "Cape May has regular horse-and-carriage and antique auto tours of the town."

Breakfast is served in the dining room or on warm days on the veranda, where even now I was enjoying the hydrangeas, tiger lilies, and roses blooming profusely in the yard. It's a wonderful place for afternoon tea and cookies, served after the house tour, conducted at 3:30 p.m. every day for visitors and houseguests.

In addition to myriad summer activities in Cape May, an annual Shakespeare Weekend is held at the Mainstay in March, and there's always a Dickens Christmas extravaganza in December.

The Mainstay and the Carrolls offer their guests a truly opulent Victorian experience on one of the most beautiful historical streets right in the center of a beautiful seaside Victorian town.

THE MAINSTAY INN & COTTAGE, 635 Columbia Ave., Cape May, NJ 08204; 609-884-8690. A 12-guestroom inn (private baths) in a well-preserved Victorian village just one block from the ocean. All-size beds available. Breakfast served to houseguests. Open every day from mid-March to mid-December Fine restaurants, historic house tours, summer theater, sailboat trips, horse and carriage tours, concerts, military reviews, bird-watching, beach, boating, swimming, fishing, bicycles, riding, golf, tennis, and hiking nearby. Not suitable for small children. No pets. No credit cards; personal checks accepted. Tom and Sue Carroll, owners/hosts.

DIRECTIONS: From Philadelphia take the Walt Whitman Bridge to the Atlantic City Expy. Follow the Atlantic City Expy. to exit for Garden State Pkwy., south. Go south on pkwy., which ends in Cape May, where pkwy. becomes Lafayette St. Turn left at first light onto Madison. Proceed 3 blocks and turn right onto Columbia. Proceed 3 blocks to inn on right side.

New York

ADELPHI HOTEL

Saratoga Springs, New York

In the 1800s, Saratoga Springs was called Queen of the Spas. The very wealthy and artistic flocked to the resort for the concerts, garden parties, horse racing, and gala balls held in the elaborate hotel ballrooms. Today, Saratoga Springs has two distinct seasons: In July the New York City Ballet has its center at the Saratoga Performing Arts Center, and in August the social set returns to attend polo matches and horse racing.

Sheila Parkert and Gregg Siefker purchased Saratoga's Adelphi Hotel just as plans were being made to tear it down, as its more grandiose sisters had been. "It was in unimaginably bad shape, though," Sheila told me. "People thought we were crazy." But the enterprising couple literally dug in and began the almost unbelievable task of renovating the huge, 19th-century Victorian. Since money was short, they did almost all the work themselves, including construction and decorating.

In 1979, they opened the lobby and the bar. Then three guest rooms were completed. And now, there are only five rooms of thirty-nine left to finish. Through this whole process, they studied magazines, collected antiques, and traveled to little country inns in Europe to gain inspiration.

It takes a well-developed sense of personal style and natural talent to take elements that are both eclectic and eccentric and combine them to produce a work of art. Sheila and Gregg have done it. The Adelphi Hotel is just that.

The building is a spectacular example of high Victorian architecture. A facade of Lombardian brick work is fronted by three-story wooden columns adorned by elaborate masses of fretwork. The opulent lobby could now be considered Gilded Age. Gilt peeks out from corners, pillar pediments, mirror frames, and ceiling panels. Dark woods and hunter-green walls set off the period chairs and sofas. The light from tiny lamps and chandeliers creates shadows as it filters through the glossy leaves of brass-potted plants. The antiques throughout the inn are all originals and attest to the dedication of the collectors. Prints and engravings of old Saratoga adorn the walls, and fresh flowers add color.

The couples' full artistic vision is evident in the spacious guest rooms. Most are done in the Victorian style, but always with unique touches that make them lively. A few rooms are worlds unto themselves, such as the Riviera Room with its wall murals of the French Riviera and the southwest-inspired Adirondack Mission Suite. All individual window treatments in the inn have been designed and sewn by Sheila, who has a great philosophy about interior design: "a building tells you what to do."

Each room has a full bath, air-conditioning, television, and special little touches, like trays with a glass decanter and glasses, and a special bottle of wine. Sheila's handmade comforters cover the beds, and antique armoires are filled with extra pillows and blankets.

A breakfast of fresh fruits, coffee cake, and a beverage is brought to your room. But finish your morning coffee from one of the wicker rockers on the inn's loggia, just off the parlor. Coffee, tea, and cakes are also available on the parlor sideboard throughout the day.

The inn's bar has a full liquor license, and in July and August lunch and a light dinner can be enjoyed in the Cafe Adelphi, or outdoors in the cafe's courtyard. Fine restaurants are also within walking distance.

Sheila and Gregg have achieved their goal of creating "a small grand-luxe hotel in the finest European tradition," and, from the enthusiastic way Sheila was talking about a new wallpaper pattern, they have no intention of stopping.

ADELPHI HOTEL, 365 Broadway, Saratoga Springs, NY 12866; 518-587-4688. A 34-guestroom (private baths) elegant Victorian in the center of historic downtown Saratoga. Operated in the European tradition. Open May through October Queen, double, and twin beds. Continental breakfast included; lunch and light dinner available during the summer. Walk to restaurants. Close to Saratoga Performing Arts Center, Spa State Park, Saratoga Race Track, mineral baths, shopping. No pets. CCs: Visa, MC. Sheila Parkert and Gregg Siefker, owners/hosts.

DIRECTIONS: From New York City, take I-87 to Saratoga Springs; take Exit 13N.

ASA RANSOM HOUSE
Clarence, New York

"Welcome. In the fine tradition of English tea time we are pleased to offer an afternoon tea each Thursday from 2:00 to 4:00 p.m. Reservations are appreciated." I was reading from an invitation left in my room. Despite the seeming formality of the invitation, I felt friendly comfort reflected in my room furnishings.

I was occupying Room #2, which had a four-poster canopy bed and walls brightly covered with a floral print wallpaper. I had read that the room came with a TV, and after an extensive search, I discovered it. I won't tell you where! Helpful hints...within the furniture or behind the pictures! Another unusual feature...heated towel racks in the bathroom. And all the guest rooms have fireplaces. Some have balconies that overlook the gardens and pond.

Steeped in tradition, the original portion of the house was built in 1853 by Asa Ransom, and was a local tavern of farmhouse design. Bob and Judy Lenz purchased it in 1975 and proceeded to add two dining rooms and, successively, guest rooms now totally nine. Honoring the history of the old structure they named it, simply, The Asa Ransom House.

Honoring of both history and modern times becomes most apparent in the dining room. The waitress arrived at my table outfitted in a long, flowing dress and pinafore with an old-fashioned bonnet covering her hair. The health-conscious attitude of the Lenz's is reflected with one smoke-free dining, and a limited smoking area in the other. I chose to experience the third option, dining on the open veranda. The menu offered a varied selection with sections entitled Vegetarian (for the healthy eaters), Streams (featuring their famous Salmon Pond Pie), Farms (appropriately offering a selection of fowl), and Woodlands (with selections of delectable prepared beef and lamb). Completing the picture the dessert area entitled Sweets ("A beautiful and tempting array of fruit and delicacies from the Baker's oven brought to your table", the menu states.) I chose to sip a glass of fruity raspberry dessert wine in lieu of dessert. There is even a section for early diners desiring to eat between 4–5:30 in the late afternoon. Nothing like catering to all needs, even down to the delicious aroma each morning of home-made muffins and breads baking in the ovens.

I did not have to travel far to pick up a few trinkets to take home as there is a gift shop located at the inn. The shopping area of Clarence is within walking distance to present a wider selection if desired, as well as antique shops. Niagara Falls is a short 28 mile drive, and Buffalo, offering cultural opportunities is within easy driving distance also.

I was impressed to observe that Judy and Bob honor their religious beliefs and close Asa Ransom each week on Friday and Saturday.

ASA RANSOM HOUSE, 10529 Main St.,(Route 5), Clarence, New York 14031; tel:716-759-2315. Delightful former tavern with nine guestrooms only 28 mis.from Niagara Falls and 15 mis. from Buffalo. Open Sunday-Thursday. Closed Friday & Saturday. Breakfast & dinner every day, with a lunch menu only on Wednesday. Jackets required for the gentlemen at dinner. Tennis, golf, fishing & swimming nearby. Limited amusement for children under 12. Limited smoking areas and no pets please. Reservations recommended. Personal checks accepted, but no credit cards. Owners/Hosts: Bob and Judy Lenz.

DIRECTIONS: From the New York Thruway traveling west, take Exit 48A-Pembroke. Turn right onto Rte. 5, proceeding 11 mi. to Clarence. Use Exit 49 off the Thruway when traveling east, turning left on Rte. 78, proceeding 1 mi. to Rte. 5 and then travelling another 5-1/4 mi. Only 9 mi. from Buffalo Airport and 11 mi. from Amtrak train station.

BEEKMAN ARMS
Rhinebeck, New York

"I've heard lots of explanations for the name 'Rhinebeck' or 'Ryn-beck,'" said Chuck LaForge, as we sat down for dinner in the low-ceilinged Tap Room of the Beekman Arms, "but recently I learned that on the same ship with Peter Stuyvesant was a German, William Beckman, who originally came here from the Rhine Valley. His son received a land grant here in 1703 from Queen Anne of England, and he named the property Rhinebeck. 'Beckman' could have been changed to 'Beek' through a clerical error in later years."

By 1769, the Beekman Arms, which started from rather humble beginnings, had increased in size to two full stories with a roomy attic that later became a ballroom. When trouble arose with the Indians in the area, the entire community would take refuge within the inn's walls.

During the Revolution, George Washington and his staff enjoyed the fare of the inn, and the window from which he watched for his couriers is still in place. Those were anxious days also for Lafayette, Schuyler, Arnold, and Hamilton, who spent many hours at the inn. In fact, over the years hundreds of men who have helped fashion the destiny of our nation partook of the inn's hospitality.

Tonight, the light from the flickering candles was reflected in the varnished tabletops and overhead beams. The walls were hung with ancient documents and prints and sabres and muskets, many of them dating back to the days of the American Revolution. This was the same place where pioneer families and early tradesmen enjoyed a roaring fire and perhaps took a pipe similar to the white clay pipes that also adorned the walls.

While colonial Beekman Arms menus probably included such items as roast beef, venison, bear steak, pheasant, quail, and turkey, tonight's menu offered dishes of crisp free-range duck glazed with wild flower honey and garlic whipped potatoes, wood grilled pineapple chili, marinated pork chops with spicy cheese grits, and New England fried ipswich clams with a home-made tartar sauce. The restaurant has been leased to Larry Forgione, considered by many to be the leader in American regional cooking in this country. Mr. Forgione, owner of An American Place restaurant in New York City, has created an exciting and creative menu using the freshest ingredients possible.

Chuck has added a greenhouse dining area in the front of the building, the Antique Barn with thirty shops, and still another adjunct to the Beekman Arms—the Delamater House, built in 1844.

"This is the Delamater courtyard," he commented, as we walked into an open-ended square area. There were buildings on three sides, including one that had been there earlier and a Federal house, its batten-and-board design similar to the original Delamater House, which has been moved from another point in the village. It now serves as a conference center.

The guest rooms in the Delameter section are furnished with a very pleasant restraint; each has a four-poster bed and a fireplace, and there is split wood for the fire. Each of them has its own little refrigerator.

Right in the center of the bustling village of Rhinebeck, Beekman Arms offers a variety of diversions. As Chuck says, "It is a wonderful walking village with many shops of all kinds, a foreign movie house, and other interesting restaurants in addition to our own."

The Beekman Arms today is more than a historic inn, listed on the National Register of Historic Places, where thousands of guests enjoy its fascinating and authentic Colonial decor and menu; like many other village inns, it is still the community meeting place.

Caveat: because the main building sits on Rte. 9, on a corner with a signal light, those rooms facing Rte. 9 will hear traffic.

BEEKMAN ARMS, Rhinebeck, NY 12572; 914-876-7077. A 13-guestroom Colonial inn (with 40 rooms and 2 suites in nearby guest house; private baths) in the center of a busy village in the Hudson River Valley. Queen, double and twin beds. European plan. Breakfast, lunch, and dinner served to travelers daily. Open year-round. Wheelchair access at Delamater House. Amtrak station at Rhinecliff 1 mi. (2-hr. train ride from Grand Central Station). Short drive to Hyde Park with F.D.R. home and library, Rhinebeck World War I Aerodrome, and Culinary Institute of America. Golf, tennis, swimming nearby. Chuck LaForge, owner/host.

DIRECTIONS: From N.Y. Thruway, take Exit 19, cross Rhinecliff Bridge and pick up Rte. 199 south to Rte. 9. Proceed south on Rte. 9 to middle of village. From Taconic Pkwy., exit at Rhinebeck and follow Rte. 199 west 11 mi. to Rte. 308 into village.

THE GENESEE COUNTRY INN

Mumford, New York

What a great place for breakfast! Seated on the airy sun porch of The Genesee Country Inn, looking over a beautiful millpond surrounded by woods, I had just finished a delightful cheddar cheese egg bake with Dijon mustard and broccoli. After a final freshly baked muffin covered with quince jelly, innkeeper Glenda Barcklow invited me to join her on a walk around the grounds.

We passed the pretty gardens and the gazebo under the pines, and Glenda said good morning to the ducks as they came waddling toward us. "Sometimes I'll see a blue heron out here on the water," she said. As we walked to the brook, I saw a brown trout flash by, rippling the water. "Yes," Glenda added, "I have both rainbow and brown trout, and people do fish in the spring-fed ponds. Spring Creek and Allen Creek come together here and they flow down to a waterfall farther on in the woods. I'm going to create a picnic area overlooking the falls. There were about forty mills in this area during the 1800s, and you can see the ruins of many of them when you walk through the woods."

The Genesee Country Inn actually began its life in 1883 as a mill, and the original section had two-foot-thick walls of native limestone, with later additions completed in plaster and clapboard. The original mill was used as the residence of the company manager in the 1900s. Glenda Barcklow bought the property in 1982 and turned it into a lovely inn.

I was really taken with the very fine stenciling in several of the rooms. The stenciling was done by Glenda and two local artists, one of whom also painted a charming fire board and the inn's sign.

Glenda is very proud of her Garden Rooms with fireplaces and French doors opening onto private balconies overlooking the millponds and gardens. All of the rooms are most attractively furnished with some antiques, country prints and fabrics, and a guest diary.

"I suppose many of your guests take the twenty-minute drive over to Rochester, for all the cultural programs and historic attractions," I said.

Glenda nodded in agreement. "But there are all sorts of things to do and see right here in Mumford," she replied. "The Genesee Country Village is less than a mile from here. This is a restored village—a 'living museum,' very much like Williamsburgh and Sturbridge—with about sixty buildings on 200 acres. It depicts a range of architectural styles, interior furnishings, as well as life-styles and occupations, covering the entire 19th century. They have many interesting events from spring into fall. Letchworth State Park is called the 'Grand Canyon of the East'; they have an Olympic-sized pool, hiking and nature trails along the river gorge, and beautiful waterfalls. Of course, nearby schools and colleges always have something going on."

"And I imagine it must be beautiful here in the winter," I mused. "Oh," she exclaimed, "there's just nothing like it. It's so lovely, the grounds are spectacular, and it's so peaceful and quiet. You feel as if you're in another world."

Glenda did a good job of convincing me with her enthusiastic attitude. I know I'll be back to take advantage of some of the peace and quiet this winter.

THE GENESEE COUNTRY INN, 948 George St., Mumford, NY 14311; 716-538-2500. A 9-guestroom (private baths) restored historic 1833 mill inn on 6 acres of woods with ponds and waterfalls. Queen, double and twin beds. Complimentary full breakfast is the only meal served. Afternoon tea. Seven good restaurants within walking distance. Open year-round. Queen and double beds. Trout fishing, nature walks, Genesee Country Museum, Letchworth State Park, Niagara Falls, historic sites, antiquing, biking, hiking, xc skiing, golf, swimming, and all attractions of Rochester nearby. No pets. Two cats in residence. Glenda Barcklow, owner/host.

DIRECTIONS: From N.Y. Thruway (I-90), take Exit 47 and Rte. 19 south to Le Roy. Go east on Rte. 5 to Caledonia, then north on Rte. 36 to Mumford. Turn left at George St.

THE HEDGES

Blue Mountain Lake, New York

The Hedges has remarkably maintained the truly rustic quality of the traditional country inn. The main house, with its lovely textured bark exterior, was built over a span of two years, beginning in 1880. The accompanying house, with its hand-cut stones and imported cypress shingles, was built some years later. Located on 12.5 acres on Blue Mountain Lake, The Hedges opened to its first guests in May of 1921.

The almost primitive nature of The Hedges during those first few years, with no electricity or plumbing, attracted the first guests. Now, even though modern accommodations have been added to the rustic rooms, the attractiveness of the environment, and the surrounding mountainous vistas and quiet restfulness of Blue Mountain Lake, still attract the appreciative soul.

The decorations within the hotel enhance its rustic nature. The beauty of the lodge and stone house is stunning. Large, comfortable Adirondack furniture beckons from wide porches and shaded lawns...a perfect place to write those six letters that you've put off for months. You'll be surprised at the creative inspiration that the invigorating mountain air gives to your prose.

The library houses some fun old westerns, a great collection of children's books for a dip into the world of Lewis Carroll, and a piano for evening sing-alongs. Backgammon, cards, chess, ping-pong, and other games offer entertainment at the end of the day or during inclement weather. In the afternoon, horseshoes, volleyball, tennis, or an eye-opening swim in Blue Mountain Lake can stimulate stress-weary minds. Additionally, water-skiing equipment and boats are available for rental at the hotel's boat livery.

Breakfast and dinner are included in the room fee, and are served at your reserved table. Dinner includes one entrée with vegetable, a salad selection, and crunchy homemade breads. Breakfast is hearty; on Saturday, a wonderful buffet is spread; and Sunday's midday dinner is ample. At a slight additional cost, a picnic lunch can also be arranged.

Guest rooms are cozy and comfortable with wooden-beamed ceilings and rockers. Before bed each evening, complimentary hot chocolate, coffee, and tea are served along with cookies or cakes.

I really think there can be nothing more peaceful than drifting off to sleep while the haunting sounds of a loon float across the lake. A stay at The Hedges can provide such a tranquil nocturnal experience.

THE HEDGES, Blue Mountain Lake, NY 12812; (518) 352-7325. A 14-guestroom, 14-cottage (private baths) rustic inn noted for its Adirondack resort quality. Open from mid-June to Columbus Day. Double and twin beds. Modified American plan. Boating, swimming, tennis, and water skiing on premises. No pets. Smoking restricted. Richard J. Van Yreren, owner/host.

DIRECTIONS: From west: N.Y. State Thruway to Utica, Exit 31, Rte. 12 to Alder Creek, Rte. 28 to Blue Mt. Lake. From south: N.Y. State Thruway to Exit 24 at Albany and I-87 to Exit 23 and Rte. 9 north. About 3 mi. north of Warrensburg take Rte. 28 to Blue Mt. Lake. From north: Rte. 3 or Rte. 30 to Tupper Lake; Rte. 30 to Blue Mt. Lake.

LINCKLAEN HOUSE
Cazenovia, New York

If an old-time stagecoach driver were to pull up his team in front of Lincklaen House today, he would find the hotel looking almost the same as it did in 1835, at least outwardly. The locally made brick, the fine chimneys, the broad front steps, and the columns flanking the doorway were built to last—and they have. Twenty or more stagecoaches passed through Cazenovia each day traveling over the Third Great Western Turnpike, and the snap of the drivers' whips was a familiar sound. The stages carried the mail and as many as fourteen passengers, and Lincklaen House must have been a welcome respite from hours spent in those lumbering horse-drawn conveyances.

Lincklaen House has been called one of the best examples of early-19th-century architecture in central New York State. Its Greek

Revival lines are in harmony with other buildings in this college town. The inn was named after the founder of the village, and over the years, many famous guests have enjoyed its hospitality.

Owner Ed Tobin, who grew up in Lincklaen House, has many plans of his own for the inn's future, and he has been knee-deep in a number of projects, including painting, wallpapering, and the more mundane but necessary things like plumbing and electrical repairs.

"We are getting to be a very special-event-minded community," Ed tells me. "The quaint shops and architecture of local homes and village buildings are spectacular. We have the winter festival every February; the Lorenzo needlework exhibit the whole month of June; arts and crafts on our village green; plus a parade and fireworks over the 4th of July; the Lorenzo driving competition, which takes place in July; the Franklin car reunion each year in August; and our own events here at Lincklaen House at Christmastime."

Cazenovia is one of the attractive towns along Route 20 in central New York State. This road, by the way, is a very interesting alternative to traveling across the state entirely on the Thruway, just a few miles to the north.

Aside from all the special events, Cazenovia provides a wide variety of sports and diversions year-round. Swimming, fishing, sailing, waterskiing, and in winter ice skating and ice fishing are available on the lake, and there is also tennis, horseback riding, and skiing nearby. A small folder outlines five lovely motor tours in the vicinity of the town, and eventually all roads lead back to Lincklaen House for afternoon tea.

LINCKLAEN HOUSE, Cazenovia, NY 13035; 315-655-3461. A 21-guestroom (private baths) village inn, 20 mi. east of Syracuse. All-sized beds available. European plan. Modified American plan upon request. Breakfast, lunch, and dinner served to travelers daily. Open year-round. Near several state parks, the Erie Canal Museum, and the Canal Trail. Tennis, golf, bicycles, alpine and xc skiing nearby. CCs: Visa, MC. Ed Tobin, owner/host. (See Index for rates.)

DIRECTIONS: From west on N.Y. Thruway, take Exit 34A, follow Rte. 481 south, take Exit 3E and follow Rte. 92 east to Cazenovia. From east on N.Y. Thruway, take Exit 34 and follow Rte. 13 south to Cazenovia. From Rte. 81, take Exit 15 (Lafayette) and follow Rte. 20 east, 18 mi. to inn.

MARSHFIELD
Amenia, New York

Ruth Lyn Bontecou has a generous heart and a very humble opinion of herself. The owner of Marshfield, a lovely rambling early-American farm house, apparently hasn't been influenced by the women's movement. When asked what her occupation had been prior to that of an innkeeper, she modestly replied, "None. I was a mom and raised four children while helping my husband with a 3,000-acre farm which included angus cattle, sheep, riding horses, and gardening."

My wife and I were incredulous as this powerhouse of a lady matter-of-factly proceeded to tell us how, in 1947, she restored a wreck of an old 1700s grist mill, turning it into this comfortable inn, painted a soft yellow with black shutters. Ruth calls it "my labor of love." Her energy seems boundless. Over our continental breakfast, served in the inn's beautiful dining room, I discovered that she also seems to find time to pursue her hobbies of sculpting, painting flower arranging and sailing.

Ruth's eye for artistry is apparent throughout the inn's common rooms in her arrangements of china and crystal and the highly polished wood of family heirloom antiques. The pine panelling in the den mellows with firelight as you walk from the dining room to the elegant living room. Another attractive sitting room offers a gaming table, fireplace and television.

The five guest rooms, all with private baths, are quite comfortable. We stayed in the Nesbit Suite, which had a wonderful old pencil post queen-sized bed and a large dressing room. The linens were soft, and the comforter fluffy.

Marshfield is located on 29 acres of the Duchess Land Conservancy, where the nearest town is five miles away. Millbrook, New York, considered the Southampton of the north, is only a seven-mile drive. Located in the center of Millbrook's fox hunting country, the area offers cross-country skiing, biking, hiking, bird watching, and fishing. Here, nature is the focus. Sitting on the porch in the evening, watching the fireflies illumine the twilight, it's hard to believe that Manhattan is only two hours to the south.

MARSHFIELD, Rte. 86, RR1, Box 432, Amenia, NY 12501; 914-868-7833. A 5-guestroom (private baths) early-American farm house on 29 rural acres. Twin, queen and king beds. Open all year. All outdoor sports. Two hours from Manhattan. No pets. One cat in residence. Ruth Lyn Bontecou, owner/host.

DIRECTIONS: From Rte. 44, go 4-plus mi. to Rte. 86. Turn right and go 3-2/10 mi. to Marshfield.

OLD DROVERS INN

Dover Plains, New York

"You know, New England had cowboys in the 1700s," innkeeper Alice Pitcher told me, much to my surprise. "During the early days when John and Ebenezer Preston opened this inn as the Clear Water Tavern, cattle drovers used to drive their herds down this post road to New York City markets and stop in here for their hot buttered rum and mulled ale—and some pretty wild midnight gambling sessions!"

So well has the inn's old-world ambience been preserved that it's easy to imagine the dusty, rough-booted drovers as they relaxed in the stone-walled tap room by a crackling fire, swapping stories of wild-eyed heifers and their balling, spindly legged calves. In fact, a portion of the inn has even been relocated intact, to be used as a museum display.

The Old Drovers Inn is nestled in the Berkshire foothills on 12

rural acres. The charming white clapboard colonial is surrounded by majestic maples and gardens. Alice and her partner, Kemper Peacock, had been patrons of the inn for many years before purchasing it in 1988. "We've tried to keep the feeling of days gone by," Kemper explained, "but we've also made sure our guests have the comforts of modern conveniences."

Cable television and a VCR are available in the parlor, and the library has an extensive collection of books. The sitting rooms are comfortable with down-filled couches and fireplaces. Hooked rugs warm polished pine floors, and antiques furnish most of the rooms.

As Alice showed me to my room, a small gray dynamo flashed past us on the stair. "That's Jed, our Yorkie," Alice laughed, following my questioning glance. "His ears are too big for his head, but he can sure zip around." Antique double beds covered in satin comforters, and bureaus and wing-back chairs are featured in each room. Chintz cheerfully frames the windows. All rooms have private baths, two with old-fashioned claw-foot tubs.

Guests enjoy a complimentary breakfast that includes three meats, eggs, griddle cakes, French toast or grits, and homemade baked goods served on polished mahogany tables in the Federal Room. Murals depicting the area's historical landmarks decorate the walls.

Lunch and dinner are served in the old tap room. The original low, smoke-darkened wood-beamed ceilings are illuminated by candles on table set with lustrous old glassware and Georgian flatware. The room's 18th-century character has been so well preserved that as I glanced into a softly lighted corner I half expected to see General Lafayette creating a historically rumored scandal by dining with two question-able ladies.

The menu is American but also features excellent English chop-house-style meats. Soups, like New England scallop chowder and ched-dar cheese soup drizzled with sherry, are served with fantastic hot popovers. I had the double-cut prime rack of lamb chops, crusty-charred and succulent, accompanied by a spicy tomato chutney. The inn's full-service bar also has an extensive wine cellar.

The area surrounding the Old Drovers Inn has a rich selection of sites to explore. Nearby, the museums at the Roosevelt and Vanderbilt estates are certainly of interest. Golf, downhill skiing, and horseback riding are a short drive away. In summer, music lovers can enjoy the Berkshire Music Festival at Tanglewood, and gourmet cooks can visit the Culinary Institute of America in Hyde Park.

The traditional hospitality of the Old Drovers Inn has survived for more than 250 years, and the comfortable warmth that greeted those early drovers still greets you today.

OLD DROVERS INN, Old Rte. 22, Dover Plains, NY 12522; 914-832-9311. A 6-gue-stroom (private baths) traditional country inn at the end of a narrow country road in the Berkshire foothills. Open all year. Queen and double beds. Complimentary full country breakfast; dinner reservations suggested. Croquet, badminton, bicycling, golf, skiing, horseback riding. Museums and antique shops nearby. Pets by arrangement. CCs: Visa, MC, DC. Alice Pitcher and Kemper Peacock, owners/hosts.

DIRECTIONS: Take Major Deegan Expwy. to the N.Y.S. Thruway; go north to Exit 7A, then north on Saw Mill River Pkwy. until it merges with Rte. 684 north. Follow Rte. 684 until it becomes Rte. 22 north; the inn is 23 mi. along Rte. 22.

OLIVER LOUD'S INN
Pittsford, New York

For nearly ten years Richardson's Canal House, the oldest surviving tavern on the Erie Canal, offered superb dining in a beautifully restored building, but there were no overnight accommodations. Then, in 1985, owner Vivienne Tellier learned that the Oliver Loud Tavern in Egypt, four miles away, was scheduled for demolition. Within twelve months, the building was moved to its present site near Richardson's, fully restored to its 1812 Federal and Greek Revival splendor, and taking overnight guests.

Oliver Loud had built his tavern in the style of the clapboard farm-houses of Massachusetts, where he was born. In 1812 the hamlet of Egypt was a busy stagecoach stop on the road to Syracuse, and Mr. Loud was something of an entrepreneur, providing bed and board to

travelers, operating the first sawmill in the area, writing pamphlets, and as an amateur astronomer, watching the heavens and probably forecasting the weather.

He had introduced considerable refinements to his inn, and Vivienne wasted no effort in recreating such special features as the Federal moldings, French and English wallpapers and borders, and paint colors. Mr. Loud's "receipt for making any wood look like mahogany" was used as an inspiration for the present hand-grained "mahogany" doors.

Vivienne has filled the rooms with fine reproductions of antique furniture and Early American paintings and artifacts. A display in the common room of the "Nanking Cargo" porcelain plates over the Federal-style mantel, which boasts gold-leaf panels and marbleized insets, was part of the cargo of a Dutch ship that sank in 1752 in the South China seas. Vivienne bought them at an auction in Amsterdam.

The guest rooms have king-sized and canopied beds and beautiful 1800s documentary and handscreened borders; four of them have a view of the canal.

You will find a chilled split of champagne, Saratoga water, fresh fruit, crackers and cheese, and homemade cookies when you arrive in your room. A continental breakfast basket will be delivered with the morning paper to your door, or you may enjoy it in a rocking chair on the porch overlooking the canal.

Lunch and dinner are available at Richardson's Canal House, a few steps away. Built in 1818, it retains virtually all of the original exterior and interior architectural detail. There are two-storied porches on the front and rear, a great cooking fireplace in the old kitchen, and delicate but simple Federal trim in its public rooms, which are painted in the intense original colors.

"For the most part the cuisine gets its inspiration from French and American regional cooking," Vivienne told me as we sat under the gay umbrellas on the terrace of the inn, which is separated from the canal by a lovely grassy bank.

"For dinner we present a five-course, fixed-price meal, including appetizers, soup, a main dish, salad, and dessert. Everything is made right here. We have our own herb garden and bake all our own breads. There's always a variation of fish, fowl, a beef dish, and perhaps one or two others on the evening menu. For instance, we get very good veal from Wisconsin and duckling from Long Island. Our area has a lot of beef eaters and they seem to like our tenderloin of beef and New York strip steaks. We frequently have entertainment on Friday nights with musicians playing original instruments and tunes from the 1800s."

This is a most appealing country setting in an Erie Canal village with its century-old locust trees.

OLIVER LOUD'S INN, 1474 Marsh Rd., Pittsford, NY 14534; 716-248-5200. An 8-guestroom (private baths) historic inn on the Erie Canal, 10 mi. east of Rochester. King and double beds. Continental breakfast included. Lunch served Monday thru Friday, and dinner served Monday thru Saturday at the famous Richardson's Canal House, on the National Register of Historic Places. Open year-round. Canal towpath for walking or running, xc skiing, scenic Finger Lakes, Letchworth State Park, museums and galleries, and other sightseeing and historical landmarks nearby. No pets. Vivienne Tellier, owner/host.

DIRECTIONS: From NY Thruway, take Exit 45 to I-490 west to Bushnell's Basin exit. Turn right off ramp, and proceed to Richardson's Canal House and Oliver Loud's Inn.

THE ROSE INN
Ithaca, New York

Perhaps it is because I am so attuned to the characteristics of central New York State that the flat-topped cupola of the Rose Inn attracted my eye. Many 19th-century homes have such cupolas. I was driving north from Ithaca along the shore of Cayuga Lake, and there on top of a small hill was a gorgeous mansion with the easily recognizable, graceful lines of a mid-19th-century Italianate home. Innkeeper Charles Rosemann met me as I was parking the car, and together we started on a lovely tour of the inn.

About the first thing I learned is that the Rose Inn is known locally as "the house with the circular staircase."

As Charles explained, "The house is a gem of woodcraft, built of

heavy timbers with large, heavy handcut doors of chestnut. The floors are laid with quarter-sawn oak, inlaid in parquet fashion. It was built and completed in 1851, with the exception of a center staircase that would have led to the cupola. No one capable of completing it could be found. Hundreds of feet of priceless Honduras mahogany were stored for over half a century. In 1922 a master craftsman appeared, and he worked for two years building a circular staircase of that solid mahogany, which extended from the main hall through two stories to the cupola."

The inn displays the ambience of its period. High ceilings, the warm glow of woods from indigenous American trees long gone, marble fireplaces, and period antiques provide an elegant but surprisingly comfortable setting. Sherry and Charles really have been ingenious in adding new rooms—it's hard to distinguish the old from the new. The honeymoon suite has a king-sized bed, a working fireplace with an antique mantel, a sunken whirlpool bath for two, and a solarium overlooking the apple orchard and the fish pond. All of the rooms display Sherry's creative touch. One room with forest green walls has a beautiful 1850s walnut bed and a fine armoire imported from England. The new addition has its own elegant parlor with a TV set and a well-stocked refrigerator.

Dinner is something special. Sterling silver settings and candlelight set the mood for prix fixe four-course dinners as rack of lamb with an herbed sauce or scampi Mediterranean cooked in a light curry and cream sauce. There is Chateaubriand grilled over charcoals, and for those who like surprises there is the chef's *entrée du jour*. Eclectic and ethnic meals are also available, and since dinners are served only with advance reservations, the innkeepers have a chance to create something quite different.

My visit was true to form and I was delighted. At breakfast (Sherry cooks the evening meal and Charles cooks breakfast), Charles explained, "We like to give our guests a good start, and so we have full breakfasts, including hand-squeezed orange juice, our own blend of coffee, homemade jams and jellies, along with fresh fruits, German apple pancakes, French toast, or bagels, cream and lox."

There are many, many more things to share about the Rose Inn, but I think the best way for such sharing is a visit to the inn itself.

THE ROSE INN, 813 Auburn Rd., Rte. 34, P.O. Box 6576, Ithaca, NY 14851; 607-533-7905. A 12-guestroom and 3-suite (private baths) elegant New York State mansion just a few minutes from Cornell University. All-sized beds available. Breakfast included in room rate; gourmet dinner offered by advance reservation. Open all year. Conveniently situated to enjoy the beautiful Finger Lakes scenery and attractions, including Cayuga Lake, wineries, and college campuses. Arrangements can be made for pets. One dog and one cat cat in residence. No smoking anywhere in the inn. CCs: Visa, MC. Charles and Sherry Rosemann, innkeepers.

DIRECTIONS: From N.Y. State Thruway take Exit 40 and Rte. 34 south about 36 mi. The inn will be on your left before arriving in Ithaca. From I-81 use Exit 11 (Cortland) to Rte. 13 to Ithaca. Take No. Triphammer Rd. right, 7.4 mi. to inn.

SIMMONS' WAY VILLAGE INN

Millerton, New York

For me, one of the most memorable things about the Simmons' Way Village Inn is that it is indeed a *village* inn. There is no typical village inn; each is a unique establishment. Yet I always look for a special feeling of communal social activity that characterizes innkeepers' involvement with guests, and with their community. Simmons' Way fits my criteria perfectly.

The twin of an English inn—the Manor House, Moreton-in-Marsh—this gracious Victorian mansion is located on the village square of Millerton. Although on a highway, the inn is set back on a hill, with an expansive, shaded lawn stretching to the street. Striding up the walkway to steps lined with Halloween jack-o'-lanterns, I was appreciating the spacious front porch when innkeeper Nancy Carter poked her head out the door. "You're just in time! We're serving cocktails in the drawing room. Come and join us."

Prior to their purchase and renovation of the inn in 1987, Richard had had an interesting career as a United Nations official, and Nancy

was a vice-president in banking and financial services. They have made many friends during their years at Simmons' Way. "Our repeat clientele first stay with us as inn guests, and some later purchase second homes in the area and continue their relationship with us as dining guests and friends," Richard told me. "I guess that's 'proof of the pudding.'"

Highly photographable, the majestic wooden-frame house has a porte cochere, a third floor, and several balconies. The interior has been almost completely renovated. From the broad front veranda, tall doors open onto the center hall, which separates the comfortable lounge area from the smaller, charming parlor. Wicker furnishings, cozy couches, antiques, Oriental rugs, and wood-burning fireplaces offer a relaxing environment. The finish has been removed from the original wood in all the inn's rooms, resulting in glowing, honey-toned floors and wainscoting.

Climbing a twisty little paneled-oak staircase, illuminated by two stained-glass windows, I made my way to my room. The guest rooms are most romantic, truly within the European tradition. All rooms are light and airy, with distinctive color themes. Spool beds, four-poster beds, brass beds, and draped-canopy beds all have down pillows, lush linens, and antique furnishings to comfort the weary traveler. Some rooms have fireplaces, and most have restful sitting areas. All rooms have private shower/baths.

You may enjoy chess, cocktails or camaraderie in the cozy commons areas or on the verandah overlooking a sloping English lawn. Specialty teas and Pisco sours are afternoon signature pleasures.

The inviting Simmons' Way ambiance is highlighted in theHoag dining room featuring seasonal game, tableside service and a rotation of over 300 entrée items. Grand Cru wines, including first growth vintages, antique silver table service and hand blown oil lamps provide a memorable dining experience.

A wonderful breakfast of home-baked muffins, granola, fresh fruit, goat's cheese, ham, eggs and coffee cake or croissants is served in the smaller dining room, on the lovely front veranda, or most decadently in your suite.

The Carters' pets—Baden, an enormous but absolutely loving two-year-old Bernese mountain dog, and discriminating Sam, a black Siamese-mix cat—are pleased to act as surrogate pets for those travelers who might be pinning for their "pup" or "kitty" left behind.

While visiting at Simmons' Way, you will be close to music festivals, theater, historic homes, and hiking and outdoor sports. Furthermore, the inn is in a perfect place for parents to make private school visits with their children, since there are at least a half-dozen schools within a short distance.

SIMMONS' WAY VILLAGE INN, 33 Main St., Millerton, NY 12546; 518-789-6235. A 9-guestroom (private baths) Victorian village inn in a rural environment only 2 hours from Manhattan. Open year-round. All-size beds. Convenient to cultural and recreational activities, antiquing, and shopping. No pets. Sam the cat and Baden the Bernese Mountain dog in residence. Nancy and Richard Carter, owners/hosts.

DIRECTIONS: From New York City, take Henry Hudson Pkwy. to Sawmill River Pkwy. to Rte. 684 north, and follow Rte. 22 to Millerton.

THE WHITE INN
Fredonia, New York

This is the story of the renaissance of an inn and a village, and of how two professors of philosophy became experts on historical restoration. Sounds ponderous, doesn't it? Actually, Dave Palmer and Dave Bryant are two great guys, who laugh about the way people get them mixed up—they look a lot alike.

The day I met them, Dave Palmer was wearing a tie and Dave Bryant was in work clothes, repairing the air conditioning, so I had no problem. "How did two university professors get involved in historical restoration and innkeeping?" I wanted to know.

"We became friends in 1970 when we both arrived at the State University of New York here," Dave Palmer replied, "and Dave, being a very skilled craftsman, got me interested in renovating some historic buildings in our spare time. My wife, Nancy, who is an art historian, also joined us in developing the design and decoration of the buildings."

Dave Bryant took up the story. "By 1980 when we bought the White Inn, I had given up my teaching career for the world of restora-

tion, and although Dave still teaches philosophy at the university, he is very much involved with the inn and continuing restoration projects." As I learned later, these two men were the catalysts for what developed into a major restoration of historic buildings in Fredonia and nearby Dunkirk. Part of the town is now listed on the National Register of Historic Places.

I was impressed with the White Inn from the moment I saw the beautiful lawn, the flowers and two ancient maples beyond the wrought iron fence, and walked up to the two-story, pillared portico with a long, spacious porch extending on both sides across the front. As we walked through the inn, every room seemed more beautiful than the last. Nancy Palmer has furnished and decorated the rooms with a great sense of style. She uses designer wallpapers and fabrics, and many handsome antique pieces and special touches that make each guest room different and delightful. There are several two-room suites, and they are all quite spacious.

From 1868, when Dr. Squire White's son replaced the original 1821 house with a brick mansion, until the early 1900s, this was a private residence. As the White Inn, it has undergone many changes and additions; in the early 1930s it was included in the first edition of *Adventures in Good Eating* by Duncan Hines.

Dave Palmer pointed out that they are very community oriented, as shown by some wonderful displays of memorabilia donated by area residents. There are displays of Victorian lace, Oriental silks, drawings, paintings, photographs, posters, and old newspaper clippings about the

White Inn. The antique stained-glass and brass tulip chandelier hanging over the registration desk was donated by a community member.

Their three dining rooms have an enthusiastic following among townsfolk, and the meals have established the White Inn's reputation for fine dining. Dinner menus might feature rainbow trout stuffed with a mousseline of scallops, shrimp, and whitefish and served with a dill sauce and fresh vegetables, or medallions of pork with wild rice and a basil brandy sauce, as well as a number of other equally tantalizing dishes.

Congratulations to the two Daves for their impressive work of preservation and restoration.

THE WHITE INN, 52 E. Main St. (Rte. 20), Fredonia, NY 14063; 716-672-2103. A 23-guestroom (private baths) village inn, off U.S. Rte. 20 and 1 mi. from Lake Erie in Chautauqua County. All-size beds available. Full breakfast included in rates. Full breakfast, lunch, and dinner served daily to public. Open year-round. Wheelchair access with assistance. Bicycles, croquet, home decor and gift shop on premises, sailing on Lake Erie on inn's sloop. Sightseeing in historic area, wineries, and the many events at SUNY and Chautauqua nearby. No pets. CCs: Visa, MC, DC, AE, Disc. David Palmer and David Bryant, owners/hosts.

DIRECTIONS: From N.Y. Thruway, take Exit 59 and follow Rte. 60 to Rte. 20. Turn right to the inn.

Ontario

THE BRIARS
Jackson's Point, Ontario, Canada

One of Canada's most delightful and elegant Country Inns can be found just an one hour drive north of Toronto. Open all year, The Briars, in its unique way offers traditional hospitality on a Canadian lakeland estate of the mid 1800s.

John Sibbald, "The Squire", is justifiably proud of this family estate, now home to the fifth generation of Sibbalds. The 200 acre property combines a wide variety of buildings from an 1840 Manor House with a new 65 foot observation tower, built to replace the original, a marvelous golf course, all kinds of swiming, boating, tennis and other resort facilities. Nestled into the mature forests and gently rolling land of the region, the golf course at the Briars captures the relaxing character of a Scottish woodlands design. Each hole is framed by majestic old pine, oak and maple trees with inviting greens often guarded by crafted bunkers. Select cottages amongst the trees have beautiful views of the couse, and others along the shoreline look beyhond Jackson's Point to the far shores of Lake Simcoe at least 15 miles away. The sunsets are wonderful.

Along the Hedge Road, or a short walk by Golfers Lane you will pass extensive lawns and gardens and arrive at the main Inn. Walk up the steps from the lawn to the grand verandah of Manor House. Built in the Palladion cottage style, one finds rooms furnished with family antiques and John's personal art collection.

In addition to the outdoor heated pools, the inn has a large indoor pool and aquatic centre, a fitness area and a large game room

From the tower Lookout you see vistas of flower and vegetable gardens, tennis courts and the Red Barn Theatre located on the grounds.

Owners John and Barbara Sibbald have prepared an unusually large full-color map of the Briars and Lake Simcoe, in addition to some very informative literature about the area, all of which you can obtain by writing the Briars.

In one corner the map details a most interesting history since 1819, tracing the building's ownership through more than 170 years to the present Sibbald family. It shows the locations of all of the many lakeside cottages and the golf clubhouse, as well as Saint George's Church. With this map in hand it's easy for guests to locate the many recreational possibilities at the Briars. In winter the property becomes a snowy paradise for walking and cross-country skiing, skating, tobogganing, and snowshoeing.

———————

THE BRIARS, Jackson's Point, Ontario, L0E 1L0 Canada; 800-465-2376. A 92-guestroom country resort-inn (private bath) on the shores of Lake Simcoe, approx. 45 mi. north of Toronto. Queen, double, and twin beds. Open every day. Breakfast, lunch, and dinner served to travelers. Summer activities include 18-hole golf course, two outdoor swimming pools, indoor swimming pool, whirlpool, sauna, lakeshore swimming, 5 all-weather tennis courts, and many lawn sports. Winter sports include xc skiing, skating, tobogganing, snowmobiling, ice-fishing, and curling. There is a children's program during the summer and Christmas holidays. Excellent for families in all seasons. CCs: Visa, MC, AE. John and Barbara Sibbald, owners/hosts.

DIRECTIONS: Jackson's Point is located near Sutton, Ontario. From Hwy. 401, via Hwy. 404/Woodbine. Continue to Sutton and then Jackson's Point, 1/2 mi. east on Hedge Rd.

Pennsylvania

GLASBERN
Fogelsville, Pennsylvania

Dusk was gathering as I turned off old Route 22 and followed first one back road, and then another, deep into Pennsylvania Dutch farmland. I thought the tiny lights I glimpsed in the hills before me were Glasbern's, but I wasn't sure. Then, down a dip and over a bridge, I turned into the driveway, bordered with split-rail fences. Up ahead loomed the outline of a huge, impressive barn.

Al and Beth Granger welcomed me into the awesome Great Room of the Barn, which they have reconstructed and converted into an inviting country inn. The incredibly high vaulted ceiling soars twenty-six feet into the air, banded by many hand-hewn beams and punctuated with several skylights. The farmer's ladders still climb to where the hay mow once was. The original stonework of the massive walls provides interesting textural contrast to the smooth, clean line of the plaster fireplace and chimney.

As we sat comfortably ensconced before a cheery fire that danced on the hearth, the Grangers told me that the barn is a 19th-century post-and-beam Pennsylvania German bank barn. "I named it Glasbern, which means 'glass barn' in Middle English," Beth said, "because I felt as if all of the windows across the front give it a kind of all-glass look."

Beth and Al are a very cordial and accommodating couple, who formerly owned a bed-and-breakfast inn and come from a background of business and teaching. "When we saw this fabulous barn and the beautiful country surrounding it," Al said, "we knew it would make a great country inn."

In addition to the Barn, where there are several guest rooms, the Carriage House is a converted tractor shed with paneled barn-siding walls, and the original Farmhouse has suites with kitchen facilities. The Carriage House rooms all have skylights, fireplaces, and whirlpool baths; in fact, in two corner rooms you can relax in a double whirlpool bath and enjoy a view of the countryside. All of the guest rooms are attractively and comfortably furnished with queen- and king-sized beds, air conditioning, telephones, and cable television.

Tucked into a fold of rolling meadows and woods, the inn's grounds encompass sixteen acres with trails for nature walks in the clear, pure air and, when there's snow, cross-country skiing. A flagstone patio surrounds the swimming pool, where a cooling splash could be followed by an hour of tranquil reflection, broken only by the distant buzz of bees, the twitter of birds, the rustle of the busy little nearby stream. In autumn the color must be breathtaking because of all the wonderful trees.

Hearty breakfasts are served at the large oval mahogany table in the dining area of the Great Room, where guests can exchange plans for the day or their adventures. Sometimes breakfast is in the Sun Room, overlooking the valley, and might include something as scrumptious as whole-wheat pecan pancakes with maple syrup and bacon. Arrangements for a fixed-price, family-style dinner can be made in advance.

"We like to think that this is a place where our guests can find sanctuary," Beth commented, "a respite from the world in a peaceful, pastoral setting."

GLASBERN, Pack House Rd., R.D. 1, Box 250, Fogelsville, PA 18051-9743; 215-285-4723, 1-800-654-9296. A 21-guestroom (private baths) country inn on a back road in rolling Pennsylvania Dutch farmland, 10 mi. west of Allentown. King and queen beds available. Hearty breakfast included. Dinner can be arranged in advance. Open year-round. Minimum 2-night stay on weekends. Wheelchair access. Swimming pool, nature walks, xc skiing, and hot air ballooning on grounds. Hawk Mountain Sanctuary, Blue Mountain Ski Area, festivals, antiquing, covered bridge tours, and wineries nearby. No pets. One gorilla in residence named Jerry. Beth and Al Granger, owners/hosts.

DIRECTIONS: From I-78 take Rte. 100 north, turning left at 1st light north of I-78 onto Old Rte. 22. Turn right on No. Church St., continue about 1/2 mi. to right turn at Pack House Rd. Continue about 1 mi. to inn.

HICKORY BRIDGE FARM
Orrtanna, Pennsylvania

The breakfast deck over the creek behind the farmhouse is a wonderful place to sit and listen to the gurgling waters as they flow under the deck. The remnants of breakfast had been cleared away, and overnight guests had gone off on their various pursuits. Nancy Jeane Hammett

took advantage of a quiet moment to sit with me. "Sometimes our guests stay out here so long I have to shoo them out so that we can get the breakfast dishes done," she said. "This is a great place for birders—they come out with their spyglasses."

"Has it been a busy summer?" I inquired. "Oh, my, yes," she replied. "We just finished canning some of the best peaches we've ever had from our neighbor's orchard, and of course we always do apple butter. Although it's been a long, hot summer, the gardens and orchards have done well. Our vegetables, honeydew melons, and cantaloupes were fine. Being at the foot of the south mountain range, we have a wonderful water supply. Our guests really appreciate a good glass of water. They say that's why my coffee and tea taste so good."

She left me to answer the summons from a telephone, and I thought about my drive over here. The road from Fairfield to Orrtanna is one of my favorite back roads. There are great cornfields on one side and apple orchards on the other and, in the midst of all, a large farmstand with a wonderful collection of pumpkins out in front, and every imaginable type of the fresh farm produce that is abundant in this highly agricultural area.

I turned at the inn sign, passed over the railroad track, and was in sight of Nancy Jeane and Doctor Jim Hammett's Hickory Bridge Farm. There were the big red barn, the many flowers gardens, the old farmhouse, and the ever-growing collection of old farm machinery and carts. All of this was set against the background of beautiful, swaying trees, which in late September were beginning to take on their autumnal colors.

When Nancy Jeane returned, I asked her if that was her son-in-law, Robert, I saw out in the field. "Yes, indeed," she replied, "Robert and Mary Lynn are taking on more responsibilities here. Dr. Jim and I are gradually exchanging hats with Mary Lynn and Robert, who will be the official innkeepers in the near future. However, Dr. Jim is always busy around the farm on his days off, and I will always be on hand to serve our guests. This is truly a family operation. Even our grandchildren love to entertain the guests."

The guest rooms in the main house are Pennsylvania farm bedrooms. Many have washstands and one even has an old-fashioned radio on the shelf. There are many additional touches, such as good country-type fixtures on the walls, that make the bedrooms very pleasant, including a rocking chair for two in one room. Additional accommodations are in two cottages beside the brook in the woods.

We took a little tour around the grounds, assisted by one of the eight grandchildren. One of the points of interest is a country store museum, where there is penny candy, molasses, sarsaparilla, and apple butter for sale. However, it is basically a museum store, with an old post office money window, and it provides a great deal of amusement for guests.

———————

HICKORY BRIDGE FARM, 96 Hickory Bridge Rd., Orrtanna, PA 17353; 717-642-5261. A 7-guestroom (private baths) country inn on a farm (with cottages) 3 mi. from Fairfield and 8 mi. west of Gettysburg. Queen and double beds. Open year-round except December 20-January 1. Deposit required. Full breakfast included in rates. Dinner served to guests and travelers some weekdays and every weekend by reservation. Less than 2 hrs. from Wash., D.C., Baltimore, Lancaster, Amish country, and Hershey, Pa. Near Gettysburg Battlefield Natl. Park, Caledonia State Park, and Totem Pole Playhouse. Hiking, biking, fishing, and country store museum on grounds. Golfing, horseback riding and antiquing nearby. The Hammett & Martin Families, innkeepers.

DIRECTIONS: From Gettysburg take Rte. 116 west to Fairfield and follow signs 3 mi. north to Orrtanna. From south, take U.S. 81 north to Greencastle, PA. Then east on Rte. 16 to 116 east to Fairfield. From south, take U.S. 270 to Rte. 15 to Emmittsburg, MD, then west on 16 to Rte. 116 east through Fairfield. From west of PA Tpke., get off at Blue Mt. exit and go south on Rte. 977 to Rte. 30 east for 9 mi. Turn south at Cashtown and follow the signs.

THE INN AT STARLIGHT LAKE
Starlight, Pennsylvania

The peepers were peeping and the sunset afterglow was lighting the western sky. I wandered down the steps through the little grove of trees next to the lake and out onto the long dock, off of which were moored boats and sailboats.

I turned around to look at the lights of the inn and realized that what we have hear is a sophisticated rural inn. The trees along the shore created lacy silhouettes against the darkening blue sky.

This wonderful old white and green trim inn is on a back road, overlooking beautiful Starlight Lake. It is an old-fashioned, comfortable place with an accumulation of furniture from over the years. The combination lobby/living room has a fireplace in one corner, and there are reminders that the McMahons are originally from show business. Besides the piano and the guitar, books of plays or sheet music may be found on the tables or on the bookshelves.

Guest rooms are in the main building and also in adjacent cottages that have been redecorated and winterized.

There's a TV room, a game room in the main house,(where I won ping pong against the best the inn had to offer) and lots of outdoor activity, from canoeing, sailing, swimming, and bicycling to ice skating on the forty-five-acre lake and cross-country skiing on eighteen miles of marked trails. Incidentally, their bicycle built for two is a real test of togetherness for their guests. There is a very pleasant lakeside play area, and many lovely walks and dirt roads for backroading in the picturesque woods. By the way, the McMahons have a fabulous collection of old films.

Their chef creates some wonderful dishes. I had the salmon steamed with fennel, and smoked trout for an appetizer. There was also lobster and shrimp marinara over homemade fettucini. The chef makes

his own pasta, mayonnaise, stock, sauces, sherbets and ice cream. And for breakfast try the brioche and nut French toast.

The newest feature is Starlight's occasional murder mystery weekend and a series of weekends on fly fishing. Because the inn is not near any major tourist attractions, the innkeepers go out of their way to show you where to drive for pleasant outings and antiquing.

The next morning I awoke to honking geese. The lake was like a mirror. What a difficult job I have.

THE INN AT STARLIGHT LAKE, Starlight, PA 18461; 717-798-2519. A 26-guestroom (20 private baths) resort-inn, 5 mi. from Hancock, NY. All-sized beds available. Modified American plan. Breakfast, lunch, and dinner served daily May 15-April 1. Closed April 1-April 15. Wheelchair access. Swimming, boating, canoeing, sailing, fishing, hunting, tennis, hiking, bicycling, xc skiing, and lawn sports on grounds. Golf nearby. No pets. Judy and Jack McMahon, innkeepers.

DIRECTIONS: From NY Rte. 17, exit at Hancock, NY. Take Rte. 191S over Delaware River to Rte. 370. Turn right, proceed 3-1/2 mi.; turn right, 1 mi. to inn. From I-81, take Exit 62 at Tompkinsville. Follow Rte. 107 east 4 mi. to Rte. 247N and Forest City. Turn left on Rte. 171 (the main street), and continue 10 mi. north to Rte. 370. Turn right and go 13 mi. east to Starlight. Turn left, 1 mi. to inn.

THE MERCERSBURG INN
Mercersburg, Pennsylvania

The colonial village of Mercersburg, located in the beautiful Cumberland Valley at the foot of the Tuscarora Mountains, has maintained its historic architecture and small-town character. Once a frontier trading post, rumor has it that the property was purchased from Indians with guns and beads. As I drove down Main Street, dotted on either side with historic structures of limestone, brick, and log, most dating back to the early 1700s, I was unprepared for my first sight of the elegant Mercersburg Inn.

Constructed in 1909 of Berlin brick, the Georgian mansion's impressive main entrance is accentuated by six massive columns. Large double porches at either end overlook 5 acres of gently terraced lawns. In 1986, Fran Wolfe, an artist with more than eighteen years of renovation experience, purchased the three-story mansion and began extensive restoration. "I attended a boarding school near here, in Chambersburg," she explained, "and during the summer I would help my mother's resort on the Eastern Shore of Deleware." The combination of business skills she learned from her mother, and her renovation and artistic skills learned as an adult, proved to be invaluable when she purchased The Mercersburg Inn.

The inn's grand entrance features polished chestnut paneling. Walking between two rose-colored scagliola columns, you can climb to the second floor by way of a graceful, curving double staircase, with unusual serpentine banisters. Sunlight filters through stained-glass windows.

The public rooms are all elegant but comfortable. The grand hall has four sets of French doors that are opened during balmy summer

evenings, and a fireplace to warm the room in the chill winter. But it's the large, airy sunroom that seems to offer the most luxurious setting for relaxation. White wicker furnishings and floral cushions on the window seats create a perfect atmosphere for sipping mint-laced iced tea. In the winter the fireplace roars, and scenes of snowy delight can be seen through the large windows.

For indoor entertainment, the bowling alley that once took up the basement has been removed and made into a game room, where guests can play billiards and board games, or watch television or a VCR.

Fran's artistry is quite evident in the inn's spacious guest rooms, each uniquely decorated. Most of the rooms have handmade cherry canopy beds and down comforters. She has made excellent use of fabrics for swagging, around beds and windows, to create a sense of romance. Antiques and tastefully hung artwork complete the mood. All rooms have meticulously restored baths.

The chef at the Inn prepares a six-course meal every evening. As you sit in the mahogany-paneled dining room amidst leaded glass chandeliers, antique cabinets, sideboards, and a crackling fire, you will be served an exquisite meal, both in flavor and beauty, on Limoges china.

I began my meal with a curried butternut squash and apple-almond soup that had a smooth texture and subtle flavoring. After an appetizer of grilled sea scallops with saffron poached potatoes, I was served a tender breast of duck, lightly coated with a port wine sauce, and accompanied by grilled quince and persimmons. A salad and dessert followed, and were of equal merit. The flavors of herbs from the inn's gardens and the freshness of the locally grown vegetables are evident in each dish.

A continental breakfast is also available, and can be enjoyed in your own room in you choose. By the way, the wallpaper in the sunroom is a pattern that was used by Thomas Jefferson at Monticello.

Be sure to take advantage of the historical richness of the area and stroll through Mercersburg. The inn is also only an hour's drive to Harper's Ferry and the Gettysburg Battlefield. A stay at The Mercersburg Inn is country elegance at its best. For those interested in the enviornment, the Inn is the host to many leaders in the national movement. Recycling is practiced at the Inn, and Fran spearheaded the effort to get the community to recycle all of its sewage. Mercenberg will be the first city in the Chesapeake Basin to eliminate the discharge of pollutants.

THE MERCERSBURG INN, 405 S. Main St., Mercersburg, PA 17236; 717-328-5231. A 15-guestroom (private baths) elegant country inn located in historical Mercersburg. All-size beds. Open year-round. Six-course gourmet meal. Close to Harper's Ferry,

Gettysburg Battlefield, hiking, skiing, boating. No smoking. Pets by special arrangement. One dog in residence. Fran Wolfe, owner/host.

DIRECTIONS: Take PA Exit 3 from I-81 west on PA Rte. 16 to Mercersburg. The inn is on the left (PA Rtes. 16 and 75).

SMITHTON INN
Ephrata, Pennsylvania

"We want our guests to have a great Lancaster County experience. The Old Order people who live in this part of Pennsylvania live exactly as most of our forebears did. Customs have remained unchanged here. It's like being in touch with your own family's past."

I was to ponder that thought, expressed by Dorothy Graybill, many, many times during my visit to the Smithton Inn and the surrounding countryside at Ephrata, a predominantly Pennsylvania Dutch community.

"Unfortunately, the image of the Pennsylvania Dutch has been considerably distorted over the years, largely because of the efforts to commercialize some of the customs, language, and artifacts. We have developed a booklet with suggestions for touring and shopping that completely eliminates any of these places," Dorothy continued. "Both Allan and I make extensive and continuing trips throughout the countryside to make certain that our guests see the 'real' Pennsylvania Dutch life."

Dorothy was speaking of her associate at the Smithton Inn, Allan Smith, who is, among many other things, an excellent architect and woodcraftsman. We were having a chat in the truly handsome Great Room of the inn, and I couldn't help but feel that this room, with its fireplace, braided rug, comfortable furniture, and brightly polished hardwood floors, was an excellent place to start any adventure of this nature.

The inn is a pre-Revolutionary inn and stagecoach stop, built in 1763, and has been an inn for most of its many years. Each of the guest rooms has its own working fireplace and can be candlelighted during the evening hours. Beds have canopies, soft goose-down pillows, and bright handmade Pennsylvania Dutch quilts. Red flannel nightshirts are an amusing touch for guests to wear if they wish. Something I particularly appreciate is the speaker on every bedside table with a volume control, so that guests can enjoy the tasteful selection of chamber music. And on cold winter evenings you may have your bed made with a featherbed. Allan is pleased to escort inn guests through the inn, pointing out many of the marvelously designed and constructed features, not only in the original building, but in the additions that are being made. He has a wonderful sense of history and an obvious affection for good craftsmanship.

"We serve a full country breakfast and a rather simple but nourishing evening meal at our guests' request," Dorothy told me. "It consists of an appetizer, soup, salad, and a meat pie. Dessert is a homemade ice cream with our exceptional chocolate sauce, which is a story in itself."

The well-known Ephrata Cloister, an 18th-century German Protestant monastic society, is situated just a few steps away.

The entire area abounds in museums, crafts shops, antiques malls, summer and winter theater, concerts, winery tours, and art exhibits. There are daily farm auctions which include antiques and furniture, farm markets every Tuesday and Friday, live stock autions weekdays, antique market every Sunday with 3000 dealers and a summer-long Renaissance fair. Among several fine Pennsylvania Dutch restaurants are some located on picturesque Dutch farms.

I strongly suggest that our readers plan on staying at the Smithton Inn for a minimum of two nights and, if possible, three or more. The expert and caring guidance from the innkeepers provides everyone with a "real Lancaster County experience."

SMITHTON INN, 900 W. Main St., Ephrata, PA 17522; 717-733-6094. A 8-guestroom (private baths) pre-Revolutionary inn in Pennsylvania Dutch country near Lancaster. King, queen, and double beds available. Breakfast included in room rate. Dinner served to houseguests by advance reservation. Those sensitive to traffic noise should ask for an inside room or the Gold Room, although the owners have triple-paned the windows on the noisy street side so all rooms may now be quiet. CCs: Visa, MC, AE. Open all year. Wheelchair access. Convenient to all of Lancaster County's cultural, historic, and recreational attractions. Ephrata Cloister nearby. Dorothy Graybill, owner/host.

DIRECTIONS: Smithton is located 11 mi. north of Lancaster, an 5 mi. south of PA Tpke. Exit 21. From north or south, take Hwy. 222 to Ephrata exit. Turn west on Rte. 322 for 2.5 mi. to inn.

Upper South

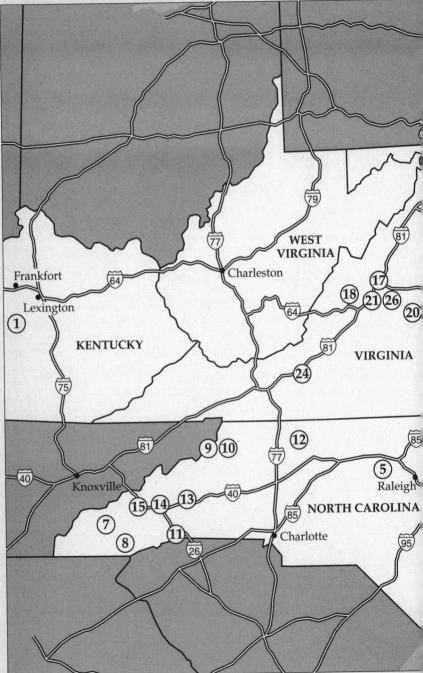

Upper South

KENTUCKY
1. Harrodsburg, BEAUMONT INN

MARYLAND
2. Baltimore, ADMIRAL FELL INN
3. Buckeystown, THE INN AT BUCKEYSTOWN
4. Oxford, ROBERT MORRIS INN

NORTH CAROLINA
5. Chapel Hill, THE FEARRINGTON HOUSE
6. Edenton, GRANVILLE QUEEN INN
7. Bryson City, HEMLOCK INN
8. Highlands, HIGHLANDS INN-THE OLD EDWARDS INN
9. Valle Crucis, THE INN AT THE TAYLOR HOUSE
10. Valle Crucis, MAST FARM INN
11. Saluda, THE ORCHARD INN
12. Pilot Mountain, PILOT KNOB INN
13. Black Mountain, RED ROCKER INN
14. Ashville, RICHMOND HILL INN
15. Clyde, WINDSONG: A MOUNTAIN INN

VIRGINIA
16. Fairfax, BAILIWICK INN
17. Staunton, BELLE GRAE INN
18. Millboro, FORT LEWIS LODGE
19. Orange, HIDDEN INN
20. Scottsville, HIGH MEADOWS INN
21. Vesuvius, IRISH GAP INNS
22. White Post, L'AUBERGE PROVENCALE
23. Alexandria, MORRISON HOUSE
24. Christianburg, THE OAKS
25. Trevilians, PROSPECT HILL
26. Nellysford, TRILLIUM HOUSE

WASHINGTON DC
27. Washington DC, HENLEY PARK HOTEL

WEST VIRGINIA
28. Berkeley Springs, THE COUNTRY INN
29. Charles Town, HILLBROOK INN

Kentucky

BEAUMONT INN

Harrodsburg, Kentucky

I love to visit Kentucky! There is a gentle quality to this landscape that matches the soft, unhurried accents of its people.

I paused for a moment in front of the Beaumont Inn, which dates well back into the days before the War Between the States, and tried to imagine what it was like when it began its career as as school for young ladies in 1845. Some years later it was Beaumont College, and in 1916 it was purchased by Mr. and Mrs. Glave Goddard and converted into the Beaumont Inn.

The ownership and management passed from Mrs. Goddard to her daughter, Mrs. Dedman, and then to Mrs. Dedman's two sons. Today, Bud Dedman is the owner, and his son, Chuck, following tradition, has become the fourth-generation innkeeper. To make it even more interesting, Chuck and his wife, Helen, have two children, one of whom, Dixon, is already showing great promise as an innkeeper of the future.

Grasping the solid handle of the big front door, I stepped inside, and there was Chuck Dedman. "I can see that you're looking around for Dixon," Chuck said. "He had to go on a very important errand for me, but he'll be back soon. Come on, I'll show you to your room."

I trotted along behind him, once again impressed by the number of rare items that have been collected and put in proper cases here at the inn. A group of antique fishing lures caught my eye, along with other Beaumont memorabilia, such as the collection of saltcellars—handsome small dishes that were used before the saltshaker came into being. Chuck's mother, Mary Elizabeth, had gathered together at least one hundred or more in a glass case.

"Oh yes, mother just loves things like that, and her history of the inn is always appreciated by our guests," he remarked.

The decorations and furniture in all the parlors and guest rooms reflect American history. The hallways on the main floor have several cabinets with beautiful old china and silverware, and the sitting rooms have elegant fireplaces and rose-patterned wallpaper. And much memorabilia is presented thoughout the rooms such as antique carpenter planes, dolls, and Haviland china.

Goddard Hall, across from the main building, has been completely renovated with the decor centered around the family's heirlooms, such as vintage clothing, and old family photographs (1830 to 1920).

The bill of fare is really down to earth. Probably topping everything is "yellow-legged" fried chicken and two-year-old Kentucky-cured country ham. Let me assure you that these taste nothing like any other food that bears the same name. The chicken almost falls off the bone and it's just about perfect, only exceeded perhaps by the tangy taste of real Kentucky ham, which is darker than some others you might have seen. These can be ordered at dinner in combination, and in spite of the fact that the menu has many other things I almost always end up ordering it. Also wonderful is the corn pudding and General Robert E. Lee Orange-Lemon Cake.

The Beaumont is a wonderful place for an early spring vacation. There are three championship golf courses close by and some wonderful shopping. The food department of the gift shop at the inn features Beaumont Inn cornmeal batter mix, brown sugar syrup, green tomato relish, sweet pickle relish, chicken-cheese casserole, frozen fruit salad, and chopped country ham. These tempting foods are also served in the dining room. Let me recommend to one and all the cornmeal cakes that are served at breakfast. They have a taste like nothing else I have ever tried.

Chuck and I returned to the front hall and, sure enough, there was Dixon already greeting new guests and giving them some suggestions about things they might like to do.

It looked to me like it was going to be another splendid visit at the Beaumont Inn.

BEAUMONT INN, Harrodsburg, KY 40330; 606-734-3381. A 33-guestroom (private baths) country inn in the heart of Kentucky's historic bluegrass country. All bed sizes.

European plan. Lunch and dinner served to travelers; all three meals to houseguests. Lunch not available Monday. Open every day from mid-March to mid-December. Tennis, swimming pool, shuffleboard on grounds. Golf courses and a wide range of recreational and historic attractions nearby. No pets. All major CCs. The Dedman Family, owners/hosts.

DIRECTIONS: From Louisville, take Exit 48 from east I-64 and go south on KY 151 to U.S. 127 and on south to Harrodsburg. From Lexington, take U.S. 60 west, then west on Bluegrass Parkway to U.S. 127. From Nashville, take Exit I-65 to Bluegrass Parkway near Elizabethton, KY, then east to U.S. 127.

Maryland

ADMIRAL FELL INN
Baltimore, Maryland

If you've always yearned for the free life of a sailor, spend some time at the Admiral Fell Inn and voyage back to Colonial Baltimore. Located in the rejuvenated, working waterfront community of Fells Point, the Admiral Fell Inn is the only historic inn on the waterfront.

Originally known as the Anchorage Hotel, the three connected buildings, constructed between 1850 and 1910, were used as a 28-room boarding house for sailors, then as a vinegar factory. Owner Jim Widman purchased the inn in 1984, and began what had to be a difficult renovation project. "Being an ex-navy officer, I never did quite shake the call of the sea," he told me as I registered. The friendly atmosphere of the inn is immediately noticeable; a partners desk adds a more personal flair than the standard hotel front desk.

Jim's attention to historical accuracy is apparent in both the interior and the exterior. The oldest of the inn's buildings is a three-story columned structure of red brick with an early Victorian-style facade. The other two buildings are four-story, rough-cut tan brick, with facades of simplified Georgian detailing. Standing at the inn's white front doors, I thought I could almost hear the heavy hobnail boots of sailors as they passed on the cobblestones.

Each guest room is unique in design, and decorated with antique treasures and period pieces found along the Eastern Seaboard. Every room bears the name and displays a biographical sketch of a famous Baltimorian. My room was luxurious, with two pencil-point four-poster beds, canopied in intricate lace work. All rooms have private baths (some with Jacuzzis), telephones, and television. Three rooms are designed to accommodate the handicapped.

Visiting the Admiral Fell Inn offers the same feeling as a stay at the home of a wealthy friend, so well are comfort and luxury married. The wood-burning fireplace in the large gracious sitting area of the drawing room highlights the room's emerald greens and warm reds, while the deep browns of Federal furniture are reflected in the polished brass fixtures.

In contrast, the skylit, four-story first-floor atrium, with its lush plants, is flooded with warmth and light all year. The library has a selection of reading material and also serves as a cozy spot to share a continental breakfast with other guests. Or, you may choose to breakfast in your room.

The inn's English-style pub is a delightful place to sip a glass of beer and listen to local lore of the 18th-century waterfront. The pub offers lunch and light fare daily. Dinner can be enjoyed by candlelight in the restaurant, featuring continental cuisine and fresh seafood. Baltimore has long been known for its ethnically diverse restaurants where you can satisfy a craving for anything from Mexican to traditional New England cuisine. Many excellent restaurants are within walking distance, or you can take advantage of the inn's complimentary van transportation. For a romantic evening excursion, take the water taxi.

Baltimore is a fascinating city to explore. Theaters, taverns, markets, jazz clubs, landmark homes, quaint shops, and boating facilities are close to the inn. For example, a short stroll through the Fells Point area will bring you to China Sea Trading, a curiosity shop worth at least an hour's investigation.

The Admiral Fell Inn has the kind of gracious hospitality and subtle elegance that inspired the comment of the couple who shared my table during breakfast: "We came for a weekend. We wish we'd come for a week." I echo their thoughts.

ADMIRAL FELL INN, 888 S. Broadway, Baltimore, MD 21231; 301-522-7377 or 800-292-INNS. A 38-guestroom (private baths) charming inn on the historic Fells Point waterfront. Large expansion during 1993 will add many more rooms. Open all year. Double and king beds. Continental breakfast included. Light fare in the pub, and dinner in the restaurant, all week. Complimentary van service. Pet boarding service available. CCs: Visa, MC, AE. Jim Widman, Dominik Eckenstein, owner/hosts.

DIRECTIONS: From I-95 South, exit Downtown left to Pratt St. Turn right and continue east for 1 mi. around Inner Harbor on President St. (I-83) and Fleet St. to Broadway.

Go right on Broadway and continue to end. From I-95 North, exit Eastern Avenue. Go on Eastern street for 4 miles to Broadway. Go left on Broadway to end.

THE INN AT BUCKEYSTOWN

Buckeystown, Maryland

Buckeystown is a Nationally Registered Historic Village full of architectural delights from early log cabins to large brick and stone Federal homes and elegant Victorian clapboard mansions. There are also many Victorian houses, but by far the most impressive is the Inn with its huge wrap-around porch. The village is in the heart of Maryland's Civil War country and on the banks of the Monocacy River. The Battle of the Monocacy saved the nation's capital from the Confederates.

The Inn occupies an 1897 Victorian mansion and a small but elegant 1884 Gothic brick church, purchased in 1981, restored and converted. All rooms have been decorated with authentic period pieces and displays of memorabilia by owners Dan Pelz and Chase Barnett.

A dinner bell at 7:30 p.m. sharp summoned us into the elegant main dining room, where two oak tables of eight were set with antique china, glassware, and silver. The room is grandly Victorian, with a bold butterfly, bird-and-flower-patterned wallpaper, Oriental rugs, oak sideboards and cabinets, and a magnificent crystal chandelier.

Dan and his helpers had cooked a burgundy toast, autumn melon with prawns and fresh lime, Jack-O-Lantern soup, romaine dijon with

sunflower seeds, honey-garlic glazed roast loin of pork on a bed of herb stuffings, snowpeas with pimentos, fried apples, corn muffins, pecan tarts and coffee.

As Dan explained later, they have one seating for both breakfast and dinner, and there's always a set menu for dinner with complimentary wine and special breads.

There are eight guest rooms and two cottages, all charmingly furnished with period pieces, as well as such modern comforts as good mattresses, electric blankets, and air conditioning.

There are interesting walks near the inn—the Monocacy River, where fisherman cast for bass, an ancient Indian dig in a rocky cliff, woods and farmlands—Dan calls the area a paradise for architecture buffs, historians, antiquers, and outdoors people. Buckeystown is within an hour of Washington, D.C., Baltimore, and Gettysburg, and within a half-hour of Harper's Ferry, Leesburg, and New Market (the antiques capital of Maryland). Nearby Frederick is a beautifully restored historic town with many sites of interest, nice shops, and all city conveniences.

THE INN AT BUCKEYSTOWN, Buckeystown, MD 21717-9999; 301-874-5755. A 9-guestroom (private baths) inn in a historic village, consisting of 2 bedroom cottage, 1 bedroom cottage, 2 suites and 3 doubles. Queen, double and twin beds. Rates include dinner and breakfast. Dinner served to travelers with 24-hr. advance reservation. Open year-round. Minimum stay of 2 days required on all holidays and on weekends from October 1–January 1 and from April 1–July 1. Conveniently located to enjoy all of the historical and cultural attractions of the region. No pets. Two cats in residence. No smoking in dining room. Dan Pelz and Chase Barnett, owners/hosts; Rebecca Shipman-Smith, manager.

DIRECTIONS: Buckeystown lies 4 mi. to the south of the Buckeystown exit off I-270 in Frederick, and 5 mi. to the south of the Buckeystown exit off I-70 in Frederick. Inn is located on Maryland Rte. 85.

ROBERT MORRIS INN
Oxford, Maryland

The Robert Morris is on the eastern shore of Maryland beside the Tred Avon River. One of the ways to reach it is via the famous Cape May—Lewes ferry, which I've been riding ever since my first visit. Oxford is, surprisingly enough, still one of the most unspoiled villages in North America. It has several pre-Revolutionary and Federalist houses that are remarkably well preserved. Incidentally, you can get a copy of "This and That About Olde Oxford, Maryland" by Howard B. Gerhardt at the front desk of the inn. It's an extremely well-written informal history of Oxford.

The original house of Robert Morris still stands and four of the original bedrooms with side views of the water are the most popular accommodations. Robert Morris Jr., a friend to George Washington, was a signer of the Declaration of Independence, the Articles of Confederation, and the Constitution.

This past year Wendy and Ken Gibson celebrated 20 years of inkeeping and received the governor's award of excellence at a special luncheon in their honor. As Wendy said, "It took 20 years to get all the private baths in and 20 years of renovations. This will be the first year we don't have to do something major!"

The decorations in the main house have always attracted attention, and the murals in the dining room, made from 140-year-old wallpaper samples, depict scenes from other places in North America—including Natural Bridge, Virginia, and Boston Harbor. The guest rooms in the main house are decorated in a casual motif with country rugs and coverlets and a variety of interesting knickknacks on the walls, among which are the tops of china serving dishes of many different designs.

Just down the block on the waterfront is Sandaway, with six guest rooms decorated in a country-romantic style. All have a view of the river and some have porches. They are reserved for nonsmokers. As a matter of fact, in the main house, the entire third floor is restricted to nonsmokers.

"Guests love our private beach on the Sandaway property, the million dollar view down the river, and watching all the variety of boat traffic that cruises by," Wendy said.

The inn's location in the Chesapeake Bay area means that there is considerable emphasis on seafood at lunch and dinner—crabcakes, crab Imperial, oysters Gino, stuffed shrimp, and stuffed fish. There are, of course, poultry and meat offerings as well.

One of their favorite stories about their legendary "light and lumpy" crabcakes is how Wendy and Ken sent some Robert Morris crabcakes to author James Michener in Sitka, Alaska, when he was working on a book there. "We heard that he was homesick for the Eastern Shore and our crabcakes. They made it via Federal Express in under forty-eight hours."

The Robert Morris is very much a family operation, with Ken's brother, Jay, handling the major innkeeping duties, while Wendy and Ken are very active and involved "behind the scenes," as Wendy puts it. Their son Ben has designed T-shirts that depict all the things guests remember about the inn and Oxford. I hear they're selling like hotcakes. His corn business allows the guests to feed the wild ducks.

A stay in this lovely inn beside the Tred Avon River is completely peaceful and quiet—a place to relax and enjoy the incredible sunsets.

ROBERT MORRIS INN, Oxford, MD 21654; 301-226-5111. A 35-guestroom (private baths) waterside inn and lodge in a secluded Colonial community on the Tred Avon, 10 mi. from Easton, Md. All-sized beds available. (Some rooms with private porches and some nonsmoking rooms.) Closed week after Thanksgiving to April 1st. European plan. Breakfast, lunch, and dinner served to travelers and guests daily Wednesday-Sunday; winter hours vary. Wheelchair access to restaurant. Tennis, golf, seasonal river swimming, sailing, fishing, and bicycles nearby. No pets. CCs: V, MC. Wendy and Ken Gibson, owners/hosts; Jay Gibson, manager.

DIRECTIONS: From Delaware Memorial Bridge, follow Rte. 13 south to Rte. 301 and proceed south to Rte. 50, then east on Rte. 50 to Easton. From Chesapeake Bay Bridge, follow Rte. 50/301 to Rte. 50 and proceed east to Easton. From Chesapeake Bay Bridge Tunnel, follow Rte. 13 north to Rte. 50 and proceed west to Easton. From Easton, follow Rte. 322 to Rte. 333 to Oxford and inn.

North Carolina

THE FEARRINGTON HOUSE
Chapel Hill, North Carolina

In the 17th and 18th centuries, many English immigrants to America settled in North Carolina. That's why I was interested to learn that R.B. Fitch, a native North Carolinian, went back to England for inspiration in the design of the Fearrington House. When I saw the arrangement of attractive, low buildings with their roofs pitched at different levels, grouped around the courtyard, with the pump in the middle and all the little gardens, I immediately thought of the Bell Inn in Buckinghamshire.

And sure enough, R.B., as he prefers being called, told me that a visit to the Bell Inn provided him and his wife with their inspiration.

"Jenny and I have made several trips to England, collecting old furniture and antiques and original art. The old pine flooring, for instance, came from an 1850 London workhouse."

Included in the group of inn buildings is the sun room, where afternoon tea is available, and the garden house, which is a living room where guests can get together.

Jenny, R.B.'s wife, has created fourteen superb guest rooms, mostly suites, every one of which is completely different from the others. I thought I could hear the pristine strains of a Mozart quartet as R.B. was showing me the guest rooms, and I asked him where that heavenly sound was coming from. "We have a wonderful sound system in all the rooms, including speakers in the bathroom. It's a great way to brush your teeth," he laughed. He's got heated towel racks in the bathrooms too.

The village is a story in itself. R.B. has turned a farmstead of over 600 acres into a tiny rural community where the homes of about 800 inhabitants nestle unobtrusively in the surrounding forest. The village center was once a cluster of old farm buildings.

Today, the old milking barn is a pottery with a resident potter, another farm building is now an excellent, well-stocked market and general store, and there is even a post office in the old blacksmith shop. Jennie's passion for gardening has resulted in the Dovecote, a wonderful country garden shop. The restaurant, a lovely white-columned farmhouse, is in the old Fearrington home, built in 1926.

Food, I discovered, was of paramount importance in their plans. They wanted to bring back Southern cooking at its finest, and the menu offers such interesting items as Carolina crab cakes with tomato and corn relish, Chatham County goat cheese salad, corn chowder with hickory-smoked duck sausage, crayfish fritters and creole butter, and grilled Carolina quail with savory cabbage and a ginger sherry sauce. Many of their dishes are featured in the handsome *Fearrington House Cookbook*.

There are many other more usual dishes, but everything is cooked and served with a special flair and accompanied by buttermilk biscuits and homemade breads. I couldn't make up my mind between the lemon meringue pie and a hazelnut meringue with chocolate ice cream and fresh raspberry sauce. They were both incredible.

I asked R.B. what his philosophy had been in creating this very interesting and outstanding settlement. "We've tried to blend it into the rolling countryside so that it looks like it's been around for a long time. The 650 acres that make up the village were in the Fearrington family for over 200 years, and when we bought it in 1974 our commitment was to preserve its heritage and beauty."

THE FEARRINGTON HOUSE, Fearrington Village Center, Pittsboro, NC 27312; 919-542-2121. A 14-guestroom (private baths) (mostly suites) luxury inn and village in rolling farm country 8 mi. south of Chapel Hill, the home of the Univ. of No. Carolina. King, queen and twin beds available. Breakfast included in room rate. Picnics available. Restaurant is open for dinner Tuesday thru Saturday and Sunday brunch. Open year-round. Swimming pool, croquet lawn, crafts shops, country walks on premises. Cultural, social, and athletic events at Univ. of No. Carolina; also Duke Univ. and No. Carolina State Univ. nearby. Children over 12 welcome. Nearby kennels available for pets. No smoking in dining rooms. Jenny and R.B. Fitch, owners/hosts.

DIRECTIONS: The Fearrington House is located halfway between Chapel Hill and Pittsboro on U.S. 15/501.

GRANVILLE QUEEN INN
Edenton, North Carolina

Startled by two pair of ebony eyes staring at me, I shut my eyes quickly to allow myself a moment to recall where I was. Oh yes, I was in the Egyptian Queen room at Granville Queen Inn. My roommates, owners of the eyes, were two large cast bronze sphinxes. They wer not the least of the unique items around me. Between the stately sentinels were two black lacquer chairs placed as if waiting for the Pharaoh and his Queen to arrive. The windows were hidden by shiny gold satin and billowing sheer drapes. My toes sank into plush carpet as I rose from a restful night's sleep under the leopard-skin comforter on the bed. The luxury extended itself to the bath's marble countertops and large tub with Egyptian paintings along its side. The sink had cobra-handled faucets.

Each of the nine guest rooms, in fact, are filled with furnishings imported from Italy, Holland, China, Thailand, England, and Egypt, arranged thematically. Several of the rooms have their own fireplaces and private balconies.

Eager to experience the five-course breakfast, my wife, Louise, and I dressed quickly. The murmur of conversation and enticing smells gave us direction and soon we found the entrance to the elegant formal dining room.

"Look at those chairs," I exclaimed. The chair backs were carved into large wooden butterflies. Heavy gold statuettes adorned the mantle of an ornately carved fireplace. Deep burgundy carpet was warmed by beige walls and peach table linens. White pillars extended to the ceilings.

"Good morning," greeted Marilyn Miller, co-owner of the inn. "Would you prefer to eat in the dining room or outdoors on the Plantation Porch?" We chose to enjoy the sunlit warmth of the porch, with its small wrought-iron tables and wicker chairs. White plantation fans were circulating overhead. Looking over the menu, we soon realized this could be a meal to remember! We began with apple crunch and pumpkin spice muffins, followed by a fresh fruit cup of juicy melons. Next came the Yogurt Carousel accompanied by raisins, peanuts, granola, spiced apples and peaches. I loosened my belt with the appearance of my entrée of grilled chicken breast smothered in a tarragon sauce. Louise sampled the grilled Filet Mignon. Our dessert choices included the Southern Pancake, a concoction similar to a souffle that's topped by warm lemon butter and sprinkles of powdered sugar and toasted almonds, or a warm blueberry and cream cheese crepe. As we enjoyed this sumptuous meal, Marilyn dropped by our table to answer some of my questions about the inn's history.

Built in 1907, the plantation style mansion was purchased by Marilyn and her partner, Greg Haden, in 1989. Greg, a general contractor, brought all his talents and skills to the project, while Marilyn's past occupation in advertising graphics aided her in decorating and furnishing the old structure. As one views the exterior, it evokes romantic fantasies of the "Old South," with massive white columns, dormer windows, and low fenced balconies. Yet it also has classical accents typical of Edwardian times.

"It was quite a challenge to rebuild this old southern mansion," concurred Greg, arriving at our table to reclaim Marilyn's attention to the details of innkeeping. We were ready to do some local exploring.

Granville Queen is in the Historic District of Edenton, just blocks from the center of Edenton, which was the first provincial capital of North Carolina. A favorite lair for the infamous pirate Blackbeard, it was also home to Revolutionary patriots. Located on Edenton Bay, it since prospered as a port town. After sight-seeing and shopping, we took a leisurely walk along the marina.

Arriving back at the inn, we joined other guests for an evening of wine tasting in the parlor, a room of breathtaking design. The beaks of two bronze flamingos pointed upward to a ceiling with intricate inlaid carvings set between its wooden beams. Thick foliaged indoor plants sat on glistening table tops. Queen Anne chairs of gold brocade were placed before the large marble fireplace. In the corner, a staircase wound upward to the second floor. We sipped our wine, visiting quietly with fellow guests in this atmosphere of elegance.

GRANVILLE QUEEN INN, 108 S. Granville St., Edenton, NC 27932; 919-482-5296. A 9-guestroom (private baths) renovated mansion of grand southern style in Historic District. King, queen and double beds. Five course breakfast included. Smoking allowed on outside porches only. Open all year. Two blocks from downtown Edenton and one block from marina. No pets. Marilyn Miller and Greg Haden, owners/hosts.

DIRECTIONS: Take US 17 Bypass to US 17 Business. Inn located on US 17 Business on the corner of Granville and Queen Sts.

HEMLOCK INN

Bryson City, North Carolina

In the Hemlock Inn reception area, there are two framed cross-stitched sayings. The first one says "This establishment serves country charm and hospitality." The second one says "In the mountains at Hemlock Inn, we forget to count the days." Both cross-stitches, made by guests of the Inn, say in simple terms what the Inn is all about.

The first thing that strikes a new guest is the marvelous view from the front porch stretching over three valleys to the mountains beyond. Sitting on 64 acres of wooded land, the Inn exists in a mountain world of its own, surrounded by nature's masterpieces. The atmosphere is friendly, relaxed and informal.

The Inn has been owned and operated by Ella Jo and John Shell since 1968. In 1988, their daughter, Elaine, and her husband, Morris White, came into the business with them. There are twenty-six rooms including several cottages and a secluded cabin. The decorations are simple and include what the innkeepers call "mountain furniture." You won't find a swimming pool, room telephones, televisions...or traffic noise. Ceiling fans create a pleasant breeze on rare days when needed.

Nor does the inn have extensive planned activities. You may play ping-pong, shuffleboard, skittles, and various board games; walk in the woods; read a book from the Inn's library; and, of course, sit in those rocking chairs on the front porch.

Three miles away is the Great Smoky Mountain National Park which has some wonderful walks, fishing and views.

The Inn serves two meals daily, eliminating lunch. Local women do all the cooking, and many have been working here for years. Guests are seated at a round table and serve themselves from a lazy Susan laden with country ham, fried chicken, beef pie, fresh vegetables, homemade hot biscuits and old-fashioned desserts.

This family-style inn is not a place for a solitary getaway. It's an inn that lets you get away and meet other people.

HEMLOCK INN, Bryson City, NC 28713-704-488-2885. A 25-guestroom (private baths) Smoky Mountain inn, 4 mi. from Bryson City and 60 mi. from Asheville. Double and twin beds. Modified American plan omits lunch. Breakfast and dinner served to travelers by reservation only. Sunday dinner served at noontime. Open late April to early November Wheelchair access. Near Fontana Dam, Cherokee, and Pisgah National Forest. Shuffleboard, skittles, table tennis, hiking trails on grounds. Tubing, rafting, and tennis nearby. No pets. No credit cards. Ella Jo and John Shell; Morris and Elaine White, owners/hosts.

DIRECTIONS: From Hwy. 74 take the Hyatt Creek Rd.-Ela exit. Bear right until you reach Rte. 19. Turn left on Rte. 19 for approx. 1 mi., and turn right at inn sign. Take county road to top of mountain.

HIGHLANDS INN-THE OLD EDWARDS INN
Highlands, North Carolina

I arrived in the beautiful mountain town of Highlands after chartering my way on Rte. 64 through the Cullasaja Gorge in a fog that was rolling in faster than those of us winding our way up the narrow two-lane road from Franklin. Cascades and waterfalls are evident along this path, and one has to admire the engineers who blasted their way through this area when the first road was built in the early 1930s. Despite the limited view, I still wanted to stop to see Dry Falls and

Bridal Veil Falls, where you can drive your car behind a 120-foot waterfall.

Cool air had arrived ahead of me and the welcome lamps from the Highlands Inn were inviting; once inside, a crackling fire was an indication of the warm hospitality I would receive here. Pat Benton, although busy with guests and helping people get reservations at the Central House Restaurant across the street, encouraged me to settle in for the night, enjoy the fireside, and be sure to join the guests downstairs at 9:00 for homemade cookies, coffee, milk or tea. Who could resist?

The Benton family purchased and renovated the Old Edwards Inn in 1981 and The Central House, part of the original structure, in 1983. The Highlands Inn, just across the street, was purchased in 1989 and has been renovated with flair. Built in 1879 and originally known as the Smith Hotel—the town's first inn—the Highlands Inn attracted a number of guests seeking the restorative qualities of the mountain air. Today guests come from all over the world to enjoy the area's golf, shopping, clear air and scenic surroundings.

My spacious second floor room featured a semi-canopied queen-sized bed, covered with a downy quilt and generous-sized pillows. There were bedside tables with reading lamps, a fainting couch, and two wing-back chairs on either side of the fireplace that invited quiet reading or friendly conversation. A door opened out to the second floor porch, bedecked with rocking chairs and geraniums. The special "soap box" I received from Carolyn provided some nice toiletries as well as a delightful surprise—I won't ruin it for you. All the rooms provide showers, and some also have baths.

As enchanting as my room was, I was also drawn to the garden room, off the parlor. White wicker furniture, splashes of greens and reds, and an aviary filled with some of the most beautiful finches I have ever seen, living in a variety of unique birdcages, offered another view of the Bentons' effort in restoring the inn in the country manner. Later, some heavy competition was in the air with challenges for chess, Trivial Pursuit, or bridge at the wicker tables. But with the fire glowing, comfortable sofas, and shelves full of books and magazines for browsing, the parlor was also a popular spot. A large-screen television is provided in a separate room, with ample seating for groups.

A number of Scottish and English accents could be detected among the guests. Many guests return here year after year, often requesting "their room."

Across the street at the Edwards Inn another fire was roaring in a smaller, but equally cozy parlor, known as the Moose Room. Guestrooms here are not as spacious, but all feature private baths and a variety of bed sizes. I talked with several couples who meet here every fall, each comparing their rooms, but returning to the same one "because they are just like another home to us."

Guests enjoy a very generous, buffet-style continental breakfast in the dining area of the Highlands Inn. Cereal, fresh fruit, freshly-baked breads ("They have something different every morning," one lady said) and coffee, tea, and juices are offered. Although tables are separate, there's so much camaraderie here that people talk between the tables or pull up chairs and enjoy a second cup of coffee. Dinner is not included in the room rate, but you're just a few steps from the Central House, where diners enjoy seafood and steak specialties, along with lighter fare, in the ambience of a colonial restaurant. Reservations, particularly during the high season of April through October, are highly recommended for all Highland restaurants.

Highlands offers galleries, antique shops, boutiques, the theater, and a library. Just down the road is golfing at the Cullasaja Club, tennis and swimming, along with rock hounding, river rafting, horseback riding and hiking. But if you don't feel like doing much beside enjoying the rockers on the front porches, that's OK. Even the townspeople say the best thing to do here is relax.

HIGHLANDS INN & OLD EDWARDS INN, Main Street, Box 1030, Highlands, NC 28841; 704-526-5036. Combined 50-guestroom (private baths) historic inns located in the mountain town of Highlands. All-sized beds. Continental breakfast included in

rates, lunch and dinner available. Open April-November Restaurants, galleries, boutiques and outdoor recreation within walking distance or short drive. No pets. CCs:
Visa, MC, AE. Rip and Pat Benton, owners/hosts.

DIRECTIONS: Take 64 to Highlands. The inn is on Main Street at the interesection of
64 and Route 28.

THE INN AT THE TAYLOR HOUSE

Valle Crucis, North Carolina

The sign of a rooster greeting a sunrise was my first welcome to The
Inn at the Taylor House. As I entered slowly up the gravel drive, the
inn, nestled within the trees, came into view. The pristine two-story is
typical of farmhouses built in the early 1900s. Three large dormers project outward under the dark gray roofline. Ladened with luggage, I
climbed the stairs onto a large wrap-around veranda. An old-fashioned

porch swing slightly swayed in the breeze. A young couple seated at
one of several wicker tables were sharing a bottle of wine.

"Everyone who stays here seems to pick their own special place on
the porch," said a friendly-looking woman standing at the front door.
"We can even serve breakfast out here if you like."

At the mention of the word "breakfast" I realized I was face-to-face
with Chip Schwab, renowned in B&B circles for her culinary talents.

Chip and her husband, Roland, brought years of training with
them to the Inn. Chip once operated the Truffles Cooking School,
while Roland grew up in his family's inn in Switzerland and holds a

degree from one of the world's top hotel schools. He commutes between Valle Crucis and Atlanta, where the Schwabs co-own a restaurant with his brother. Breakfast is Chip's specialty, but Roland sometimes adds his expertise in preparing dinners for special parties.

Tiring of their hectic city lifestyle, they searched all over the United States for a country inn. Chip was familiar with Valle Crucis from her college days, and was delighted when the Taylor home, situated on three acres, came up for sale. The conversion from farmhouse to inn was quite a project, all the time working to retain the original style.

Following her inside, I approved wholeheartedly of their efforts. Refinished hardwood floors border the rich red and black design of Oriental area rugs in the living room. The antique coffee table, magazines fanned across one corner, is surrounded by plump-cushioned chairs and sofa. Similarly decorated, but smaller, the cozy den has a good supply of books and a VCR for movie viewing.

I had to laugh when Chip told me the old kitchen had to be removed with a chainsaw! Its replacement is a restaurant-grade kitchen well suited to their love of food preparation. I asked her what taste treats might be in store during my stay. Usually served in two courses, breakfast may start with Eggs Benedict or Birchermusli—a cereal of nuts, berries, oats, and yogurt and a favorite of the Swiss—followed by sour cream pancakes topped with fresh strawberries or poached pears covered with a tangy bleu cheese sauce. Chip does not hesitate to share her recipes. Guests are served in the bright yellow dining room.

Retrieving my bags, we climbed the bannistered staircase to my room. Guestrooms, each decorated in a different style, have fluffy goose down comforters on the beds. My room had a country look, with calico and lace covering the windows, floral wallpaper, and an antique rocking chair. The claw foot tub in the adjacent bath completed this old-fashioned picture. There is also a two-room suite, complete with fireplace and sitting room, on the first floor. The River Cabin can accomodate a larger party, but accommodations there don't include breakfast.

I was looking forward to the variety of local attractions. For the physically inclined, there are several golf courses nearby, trout fishing on the Watauga River, and horseback riding and hiking in nearby mountains. For the daring, the mile-high suspension bridge at Grandfather Mountain offers panoramic views. The kids will love a ride on the 100-year-old Tweetsie Railroad in the amusement park between Boon and Blowing Rock. A full day can be spent submerged in history at Valle Crucis. So much to do, so little time...I may have to schedule a second visit.

THE INN AT THE TAYLOR HOUSE, Box 713, Hwy.194, Valle Crucis, N.C. 28691; 704-963-5581. A 6-guestroom farmhouse on three high country acres near Valle Crucis. All-sized beds. Complimentary full breakfast. Dinners available for special groups by arrangement. Afternoon tea and complimentary wine. Gift Shop. Open May-December Minimum two-night stay on weekends. No pets. Restricted smoking. Activities nearby include fishing, hiking, horseback riding, sightseeing, shopping, and golfing. No pets. CCs: Visa, MC. Chip and Roland Schwab, owners/hosts.

DIRECTIONS: Less than 1 mi. from Valle Crucis on Hwy. 194.

MAST FARM INN

Valle Crucis, North Carolina

"People in this part of North Carolina are very fond of just sittin' and talkin'." Francis and Sibyl Pressly and I were engaged in one of the most popular activities at the Mast Farm Inn: porch-rocking. They were telling me about the outbuildings around the rambling old farmhouse, which is on the National Register of Historic Places as "one of the most complete and best-presented groups of 19th-century farm buildings in western North Carolina." The Mast Farm had grown from the tiny log cabin built in 1812 by David Mast.

"The building with the bell tower is the old smokehouse," Francis continued. "Then there's the spring house. Then if you move on around, you come to the old woodshed and the apple house, or ice house, which has foot-thick walls, and we still use it for storing our potatoes and apples."

"Are any of the other buildings used for anything now?" I wondered.

"Oh, sure, we do some woodworking and keep our tools in the old woodshed," Francis replied.

"There's a nest of wrens who are using the old wash house," Sibyl added. "It was considered to be a very innovative wash house because it was built right over a stream and it had lattice work above, so the cool breezes could blow through. There are still two big old iron pots in there."

"Actually," Francis said, "we've restored these buildings to show what an old mountain farmstead was like. We have really made every effort to remain faithful to the past in this entire restoration."

I would say that Francis and Sibyl have succeeded admirably in their objectives. The main house, its long porch stretching around the side with rocking chairs and swings, must look very much as it did in the early 1900s, when it was first turned into an inn. A stay at the inn feels very much like a step back in time, with no telephones or television to shatter the peaceful country atmosphere.

Both originally from North Carolina, Francis and Sibyl had been living in Washington, D.C., where Francis was an administrator with the National 4-H Council, and Sibyl a physical therapist in geriatrics.

In the few years since they began renovating the farmhouse, they have shored up foundations, buttressed walls and floors, painted, papered, brought in craftsmen for woodworking, and done all those things that are necessary to bring a neglected and derelict old house back to its former dignity and beauty.

Today, the rooms fairly sparkle with turn-of-the-century antique furnishings and mountain crafts. There are fresh flowers everywhere and as one of their guests told me, "The inn is squeaky clean from one end to the other, and the room appointments seem to have been chosen not for their country atmosphere, but to make the guests comfortable."

I can see that the Presslys are very good at putting their guests at ease. They are very welcoming and make a point of introducing everyone. When it comes to meals, Sibyl says, "We serve our guests the kind of food that we enjoy."

They describe it as "country cooking with a gourmet flair." That means vegetables and fruit from their garden down by the river. The menu is prix fixe and dinner might be an appetizer, sautéed mountain trout, vegetable strudel, corn pudding, garden vegetables, salad, fresh-baked rolls and cornbread. Dessert could be a fruit cobbler with ice cream, hot fudge cake, fudge nut cake, sour cream apple pie, or Shaker lemon pie.

As we were sat out on the porch, rocking, and Sibyl and Francis began to tell me about how they'd happened to come here, I looked out over the beautiful mountain valley. I could see just what it was about these North Carolina hills that had attracted them so much.

MAST FARM INN, P.O. Box 704, Valle Crucis, NC 28691; 704-963-5857. An 12-guestroom (10 private baths) farmhouse inn set in a beautiful mountain valley between Boone and Banner Elk in western North Carolina. All-sized beds. Modified American plan includes breakfast and dinner. Dinner served to the public Tuesday-Sunday noon. Reservations necessary. Open January to mid-March; May 1 to November 1. Fishing, canoeing, golf, hiking, skiing, country walks, crafts, and country fairs nearby. Children over 12 welcome. No pets. No smoking. Sibyl and Francis Pressly, owners/hosts.

DIRECTIONS: The Boone/Banner Elk area is accessible from any direction. Watch for Valle Crucis on NC 105. Mast Farm Inn is 3 mi. from Rte. 105 on Rte. SR 1112.

THE ORCHARD INN

Saluda, North Carolina

I had finished every last bit of the succulent chicken Madras and now I was trying to stretch out a scrumptious blackberry cobbler so it would last as long as possible. I peered through the window, where nature had just put on a marvelous sunset, high in the North Carolina mountains. A pinpoint of light in the valley far below caught my eye.

Ken Hough joined me for a moment, having completed the busiest part of his evening in the kitchen as chef. "Have you ever wondered who lives down there where we can see that light?" I asked. Ken, among a number of other careers, has been headmaster of a college preparatory school in Charleston and also an operatic tenor. He smiled broadly at my question and replied, "It's funny you should mention that because I've often wondered the same thing. Of course, we could never find it in the daytime and the chances are we could never find it by night either."

The inn is midway between Hendersonville and Tryon and, like some other North Carolina inns, has a truly spectacular view.

In the case of the Orchard Inn there are many words that come to my mind—flowers, original paintings, music, sculpture, a breathtaking view, cordiality, intellectual curiosity, good conversation, mountain tranquility, and the changing tones and colors as they are affected by the mists off the mountains at various times of the day.

The Orchard Inn combines country farmhouse warmth with many touches of southern plantation elegance. It has Oriental rugs, original artwork, baskets, quilts, and Flow Blue china. Ann has exercised splendid taste in decorating the ten guest rooms with antiques, including some with iron and brass beds and hand-woven rag rugs.

This inn has one of the most interesting second-floor hallways I have ever seen. Several bookshelves are loaded with books and magazines, including very old but readable ones. There are all kinds of unusual curious, dolls, children's toys, a dollhouse, and contemporary drawings, watercolors, and prints from the French Impressionists.

The dining room is in the wonderful, long, glassed-in porch overlooking the rolling peaks of the Warrior Mountain Range. It's really quite magical after dusk has fallen—every table is candlelit, and the strains of Schumann, Mozart, and Scarlatti float out into the gathering night.

Ann joined us at the table and mentioned that Ken's "Ladies Only" cooking school was most successful this past winter. "We're going to continue it. We include walks, massages, and concerts, and the camarderie is wonderful." If the reader is interested in learning more about not only the cooking school but other special weekends that are offered throughout the year, just drop the inn a line.

Ken and Ann excused themselves and once again I was left looking out into the darkness at that one single pinpoint of light. I wondered if perhaps they, too, might be looking up at the lights of the inn.

THE ORCHARD INN, Box 725, Saluda, NC 28773; 704-749-5471. A 12-guestroom (private baths) mountaintop (2,500 ft.) inn a short distance from Tryon in western North Carolina. Queen, double, and twin beds available. Breakfast included with room rate. Dinner available. Open year-round. Antiquing, hiking, wildflower collecting, birdwatching, and superb country roads abound. No pets. No credit cards. Ann and Ken Hough, owners/hosts.

DIRECTIONS: From Atlanta, take I-85 north to I-26. Continue north to Exit 28 and Hwy. 176. Inn is on Hwy. 176, 2 mi. off I-26. From Asheville, take I-26 south.

PILOT KNOB INN

Pilot Mountain, North Carolina

What does one do with old log tobacco barns in the foothills of North Carolina? It took Jim Rouse, with his real estate background, and the investing dollars of his silent partner, Norman Ross, to figure an answer. They purchased this inn's eleven acres and its old 40' x 40'

tobacco barn on the eastern side of Pilot Mountain in 1987. Then they purchased five separate smaller barns from the surrounding area to be transported to the property. (This meant dismantling the barns, numbering each log for reconstruction, and hauling them to the new site by truck.)

Tobacco barns, used for storage and curing of tobacco in the late 1800s, have reached near extinction and have been replaced by more modern metal buildings. These were quite a find.

Jim showed me how they used every part of each barn in rebuilding them. Rocks from the original foundations became fireplaces. Tier poles used for drying tobacco leaves are now supports and railings for front porches. The finished product is a unique inn with individual log cabins tucked in the woods on the slopes of the mountain.

My cabin had a cozy living room. A massive stone fireplace was built along one wall with a hearth extending out onto the plank hardwood floors. Red brocade loveseats faced each other across the wooden trunk that served as a coffee table. The bed in the adjoining bedroom was most unusual. The heavy headboard and footboard were made from tree trunks of stripped juniper, also called Atlantic white cedar; each piece is so large it requires four men to carry it. The footboard still had a tree limb attached. The bathroom held a whirlpool for two. The welcoming touches of fresh cut flowers, bathrobes, and snacks of ripened fruit made me feel at home.

Later I walked down the lane, dotted with log cabins, to the large restored barn, which houses the common room, breakfast room, and a dry sauna. Sounds of classical music from Norman's collection led me into the formal library, with its 300-year-old Italian marble fireplace. Flames of red and orange hues could be seen through its glass doors. The brightly colored area rug covers refinished wood floors with antique seating arrangements to match. The walls are a rich mahogany.

Following an early morning sauna the next day, I returned to enjoy breakfast in the dining room, which included sausage biscuits, fresh fruit, and several tempting varieties of coffee cake.

"Why don't you bring your coffee and I will give you a tour of the outside and some tips on interesting sights nearby," Jim suggested, just as I was finishing my last sweet bite of cake.

Strolling behind the barn, Jim pointed out the swimming pool and deck area. The hiking trails of Pilot Mountain State Park border Pilot Knob, while several other parks are a short drive away. He told me a visit to Mabry Mill is a must: corn is still ground there, and the local entertainments of music and clog dancing are provided. The nearby town of Winston-Salem offers an abundance of 18th-century history, restaurants, and shopping. I could even try a hot air balloon ride! Before returning to the many chores of an innkeeper, Jim advised me not to miss nature's sunrise show of the 115-foot rock knob of Pilot Mountain glowing at dawn.

———

PILOT KNOB INN, P.O. Box 1280, Pilot Mountain, N.C. 27041; 919-325-2502. Individual 6-guestroom (private baths) log cabins secluded in the woods. Whirlpool tubs in rooms. Breakfast included. Open year round. Swimming pool. Smoking in most areas. Nature hikes in nearby Pilot Mountain State Park, one of many parks nearby. Shopping, dining, and historical sites with short drive to Winston-Salem. No pets. CCs: Visa, MC. James Rouse and Norman Ross, owners; James Rouse, host.

DIRECTIONS: Highway 52 to Pilot Mountain State Park exit. Turn left to small gravel drive. Go about 7/10 mi.

RED ROCKER INN

Black Mountain, North Carolina

I just can't help it. Whenever I discover an inn that serves dinner *family style*, my mouth begins to water, my eyes grow wide, and I become a man possessed. It's not that I'm a glutton, it's just that I was raised on mounds of excellent mid-Western cooking, always served family style. That term brings with it other feelings—feelings of contentment, friendship, conviviality and celebration.

So, it was with high expectations that I traveled to the Red Rocker Inn where, according to innkeepers Pat and Fred Eshleman, "food is our forte," and dining is "family style." I was not disappointed.

The Eshlemans seat their guests at large tables to encourage conversation and new friendships. Each meal begins with the innkeeper's blessing—a tradition followed since 1981 when Pat and Fred opened their inn. The menu changes daily but always begins with a hearty soup, like cream of broccoli or vegetable chowder. In the warm summer months an unusual salad replaces the soup course.

"Now the fun begins!" Pat whispered to me as she removed my soup bowl. And here it came, my childhood remembrance—family style food: baskets overflowing with spicy zucchini muffins, tender buttermilk biscuits, fresh jam and creamy butter. A choice of entrée is offered and may include roast loin of pork with cornbread stuffing, country ham, or a fabulous pan-fried Southern style chicken fried steak, complete with gravy.

During the wait for the entrée, all types of tart tidbits are served: Pennsylvania Dutch chow-chow, sauerkraut salad, and marinated cucumbers. As your entrée arrives so do heaping bowls of vegetables and a variety of casseroles.

Desserts (if you have even a tiny bit of room left) are incredible. Warm wild blackberry cobbler, covered with melting ice cream, was my choice. Other dinner partners enjoyed homemade pies, including Black Mountain mud pie and coconut cream pie, and a rich "x-rated" chocolate cake.

Breakfast is just as wonderful, but I'll let you discover that for yourselves. One suggestion—try the "Georgia ice cream grits."

The Red Rocker certainly has more than food to offer. This spacious Victorian has housed guests since 1927. Originally built as a wedding gift in 1894, the two story beige clapboard still exudes a romantic countenance. Perky red geraniums frame the lawn and lofty shade trees cool the wrap-around veranda. The absence of television or a private phone encourages rest and relaxation.

The eighteen guest rooms are all homey and comfortable, and include private baths. We stayed in the Music Room, where whimsical sheet music papers the wall at the head of the king-sized bed.

The inn's common areas feature Grandma's living room, with a wooden-manteled fireplace flanked by bookcases, and the sunny game room, where I soundly trounced an opponent at gin-rummy one evening.

The Red Rocker is located in a residential area of similarly styled homes. The Eshlemans are constantly renovating and refurbishing their pampered inn, watching over it with loving care. They both love music (Fred's avocation) and enjoy traveling when they can get a few days away.

"We want our guests to feel like they're visiting at Grandma's farmhouse," Pat told me over breakfast. "We'd like people to think of us as an old-fashioned inn." And I must say, "old-fashioned" here means friendliness, comfort, wonderful food, and a relaxed stay nestled among the North Carolina mountains.

———

RED ROCKER INN, 136 North Dougherty St., Black Mountain, NC 28711; 704-669-5991. An old-fashioned country inn with 18 guestrooms (private baths) located in the mountains of North Carolina. Open May-October All sized beds. Full breakfast; lunch Monday-Friday; dinner every day. All meals additional (except during special rate periods May 1-June 15, and September 1-September 30). Two blocks to town. Hiking, picnics, golf, tennis, and antiquing nearby. No pets. Smoking restricted. Pat and Fred Eshleman, owners/hosts.

DIRECTIONS: Exit 64 from I-40, then go left into town. Take another left after crossing the railroad tracks. Proceed through red light to the top of the hill.

RICHMOND HILL INN

Asheville, North Carolina

Perched on forty-seven acres overlooking the French Board River, the stately Queen Anne-style Richmond Hill Inn, once described by North Carolina writer Thomas Wolfe as the "big, rambling, magnificent Victorian house," presides to the east, with a backdrop of smoky blue mountains. Unfortunately, this once-proud Victorian became tattered through years of neglect. That is, until Jake and Marge Michel saw the luster through the tarnish.

In 1985 Jake crested Richmond Hill during a hike. His eye fell on the sorry sight of the mansion and his years of interest in historic preservation told him that this property was very special.

"I belong to the state preservation society and receive a lot of information about helping in home restorations in different areas," Jake told me. We were seated in the glass-enclosed sun porch on a gorgeous Saturday morning and I was sinking my teeth into heavenly apple-raisin pancakes, so he did most of the talking.

"I was so fortunate to find a building of this stature waiting for someone to take care of it," he went on. And loving care they have given. After a 2.5 million dollar renovation the inn is now a high-class, yet gracious, home.

Just step into the Great Hall and you'll feel the richness of the native oak paneled walls and exposed oak beams. The front parlor is replete with a luxurious velvet sofa, floral draperies and a fireplace. The Damask Parlor looks out onto the sun porch. Other sophisticated, yet easy-living, common rooms include the Drawing Room, with a white-one-white theme accented by a burgundy-tiled fireplace, and the elegant octagonal Ballroom.

But my favorite haunt was the Library. Warm pine paneling, stained a deep walnut, backs a fine collection of works by Western North Carolina authors and books about Western North Carolina. In fact, many of Richmond Hill's twelve comfortable guest rooms take their names from the authors of the library's first editions.

Canopy beds, lacy curtains, antiques, and Oriental rugs dominate the guest rooms. The second floor rooms are spacious, and the third floor rooms are tucked into the former attic. There are a few rooms on the first floor for those who choose not to climb stairs. I spent a magical rainy afternoon in the Sandburg Room curled up on the windowseat, just daydreaming.

All rooms enjoy private baths with claw-footed tubs and creature comforts like fluffy down pillows, fresh flowers, television and a telephone.

A charming group of guest cottages has recently been added to the estate. The Croquet Cottages are situated around a croquet courtyard in a tranquil setting reminiscent of a Victorian country retreat. Each has a large furnished porch, a fireplace and a spacious private bath.

Inspired by the romance and history of the mansion, I looked forward to dinner in the elegant Victorian dining room. White linen, the soft glow of candles, views to the surrounding mountains in twilight, and one of the juiciest rib-eye steaks I've ever had, made this a night to remember. Other entrée choices might be grilled yellow fin tuna, veal marsala, or pork loin with saffron beurre blan, for example. Entrees include salad, vegetable soup, and rice, pasta or potato. The desserts are all homemade.

The following day I explored the area, starting at the National Smoky Mountain National Park, about an hour's drive away, then wending my way back via Carl Sandburg's house and Thomas Wolfe's home.

When my weekend was up I was really reluctant to leave Richmond Hill, and my windowseat.

RICHMOND HILL INN, 87 Richmond Hill Drive, Asheville, NC 28806; 800-545-9238, 704-252-7313. A 12-guestroom 11 cottages (private baths) restored grand Victorian mansion overlooking the French Broad River with nine cottages. Open all year. Queen, double, and twin beds. Breakfast included; lunch Monday-Friday; dinner all week. Historical points of interest within an hour's drive. No pets. Smoking restricted. CCs: Visa, MC, AE. The Education Center, Inc., Jake and Marge Michel, owners; Charles Frye, manager.

DIRECTIONS: From I-240 take the 19/23 Weaverville Exit. Continue on 19/23 and turn at Exit 251 (UNC-Asheville). At the bottom of the ramp, turn left. At the first stoplight, turn left again on Riverside Dr. Turn right on Pearson Bridge Rd. and cross the bridge. At the sharp curve, turn right on Richmond Hill Dr.

WINDSONG: A MOUNTAIN INN

Clyde, North Carolina

It's not unusual to find a log home in the mountains, but it is unusual to find one as beautiful and unique as Windsong. Donna and Gale Livengood built Windsong in 1989 and with the help of Donna's brother, a design architect, proceeded to create a mountain haven.

To keep the inn bright and airy, the interior logs were sandblasted and treated to maintain their light finish. The spacious dining and living areas have high, beamed ceilings, and are unified by Mexican saltillo floor tiles.

The Livengoods' collection of Native American accessories, including colorful Indian motif rugs, handwoven pillows, and a carved totem on the mantel of the Great Room's mammoth stone fireplace, are comfortably juxtaposed with the richness of leather sofas and the stripped pine of the breakfast tables. Walls of windows open onto a spectacular view of the Smoky Mountains. Afternoon wine and hors d'oeuvres, and evening coffee and dessert, are served in this comfortable room.

The guest lounge offers a wet bar, a pool table, games and books. The influence of Gale's previous career as a distributor of educational films is apparent in the inn's large library of cassettes and videos which can be viewed in your room.

Each of the guest rooms has a fantasy theme, which was quite unexpected and fun. The Safari Room was my favorite. A bamboo frame is swathed in a netting canopy over the bed. Primitive artifacts decorate the room, including hand-carved African animals migrating across the beam above the bed. A ceiling fan gently stirs the air.

The Alaska Room, Santa Fe Room and Country Room are also appropriately decorated to their themes. All have private baths with wonderful steeping tubs and separate showers, fireplaces, private patios or decks, and breathtaking mountain views.

I chose to take my breakfast to the deck so I could soak up its view of pastures and woodlands, and breathe in the invigorating mountain air. The inn is located at 3000 feet on 25 acres of mountainside, so hiking is a real treat, as is their new herd of llamas. A swimming pool and tennis courts are also available.

WINDSONG: A MOUNTAIN INN, 120 Ferguson Ridge, Clyde, NC 28721; 704-627-6111. A 5-guestroom (private baths) serene mountain retreat overlooking the Smoky Mountains. Queen and twin beds. Full breakfast. Open all year. Close to Biltmore House gardens and winery, the Appalachian Trail, hiking, white water rafting. No pets. One dog in residence. Smoking restricted. CCs: Visa, MC. Donna and Gale Livengood, owners/hosts.

DIRECTIONS: Take Exit 24 off I-40. Go north on US 209, 2.5 mi. Turn left on Riverside Dr.; go 2 mi. Turn right on Ferguson Cove Loop. Stay left; go 1 mi.

Virginia

BAILIWICK INN

Fairfax, Virginia

One wonders what Joshua Gunnel would think if he stepped inside The Bailiwick Inn today and enjoyed high tea or soft music by the parlor fireside. No doubt he'd recall the first Confederate casualty of the Civil War, Captain John Quincy Marr of the Warrenton Rifles, shot in a skirmish fought on the front lawn. He'd remember how Virginia governor "Extra Billy" Smith began his military career that night when he rushed across the street and took command.

During the first decade of the 1800s, Gunnell built, "across the street from the Court House," a Federal-style brick home that remained in the county sheriff's family until the end of the century. Along with Fairfax itself, with its convenient location to the Capital, quaint shops and restaurants, and access to Civil War battlefields, the Bailiwick is now part of the National Historic Register.

When Anne and Ray Smith acquired the dwelling in 1989, they gave the inn its present name ("bailiwick," in its oldest form, means "the area around the court") and began a meticulous renovation. Many structural details of the Federal period were preserved; even the heart-of-pine floors in the original portion were matched in the new section by planks of pine sawn from support timbers salvaged from old warehouses. With the assistance of the staff of the Virginia Room of the Fairfax County Library, decorators furnished the common areas and fourteen guest rooms and baths, each named for a Virginian. According to Anne, visiting circuit judges and many other business and leisure travelers enjoy choosing a room of one of their favorite historical figures, each one decorated in a style appropriate to that famous individual. Several rooms have fireplaces and the Antonia Ford Bridal Suite, named after the Confederate spy, features a Jacuzzi and a separate sitting room.

Ray's hearty breakfasts are served in the dining room—the decor of which was inspired by Belvoir, home of William Fairfax—or in the courtyard garden featuring an herb garden, grape vines and a small fountain.

A new addition is its restaurant for dinner guests. An attempt is being made for authentic recipes from the area such as cornsticks and "Sally Lund" bread. The chef uses Virginia products as much as possible including Shenandoah trout, rockfish, blue crabs, Chesapeake oysters and venison. The produce is mostly grown locally.

Despite its elegant furnishings, the Bailiwick is an inviting respite from the bustle of the city traffic as well as a comfortable escape to step back in time, soak up some local history, and spend an evening in the midst of some American heritage.

BAILIWICK INN, 4023 Chain Bridge Road, Fairfax, Virginia 22030; 703-691-2266 or 800-366-7666. A 14-guestroom (private baths) restored 19th century home in the heart of Fairfax City, just minutes from George Mason University and 15 minutes west of Washington, DC. Open all year. Local shuttle to Metrorail; midway between National and Dulles Airports. No pets. Smoking in garden and courtyard only. Anne and Ray smith, Owners/hosts.

DIRECTIONS: From I-66 take Rte. 123 one mile south of the Interstate, or from I-495 and I-95 take Rte. 50 to Rte. 123. Inn is directly across from the Courthouse.

BELLE GRAE INN

Staunton, Virginia

Between the Allegheny Mountains on the west and the Blue Ridge Mountains on the east lies the fertile, green Shenandoah Valley. It's no wonder that this valley has been celebrated in song with the words, "Oh Shenandoah, I long to see you..." Known as America's First Frontier, the limestone-dotted hills, picturesque towns, stone farmhouses, and log cabins have seen early settlers pass from Pennsylvania on their way to historic towns like Lexington and Staunton.

Many of the inns in the valley have offered hospitality to travelers for over a hundred years. The Belle Grae Inn in Staunton is one of these. The Federal-style mansion was originally built in 1870. Innkeeper Michael Organ, a communications professor, saw the potential of the stately old home and restored it to its original splendor in 1983. While many of Virginia's inns are country inns, the Belle Grae revels in her classification as a city inn.

The inn takes its name from two of the seven hills on which the city of Staunton is built: Betsy Belle and Mary Grae. As you sit on the inn's spacious veranda, you get a splendid view of these two old Scottish ladies. The rambling Victorian is located in a quiet residential neighborhood in the center of the Newtown Historic District. Dogwoods, azaleas, and lilacs surround the house with lovely colors and scents during the spring.

Michael calls the inn's furnishings *collectics*, a most charming word for his collection of antiques, keepsakes, and reproductions that decorate the common rooms. The ten guest rooms are decorated in traditional Victorian colors of mauve, forest green, dusty rose, and steel blue, which accent the hardwood floors and antique furnishings. My room had a wonderful queen-sized canopy bed, a desk with a comfortable chair, and a cozy fireplace. Some of the rooms have sitting areas, and one room, whimsically called the Pullman Car, has an antique Murphy bed. The private baths have pedestal sinks, along with full tub and shower units.

Suites are more luxurious, with four-poster beds, fireplaces, Oriental carpets, sitting areas, large dressing rooms, private baths, and telephones and televisions. The vintage brick townhouse suite is joined to the main inn by a footbridge, and from the suite's windows, the comings and goings of Staunton can be heard.

Belle Grae is the only inn I know of with a 24-hour Bellboy...he's a boxer. Bellboy was the inn's first full-time employee and began service in October 1983 when he was two months old. His biggest contribution is to carry small packages for guests when the innkeepers aren't sure about them. At last communication he was bucking to be named Chief of Security.

Afternoon tea is served with tasty tea cakes and cookies. I enjoyed my cup and shared my cakes with Bellboy as I sat in a wicker rocker in the peaceful courtyard.

The Belle-Grae Bistro is Staunton's only indoor/outdoor cafe. Guests can enjoy à la carte dining on the terrace patio under umbrellas, and listen to live evening entertainment. Indoors, the Bistro's bright, sunny room overlooking the expansive lawn is a wonderful place to begin your leisurely breakfast with coffee, juice, and pastries, followed by an omelet, fried tomatoes, and cheese grits. Dinner is served in the more formal dining rooms of the original house or on the veranda.

The Belle Grae Inn is on the walking tour of Staunton, President Woodrow Wilson's birthplace is just seven blocks away, and the Statler Brothers' Museum, antique stores, and specialty shops are all nearby.

BELLE GRAE INN, 515 W. Frederick St., Staunton, VA 24401; 703-886-5151. A 18-guestroom (private baths) historic Victorian inn located in Virginia's Shenandoah Valley. Breakfast included; dinner Wednesday-Sunday, lunch Tuesday-Sunday Open year-round. Queen, double, and twin beds. Monthly celebrations and seasonal activities. Near specialty shops and historical sites. Children over 10 welcome. No pets. One boxer named Bellboy in residence. Michael Organ, owner/host.

DIRECTIONS: From I-81 take Exit 57 west (Rte. 250W to center of Staunton). Rte. 250W intersects Rte. 254W (Frederick St.). Go left 6 blocks to inn.

FORT LEWIS LODGE
Millboro, Virginia

A breathtaking view of Goshen Pass and a glimpse at two deer feeding by the winding mountain road forecasted what lay ahead. Knowing that Fort Lewis Lodge had been a working farm for the past decade as well as one of the most coveted hunting spots east of the Mississippi, my expectations were more on the rustic side. But by the time I'd

reached the end of the gravel road leading to the Lodge, past cattle and acres of farmland, I knew that I'd found a wonderful slice of Virginia farmland, quiet, comfortable surroundings, warm hospitality, and the home of friends. John Cowden waved from the front of the gristmill he and his wife Caryl almost single-handedly restored to become the inn's kitchen and dining area. Even Max, the chocolate Lab, wiggled his way towards the car welcoming another guest.

Snuggled between the Allegheny Mountains near Millboro Springs, Virginia, Fort Lewis Lodge stretches over 3,200 bucolic acres of farmland, cow pastures, hiking trails, hunting grounds, wilderness camping retreats, and plenty of room for tubing, fishing and swimming in the Cowpasture River. John and I strolled down by the swimming hole and along rows of corn and soybeans, enjoying the late afternoon sunset. His love of the outdoors, as well as his extensive knowledge of the natural habitat surounding the lodge, provided plenty of background for an informal tour—my introduction to what lay beyond the trees.

"Hear that?" he said, stopping in his tracks. "That's a deer blowing. She knows there's someone around and she's sending out a warning. We'll see if we can spot some later." A pheasant crossed the path ahead of us. This was definitely a nature lover's retreat.

After enjoying Caryl's Fort Lewis Harvest Roast, scalloped apples, fresh vegetables, fresh biscuits, a piece of very sinful chocolate pie, and conversation with the Cowdens, their children and other guests, John invited us all for a ride around the farm to find those deer. Equipped with a spotlight and sweaters, we spent the next half hour watching the deer feeding and scampering in the fields. Even John was excited when he spotted two large bucks standing guard on a hillside. Seeing over three dozen wild deer in such a short time was a first for me.

In 1755, Colonel Charles Lewis built a stockade here to protect his family from Indian raids. Lewis died in 1774 at the Battle of Point Pleasant, considered by some historians to have been the first engagement of the American Revolution. The manor house on the hill, which John also restored and in which he now resides with his family, was built by Benjamin Crawford, a merchant from nearby Staunton. Although the farmland has been in the Cowden family since the late 1950s, John and Caryl first came here in 1978. With his background in agronomy and farm management and his obvious talent for carpentry and architecture, the challenge of tackling the property was intriguing. But only after the downturn of the farm economy in the 1980s did the Cowdens decide to establish a hunting retreat. At that point, since "it was a shame not to share all this with more people," John and Caryl opened the lodge to bed and breakfast guests from May to October.

Attached to a renovated silo, now used as an observation tower, is the two-story cedar shake lodge with 12 guest rooms furnished in a blend of Shaker and country furnishings crafted by a local artisan. Hooked rugs are scattered on the milled pine floors and cheery patchwork quilts cover the beds, which vary from twin to king-size. A family room in the tower features a couch, bunks, double beds, and TV. Downstairs guests are drawn to the spacious "gathering room," with a fireplace, a bar area, and upholstered furniture arranged to invite conversation. Games and puzzles, as well as a photo album tracking the renovation of the property, are kept here. Guests are also invited to gather around the wood stove in the dining area for a cup of coffee or some music from the piano.

By morning, everyone is gathered there to enjoy another one of Caryl's delightful meals. Breakfast is hearty enough to keep even hikers and spelunkers satisfied until noon. Caryl loves to cook, and it shows. She also insists that calories don't really count in the mountains. The Cowdens will prepare picnic lunches with advance notice. In fact, for those who want to try some wilderness camping for at least one night, John has built a shelter about two miles from the lodge. They'll even provide the gear and bring you meals. (Sounds like my kind of camping!)

"We have a lot of people who want to go out for a night but don't want to buy all the equipment or worry about meals and where to go," said John, who also sponsors photography, wildflower and Elderhostel weekends. "We just make it easy for them, and they can also come back the next night and enjoy the comforts of a guest room."

No matter what your purpose for visiting may be, the Cowdens offer what they call rustic elegance, delicious food, and most of all a feeling of belonging. And while you might feel away from it all, nearby attractions include historic Lexington and Staunton, the Warm Springs Pools, the Homestead resort and shopping in Hot Springs.

FORT LEWIS LODGE, Millboro, VA 24460; 703-925-2314. A 15-guestroom, three round rooms in silo (private baths except for shared family room) country inn/hunting retreat in the Allegheny Mountains and surrounded by the George Washington National Forest. All bed sizes. Open May-October summer guests; October-December deer and turkey season; April-May turkey season. Closed January-March Fishing on a catch-and-release basis except for trophy class. Breakfast and dinner included in rates. Pets by advance arrangement. No smoking in rooms. CCs: Visa, MC. John and Caryl Cowden, owners/hosts.

DIRECTIONS: From I-81 in Staunton take 254 west, onto 42 west at Buffalo Gap. Straight on 39 west at Millboro Springs, right on Rte. 678 and left on Rte. 625. From Millboro Springs, take 39 west to Rte. 678, turn right and go 10.8 mi. to Rte. 625, 1/4 mi. to Lodge on left.

HIDDEN INN
Orange, Virginia

It's easy to see why James Madison, the father of the Constitution, drew inspiration from his surroundings; this is some of the most scenic countryside in Virginia. Madison's home, Montpelier, is only a short distance from Orange. I spent a fascinating afternoon learning more about Madison and the history of the area at the town's James Madison Museum before I strolled back to the Hidden Inn.

This colorful blue Victorian has brick red shutters and fresh white trim. It regally sits on a wide expanse of lawn under many lovely shade trees. As I stepped up onto the wrap-around-porch past the American

flag I was met by Duke, the inn's perky Chinese pug. Right behind came innkeeper Barbara Lonick. "Well, I think you've made a friend for life," she laughed as Duke squirmed at my feet.

Barbara is very friendly and, by her own admission, loves to talk. Her husband, Ray, enjoys innkeeping because it offers a variety tasks which make use of his skills. The Lonicks used to drive through the area around Orange when they took their daughter to Sweet Briar College. "We really fell in love with the countryside," Barbara told me, "and the small towns." Orange, a town of approximately 2,500 residents, turned out to be just the right size, and the Hidden Inn just happened to be for sale, so they snapped it up.

The inn's interior, painted a soft salmon and blue, has a light, airy quality. The Lonicks have done a wonderful job of restoration. Lace and fresh cut flowers highlight the Victorian-style common areas and guest rooms.

Afternoon tea (usually Earl Grey) and cakes are served from the silver tea service in the roomy living room. The fireplace is framed by a large, comfortable sofa, wing backed chair and rocker. Champagne, California and Virginia wines, and imported micro-brewery beers are available and are served at the wine bar at the opposite end of the room. In the evening firelight falls across the Oriental rug and the room becomes a perfect spot for quiet conversation.

The Victorian dining room, the setting for the inn's full breakfast, is transformed by candlelight for a gourmet five-course dinner. On the recommendation of a gentleman at a neighboring table, I ordered the grilled swordfish.

An appetizer of mushrooms layered in a light phyllo dough and a delicately flavored carrot-orange soup began the meal, followed by a salad of deep green spinach dotted with pine nuts. The swordfish, fresh, moist and flaky, was accompanied by a side dish of vegetables and fluffy risotto.

A number of entrées are offered Thursday through Sunday, all completed by seasonal desserts and the Hidden Inn's own blend of coffee. And don't worry if you arrive too late for dinner; the Lonicks will bring a romantic candlelight picnic to your room. (Reason enough to arrive late!)

The ten guest rooms are cheerfully papered in floral prints. Handmade quilts accent canopied or brass beds, and antiques furnish the rooms. Two rooms have their own fireplaces, and all have private baths, four with Jacuzzis. The newly completed Rose Garden cottage adjoining the main house has its own private veranda, perfect for balmy summer evening sitting.

Ray and Barbara have been adding extras around the inn to make the outdoors more inviting. Besides the completion of the Rose Garden cottage, they have constructed a thirty-two foot deck, built a picturesque gazebo, and bricked in a new patio.

I know you'll enjoy your visit to this wonderful inn, and to the historical area around Orange.

HIDDEN INN, 249 Caroline St., Orange, VA 22960; 703-672-3625. A 10-guestroom (private baths) Victorian on six acres of grounds. King, queen, and full beds. Open year-round. Full breakfast and tea included; gourmet dinner available Thursday-Sunday Close to historic sites. No smoking or pets. CCs: Visa, MC. Barbara and Ray Lonick, owners-hosts.

DIRECTIONS: From Washington, D.C., take Rte. 66 to Rte. 15 south to Orange. Inn is at the intersection of Rte. 20.

HIGH MEADOWS INN
Scottsville, Virginia

Occasionally I get a bit jaded as a travel writer. Difficult as it may be to believe, just as any job has its moments of boredom, so does mine. And then I stay at an inn like the High Meadows, and all of a sudden the world takes on a new glow, and I can't imagine having any other profession.

This gracious inn is located on the Constitution Route in the midst of the Virginia wine country. Located on 23 acres, the stately home is actually two separate houses joined by a great hall: one a Federal style and the other a Victorian. The home with its seventeen rooms, nine

fireplaces, and original grained woodwork was recently placed on the National Register of Historic Homes.

When I arrived at High Meadows Inn I was greeted by innkeeper Mary Jae Sushka. Later during the weekend I was surprised to discover that Mary Jae has a chameleon career. During the week she is a securities and exchange commission senior analyst. After four years in Britain where Peter, her husband and fellow innkeeper, served as a liaison to the Royal Navy, the Sushkas returned to the United States to search for an inn. "We read a real estate ad for a 'restoration gem'," Mary Jae recalled. "What we saw was a hulk. No electricity. No plumbing." But the Sushkas saw the possibilities, and purchased the property the year Peter retired.

The surroundings are relaxed and pleasant. Guests can stroll through the rose gardens or spend time in the Pinot Noir vineyards. Numerous footpaths around two ponds and meandering creeks present tranquil, pastoral settings for contemplation.

Each of the seven guest rooms is quite unique and furnished with period antiques, some dating from the 1700s. Sitting areas with writing desks, reading materials and reading lamps, and at least one soft chair provide reason enough to stay in your room. A small crystal decanter of port wine and two small stemmed glasses invite a late-night toast. I was interested in each room's individualized leather-bound memorabilia book, containing before and after restoration pictures and a three- or four-page history describing the room's furnishings and method of restoration.

We stayed in the spacious Highview Room, one of two air-conditioned rooms on the upper level of the Victorian house, with its huge windows and original comb graining. All guest rooms include private baths, some with sitting showers and others with claw-foot tubs. As I sat reading in the room's Chippendale chair, I happened to glance up and notice an original steel engraving of "George Washington's First Interview with His Wife Martha." His hand was firmly planted on a similar splat-backed chair.

Rates include breakfast, afternoon tea, and Virginia wine with hors d'oeuvres before dining. Everything served at the inn is made on the premises. Dinner is by candlelight and includes four courses. Coffee and peach wine are served afterward in either the main hall or on the west terrace. Specialties are Smoked Alaskan Salmon Encroute with herbed feta cheese; Veal Escalops in Pommery sauce; Medallions of Pork Tenderloin with Bing Cherries. For dessert I had the Capucciano Torte with cream and cinnamon and tried their wonderful Bourbon Street Fudge Cake. During the week, a European picnic supper basket can be filled with such choice goodies as Roman beef loaf on fettuccine, lemon cole slaw with apples and currants, fresh fruits, brownies, fresh daisies, and the traditional red-and-white-checked tablecloth.

Tubing, canoeing, and fishing on the lazy James River can fill an afternoon, or you may prefer a more history-infused visit to nearby Monticello and the presidential homes of Monroe and Madison. I just stayed put, enjoying the pastoral surroundings. When I left, I was rejuvenated and happy to be the travel writer that I am.

HIGH MEADOWS INN, Rte. 20 South, Rte. 4, Box 6, Scottsville, VA 24590; 804-286-2218. A 13-guestroom (private baths) and cottage historic, restored country inn located just minutes from Charlottesville. 50 acres. Open year-round. All bed sizes. Full breakfast, tea, and wine and hors d'oeuvres included. Dinner on weekends; gourmet picnic baskets on weekdays. Close to outdoor activities and historic tours. Pets by prior arrangement. CCs: Visa, MC. Peter and Mary Jae Sushka, owners-hosts.

DIRECTIONS: Take Exit 24 on I-64 in Charlottesville and proceed on Rte. 20 south for 17 mi. Cross Rte. 726 and the inn's private drive is 3/10 mi. further on your left.

IRISH GAP INNS
Vesuvius, Virginia

I was on my way to a tea party! And the most intriguing aspect of this tea party was its other guests: Holland Lops, English Lops, French Lops, and Netherland Dwarfs. I was particularly pleased that I would be enjoying my toast and marmalade with such international guests. Well, of course, I'm teasing. The other guests are really pedigreed rabbits belonging to the Irish Gap Inns' owner, Dillard Saunders. When she heard that I would be visiting, she invited me to join her, and the menagerie, at an Easter tea held for the children of Irish Gap, Virginia.

The Irish Gap Inns are tucked off the Blue Ridge Parkway on 285 acres of beautiful Virginia mountaintop woodlands and fields. Even though the parkway is close, the location is both remote and private. A gravel drive leads to the Bee Skep Inn and its partner, the Gatehouse B&B, that comprise the Inns. Dillard, a native Virginian, purchased the property in 1984, and lived in the old farmhouse while work was done on the inns.

With a background in interior design, Ms. Saunders successfully constructed the inns to look like turn-of-the-century hostelries: old in appearance yet modern on the interiors. "I wanted the inns to reflect an understated elegance," Dillard told me. Behind the inn, water cascades from a mountain-fed spring down a hand-built rock wall and into one of two ponds.

The Bee Skep Inn is built on the site of the property's original log cabin. Its large common rooms, built of oak beams with timber framing, overlook the ponds. The living room is spacious, with a dining area. English pine antiques, heart-pine floors, and colors of blue, white, and coral create an old-world ambience.

The four guest rooms have charming woodland names with decorative themes to fit. For example, the fox hunter room is done in red with navy plaid fabrics, has dark woods, oil paintings of fox hunts, and features four-poster beds and antique and reproduction furnishings. Each room has two beds, a private bath, television, and a small refrigerator and coffee maker. Window boxes, spilling over with flowers, and comfortable rockers await on each room's private sitting porch.

Dillard took me on a hike along the fern-covered banks of the creek, and we ended up at the back deck of the Gatehouse. This tidy white Victorian cottage has an airy wraparound front porch also. The great room is furnished with Early American primitive antiques and reproductions, and has a large fireplace for intimate winter evenings. A bedroom with a private bath is located on the main floor, and two other bedrooms share a bath upstairs. A small kitchen is available.

A complimentary breakfast is served at the Bee Skep and includes fruit, French toast, eggs, sausage, tea and coffee, and an inn specialty, chocolate squash bread.

Dinner is by reservation, and can include such gourmet choices as veal scallops with lemon-garlic cream sauce, broccoli vinaigrette, and yellow squash parmigiana. Desserts are luscious. I sampled the fresh fruit cobbler and ended up having two servings. Most of the vegetables are garden fresh.

There are great outdoor activities available around the area that include bicycling on the Blue Ridge Parkway and fishing and swimming in the ponds. You might also like to give Dillard a hand when she feeds the rest of her farm family: seven dogs, five goats, turkeys, chickens, and three horses.

Oh, by the way, our tea party was quite elegant. The rabbits chose the watercress sandwiches and left the sweets for the children and me. It was an affair that would have satisfied even the Mad Hatter's expectations.

IRISH GAP INNS, Rte. 1, Box 40, Vesuvius, VA 24483; 804-922-7701. A 7-guestroom (4 in the Inn, all private baths; 3 in the Gatehouse, 1 private bath, 1 shared) inn on 285 acres of rural woodlands. All-size beds. Complimentary breakfast; dinner by reservation. Open all year. Bicycling, fishing, swimming. Near historic Lexington. Handicap accessibility. No pets. Dillard Saunders, owner-host.

DIRECTIONS: Located between milepost 37 and 38 on the Blue Ridge Parkway at Irish Gap. Take Parkway exit, then turn left at Private Road sign.

L'AUBERGE PROVENÇALE
White Post, Virginia

Swinging gently in the hanging wooden swing on the wide front porch, Celeste Borel and I had been talking about how she and Alain, her husband, had found this beautiful 1753 stone farmhouse and had opened a country inn. During a lull in the conversation, I heard a flock of geese honk their way across the sky and watched as they settled on a pond in the nearby field. Crickets chirped, and far off in a pasture cattle lowed.

As reluctant as I was to leave this tranquil and bucolic scene, the aromas wafting from the kitchen, where Alain was practicing his art, were too much for me, and I eagerly followed Celeste into one of the three cozy dining rooms, where other guests were just sitting down to tables set with Provencal fabrics from France, sparkling crystal, and fresh flowers from the garden. It was a very pleasant dining room with a fireplace, polished wood floors, and walls lined with French paintings and prints, including a Picasso.

"How do you happen to have a picture of the Pope's palace and the bridge of Avignon on your menu?" I asked Celeste.

"Alain was born and raised in Avignon," she replied. "He started working in his grandfather's restaurant there when he was thirteen, and he has been in the restaurant business ever since." Later, when I saw all of the articles that have been written about L'Auberge Provençale and Alain's cuisine, I realized he has become quite famous as a French chef. They frequently have diners who have driven from Washington, D.C., ninety minutes away, as well as international travelers.

Alain showed me the huge herb and vegetable garden. "We also have two cherry trees, a purple plum, a peach, a pear, and an apple tree."

Alain calls his menu "cuisine moderne—classic Provençale French with innovative twists and the freshest ingredients." Some of his starters include sautéed sweetbreads with port, capers, and pine nuts and capers, duck foie gras with pears and turmeric, and smoked pheasant consomme with wild mushrooms. Entrées could be roast squab with fresh peaches, cloves, and cinnamon basil served with wild rice; or Moroccan-style medallions of lamb and lobster with Tahitian vanilla beans. There are wonderful desserts, such as carmelized blueberry tart with hazelnut praline ice cream, and chocolate souffle cake with Frangelico cream."

Guest rooms in the main house and in an adjacent cottage are attractively and comfortably furnished with antiques, fabrics from Provence, and original paintings; four have poster beds and five have fireplaces.

The next morning as I sat on the porch at breakfast, savoring one of Alain's perfect omelets and watching as the landscape emerged from the lifting mists, I pondered on what an interesting set of circumstances we had here.

Deep in the farming country of the Shenandoah Valley, in the tiny early American village of White Post—so named because George Washington as a young surveyor had erected a white post there— Celeste and Alain Borel have created a French country inn and restaurant. An eclectic managerie of hand carved animals, horses, rocking rabbits, colorful hand crafted reed birds, Santon dolls from Provence and other art collectibles from around the world which are exclusive to the inn give it a unique ambience and make it a gift shopping delight.

L'AUBERGE PROVENÇALE, Rte. 340, P.O. Box 119, White Post, VA 22633; 703-837-1375: 1-800-638-1702. Fax 703-837-2004. A 10-guestroom (private baths) French country inn and restaurant in Clarke County in the Shenandoah Valley, 90 min. west of Washington, D.C. Queen and double beds. Picnic lunches by arrangement. Dinner served Wednesday-Saturday, 6-10:30 p.m.; Sunday, 4-9 p.m. Open year-round. Antiques and country shops, Burwell-Morgan Mill, Blandy Farm, White Post antique car restoration, point-to-point horse races, Skyline Drive, and magnificent backroading nearby. No pets. CCs: Visa, MC. Celeste and Alain Borel, owners/hosts.

DIRECTIONS: From Washington, D.C., take Rte. 50 to Rte. 340, where there is a 4-way traffic light. Turn left and continue 1 mi. to inn. Only 45 min. to Dulles Airport.

MORRISON HOUSE
Alexandria, Virginia

Morrison House in Old Town, Alexandria, about twenty minutes from downtown D.C., is not a country inn on a back road, but it is the answer to having quiet, elegant lodgings in an atmosphere that is quite reminiscent of Knightsbridge, London. Further, if you have business or pleasure in the nearby nation's capital it is a most rewarding experience to return to Old Town, with its rows of 18th- and 19th-century houses, diverting shops, and safe walking at night.

The four-story, Federal-style building is red brick with black shutters, with a porticoed entrance, supported by four Greek columns and reached by twin curved staircases encircling a fountain sculpture.

Seated in the small courtyard in front of the hotel, I was enjoying the freshness of the early morning air and thinking back over the events of my arrival the previous evening. When I pulled up in front of the entrance, my automobile door was opened by a properly attired butler—not a bellboy, but a butler. I learned that this gentleman is a very important part of the service offered at Morrison House. He was relaxed, efficient, not pompous, extremely accommodating, and a veritable fountain of information about where to go in the D.C. area and how to get there. In the meantime, my car had been whisked away to the hotel's underground parking garage.

To the right of the foyer is the parlor, pleasantly elegant with Federal-style sofas and chairs upholstered in silk brocade. Gracefully draped floor-to-ceiling windows look out over a quiet street.

If all of this talk of butlers and European elegance seems a little stiff, let me assure you that it is quite relaxed, and designed to provide a very pleasant stay.

This is also true of the guest rooms, which have mahogany four-poster and canopied beds, made up in the European style with triple sheets. The bathrooms are done in Italian marble, and there are terrycloth robes and little reminders to the effect that should a traveler have forgotten such things as a toothbrush, comb, shaving cream, and so forth, these can be obtained by calling the reception area.

All of the additional thoughtfulness and amenities reflected in this hotel are the result of the extremely broad travel experiences of owners Robert and Rosemary Morrison. I had a very enjoyable chat with them about various European and British hotels that we both have enjoyed, and, not surprisingly, one mutual favorite was La Résidence du Bois in Paris, included in the European edition of this book.

As might be expected, part of the Morrison adventure is its two restaurants, Le Chardon d'Or ("the gold thistle"), with contemporary French cuisine, and the Grill, which has an American grill-style menu. Both have an extensive wine list, with many wines available by the glass. Le Chardon d'Or, with its à la carte and prix-fixe menus, is open for Sunday brunch and dinner Monday through Saturday. The Grill is open for lunch and dinner every day. Breakfast is served at Morrison House every day, and room service is available twenty-four hours every day.

MORRISON HOUSE, 116 S. Alfred St., Alexandria, VA 22314; 800-367-0800; 703-533-1808 (VA); or 703-838-8000 (local). A 45-guestroom (private baths) elegant, luxury hotel in a historic section of Alexandria, 15 min. from D.C. Restaurants open for breakfast, lunch, and dinner; Sunday brunch. Open year-round. Metro a 10-min. walk; 3 mi. to National Airport. Conveniently located to visit all of the D.C. area historic, recreational, and cultural attractions. Attractive weekend rates. Robert Morrison, owner/host.

DIRECTIONS: From National Airport, drive south on Geo. Washington Pkwy. to King St. Turn right and continue for 2 blocks and turn left on S. Alfred St. The hotel is on the left at midblock. From the Beltway/U.S. 495, take Exit U.S. 1 north to Prince St. Turn right and continue for 1 block to S. Alfred St. Hotel is on right side.

THE OAKS
Christianburg, Virginia

The New River Valley holds many pleasant surprises for the traveller—the Blue Ridge Parkway, fine restaurants, wineries, antique and craft shops. Add The Oaks to that list, an elegant lady of a Victorian home, magnificently restored by Margaret and Tom Ray.

The Rays, who left city life for innkeeping, may be as enthusiastic about this area as they are about their home. "There is just a wealth of history and beauty and places to see here," said Margaret. "You could stay busy for days."

Many of the guests are business travelers or professionals visiting nearby Virginia Tech and Radford University. Leaving the graceful surroundings of this Montogomery County landmark, built in 1883, may takes some effort, however.

The first thing I noticed on my arrival was the grand wrap-around porch with Kennedy rockers and wicker chairs that led me to the front door. Once inside the spacious foyer, with its stained-glass windows and grand staircase, I was greeted with the Rays' gracious hospitality: refreshments in the parlor, soft music in the backgound, and a welcoming guest room, complete with canopied bed—and without any pretentions. Even the delicious gourmet breakfast, served on fine china, was relaxing.

Margaret has thought of everything, from Battenburg laces and linens, desks in each guest room, terry robes and thick towels to a fine collection of art, a sunroom and patio, and a gazebo with a hot tub. Lingering at The Oaks is certainly tempting.

THE OAKS, 311 E. Main Street, Christianburg, VA 24073; 703-381-1500. A luxurious 6-guestroom (private baths) Victorian home surrounded by massive 300-year-old oaks. One dog in residence. No pets. Margaret and Tom Ray, owners/hosts.

DIRECTIONS: From I-81 take Christianburg exit 37 to Roanoke St. Go 3 mi. to E. Main. Right on E. Main, one block to the fork at Main and Park Sts. Bear right on Park to The Oaks' side yard parking. From Skyline Drive, exit Rte. 8, which becomes Main St., and follow above directions.

PROSPECT HILL
Trevilians, Virginia

As often as I have visited Prospect Hill, a restored plantation house outside Charlottesville, Virginia, I am always delighted by the wealth of information Bill Sheehan has compiled about the history of the inn.

Although the Roger Thompson family owned it in 1732, its real progress began when William Overton purchased the property and increased it to over 1,500 acres in 1840. He enlarged the original house by adding two wings and a spiral staircase.

As Bill says, "During the War Between the States the son of the owner returned to find everything in a completely rundown condition and of course the slaves were gone. I don't believe that he really ever recovered from this catastrophe."

Today, there are guest rooms decorated in a late 18th-century style in the main house and in the outbuildings formerly occupied by slaves and servants of the plantation. Some include Uncle Guy's House, with rooms both upstairs and down; the Overseer's Cottage, with a suite; the Boys' Cabin, and slave quarters.

Further restorations and renovations have been going on industriously during the last few years. "We have renovated the old Carriage House, which was built sometime in the 1840s," Bill told me. "We

have added four magnificent Palladian windows to the open archways on each end of the house to keep the original flavor of the building's use as a carriage house.

"Sancho Pansy's Cottage, named after a slave who followed his young master into war, was built in the 1800s and was last used as the hen house." Bill says that since this building was not quite as historic as the others, his wife, Mireille, decorated it to reflect her Provençal French heritage. With a working fireplace and a Jacuzzi, it is particularly popular with honeymooners.

"Perhaps equally exciting is Mammy Katie's Kitchen, which was built around 1720 and named after the slave Mammy Katie, who was one of the few slaves who remained on the plantation after the Civil War. She probably helped raise young William Overton. The kitchen building has the original fireplace, exposed beams, and ceiling joists dating to the 1720s. We, however, in our tradition of having 18th-century bedrooms and 20th-century bathrooms, added a small deck behind the kitchen for breakfast in the morning, and a large bedroom with a picture window with a beautiful view across our pasture.

"Prospect Hill retains its original character of an 18th-century plantation while having all the modern amenities for our guests."

Dinner is served daily by reservation and the menu has some very French touches because Bill and Mireille travel widely in France and the cuisine is patterned after their experiences. Their son, Michael, has been working with them since he graduated from college a few years ago, and all three of them do the cooking. This part of Virginia really offers a most impressive historical experience, particularly with Monticello, Jefferson's home, and the reproduction of the Michie Tavern nearby. There are numerous historical markers in the area, and Charlottesville itself has the impressive campus of the University of Virginia and its wonderful Georgian buildings. All of this is set in the greening countryside with the Blue Ridge Mountains just a short drive away.

PROSPECT HILL, Route 613, Trevilians, VA 23093; 1-800-277-0844 or 703-967-0844. An 11-guestroom (private baths seven with Jacuzzis) country inn on a historic plantation 15 mi. east of Charlottesville, Va., 90 mi. southwest of Washington, D.C. All bed sizes. Modified American plan with full breakfast-in-bed and full dinner. Dinner served daily by reservation. Breakfast always served to houseguests. Swimming pool. Near Monticello, Ashlawn (President Monroe's home), Univ. of Virginia, Montpelier, and Skyline Drive. Children welcome. No pets. One "Kitty" cat in residence. Bill and Mireille Sheehan, owners/hosts.

DIRECTIONS: From Washington, D.C.: Beltway to I-66 west to Warrenton. Follow Rte. 29 south to Culpeper, then Rte. 15 south thru Orange and Gordonsville to Zion Crossroads. Turn left on Rte. 250 east 1 mi. to Rte. 613. Turn left 3 mi. to inn on left. From Charlottesville or Richmond: take I-64 to Exit 27; Rte. 15 south 1/2 mi. to Zion Crossroads; turn left on Rte. 250 east 1 mi. to Rte. 613. Turn left 3 mi. to inn on left.

TRILLIUM HOUSE
Wintergreen, Nellysford, Virginia

First, I'd better explain Wintergreen. This is a ten-thousand-acre residential community-cum-four-season resort on the slopes of the Blue Ridge Mountains, three hours southwest of Washington, D.C., and an hour from Charlottesville. Tucked away in the mountains are two 18-hole golf courses, an extensive tennis compound, a sixteen-acre lake, land-scaped swimming pools, an equestrian center, ten ski slopes and 27 miles of hiking trails. The Wintergreen gate is just one mile from the Reeds Gap exit of the Blue Ridge Parkway.

Now, Trillium House. A rambling cedar building with dormers and pitched roofs, this country inn at Wintergreen is named after one of the many species of wildflowers that grow in abundance in these mountains.

Rustic, but quite modern, the Trillium House makes an excellent first impression. After stopping at the gate, Trillium guests receive from the courteous gatekeepers directions upward through various clusters of condominiums to Trillium, on one of the highest points at Wintergreen. It happens to be directly across the road from the Wintergarden, a recreation complex with both indoor and outdoor swimming pools, exercise rooms, and a very attractive restaurant looking out on a splendid view of the Blue Ridge Mountains. It is just a short distance to one of the many ski lifts. Strange as it may seem to some

northerners, this part of Virginia has first-rate downhill skiing.

I stepped through the double entrance doors at ground level into the "great room" with a 22-foot cathedral ceiling and Jefferson sunburst window. A massive chimney with a woodburning stove dominates the room. Across the back of this room and up a short flight of steps stretches a balcony with a most impressive library, and on the other side of the chimney is a big-screen TV-watching room and gathering place.

Hallways stretch out from both sides of this room, along which are guest rooms and suites, many of them containing heirlooms that Ed and Betty Dinwiddie have brought from their former homes.

The dining-room windows put the guest on almost intimate terms with the 17th fairway and green, and watching the chipmunks and squirrels and birds around the feeders provides entertainment at breakfast.

I would describe Trillium House as being basically informal. It is, after all, an area where one would come to enjoy all of the great outdoors, from walking and hiking to golf, tennis, and swimming. Gentlemen are comfortable with or without jackets at dinner, and Ed and Betty have a way of immediately making everyone feel at home.

Speaking of dinner, it is a single entrée and available on Friday and Saturday nights with advance reservations. "Our dinner guests tend to come again and again to enjoy stuffed tenderloin of beef and various chicken, veal, and seafood creations."

If you did not receive your confirmation in advance, it's necessary to have the gatekeeper phone ahead to Trillium House.

The Trillium House country-inn experience is much greater than I can describe in one edition. The entire area—the beauty of the mountains, the vistas, and the splendid facilities are almost beyond my descriptive powers.

———

TRILLIUM HOUSE, Wintergreen, P.O. Box 280, Nellysford, VA 22958; 804-325-9126; Fax: 1-804-325-1099. use 800-325-9126 between 9 a.m. and 8 p.m. A 12-guestroom country inn (private baths) within the resort complex of Wintergreen. Queen and twin beds. Breakfast included in room rate. Dinner served Friday and Saturday by advance reservation. Restaurant closeby. Open year-round except December 24-25. Extensive four-season recreation available, including golf, tennis, swimming (indoor and outdoor pool), and downhill skiing, hiking, bird watching, and horseback riding. One dog, Jemima, in residence. Ed and Betty Dinwiddie, owners/hosts.

DIRECTIONS: From points north and east of Charlottesville take the Crozet/Rte. 250 exit from I-64. Go west on Rte. 250 to Rte. 6 and turn left. Follow Rte. 151 south to Rte. 664; turn right on 664 to Wintergreen entrance. From Blue Ridge Pkwy., exit at Reeds Gap, going east on Rte. 664. Don't depend on brakes alone; use lower gears.

Washington, D.C.

THE HENLEY PARK HOTEL
Washington, D.C.

While the Henley Park Hotel isn't a traditional country inn, it fits my definition. And what is that? Well actually, my definition is more of a concept, or feeling, that doesn't so much specify physical considerations (although physical comforts are a primary requirement) as it does a welcoming spirit—an effort by staff to make each guest feel genuinely appreciated.

The staff at the Henley Park Hotel rise to this challenge in a supreme manner. From the moment I wandered into the Wilkes Room, just off the hotel's lobby, I felt relaxed and at home. Fresh pots of

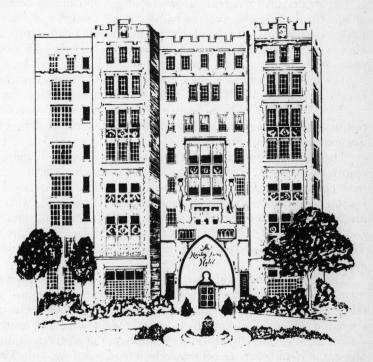

golden chrysanthemums warmed round marble tables placed among soft leather- and tapestry-covered easy chairs. Oriental rugs and a fireplace enhanced the subtle mood of this sitting room, a perfect spot to enjoy a traditional afternoon English tea—Earl Grey, cucumber finger sandwiches, scones, and bowls of heavenly Devonshire cream.

Another snug room, Marley's bar and lounge, creates intimacy with shirred fabric covered walls and leaded glass windows in mauve tones. The incoming light casts a soft, warm glow. A variety of live entertainment, including a talented and seasoned jazz trio, makes an evening in this room seem almost like a private party.

The hotel is a choice example of a Tudor-style building. Constructed in 1918, and restored in 1982, it's unique structure. Its exterior is adorned with a total of 119 gargoyles and plaques. See if you can find the original owners' faces.

Designer Andrew Thompson carefully mixed furniture styles to avoid the unimaginative "department store" groupings so typically found in many hotels. In the guest rooms traditional mahogany furnishings, chintz fabrics, and tastefully framed historical and botanical prints present a refined and relaxed atmosphere.

Ornate drapery treatments, crown moldings, and custom-designed mosaic tile floors in the gorgeous bathrooms are examples of Thompson's careful attention to detail. Details like telephones, for instance. How many country inns, or luxury hotels for that matter, have a telephone in the bedroom *and* in the bathroom? The Henley Park does.

The main dining room, the Coeur de Lion, is connected to the hotel's garden room by French doors. Featuring soft tones of grey touched with accents of beige, mauve, and taupe, the room emanates a restful, intimate elegance. Skylights draw in the sunlight during the day and the stars at night.

The cuisine is French with Asian influences. By candlelight we enjoyed an appetizer of grilled eggplant topped by plum tomatoes and fresh buffalo milk mozzarella spiced with basil, garlic and olive oil. A succulent sautéed escalope of veal tenderloin followed, with an unusual foie gras mousse in a caramelized pink grapefruit sauce. I couldn't manage dessert, although the creme brulee looked divine. The restaurant offers an extensive list of domestic and imported wines and spirits.

The Henley Park Hotel is within walking distance of fine department stores, and an extended walk will take you to the famous, and fabulous, Smithsonian Institution, among other museums. Georgetown, the National Zoo, Embassy Row, and the Capitol are all nearby.

For highly personalized service reminiscent of a private country house, the Henley Park Hotel should be a must when you visit Washington. After three days of the staff's luxurious care, I found it difficult to leave.

HENLEY PARK HOTEL, 926 Massachusetts Ave. NW, Washington, DC 20001; 202-

638-5200. A 91-guestroom (private baths) urban hotel reminiscent of a private home. All bed sizes. Open all year. European plan. An extended walk to the Smithsonian Museums and fine department stores. Georgetown and the National Zoo close by. No pets; no handicapped access. RB Associates, owners; David M. Hill, manager.

DIRECTIONS: Located in downtown Washington at the corner of 10th St. and Massachusetts Ave. NW.

West Virginia

THE COUNTRY INN
Berkeley Springs, West Virginia

"Let me tell you about our West Virginia springhouse water, which is from right here in Berkeley Springs and is shipped as far away as Miami, Florida!"

I was having lunch in the Garden Room at the Country Inn with Jack Barker.

Although it was a very warm fall day, the atmosphere in the Garden Room was really springtime. It has a wallpaper ceiling, and its many, many growing plants, and decor of colorful white, pink and green with strings of tiny white lights, create a very festive air.

Jack at 79 years young is certainly testament to the healthfulness of the water.

I had landed earlier that morning at the Washington airport and made the relatively short trip through the countryside to this eastern panhandle of West Virginia well in time for lunch.

The first thing we did was to tour Country Inn West. Each floor has a different decorative color scheme, and there is an elevator and rooms for the handicapped. Guestrooms in the new building are larger, with more sumptuous bathrooms, and provide an interesting contrast to the rooms in the older building, with their brass beds and individual furnishings.

The hallways throughout both of the buildings of the Country Inn are hung with prints, reflecting Jack's interest in paintings and art. In fact, a gallery- living room has been set aside to display these well-chosen works of art for sale to the guests. There are reproductions of Italian, Flemish, French, and English masters, as well as American primitives. In particular, there are excellent and reasonably priced reproductions of turn-of-the-century French theatrical posters.

Jack was particularly enthusiastic about the completed spa, where it is now possible "to take the mineral waters," for which this section of West Virginia is famous, right at the inn.

The talk at lunch turned to the kinds of entertainments that have been developed over the past few years. "We have live music each weekend for our guests' listening and dancing pleasure," Adele told me. "Special shows include theme nights and dinner theater."

The regular menu at the inn features varied and tempting homemade soups, with special attention to entrées of fowl, beef, seafood, and country fare to satisfy hearty as well as calorie-conscious palates.

The bakery features hot Kentucky pie, fruit pies of apple, cherry, blueberry and strawberry, along with coconut cream, pecan and their special cheese cakes.

Almost since the very start there has always been something in the works. "The completion of our Renaissance Spa provides the use of relaxing Swedish techniques and deep muscle massage," Jack commented. "And we expect that our facial massage and make-up analysis will be equally attractive to our guests."

This section of West Virginia, identified as the Potomac Highlands, offers boating and fishing as well as many, many antique shops and excellent backroading in every season. Guests come in the winter to enjoy the quiet peacefulness, and now, with the opening of Country Inn West's new spa and massage facilities, more and more people will be able to enjoy this truly country-inn hospitality.

THE COUNTRY INN, Berkeley Springs, WV 25411; 304-258-2210: 1-800-822-6630. A 72-guestroom (59 private baths) resort inn on Rte. 522, 34 mi. from Winchester, VA, and 100 mi. from Washington, D.C., or Baltimore, MD. Queen, double, and twin beds. European plan. Breakfast, lunch, and dinner served to travelers. Open every day of the year. Wheelchair access. Berkeley Springs Spa adjoins the inn. Hunting, fishing, hiking, canoeing, antiquing, championship golf nearby. Jack and Adele Barker, owners/hosts.

DIRECTIONS: Take I-70 to Hancock, MD. Inn is 6 mi. south on Rte. 522.

HILLBROOK INN
Charles Town, West Virignia

At Hillbrook Inn you can drink water from the same springhouse that slaked George Washington's thirst. Hillbrook's seventeen pastoral acres were originally a portion of Washington's "Rock Hill" estate, and his springhouse still captures the crystal waters of Bullskin Run.

At the end of the half-mile long drive a resplendent English rock garden skirts the front walk leading to the rambling wood frame and stuccoed Tudor style manor house. Actually, Hillbrook Inn rather reminds me of Anne Hathaway's cottage in Stratford-on-Avon— although, with its fifteen different levels gracefully spilling down a picturesque limestone ridge, the inn is certainly more spacious than the birthplace of Shakespeare's wife.

In contrast to the usual dark woodwork and white walls of many inns, Hillbrook's twenty-foot-high living room offers the reverse, the simplicity of bright white woodwork set against deep teracotta-shaded walls. A blend of antique wooden tables, tapestry covered easy chairs, and richly colored Oriental rugs whose comfortable age complements polished wood floors, are juxtaposed with innkeeper Gretchen Carroll's eclectic collection of primitive and modern pottery and art treasures.

Gathered during her trips with her father and her ex-husband— both of whom had careers with the Foreign Service—pieces from Italy, Vietnam, Turkey, Thailand, and the exotic Ivory Coast, appear throughout the inn creating a pleasing contrast to the more formal English manor house furnishings. "I can stand in the living room and re-create my travels," Gretchen told me as she fondly palmed a pod-shaped statue from Senegal.

When Hillbrook was renovated it was built around the original 1922 log frame, creating intriguing nooks, crannies, twists and turns in the guest rooms. The most sought-after is The Point. A mysterious tunnel lures guests to this cozy room tucked under the kitchen eaves. Paisely-print linens on the double bed, and dramatic wallpaper, enchance the European and Asian paintings and prints on the walls.

Though The Point was occupied when we visited, our stay in The Lookout (named for the precarious slant of the ceiling: "Look out!"), couldn't have been more enjoyable. Spacious windows on three sides bring in the verdant countryside. A minature teak Thai Spirit House ensures safety and good luck.

The Cottage, reached through a private entrance just past the fragrant herb garden, is heated by a wood-burning stove. From the room's two balconies you'll have a sweeping view of the woods and lawns, and the inn's endearingly pompous ducks.

A seven-course dinner in Hillbrook's dining room is lighted by brass chandeliers and old oil lamps casting romantic shadows on the fine crystal and polished wood of antique tables. Gretchen's brass teapot collection winks from the buffet across the room.

A pate with walnuts and brandy started our elegant evening meal. Next, we savored a Creole fish stew; fresh pasta with garlic, olive oil, cashews and basil; and an entrée of chicken breasts drizzled with a sweet-hot pimento sauce and coriander. And in the English tradition, a cheese and fruit plate, along with more sinful delights, was offered for dessert. Wine is included with the price of dinner.

Pecan pancakes sopped in ginger butter are served in the airy glass-enclosed breakfast room in the morning. But beware—Crumpet, the endearing house cat, may just be hunting about for affection. "We call her 'crummy-pet' when she's bad," Gretchen secretly told me.

Gretchen can give you tips on antique hunting and informed suggestions on how to entertain yourselves in the area. We spent a fascinating afternoon at Harper's Ferry, a national park with scads of historical significance, visiting museums and working archeological digs.

Afterwards we returned to the inn's Bullskin Tavern for cappuccino and dessert. Feeling quite blessed, I saved a few crumbs for the Thai Spirit House.

HILLBROOK INN, Rte. 2, Box 152, Charles Town, WV 25414; 304-725-4223. A 5-guestroom (private baths) Tudor-style country house. Open all year; closed Monday and Tuesday. Double beds. Breakfast included; lunch Sunday, 7-course dinner Wednesday-Sunday. 5 mi. from Charles Town. Visit Harper's Ferry; antiquing, rafting, trail rides. No pets. Gretchen Carroll, owner/host.

DIRECTIONS: From Charles Town, take Rte. 51 west to Rte. 13. Bear left on Rte. 13 and go 4.8 mi. to inn.

Deep South

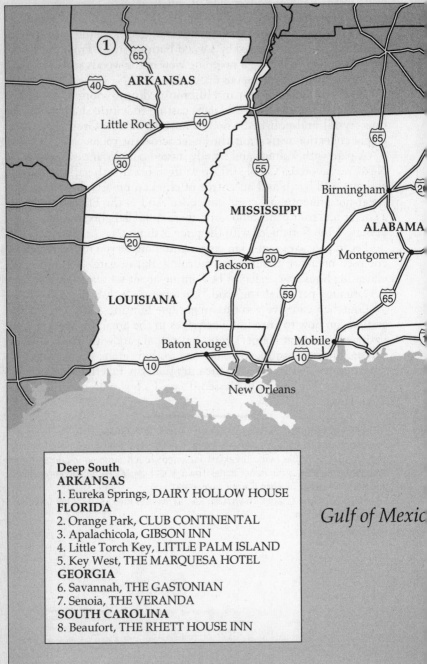

Gulf of Mexic

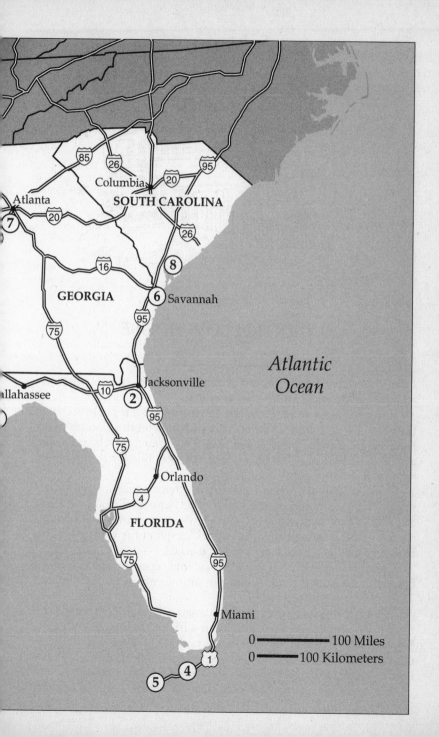

Arkansas

DAIRY HOLLOW HOUSE
Eureka Springs, Arkansas

It isn't often that I have the opportunity to explore a new country inn and discuss "the muse" with a fellow writer.

Innkeeper and writer Crescent Dragonwagon has published over thirty books, including children's books (she won the Coretta Scott King Award for *Half a Moon and One Whole Star*), novels, magazine articles, and her *Dairy Hollow House Cookbook*, filled with the savory recipes served at the inn's restaurant.

Crescent laughed when I asked the obvious question about her name. "That's a long one," she said, rolling her eyes skyward. "If I had any *idea* of how many times I would have to explain this ridiculous name...!" (But I rather think she gets a kick out of the explanation, so be sure to ask her for the story when you visit.)

Crescent met her husband and fellow innkeeper, Ned Shank, when he came to Arkansas to do research as an internist with the National Trust for Historic Preservation.

Eureka Springs is located in the dramatically beautiful heart of the Ozarks. The resort town has long been a haven for writers, craftspeople, and artists. It also has excellent examples of Victorian architecture. But when Crescent and Ned opened their inn, new development was "in"; historic architecture was viewed as "old and backwards."

Ned and Crescent had another idea. "We wanted deeply to show that tourism and preservation were natural partners," they told me, "and hoped Dairy Hollow House would demonstrate this to our community." After ten years of operational success, their goal has certainly been met.

The two buildings which comprise the Dairy Hollow House are an 1880s "Ozark Vernacular" farmhouse and an American/southern style cottage from the 1940s. Ned's trained preservationist's eye provided the vision, first with the main house and later with the cottage, that led to the inevitable energy-intensive refurbishing.

The common areas of the inn feel lazy and unpretentious. Comfortable chairs, warm rose tones, and a close, caring staff create a sense of home. There are also numerous porches where the lovely Ozark scenery can be enjoyed—and the secluded hot tub/Jacuzzi in the woods is a must!

Crescent's enjoyment of creative detail is apparent throughout the inn. In the six guest rooms regional antiques are complimented by traditionally-patterned handmade quilts, framed children's book illustrations, and fresh flowers. Each room has an individual color scheme, a romantic fireplace (one has a pot-bellied stove), and a private bath.

In the restaurant's dining room nine lace-framed windows open onto a park setting, bringing the woodsy outdoors in. Crescent has enhanced this mood with a Victorian-inspired fernlike carpet, English floral padded wainscotting, and soft late-summer shades of cream and pale yellow with accents of rose, fern and blue.

The restaurant has developed a reputation for serving innovative regional cuisine with a stylish simplicity. "We call our brand of regionalism, of course, 'Noveau 'Zarks'," Crescent explained. "We emphasize local foods, like fresh vegetables from Dripping Springs Organic Farm and herbs from Bleumarie Herb Farm."

A scrumptious full breakfast, offering all sorts of homemade goodies, is included with your room rate. Dinner is a six-course delight served seven nights a week. If it's on the evening's menu, be sure to sample the old-fashioned rabbit fricassee.

I can't think of a more peaceful, welcoming setting from which to enjoy the Ozarks than Dairy Hollow House.

DAIRY HOLLOW HOUSE, 515 Spring, Eureka Springs, AR 72632; 501-253-7444. A 6-guestroom (private baths) country inn and restaurant in the heart of the Ozark mountains. Queen, double and twin beds. Open year-round; restaurant open April 1–January 1. Breakfast included; six-course dinner all week. Close to hiking, lakes, King's River for floating and fishing, antiquing, galleries. No pets. Crescent Dragonwagon and Ned Shank, owners/hosts.

DIRECTIONS: From 62 E/W, come to Historic Loop (old 62B). Loop from downtown to Spring St. Main house is at 515 Spring, next to Harmon Park.

Florida

CLUB CONTINENTAL

Orange Park, Florida

House, town, and family history are one, as I discovered on my first tour with Frica Massee and her children around the grounds of the Club Continental. The club is two things, a membership club that mostly uses facilities removed from the inn, and the intimate lodging where guests have access to all member facilities.

The house itself is known as Mira Rio because its Mediterranean setting overlooks the St. Johns River, where it flows three miles wide past the historic shore of Orange Park. The town was incorporated in 1877, and 10 years later Mira Rio became the winter home of the Massees, the founding family of the Palmolive Soap Company. For the past 25 years the home has been the lodging that drew me.

Managed by Frica's late husband Jon, and now by Frica and Jon's son Caleb, the seven-suite lodging is one of the finest in Florida. Certainly nothing this intimate, yet still this luxurious, is likely to be built ever again. The patina of age has everything to do with its quality. Guest rooms, public spaces, and grounds are all in the great tradition of imagination inspired by wealth.

The six-acre grounds (the estate once included 17) fan from the lyrically beautiful Mira Rio into an enclave of gardens and pools. The architecture is of limestone, ornamental archways, filigreed ironwork, and sumptuous carpets on tile. In other words, an adaptation of a Renaissance palazzo. Newer buildings set unobtrusively to the south adapt the traditional stone look for the low-rise condominium dwellings of more recent residents, clustered around a marina with tennis courts that are also available to guests. More intriguing are two older buildings to the north. One is Winterbourne ("winter waterway" in Scottish), a white wooden clapboard structure of dignified bearing leased by Massee forebears after their first winters at a local resort hotel. This house became the seed of the present estate when Jon Massee's grand-uncle acquired it in 1906. Waterbourne's four housekeeping units are leased for long-term stays.

Nearby and extended over the water is a pre-Civil War cottage that Frica rescued from a mouldering oblivion five miles south. She had it barged to the site and restored. It was later expanded by Frica's daughter Jeanne and her husband Bill Patterson into a popular patio-pub called the River House that today—behind huge cypress, hickory, and palm trees, and seasonally bordered by impatiens and wildflowers—is greatly enjoyed by Club Continental members.

"Enjoyed so much," says Frica, "that when a big storm struck and the whole area lost electricity, one fellow, a member with a generator, brought it here instead of home to keep the River House lit and in use. I'm sure he got in big trouble at home." Guests bed down in rooms composed of antiques acquired by Jon Massee's mother on her round-the-world travels. The decor is variously English, country French, Mexican, and continental. Guests luxuriate in carved Italian beds, some with theatrical canopies. The Continental Suite has a Jacobean sideboard, and a beautiful Jamaican wall painting on four sides of the bathroom, as well as a marble shower stall. The French Room has elaborately swagged drapes that frame three pairs of push-out windows. The bed has a gesso-like finish of rustic scenes in its arched headboards, topped by a gathered crown canopy in a viney fabric matched by bedcover and drapes. The rooms have magnificent views through oaks and palm to the river. Frica tells the story about the Sicilian donkey cart that now, full of flowers, graces the second-story sitting area. "When mother Massee approached the vendor he thought she wanted all the flowers. What she wanted was the cart, the donkey—and the flowers. And she had her way!"

The dining room features fine continental cuisine in a splendid seating behind a row of Palladian fanlight windows. Candles in crystal holders and a rose in a vase adorn every table, each set with white linen, on English-garden carpets. So I dined on an appetizer of crispy pee wee softshell crabs on a bed of fried spinach, on the grouper beurre blanc nippy with bacon bits, the house salad with its home grown arugula, and for dessert, fresh raspberries with cream. Throughout, views of the carpet-like lawns beneath towering oaks leading to the stone balustrades that rim the river stole my gaze. I found the setting magical and look forward to many returns.

CLUB CONTINENTAL, 2143 Astor St., P.O.Box 7059, Orange Park, FL 32073; 904-264-6070. A 7-room/suite (private baths) version of an Italian palazzo along the widest part of the St. Johns River, 15 miles south of Jacksonville. King and queen beds. Open year-round. Scenic river tours, fishing, tennis, freshwater pool swimming, boating available on premises. No pets. Caleb Massee, general manager.

DIRECTIONS: From Jacksonville, south on I-275, exit U.S. 17 south to Kingsley Avenue, left to river, right on Astor Street to gatehouse.

GIBSON INN
Apalachicola, Florida

I came to Apalachicola wanting to find out about the Gibson Inn, and all Michael Koun wanted to talk about was the "Governor Stone." Launched in 1877, the "Governor Stone" is the last known upper Gulf coasting schooner of the South. Michael heads the committee that funds its upkeep by grants and training charters. He sees the little vessel as a treasured asset for reviving Apalachicola.

Michael came to Apalach (as everyone calls the town) in the early 1980s after one of his brothers stumbled upon the Gibson and organized a partnership to restore it. Michael, though still a young man, was ready to exit the corporate world for a more personal challenge and became managing partner for the project.

You can hardly imagine any place more different from Chicago, where Michael came from. Apalachicola has a year-round population of perhaps 3,000. Surrounding Franklin County is the poorest in Florida. Only one road comes through town. First-time visitors usually show up because they've seen U.S. Highway 98 on the map and have driven off the Interstate curious about a road that skirts the shore for 200 miles. Next time they come for the Gibson Inn, built in 1907, and crown jewel in a district of dozens of buildings on the National Register of Historic Places.

Gingerbread blue and white, the Gibson Inn sits moored at the front of town where the new high bridge sweeps across the river with a ninety-degree flourish. From its rocking-chair porches to its widow's walk cupola, the Gibson stylishly beckons visitors to stay awhile and explore this seafaring town.

The inn's downstairs porch, its big lobby, cypress bar, and long dining room full of historic photos attract visitors and locals alike. Rooms upstairs on two floors feature period antiques and reproduction hardware in modern bathrooms. Yesteryear further abides in bullseye door surrounds, in boxcar siding ceilings, and transoms in most rooms which, while they no longer open, have not been covered over either.

Beds are four-poster and white iron, armoires antique pine or mahogany. Pedestal sinks are in the bedchambers.

The dining room feels like the least re-touched of the inn's spaces. Its swinging kitchen doors stay busy and its black cypress plank floors creak under the footfalls of waitresses bringing garlicky-fresh seafood. I particularly enjoyed an okra-rich gumbo, springy little scallops, buttery-tender oysters, and a simply grilled snapper. I barely had room for the authentic Key lime pie, yellow and tart. Guests often dine in shorts and jeans, though some dress in jackets and ties. The Gibson is very "live and let live."

The pleasures of the lobby include its intricately hand-carved newel posts that flank the mahogany stairway, and the handsome bar, dark and winey, set about with captain's stools. High narrow wainscotting is topped by a mellow blue, the same color as the inn's exterior, with shiplike green lampshades. Outside the sets of French doors, their traipsing moldings lately painted in red, white and blue like a primer drawing, the porch is busy with guests who gather all day, from morning coffee to evening beer. Most fun in Apalach is a walk through the historic district. The pride of the town is the John Gorrie Museum, named for the MD who invented the ice-making machine. Trinity Episcopal Church is a Greek Revival building shipped in sections from New York in 1837–38. Chestnut Street Cemetery dates from 1831. Michael allowed how he was lately flown to Dallas by a corporate recruiter. He says he took one look down at the North-Central Expressway and knew he could never return to life in the congested lane. He's now back in Apalach as president of the St. Patrick's Parish Council, a director of the Florida Seafood Festival, and a member of the Chamber of Commerce."

I enjoy sailing, history, and old wooden buildings too much to ever go back," says Michael. And I look forward to seeing him again in that beautifully restored Gibson Inn of his, talking about old ships and the revival of his adopted town where he's making such a fine contribution.

GIBSON INN, Apalachicola, FL 32320; 904-653-2191, 904-653-8282. A 31-guestroom (private baths) Victorian inn built in 1907 at the foot of the high bridge into town, 75 miles southwest of Tallahassee, 65 miles east of Panama City on Florida's northwest gulf coast. King, queen and twin beds. European plan. Upper stories overlook Apalachicola Bay. Open year-round. In a National Register Historic District, and close to St. Vincent Natinal Wildlife Refuge, St. Joseph Peninsula State Park, St. George Island State Park. Self-guided historic walking tours, swimming, fishing. Pets accepted. Michael Koun, owner/host.

DIRECTIONS: From Tallahassee, 75 miles south and west on U.S. 319 & U.S. 98 to Apalachicola; from Panama City east on U.S. 98, 65 miles to Apalachicola, to the foot of the high bridge.

LITTLE PALM ISLAND
Little Torch Key, Florida

Only Ben Woodson knows how fine is the line between beekeeping and innkeeping. I learned it's a sliver of 24 hours. That was the wink of time Ben and his partners had to get plans approved for their hideaway before the new Florida Keys land use plan said "NO" forever to commerce of any kind on unbridged islands. Except beekeeping. Ben and his partners, all from Memphis, were hardly the rapscallions who had given the Keys' developers their woeful reputation. All were successful in other fields—medicine, manufacturing, chain resorts, commodities trading. Little Palm Island was their inspiration for change-of-pace fun in the sun.

Little Palm Island is 30 suites up on stilts under thatch roofs—a mere five acres of sand and palm trees at the edge of the Atlantic. That, plus a gourmet dining room—one of Florida's most outstanding—and things to do of the quiet and indulgent kind. Guests have kayaks and windsailers to use, a boutique, a dive shop, a pool with fresh water, as well as the sea.

But the impression I like best on Little Palm Island is how, on the first night, you realize how out of this world you are. Three miles off the Keys highway, only the flat Bahamas far to the east stands between you and Africa. Subtleties signal the difference: mosquito netting-protected sleep, rain that falls like the thrum of an ancient instrument, nights full of stars long disappeared from city skies, sunrises and sunsets with the Master's original intensity.

Nature all the time pokes into this world.

Not long ago, Ben told me, the endangered Key deer were swimming over to feed on Little Palm Island's hibiscus plants and the chef's herb garden. Wildlife authorities didn't want these shy animals becoming domesticated and asked Ben to install a single strand of electric fencing to discourage the deers' intrusion. Ben complied. No problem for guests who are quicklly informed about the installation.

Nor does the mosquito netting mean problems. "It's strictly for effect," says Ben. "The roofs of our suites are pitched so high that the bamboo rigging that secures the netting above the beds breaks the sheer expanse. At the same time the netting takes guests out of their ordinary state of mind. It helps them further shake loose of the pressures of daily life and accept the wonderful relaxation this island offers."

Relaxation begins the moment guests arrive at the Little Palm Island shore station at mile marker 28.5 of the Overseas Highway on Little Torch Key. Bags are checked in (next appearing in suites) while guests enjoy a tropical drink before boarding the launch that leaves for the island hourly.

The launch ferries guests across Coupon Bight Aquatic Preserve. Even at high tide as you step ashore you'll notice the flats that, dawn and dusk (and especially at low tide), attract an extraordinary variety of water birds. Reserving your dinner hour in the casually elegant indoor-outdoor dining room is the most challenging decision you're obliged to make. After a brief tour of the island you're ensconced.

Suites are arranged two to a villa—28 altogether, plus two additional suites in the great house where meals are served. Each includes a sitting room, bathroom/dressing room, and bedchamber. All are spacious, furnished in sturdy and stylish wicker and rattan with lots of color, and each guest is supplied with a robe. Why not? This is as close to the tropics as continental America gets. Oversized floral prints on sofa cushions and bold art draw guests into the romance of island life.

Equally tropical are the magnificent coral reefs close by that enchant divers and snorkelers. Nowhere in America but Hawaii are reefs so colorful. Fishing is challenging offshore and on the flats, where dozens of varieties have provided sport and food for generations. Little Palm Island provides some of the area's best guides.

Three meals are included in the room rate, and they are of award-winning gourmet quality. Dishes include fresh Keys seafood expertly prepared (snapper, swordfish, grouper, dolphin, shrimps, and Florida lobster are favorites), along with light French cuisine and a long list of wines that, bottle by bottle, might reach from one end of the island to the other. I felt I was leaving paradise after my visit. I couldn't believe I wouldn't have to show a passport to return home.

LITTLE PALM ISLAND, Rte. 4, Box 1036, Little Torch Key, FL 33042, mile marker 28.5, Overseas Highway; 800-343-8567, 305-872-2524. A 30-suite (private baths) South Seas-style hideaway in the Coupon Bight Aquatic Preserve, 150 miles south of Miami. King and twin beds and queen sofa beds. American Plan. Open year round. Snorkeling, diving, deepwater and backcountry fishing, freshwater pool, beach, kayaking, canoeing, windsailing. Near National Key Deer Refuge, Great White Heron National Wildlife Refuge, Looe Key National Marine Sanctuary, Coupon Bight Aquatic Preserve, The Museum of Natural History of the Florida Keys. No pets. Ben Woodson, owner/host.

DIRECTIONS: From Miami International Airport take Florida's Turnpike south to its end. Drive U.S. 1 (Overseas Highway) approx. 120 mi. to Little Torch Key at mile marker 28.5. Look for Little Palm Island Ferry Service sign. Turn left into Dolphin Marina to Little Palm Island Shore Station. From Marathon Airport drive 22.5 mi. south to Little Torch Key. From Key West Airport drive north 27 mi. to Little Torch Key.

THE MARQUESA HOTEL
Key West, Florida

Even on rainy mornings, Key West has its rewards. I was lately able to enjoy a light breakfast under the big dripping eave of the front porch at the Marquesa with its manager Carol Wightman. While I devoured a meal of her sinfully candy-like home-made granola with Michigan dried cherries (drenched in milk), Carol was greeting a colorful assortment of the characters for which Key West is known.

Here was "Do" the doberman in her protective tee shirt trotting along with J.T. of the Solares Hill Design Group, he on his clunker

bike, "Do" with her shirt hiding her double row of pearls. Almost every bypasser just off the Simonton Street corner of Fleming Street waved or called a greeting.

Carol is wife of one of the partners of this 15-room landmark restoration, which is listed in the National Register of Historic Places. Carol's husband Erik deBoer and Richard Manley are general contractors specializing in historic preservation whose work has won more than a dozen design awards in the 10 years they've been in business.

The Marquesa stands out so successfully, even in this town renowned for preservation, that its pale green clapboard and blue shutters with white trim are now popularly known among restorers as Marquesa green and Marquesa blue.

Carol relates how Erik and Richard acquired the property early in 1987 expressly to convert its existing buildings into a fine little hotel. In their time the two buildings had been a dry goods store, a furniture store, a grocery store and a forlorn apartment building. With the help of dozens of craftsmen and the infusion of close to $2 million, eight months later the Marquesa was born. Its smart row of dormers trailing behind the sharply eaved roof hint at nothing so much as a row of ducklings—a look which, in this section of Key West called Old Town, seems to capture time.

From the parlor to the tidy pool, the little restaurant, and the guest rooms, the Marquesa suggests the home of a beloved American family, for it isn't so much all of a period as it is the selected accumulation of generations.

The parlor welcomes guests with a brilliant burst of tropical flowers and the complementing oils of Key West modern abstractionist Beth Nable. Walls expose the original tongue-and-groove siding. Furniture combines a French provincial desk with a starkly modern glass-topped table.

Guest rooms and suites are up and around a maze of textured spaces inside and out. The upstairs rooms have especially high peaked ceilings, though all extend to almost 12 feet. Four rooms are in a boxy new structure so skillfully added to a next-door Fleming Street lot that guests will likely notice no difference in essential style and quality. Rooms may have a Heppelwhite dresser, a Queen Anne desk, antique wicker armchairs, a three-doored mahogany armoire, or a split-pediment headboard in the softest blue (at the end of beds firm as old-style handshakes). They also have ultra-modern telephones, Italian chrome bathroom fixtures, and art deco sconces. These are rooms that feel right for living in rather than collector' ideals.

And the living is good here, so that given Old Town's historic and revelrous attractions (which hardly anyone passes up), guests nonetheless spend much time relaxing on Marquesa premises. The little pool surrounded by a high board fence sits like a jewel in a setting of exotic traveler palms and fountain, lined with Marquesa green and blue tiles, embellished by potted bougainvilleas, impatiens, and roses.

Do not miss dinner in the Cafe Marquesa. Mine in this intimate dining room, with its emerald greens and warm golden yellows, was a half-serving of the home-made angel hair pasta with duck patties and wild mushrooms, the grilled dolphin marinated in sesame oil, light soy, and wasabi, extra helpings of the zesty flatbread sprinkled with white and black sesame seeds and crisply baked, and for dessert the melt-in-your-mouth flourless chocolate and walnut cake with raspberry sauce and a creme anglaise.

Others, I noticed, enjoyed their meals directly at the handsome mahogany bar where, through the multi-paned bay windows, they could enjoy the passing parade along Fleming Street—a pleasure, I learned from my visit, to be enjoyed rain or shine.

THE MARQUESA HOTEL, 600 Fleming Street, Key West, FL 33040; 800-869-4631, 305-292-1919. A 15-room/suite (private baths) Victorian revival inn completed in 1987 in Old Town. Queen beds, and double bed sofas. Open year-round. In a National Register Historic District within walking distance of many sites including the Hemingway House, Audubon House, Wrecker's Museum, Lighthouse Museum, sunset carrying-on at Mallory Square. Conch Tour Train and Old Town Trolley offer guided tours. Swimming, fishing, boating. No pets. Carol Wightman, manager/host.

DIRECTIONS: U.S. 1 to Simonton Street, right 6 blocks to Fleming.

Georgia

THE GASTONIAN
Savannah, Georgia

Light splashes down the steps and across the sidewalk when the door opens to welcome frock-coated gentlemen with their bejewelled ladies in silks and satins alighting from their carriages. Sounds of gaiety and music spill out of the open windows. It is 1868 and another brilliant party is in progress at the opulent townhouse of insurance broker R.H. Footman. Next door, the equally opulent house is dim, as Aaron Champion and his wife join their neighbor's gathering. The Civil War has been over for three years, and Savannah society, spared General Sherman's wrath, is returning to sparkling life.

    Well, I'm just daydreaming, but that's the sort of thing one does in this lavishly restored and decorated home. Hugh and Roberta Lineberger encourage such fantasies. After all, it was their own fantasy that brought them here in the first place. "We were on vacation from our home in California, passing through Savannah on our way to a golfing holiday in South Carolina," Roberta told me, "when we started looking at some of these lovely old housed and dreaming about running a bed-and-breakfast inn." Within a matter of weeks they found themselves the owners of not one but two Italianate Regency homes, side by side, and were deep in the intricacies of renovation.

I must say, the Linebergers have done a magnificent job of creating a truly elegant inn out of these two historic homes. The houses are connected by an attractive curving walkway, elevated over the garden filled with fragrant myrtle and flowering dogwood.

I could go on at great lengths about the beautiful architectural features and the equally beautiful American and European antique furnishings of the Gastonian. Roberta has decorated every room with great flair and taste, with lush fabrics and authentic Savannah colors. The rooms have working fireplaces, plants and fresh flowers.

Some of the bathrooms are the most unusual I've ever seen. Many of the tubs are the kind, as Hugh put it, "you can fill up to your earlobes and soak away in." One of them, fit for a Roman emperor, is in the Caracalla Suite, which has an eight-foot round whirlpool bathtub in front of a fireplace.

More important to me is the feeling of gracious hospitality. Having tea with Hugh and Roberta in the elegant Chippendale and Sheraton sitting room, facing a charming portrait of a lovely lady over the carved white-marble fireplace, I found them very warm and easy to talk with.

Roberta explained that, although breakfast is sometimes served in the formal dining room, she usually cooks and served it in the large, sunny kitchen. In addition to her legendary Southern-style breakfasts, "We welcome our guest with fresh fruit and wine," she said, "and have little extras, like turn-down service and Savannah sweets and cordials." They have many amusing stories of their adventures in bringing the Gastonian into being, and their travels in Europe, collecting treasures for it. "I'm sure there's a story about that portrait of the lovely lady," I said. "Yes, indeed, there is," Roberta replied. "The antiques dealer in southeastern England where we saw her had made a solemn vow to find the right home for her, and we had to promise him we would provide her with a most beautiful setting."

"Actually," Hugh commented with a smile, "we like to provide all our guests with a beautiful setting, as well as with real Southern hospitality."

THE GASTONIAN, 220 E. Gaston St., Savannah, GA 31401; 912-232-2869. A 13-guestroom/suite (private baths) luxurious inn in twin townhouses in the Historic Landmark District of Savannah. Complimentary full breakfast only meal served. Open year-round. Arrangements for horse-drawn carriage historical tours, dinner reservations, hot tub on premises. Golf and athletic club privileges, tennis, deep-sea fishing, Savannah River within walking distance, and all of the historic and cultural attractions in the largest Historic District in the U.S. nearby. No children under 12. Smoking limited. Hugh and Roberta Lineberger, innkeepers.

DIRECTIONS: From I-95 take I-16 to Savannah. Take W. Broad St. exit, crossing Broad St. and continuing to Gaston St. and the inn at the corner of Lincoln St.

THE VERANDA
Senoia, Georgia

For a real taste of old-fashioned Georgia country hospitality, you can't beat the Veranda in the sleepy little town of Senoia (pronounced senoy). The Veranda is listed on the National Register of Historic Places, along with 113 other buildings, virtually the whole town. The local hardware store, with one or more of "everything," is located across the street and has been selected featured on TV and in magazine articles.

Jan and Bobby Boal at the Veranda have a few museum-quality collections themselves. I loved Bobby's array of over 100 walking sticks, many of them made by her father and grandfather and others purchased all over the world, including one that belonged to Senator Robert A. Taft. Some other things that are a lot of fun are a huge old Wurlitzer player piano-organ with chimes, and a lot of music rolls, and the 1860s Estey pump organ with all kinds of turn-of-the-century sheet music and songbooks. They also have a vast and fascinating collection of kaleidoscopes and unusual puzzles and games.

When Jan and Bobby bought the house in 1985, it had been a private residence since the 1930s. Before that, it had been the Hollberg Hotel, built in 1906 when Senoia was a thriving cotton town with a new rail station. A rambling white clapboard building with a Doric-columned wraparound porch, it was built entirely with heart-pine lumber. Several rooms have the original pressed-tin ceilings, unusual prismed chandeliers, stained-glass window insets, and thin-planked wainscotting.

The Boals have completed the feeling of authenticity with their own heirlooms and antiques, including eclectic furnishings, Oriental rugs, fine old books, prints, and etchings and a massive set of walnut book cases, once owned by President William McKinley.

All of the guest rooms are most attractively furnished with queen-sized beds, armoires, handmade quilts, rocking chairs, and fresh flowers. When I retired for the night, I found my bed had been turned down and a miniature kaleidoscope was on the pillow.

The Boals are two of the friendliest people you'd ever want to meet. While Bobby was busy in the kitchen, Jan entertained us with a tune on the pump organ. When he isn't playing the organ, serving meals, making French toast for breakfast, and just generally innkeeping, Jan, a retired mathematics professor from Georgia State University will converse on a broad range of subjects including movie making. Yes, Senoia now has a fine movie studio and many films are being made there. Jessica Tandy & Kathy Bates were guests at the Veranda when Fried Green Tomatoes was filmed around the corner from the Inn.

Bobby says innkeeping is hard work but the rewards are many. She loves it when guests share her interest in the history of the area.

Be sure to make advance reservations for dinner, as you won't want to miss one of her "made from scratch" meals, including the crisp Georgia crackers that accompany the fresh fruit salad. Bobby has a large collection of regional and old family-secret recipes, along with many of her own original ones. Everyone tells her she should write a cookbook. One of her dinners might include cold peach soup, veal in puffed pastry, a ham and chicken casserole, homemade fruit sorbet, sourdough biscuits or sourdough bread, fresh vegetables, and some delectable dessert like lemon meringue sundae, Black Forest torte, or homemade angel food cake with fresh strawberries and whipped cream.

There's so much more to tell, but I'll leave it to you to discover the delights of a visit to this homey, comfortable inn where Southern hospitality reigns.

THE VERANDA, 252 Seavy St., Senoia, GA 30276; 404-599-3905. A 9-guestroom (private baths) homey Victorian inn on the National Register of Historic Places in a quiet small town, 36 mi. south of Atlanta. Queen and twin beds available. Deluxe breakfast included; all meals available by reservation. Open year-round. Library, music, puzzles, games, gift shop, porch swings and rocking chairs, and special theme weekends on premises. Golf, tennis, fishing, historic walking tours, festivals, antiquing, Callaway Gardens, Warm Springs, private museum, and great hardware store nearby. No pets. Limited smoking. Bobby and Jan Boal, owners/hosts.

DIRECTIONS: From Atlanta, take Rte. 85 through Riverdale and Fayetteville to Senoia city limit. Turn right at Seavy St. Inn is on corner of Barnes and Seavy Sts.

South Carolina

THE RHETT HOUSE INN
Beaufort, South Carolina

Southerners appreciate the finer things in life: architecture, food, drink, and trees. Yes, trees—and particularly oak trees. I recently toured the South and discovered that their colossal oaks are endowed with respectful names when they reach the age of 300 years. I was reminded of this tradition as I swayed in a hammock on the upper veranda of the Rhett House, watching the breeze nudge the Spanish moss draped on a mammoth oak.

This plantation house is typical of the grand homes built during the 1820s. Corinthian columns support a classic two-story veranda that loops around both sides. Guests climb an unusual exterior stairway set to the side before they walk across the veranda to the front door and the antebellum elegance of the entrance hall beyond.

Steve and Marianne Harrison transferred their impeccable style from Manhattan's fashion industry to the Rhett House. Using a beginning canvas of polished heart pine floors and pristine white walls, Marianne has added Oriental carpets, a mix of contemporary and antique furnishings, floral print fabrics, and tastefully chosen art work to paint a picture of gracious refinement.

In the sun-drenched living room, guests can sip sherry and loll on one of the sofas, or try their hand at a game of pool on the antique billiards table. Here, and in the dining room, you can see excellent examples of Adams-style mantlepieces over the fireplaces. Family photographs are placed here and there. "This is a big house," Marianne told me, "and it could be very intimidating, but we decorated it to give it a warm, personal feel."

The spacious guest rooms have private baths and comfortable sitting areas decorated with English and American antiques and cotton chintz. Some have fireplaces and all have good reading lights, thick towels, and extra pillows.

The Harrisons whip up a tasty full breakfast which is served at the long pine table in the dining room. A small vase of wildflowers and sprigs of rosemary from Marianne's herb garden provide a centerpiece.

Knowing my penchant for history, Steve showed me a picture of the home made during the Civil War when it was used as a hospital for Union troops. There, in almost the same spot on the veranda where I had been, sat a recuperating Union soldier—and shading him was the same old oak.

THE RHETT HOUSE INN, 1009 Craven St., Beaufort, SC 29902; 803-524-9030. An 8-guestroom (private baths) elegant Plantation inn. Queen, double, and twin beds. Open all year. Bikes provided. Swimming, golfing, fishing. Historic house tours. No pets. Smoking restricted. CCs: Visa, MC. Marianne and Steve Harrison, owners/hosts.

DIRECTIONS: Contact the inn.

Midwest

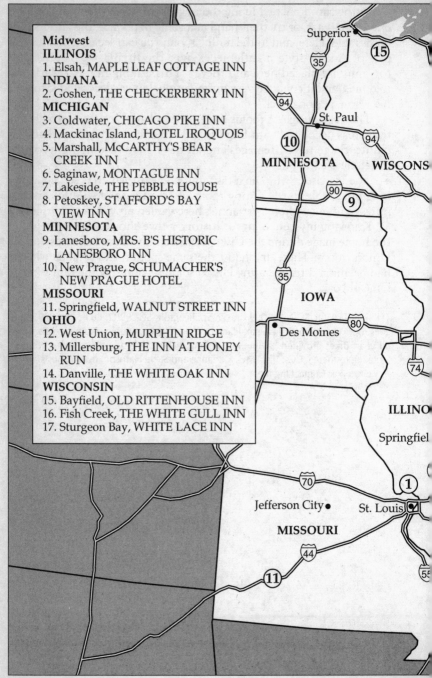

Superior

St. Paul

MINNESOTA   WISCONS

IOWA

Des Moines

ILLINO

Springfiel

Jefferson City   St. Louis

MISSOURI

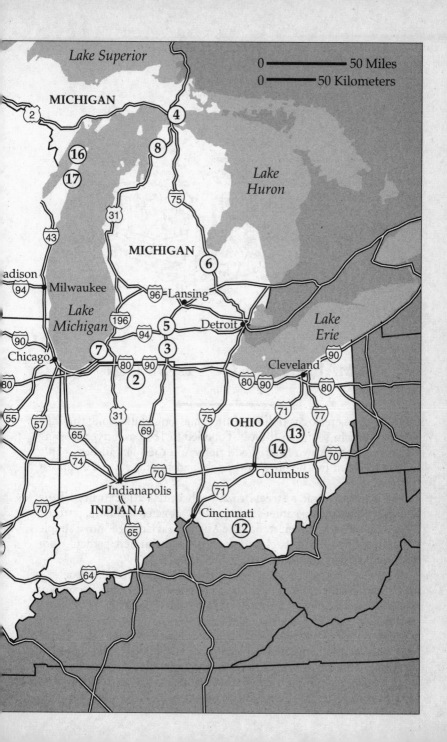

Illinois

MAPLE LEAF COTTAGE INN
Elsah, Illinois

Elsah lies in a creek-cut hollow of the limestone bluffs along the Mississippi River in southern Illinois. Founded in 1853 as a river crossing for travelers, the town flourished briefly and then languished—only lightly touched by the growth that shaped so many other Midwest towns.

As a result, Elsah's streets today echo the 19th century: stone houses with sprawling gardens, a ruined ivy-covered icehouse, an 1887 village hall. Among them stands the Maple Leaf Cottage Inn, a simple white frame house with backyard guest cottages, an herb garden, wildflowers and a perennial garden.

These gardens were once part of the estate of Christian Loehr, a prominent Elsah citizen. When a 1918 fire destroyed all but his smokehouse and wash house, another house was built—one with a cozy front porch, a low roof, and plenty of windows.

New owners Patricia and Jerry Taetz have renovated the Maple Leaf with artistic reminders of Elsah's past and present. Silhouettes of the Elsah streetscape are painted on the wall of one cottage. Parlor stencils were taken from tracings of actual maple leaves from the front yard. Says Patricia: "It's important to preserve Elsah's heritage."

Weather permitting, guests sit in the gardens to eat and drink. Come morning, they sample a full breakfast on the screened porch or in one of two cheerful breakfast rooms. Guests can then spend the day touring Illinois' Great River Road along the Mississippi, or roaming Elsah.

What they'll see in town is interesting architecture, Midwest history, and a good deal of natural beauty. They'll not see many tourist services, although plenty of people come to tiny Elsah. There's only one restaurant, and since the town is a "dry" community, liquor is not served. "Visitors come for the serenity of the village," Patricia explains. "This way, they can appreciate Elsah's charm and historic significance."

MAPLE LEAF COTTAGE INN, P.O. Box 156, Elsah, IL 62028; 618-374-1684. A 1-guestroom pleasant white frame home with 3 cottages in the heart of a historic river town. Double beds. Full breakfast. Dinner by reservation. Open year-round. No pets. One cat in residence. No smoking. Patricia Taetz, owner/host.

DIRECTIONS: From I-70, take Rte. 3 north. Follow Great River Rd. signs to Alton; in Alton, turn west on Broadway and follow Great River Rd. signs out of town. Soon you'll see another sign for the village of Elsah. Turn right into the village, continue up Mill St. and turn at third left onto Selma. Inn begins at end of Selma Street to the corner of Maple, on Lasalle.

Indiana

THE CHECKERBERRY INN

Goshen, Indiana

Located on one hundred acres of Indiana's Amish countryside, the Checkerberry Inn offers that same sense of tranquility and peace. You'll share the six miles of road from Goshen, the nearest town, with the "plain people" and their simple, elegant Amish buggies.

John and Susan Graff operated (and still do) a villa resort on the Island of Anguilla in the British West Indies prior to their construction of the Checkerberry Inn.

"One Christmas Susie's father announced that each of his five children should choose their farm from the five he owned," John told me, "so Susie chose these hundred acres."

"These hundred acres" included an 1880s Amish farmhouse which the Graffs immediately saw as a renovating challenge. After the renovation was complete, John twiddle his thumbs for about eight months until Susie suggested opening an inn in the Midwest.

Freshly inspired, they began to search for a location, and after only a few casual nods to other Midwestern states they decided, like Kansas's Dorothy, that "happiness is in your own backyard"—or in their case, just across the road.

The result of their efforts is a striking three-story, butter-colored Georgian inn, as tidy and precise as the surrounding farmland. Black shutters frame the many windows and an expansive veranda extends the length of the building. Purple chrysanthemums and pink and red geraniums spill from earthenware pots. Fresh white wicker furniture invites "sittin' for a spell."

The veranda sets the Checkerberry mood: unpretentious and

leisurely. Whether you relax in the cozy pine-paneled library by a comforting fire or step through the French doors for a quiet evening stroll on the only professional croquet course in Indiana, tensions will evaporate.

Susie's training as an interior decorator affects all aspects of the inn. The furnishings are a combination of traditional and contemporary, but always balanced: French country to Amish; primitive with Chippendale. The accent colors are fresh. In some designer's hands the simplicity of the inn would be stark, but Susie has sculpted a relaxed and romantic ambience. In the guest rooms Amish hats hang above headboards, print pillows spice up cushy comforters, and sophisticated contemporary oil paintings offer a pleasantly contrasting stimulation to the senses.

This artistic flair for eclectic pairing appears again in the inn's continental breakfast buffet and gourmet dinners. The cheerful dining room, with its blue and white checkered table cloths and Tennessee hickory chairs, really doesn't prepare one for the not-so-simple food.

I had morning-glory muffins spread with strawberry butter at breakfast; the inn's famous tomato pie—fresh beefsteak tomatoes layered with cheeses, then baked in a tender French pastry crust, for lunch; and tender local duck breast sauteed, sliced, and served over pears, apples, and sweet onions, all drizzled with a tangy port wine sauce, for dinner.

I discovered that Susie is quite the croquet buff (she's organized a Hoosier team), so we played a bit one morning. "You know," she began, fixing me with her clear Indiana determination, "the shotmaking of billiards, the finesse of golf and the strategy of chess are all combined in this game."

Although I know I could have "sent" her with one skilled stroke and changed the game's outcome, I chose the diplomatic route and just aimed for the wickets.

THE CHECKERBERRY INN, 62644 CR 37, Goshen, IN 46526; 219-642-4445. A 12-guestroom (private baths) with a two bedroom, 2 bath suite country inn located in the heart of Amish America. Open February–December King and queen beds. Continental-plus breakfast included; lunch and dinner available. Hiking, croquet, swimming and tennis. Children accepted. No pets. Smoking restricted. Susan and John Graff, owners/hosts.

DIRECTIONS: From I-80–90, go south to Exit 107 on SR 13 to SR 4. Go west 1/2 mi. to CR 37, then south 1 mi. Inn is on the right.

Michigan

CHICAGO PIKE INN
Coldwater, Michigan

The red, white, and blue of four American flags hanging from massive columns snapped in the breeze as I climbed the wide front steps of the magnificent Chicago Pike Inn. Crossing the veranda, I entered the spacious reception room. Sturdy wooden beams framed the interior's soft yellow. Jane Schultz, co-owner with her husband Harold, told me this room was decorated in "dog theme." Noting the questioning look on my face, she pointed to the many objects depicting "man's best friend," right down to an overstuffed chair with dogs carved on the armrests and a pair of Stafforshire dog statuettes on the fireplace mantle.

Guiding me further into the room, she introduced me to her daughter Becky, who now manages the inn and worked alongside Jane in the renovation process.

"We tried to avoid the museum look by using colorful wallpapers and fabrics to brighten the dark wood paneling and antiques," Becky said. "Yet we didn't want to detract from the splendid wood work displayed throughout the house."

"And we wanted our guests to feel at home here," added Jane.

Designed and built in 1903, the elegant mansion served as the Clarke family home for years. Intricate gingerbread trim and Greek

Revival columns complimented the clean wood siding of the old structure. The Schultz family purchased the home in 1988, bringing along their tool kit to begin the renovation into an inn.

Leading the way to my room, Becky told me that the guest rooms are named with the Clarke family in mind. I stayed in the Hired Girls' Suite, one of six guest rooms, which has a sitting area decorated in black and white stripes and a brilliant red print sofa. The adjoining bedroom has red plaid window coverings with room-darkening shades beneath. A matching red floral comforter covers the white iron bed. An old-fashioned oak wash stand holds a red porcelain pitcher and basin. Braided rag rugs are scattered on the hardwood floor.

Descended the sweeping staircase to the dining room, I joined the other guests at a large walnut table surrounded by carved chairs with needlepoint cushions. The cherry wood paneling was reflected in the mirror of a built-in buffet. White and green wallpaper was softened by a rose trellis design on the beamed ceiling.

The breakfast specialty of the day included a delicious hot fruit soup followed by French toasted pound cake, dripping with cranberry syrup, and crisply fried bacon. Weekend breakfast buffets are more casual and can be enjoyed in the dining room or in the outdoor gazebo.

After breakfast I made the short drive into Allen, a nearby community known locally as the "antiques capital," spending the better part of the day strolling in and out of shops. Also nearby is the town of Marshall, which features historical sites, several lakes, and a chance to explore the surrounding Sipshewana Amish Country. Coldwater itself is a quaint village not yet flooded with tourists that offers quiet downtown walks and a popular summer theater.

Arriving back at the inn, I made my way to the cozy comfort of the library. This room has a light, airy feeling with white woodwork and bookshelves, offset by floral wallpaper in pink and mauve—something of a contrast to the dark woods used throughout the rest of the inn. The Victorian loveseat was a perfect reading spot. Later that afternoon, I enjoyed homemade scones and tea by the crackling fire.

CHICAGO PIKE INN, 215 E. Chicago St., Coldwater, MI 49036; 517-279-8744. Beautiful 6-guestroom (private baths) restored mansion in Historic District of Coldwater. Queen and twin beds. Open all year. Breakfast included. Bring own liquor. Quiet location with lakes, small villages, restaurants, and shops nearby. Restricted smoking. Leave pets at home. CCs: Visa, MC, AE. Jane and Harold Schultz, owners; Becky Schultz, host.

DIRECTIONS: I-69 to US-12 Coldwater Exit. Turn right, go through 2nd light. Inn on next NW corner.

HOTEL IROQUOIS
Mackinac Island, Michigan

Since Mackinac Island's city council banned motor vehicles in 1895, the same year Henry Ford produced his first car, there have been no automobile-produced gasoline fumes infusing the air. Instead, horse-drawn carriages provide pleasant, rhythmic transportation with a pollution quotient that I really don't mind.

And in the midst of this idyllic scene, the Hotel Iroquois offers hospitality and a gracious visit to a turn-of-the century island, Victorian style.

The inn is splashed with sunlight. Its Victorian cottage architecture makes the best use of sunporches and many, many windows. The airy common rooms, including the lobby, library, circle sunporch, and dining room/cocktail lounge, are filled with light. Fresh flowers and Victorian wicker emphasize the freshness of the floral wallpaper.

Mackinac has always been a haven for those who appreciate gracious homes, formal gardens, and elegant hotels. And the Hotel Iroquois offers all of the above.

This hotel is a sanctuary. According to Margaret McIntire, long-time owner of this lovely establishment, "The hotel is right down here on the lake and there are plenty of windows to catch the breeze." Margaret takes a very personal interest in the hotel; she loves her job—actually, her life.

"When we first bought the Iroquois in 1954, our goal was to turn this into a very choice hotel," Margaret told me. And her goal has been met. After thirty-six years in the hotel business, her vision certainly has been right on the mark.

While there are forty-seven guest rooms, the feeling is intimate.

High quality furnishings, Victorian patterned wallpaper, and cushy wall-to-wall carpets create a homey environment. Fresh spring colors of pink, green, yellow and blue make for a cheerful atmosphere. Private baths and fans are available in all the rooms. The lake-side rooms now have individual porches.

Margaret's daughter, Mary K., manages the hotel. An attorney who has chosen the more restful ("HA!" she laughed) existence as a hotel manager, Mary K. oversees, among other things, the inn's Carriage House restaurant.

"Our grilled seafood salad sandwich is just excellent," Mary K. told me as we reviewed the lunch menu. In my usual state of indecision about what to order (everything always sounds so good), her suggestion was both helpful and rewarding. Grilled crab, lobster and shrimp were married, making for a flavorful sandwich. Another choice which caught my eye was a hotel specialty: seasonal field greens, avocado, shrimp and smoked salmon. Lighter fare, like French onion soup au gratin and a lovely spinach salad dotted with feta cheese, are also available.

Dinner is excellent and includes appetizers like crab cakes with a mustard herb vinaigrette, or grilled Gulf shrimp laced with Iroquois barbeque sauce accompanied by pop-in-your-mouth tiny corn muffins. Entrees, such as roast prime rib, poached Norwegian salmon, or—an Iroquois tradition—fresh broiled whitefish, include salad and seasonal accompaniments. The homemade desserts change daily. I was lucky enough to visit when the Mackinac Island fudge ice cream puff was on the menu—gooey and luscious.

The hotel sponsors special events during the year. I was particularly interested in the annual stone skipping contest held on July 4th. I must brag a bit here; I was the stone skipping champion of my neighborhood for over four years. So next year on the 4th you may just want to visit Margaret and Mary K. at the Hotel Iroquois, and supply me with a rousing cheering section, because I've decided to take the challenge.

And even if you don't want to visit to cheer for me, you certainly should treat yourself the rejuvinating magic of this lovely place.

HOTEL IROQUOIS, 298 Main St., Box 456, Mackinac Island, MI 49757; 906-847-3321 or 906-847-6511. A 47-guestroom (private baths) sunny Victorian-styled Mackinac Island inn on the edge of Lake Michigan. All sized beds. Open mid-May to late October European plan. Bike, hike, enjoy nature. You can walk from town. No pets. Margaret McIntire, owner; Mary K. McIntire, manager.

DIRECTIONS: To reach Mackinaw City (and ferry service) take U.S. Hwy. 131 north to 31 north to I-75 from the west; take I-75 north to Mackinaw City from the east. Once you get off the ferry walk or take a horse and buggy. The hotel is just to the left.

MCCARTHY'S BEAR CREEK INN
Marshall, Michigan

This inn has so many sweet touches, it's hard to choose which ones to describe.

Perhaps the footbridge, crossing the tiny creek. Or maybe the look of its stone fences set crisply against the green lawns. Or the shaggy burr oaks, towering over the backyard barn. Or just the way it sits high on a hill, a gracious fourteen acres on the outskirts of town.

All of it was built in the 1940s by Robert Maes, a wealthy agricultural inventor. Michael and Beth McCarthy converted it to a country inn in 1985, adding plenty of choice details. Each of the guest rooms, for example, includes a reading lamp, chairs, and little radios inset with clocks. Many have delicate watercolors by local artist Maureen Reed, plus antiques and cherished family belongings that the McCarthys have collected throughout the years. Beth McCarthy has also thoughtfully set out colorful little sewing baskets for the guest with that loose button or drooping hem.

Breakfast, served on the porch, is displayed on a handsome Dutch cupboard of bird's-eye maple. It includes mason jars full of granola and cornflakes, pitchers of juice and milk, baskets of fruit, bowls of hard-boiled eggs, and plates of doughnuts, toast, or sweet breads and Michael's blueberry or raspberry muffins. Guests help themselves before sitting down to individual tables, overlooking the handsome grounds. On the morning of my visit, each table sported a bouquet of bright yellow flowers.

Downtown Marshall boasts a wealth of historic architecture. But the inn itself offers much to do, too. Inside, there are plenty of magazines and games. Outside, the grounds are perfect for a hike through the fields to the forest. Daughter Carey will show young visitors her rabbit in the barn; Tim will take them to see the ducks by the creek.

MCCARTHY'S BEAR CREEK INN, 15230 C Dr. North, Marshall, MI 49068; 616-781-8383. A 14-guestroom (private baths) country estate on 14 acres on the outskirts of town. Queen, double and twin beds. Lodgings include breakfast. Closed December 23, 24, and 25. Hiking, x-country skiing, sledding and picnics. One dog and two cats in residence. CCs: Visa, MC, AE. Mike and Beth McCarthy, owners/hosts.

DIRECTIONS: From I-69, take Exit 36 to Marshall. After you exit, turn west onto Michigan Ave. Almost immediately, turn left onto 15-Mile Rd., and then, almost immediately, right onto C Dr. North. The inn will be on your left.

MONTAGUE INN
Saginaw, Michigan

Secret panels and passageways behind the library walls? What does it all mean? I think it means that this grand Georgian mansion was built in the middle of Prohibition (1929) and the owners may have had some things they wanted to hide. Otherwise, the Montagues were pillars of the community—manufacturers of soaps and hand creams, subsequently bought by the Jergens Company.

Today, innkeeper Meg Brodie-Ideker stores their bottles of homemade herb vinegars in the secret closet, and guests sip their before-din-

ner aperitifs or wine in the book-lined library, without ever guessing what lies behind the white paneled walls.

This had been just another mouldering mansion in the once-opulent Grove area of Saginaw when Norman Kinney and his partners found it in 1985. Norman Kinney has become something of a celebrity in the field of inn restorations, and his expertise is in great demand. The National House in nearby Marshall and now the Montague Inn are prime examples of his talent.

As Norman points out, he and his wife, Kathryn, had a lot of help from the four other couples who pooled their resources and pitched in to bring this beautiful home back to vibrant and elegant life. It is now listed on the National Register of Historic Places.

Driving through busy, industrial Saginaw, I marveled at the green oasis, known as the Grove, on the east side of the city, where grand old mansions and the many huge trees reminded me that lumber barons had once prospered and lived here.

I turned off the wide boulevard and drove through the parklike grounds of the Montague Inn around to the back parking area. Meg, who was cutting flowers, greeted me with a welcoming wave and a bright, charming smile. "Do I see the glint of water over there?" I called, gesturing toward a line of trees at the edge of the lawn. "That's Lake Linton," she replied, coming over to me, her arms loaded with colorful tulips and daffodils. "Across the water is Ojibway Island—it's a wonderful spot for picnics, and the Saginaw River is just beyond that."

Meg went on to tell me, "Kathryn has a wonderful herb garden over on the side of the house. She has all of the usual herbs as well as lovage, bergamot, lemon balm, scented geraniums, baby's breath, and many edible flowers. We use them in our salad dressings, soups, and sauces, and our chef likes to dress his dishes with the edible flowers."

I knew the inn had established a reputation for gourmet dining, and my dinner that evening convinced me it was well deserved. My smoked salmon appetizer, served with fresh fruit puree and bleu cheese, was delightfully different and the medallions of tenderloin were perfectly grilled and seasoned. The black-and-white-uniformed waitresses served dinner with smooth, cheerful efficiency. The dining room was most inviting, the tables set with sparkling crystal and silver and fresh flowers, the large bay window looking out across the lawns to the lake.

This is a very gracious house, with several bay windows, fireplaces, white paneled walls, and a beautiful cantilevered, curved staircase rising above the circular foyer. Furnished in fine mahogany antiques, Oriental rugs, and original paintings, the atmosphere is one of elegance and comfort. Most of the guest rooms are spacious, and all are attractively decorated. The original tile bathrooms have unique art deco fixtures.

The architecture, atmosphere, decor, and service remind me of the country house hotels of Great Britain.

MONTAGUE INN, 1581 So. Washington Ave., Saginaw, MI 48601; 517-752-3939. An 18-guestroom (2 with shared bath) Georgian manor inn on 8 acres in a parklike setting in the Grove area of the city. All size beds. European plan. Complimentary continental breakfast. Open year-round. Wheelchair access. Picnic lunches, Lake Linton, special events on grounds. Ojibway Island, Japanese Garden and Teahouse, children's zoo, Hoyt Park with skating rink, boat races, and fishing in Saginaw River nearby. Meg Brodie-Ideker, innkeeper.

DIRECTIONS: From I-75, take Holland Ave. (Rte. 46), bearing right onto Remington Ave. Turn left at Washington Ave. and continue to inn.

THE PEBBLE HOUSE
Lakeside, Michigan

The Arts and Crafts Movement of the early 1900s influenced architecture, furnishings, fabric, pottery, jewelry, book design, and fine art. It rejected Victorian excess, poor quality, and the lack of individuality that were the result of industrial production. Craft was elevated to art.

The unique Pebble House is characterized by the best of this movement, as well it should. Innkeepers Jean and Ed Lawrence are both authorities in the field: Jean is an artist and teaches a course on the Movement at Indiana University, and Ed is compiling a directory of

inns, resorts, and hotels which reflect the Arts and Crafts influence.

The Lawrences rescued the 1912 Craftsman-style home in 1983. It had become run down when the once-popular vacation area around Lake Michigan was virtually deserted after World War II. Its close proximity to Chicago (an hour and a half by car) makes it a perfect escape from the city.

The home sits on one-plus acres just across the road from the lake. With its exterior of pebbles, decorative block, and wood, it blends perfectly with its wooded surroundings. Wooden walkways connect the main house to two other buildings, the tennis court, the skylighted summer house (complete with hammocks), and spacious decks.

The decorative features of the inn, including lamps, pottery, and rugs, are true to the Arts and Crafts Movement, creating a unity of design. Mission oak furniture graces all the spacious common areas and four of the guest rooms. Whether you sit in front of the glassed-in porch's fireplace on a rainy day, or read by the library's freestanding fireplace, you'll always find comfortable chairs and couches at the ready. Games and puzzles are also available for entertainment.

The other three guest rooms are Victorian in style with soft pastel color themes. All seven guest rooms have private baths, air conditioning, and private decks overlooking the yard or the lake.

A resplendent Scandinavian-style buffet is served at breakfast. You can sit with other guests at the large dining room table, or wander out to the deck tables for more privacy.

Since Jean considers the Pebble House an extension of her art, she is quite happy to talk about the philosophy and design features that influenced its creation. She and Ed are also very knowledgeable about galleries and shops in the area.

THE PEBBLE HOUSE, 15093 Lakeshore Rd., Lakeside, MI 49116; 616-469-1416. A 7-guestroom (private baths) unique Art and Crafts style inn beside Lake Michigan. King, queen, and double beds. Scandinavian buffet. Open all year. Ninety min. to Chicago. No pets; two cats in residence; smoking restricted. CCs: Visa, MC. Jean and Ed Lawrence, owner/hosts.

DIRECTIONS: From Exit 6 of I-94 to stop sign. Left at sign for 1-1/2 mi. through Lakeside to Lakeshore Rd. Turn left .6 mi.

STAFFORD'S BAY VIEW INN
Petoskey, Michigan

It was on April Fool's day in 1961 that Stafford and Janice Smith purchased the Bay View Inn. At that time, the inn was 75 years old. The Smiths were newlyweds in their early 20s.

The Bay View Association was founded during the Civil War years by the Methodist Church as a chautauqua program offering enrichment programs in drama, music, and art, lectures, and religious services. The inn was built in 1886 to serve those who had booked passage on railroads or lake steamer boats to reach the remote area of Petoskey. During Michigan's lumbering era at the turn of the century, the chautauqua tents were replaced with Victorian "gingerbread" cottages which have collectively survived to become a National Historic Landmark on the National Register of Historic Places.

Stafford lovingly restored the crumbling relic into a Victorian with style. After building a solid foundation, eliminating half the guest rooms to accommodate private baths, and installing insulation, he had Judy Honor design and refinish the interior of the inn using the old chairs, dressers and beds found in the storage barn. The only 'old' that remains are the outside walls, and some nooks and crannies.

No two rooms are alike. Each is wallpapered in exciting Clarence House prints with a Victorian flair and bright, bright flowers. The Staffords have even created a third floor mini-lobby for guests to gather in. All is very cozy and comfortable.

Janice's favorite room, which Judy calls Grandmother's Room because it is blue with pink rosebuds, is located in the tower and incorporates the room she lived in when she was a hostess a the inn and first met Stafford. That part is a lovely sitting room that overlooks the bay, and even the old dresser that Janice used has been refinished and fits right into the decor.

The food is delicious made from fresh, regionally produced poultry, meats and vegetables. The inn's own pastry chef creates wonderful breads and sweets, and the soups are made daily from scratch.

The floors still creak, Little Traverse Bay still serves a a stunning backdrop, and Stafford and Janice still preside here, though now with the help of their three grown children.

STAFFORD'S BAY VIEW INN, Box 3, Petoskey, MI 49770; 616-347-2771, 800-456-1917. A 30-guestroom (private baths) resort-inn on Little Traverse Bay in the Bay View section of Petoskey. Full breakfast complimentary. All size beds. Breakfast, lunch, and dinner served daily to travelers. Open daily May 6 to November 1; Thanksgiving weekend; December 26 to March 24. Wheelchair access. Lake swimming and xc skiing on grounds. Historical Festival events, 3rd weekend in June. Bay View cultural programs in July and August Golfing, boating, tennis, fishing, hiking, alpine ski trails, scenic and historic drives, and excellent shopping nearby. Stafford and Janice Smith and Judy Honor, owners-hosts.

DIRECTIONS: From Detroit, take Gaylord exit from I-75 and follow Mich. Rte. 32 to Rte. 131 north to Petoskey. From Chicago, use Rte. 131 north to Petoskey.

Minnesota

MRS. B'S HISTORIC LANESBORO INN
Lanesboro, Minnesota

Minnesota's farm country is poetically pastoral. Lush alfalfa fields are checkerboarded by black and white Holsteins and russet and white Guernseys. In this pristine environment Norman Rockwell's visions become animated.

Travel to Lanesboro via Highway 52 through Minneapolis and Rochester, then left onto Country Road 8 at Fountain. By taking this route you will have the pleasure of "discovering" Lanesboro. The view is fantastic.

Lanesboro village is Americana surrounded by hardwood forests and high bluffs: the middle fork of the Root River even meanders through the center of town. Nineteenth century buildings nod to each other across wide, tree lined streets. You can be lazy here. And for all its old town flavor, the locals here are warm and friendly.

Inside the inn, stenciled borders lead the eye down the hall to the ten guest rooms where simple comforts await: good beds, big towels, complimentary sherry, comfortable chairs with reading lamps, and an excellent selection of books. Natural fibers, like muslin, traditional colors, and pine antiques set off the character of each room. Touches of eyelet add a kiss of romance. All rooms have access to a balcony and private baths.

The living room offers cozy seating and a fireplace flanked by over-flowing bookcases. In pleasant weather, conversation and afternoon tea move out to the open wooden decks and stone patio which have been well integrated with the native limestone of the building's exterior.

Local fresh ingredients, including fruits and cheeses, are used in the delicious breakfasts that are served in the cheerful breakfast room. My favorite morning meal was oatmeal buttermilk pancakes with blueber-ries served with warm syrup and a large slab of lean cottage bacon. Owner Bill Sermeus does the cooking. While breakfast is reserved for guests only, you may be joined by other vacationers, or even local townfolk, for Mrs. B's dinners. Lunch or dinner is offered Wednesday through Sunday by reservation. A colorful hand-decorated menu is posted each day.

A typical meal may begin with an appetizer of marinated cod and tender vegetables with linguini in a unique orange and anise sauce. A salad of mushroom custard, served warm, on crisp lettuce dressed with blackberry mayonaise and garnished with wild hickory nuts and scal-lion is next, followed by a main course of turkey breast layered with garlic sausage, pistachios, and a vegetable ragu. I passed up the calories of the inviting desserts to enjoy "Mrs. B's Bedtime Bump," a heady concoction of milk, eggs, brandy, chocolate, and some very secret ingredients that would relax even the most stress-ridden soul. Cock-tails, beer, and wines, including local vintages, are also available.

For a bit of exercise Bill can suggest country hikes for all skill lev-els. Or wander next door to Landesboro's history museum. I spent an hour there just reading early settlers' letters. Oh, and be sure to buy a bag of popcorn from the celebrated Norwegian popcorn machine.

MRS. B'S HISTORIC LANESBORO INN, 101 Parkway, Lanesboro, MN 55949; 507-467-2154. A 10-guestroom (private baths) comfortable country-style inn. King, queen, and twin beds. Full breakfast; dinner by reservation Wednesday–Sunday. Open all year. Walk everywhere. Skiing, canoeing, hiking. No pets. Bill Sermeus and Mimi Abell, Owners-hosts;
   DIRECTIONS: Contact inn. Most routes are scenic.

SCHUMACHER'S NEW PRAGUE HOTEL
New Prague, Minnesota

It's not what you might expect to find in a small town in the rich prairie farmland of Minnesota. Forty-five miles from downtown Min-neapolis/St. Paul, this is a well-recognized country inn located in the Czech-American farm coummunity of New Prague, a dazzling oasis of European grand hospitality in a gracious mid-american setting.

John Schumacher, a graduate of culinary school, purchased an old hotel on the main street in 1974. The Hotel Broz had been built in 1898, designed by Cass Gilbert, the architect who later designed the Minnesota State Capitol and the Library of Congress in Washington, DC. John soon transformed its rooms with hand-painted furniture by the Bavarian folk artist Pipka, and with imported Bavarian pine wainscotting, hand-carved chairs and European chandeliers. A delightful Central European hunter's style pub was added and the eleven guest rooms, each named after a month of the year, became luxurious settings for a night's repose in old Europe.

John's wife Kathleen operates quite an extensive gift shop that offers Central European glassware, furniture, lampshades, and dolls from the Menzel workshop in Bavaria. Poland, Hungary, Rumania and Russia are also represented in the many unusual gift items.

The dining room features the original recipes of Chef John as well as authentic cuisines of Central Europe. Game dishes and veal specialties, homemade desserts and baked goods are plentiful. Kathleen is a registered dietitian and has initiated a popular "Healthy Heart" low-fat, low-cholesterol section of the menu.

The town of New Prague offers a walking tour with painted building murals depicting the town's history.

SCHUMACHER'S NEW PRAGUE HOTEL, 212 West Main St., New Prague, MN 56071; 612-758-2133. (Metro line: 612-445-7285.) An 11-guestroom (private baths) Czechoslovakian-German inn located in a small country town, approx. 45 mi. south of Minneapolis and St. Paul. King, queen, and double beds. European plan. Breakfast, lunch, and dinner served to travelers all year except 2 days at Christmas. Wheelchair access to restaurant. Good bicycling and backroading nearby; also xc skiing, tennis, and golf. No pets. John & Kathleen Schumacher, owners/hosts.

DIRECTIONS: From Minneapolis, take Rte. 494 west to Cedar Avenue South (77S). Exit onto 35E South. Take exit 69 onto Hwy. 19. Follow Hwy. 19 west into New Prague. From Minneapolis/St. Paul's western suburbs: take 169 South. Exit at Hwy. 19. Follow to the east to New Prague.

Missouri

WALNUT STREET INN
Springfield, Missouri

Passing through the beveled-glass front door of the Walnut Street Inn, my footsteps echoed upon richly finished hardwood floors. Gold-framed photos along the warm pastel walls spoke a visual tale of history. Gazing upon them, I felt the years roll away, propelling me back in time.

This building, the shining star of Springfield's Historic District was purchased in 1987 by Karol Brown, along with her parents Gary and Nancy. It was a full year before renovation was complete, with six guest rooms and the convenience of a common room on each floor.

I was staying in the Rosen Room. Lavishly draped in burgundy paisley prints underscored with delicate white lace, the room is frequently used by honeymooners. It has a high four-poster bed and a forest green chaise, with colorful pillows tucked in its corners. The antique bureau displays brown-tinged snapshots of Karol's great-grandfather atop a lace doily. A delicate spring bouquet is reflected in the heavy, gold-framed mirror above. The connecting bath is furnished with original porcelain fixtures. A unique touch is the complete supply of thick Turkish bathrobes and towels.

Later that afternoon, I visited the Jewell Room for some wine and cheese. Rays of afternoon sunlight were filtering through the delicate leaded glass windows, expanding on the softness of the pale peach walls trimmed with a pattern of teal and gold. I was fascinated with the intricate design of the rosewood piano. Observing my curiosity, a more knowledgeable guest told me it was from an era prior to the Civil War.

Sipping my wine, I wandered up the stairs to the slightly less formal Gathering Room. Two guest were engaged in friendly competition at the game table. Selecting a paperback, I settled into a comfortable chair before the glowing warmth of the fire to read a bit.

Next morning, ringing chimes called me to breakfast after a fitful night's sleep. I had my first taste of Ozark Mountain black walnut bread and persimmon muffins, both house specialties. For more hearty diners, there was a heaping platter of smoked ham and bacon. Karol joined me and, over a cup of coffee, offered information about the inn.

Sturdily supported by twenty-one hand-painted Corinthian columns, the Queen Anne Victorian has been standing for nearly 100 years. Light-colored gingerbread trims the wide veranda and gables above. Although situated within the peacefulness of the Historic District, the inn is within easy walking distance of activities, shops, and restaurants. The Southwest Missouri State University Art Exhibition Center exhibits many local talents. The inn offers a performance package to the restored Landers Theater. Also nearby are the Sports Center and Art Museum.

As Karol said to me upon my departure, "We purchased this house because it was large enough to be gracious, but small enough for guests to feel intimate and peaceful."

———————————

WALNUT STREET INN, 900 E. Walnut, Springfield, MO.65806; 417-864-6346. Queen Anne Victorian B&B with 6 guestrooms (private baths). Weekday continental breakfast, weekend full breakfast. Queen and double beds. Wine, tea and cheese in afternoons. Open all year. Limited facilities for children. Smoking outdoors only. Located in Historic District. Shopping, restaurants, and activities within walking distance. No pets. CCs: Visa, MC, AE. Gary, Nancy, and Karol Brown, owners/hosts; Karol Brown, manager.

DIRECTIONS: I-44 to 65 Bypass. Exit on Chestnut Expressway. Left on Sherman Parkway to Walnut.

Ohio

THE INN AT HONEY RUN
Millersburg, Ohio

Partially hidden in its woodsy setting, the Inn at Honey Run blends into the forest of maples, ash, oak, poplar, black walnut, butternut, and hickory. A six acre orchard is planted with 450 trees—14 varieties of apples, peaches, nectarines, cherries, and plums. Many of those woods, as well as other native materials, can be found throughout the inn. The spectacular free-standing fireplace in the living room is of native matched-vein sandstone. The many colorful quilts on the beds and the walls are made by local craftspeople.

Marge Stock's dream was to create an inn that was nearly indiscernable from the forest and fields that surround it. Floor-to-ceiling windows, outside decks that literally thrust themselves into the forest, bird feeders everywhere, all enhance the enjoyment of nature.

Although the architecture may be very contemporary and dramatic, the hospitality is old-fashioned and personal. Marge has a great staff of cheerful, friendly people who really make their guests feel at home.

Marge sent me up the hill to see her latest pet project, an earth-sheltered building with twelve new guest rooms. At first I thought they looked like great rock-rimmed cups or pockets tilted into the hill. Then I could see why Marge called them "Honeycombs"—they did bear a resemblance to a honeycomb, albeit one of giant and rock-ribbed proportions. As I came up the curving drive and gazed across the wildflower-strewn field, I marveled at how imperceptibly these new structures were tucked into the hill, and this was before the azaleas, junipers, heather, cotoneaster, and other shrubbery had grown to further camouflage them.

I'd made the trip out to Ohio specifically to see Marge's new project. "An earth shelter has so many practical advantages," she told me. "In addition, it has a feeling of great serenity and peace." This is, to my knowledge, the first earth-sheltered building with public accommodations in the country.

As I walked toward the huge square concrete arch that burrowed into the hill, I wondered if it would feel like a cave inside, but when I stepped into the entry hall, I had an instant feeling of space and light. The ceiling soared thirty feet to a skylight, and a spacious, carpeted staircase wound around to the second floor.

As with the main inn, the feeling is very contemporary. In each guest room, a massive fireplace wall of native Ohio sandstone rock has a cut-out section for a built-in cabinet, which hides a remote-control TV. Every conceivable modern convenience is provided in these rooms.

Beyond the sliding glass doors of each room is a private patio where you can almost reach out and touch the vivid wildflowers. Off in the distance are rolling forested hills, interspersed with patches of green cultivated fields. I watched from my patio as a beautiful sunrise spread its rosy fingers through the trees, as my neighbors could have done since all the rooms face east. It's a perfect place for quiet contemplation and feeling close to nature.

Meals are made from scratch, with such things as pan-fried trout from Holmes County waters, steak, baked ham, and roast loin of pork, which as Marge says, "comes with fresh applesauce."

Marge is a very special person. After spending several hours solving the world's problems and listening to her dreams, many of which have come true, I felt honored to have been in her presence and sad that my departure came so soon.

THE INN AT HONEY RUN, 6920 Country Road 203, Millerburg, OH 44654; 216-674-0011. A 37-guestroom (private baths) country inn located in north-central Ohio's beautiful, wooded countryside. King, queen, and twin beds available. Continental breakfast included in room rate. Lunch and dinner served Monday–Saturday by advance reservation only. Sunday breakfast and eve. buffet served to house guests only. Closed January 1–15. Wheelchair access. Ample opportunities for recreation and backroading in Ohio's Amish country. No pets. CCs: Visa, MC, AE. Marjorie Stock, owner-host.

DIRECTIONS: From Millersburg, proceed on E. Jackson St. (Rtes. 39 and 62) past courthouse and gas station on right. At next corner turn left onto Rte. 241. At 1 mi. the road goes downhill. At 1-3/4 mi. it crosses the bridge over Honey Run; turn right immediately around the small hill onto Rte. 203 (not well marked). After about 1-1/2 mi. turn right at inn sign. (Watch out for the Amish horse-drawn buggies.)

MURPHIN RIDGE INN

West Union, Ohio

I've always loved the word "sassafras." It conjures up old fashioned pleasures like the slow, back-and-forth of a front porch swing, the sun-scent of freshly ironed pillow cases, and that first glorious spoonful of homemade peach ice cream. But it wasn't until I spent a weekend at the Murphin Ridge Inn that I got my first chance to actually see a real sassafras tree.

Surrounded by towering oaks and sassafras, the original 1810 brick farmhouse, which serves as the inn's dining house, presides over 640 acres of woods and farmland. Only an hour west of Cincinnati, this quiet haven not only offers serenity and comfort, but fabulous French and regional cuisine.

"Actually, this is my third career," innkeeper, Bob Crosset told me as we walked down a tidy path past a log corn crib and smokehouse on our way to the ten-room guest house. "I'd always had a dream of opening a country inn," he continued, "and it finally became true when I took an early retirement."

Bob and his wife, Mary, served the Cincinnati areas as educators for over 20 years before opening Murphin Ridge Inn. They see their new careers as just another way to serve people.

"We saw the inn as a chance to bring business to an isolated and financially depressed area," Mary confided to me. "The neighbors were pretty skeptical." But the Crosset's had done their homework and the inn's success has turned the skeptics into supportive friends.

Taking one step at a time, they first opened the farmhouse for dining early in 1990. Chef Lori Bulk, a graduate of the Culinary Institute of America, focuses on what she calls "folk cuisine," borrowing from the local Amish heritage with smatterings of Swiss and Southern-style dishes included.

The dining rooms are rustic and simply furnished with polished tables and plank chairs. I sat in the Jane Harsha dining room (all dining rooms are named for former owners or their descendants). I was dipping a thick slice of Amish bread into my coffee when Bob handed me the lunch and dinner menu.

"Everything's great," he said, "but I'll suggest some of my favorites."

What choices! My taste buds were ready. I decided on the Murphin Ridge Meat Loaf, a hearty mixture of pork, beef, onion and spices, served with a special orange tomato mayonnaise for my next lunch. Dinner, served with warm muffins, homemade soup, salad, juicy little dumplings and fresh vegetables, was a mushroom-laced Blue Creek Rib Eye Steak, with a warm blue cheese sauce on the side. Heavenly flavors!!

Four months after the restaurant opened, the new, modern guest house was completed. Mary and Bill had realized their dream. When building, they used materials compatible with the custom-designed, Shaker-inspired furniture of David T. Smith. Each room is unique. Two have fireplaces and some have porches with views of the woodlands and fields. All have private baths.

The inn's high-ceilinged great room offers magazines, a game table, and, should you desire, a large screen television. The surrounding area is fun to explore with Amish shops, a harness maker, bakeries, shoemaker, greenhouse, and general store. Visits to the Cincinnati Museum of Natural History's Edge of Appalachia Preserve and the pre-historic Serpent Mount, built by the Adena Indians, are musts-to-see. There are wonderful hiking trails through dense forests for the energetic. Ask ahead and the inn's kitchen will pack up a sumptuous picnic for taking along.

After an invigorating set of singles on the inn's tennis court, I sat sipping iced tea. Bob busily clipping the grass around the wishing well. Leaning back in my chair, looking through the leaves of the sassafras, I was transported back to that old porch swing and could almost taste a spoonful of homemade peach ice cream lingering on my tongue.

MURPHIN RIDGE INN, 750 Murphin Ridge Rd., West Union, OH 45693; 513-544-2263. A ten room retreat on the edge of Appalachia. Queen beds, some fireplaces, and porches. Private baths. Full breakfast included. Lunches and dinners offered Wednesday–Saturday Light & hearty fare offered Sundays 11:30–4:00. Some non-smoking areas & rooms. Closed during January, and on Mondays & Tuesdays each week. Pool, tennis & volleyball courts, hiking trails and golf course all close by. View Amish crafts or visit the wineries and vineyards. Bob and Mary Crosset, owners/hosts.

DIRECTIONS: Two mis. west of Rte.41 at Dunkinsville. One hour east of Cincinnati, off Rte. 32.

THE WHITE OAK INN

Danville, Ohio

I think wood is the big story here at the White Oak Inn. It begins when you drive up the two-lane scenic route and you first see the inn's sign on the great white oak from which the inn takes its name. This was originally a working farm of several hundred acres. In 1915, George Crise set up a temporary sawmill on the land and, taking trees from the surrounding woods, fashioned the timbers that went into the three-story, gambrel-roofed house. As Jim Acton says, "He was a real craftsman." All of the doors, moldings, and cabinetry throughout the house are testimony to his craftsmanship. The guest rooms are named for the woods with which they are furnished—oak, poplar, ash, maple, walnut and cherry.

When James and Joyce Acton were looking for an inn, they took a drive through the hills and down into the oil-drilling and farming community near Danville, across from the Kokosing River. "The moment we saw the house," Joyce exclaimed, "we knew this was it, it was so big and so nice."

A bearded Jim Acton greeted me as I drove up and pointed out some of the grand old trees on the property. Two friendly Labradors—Lady Chardonnay, or Charlie, and Captain—frolicked around us. Joyce and Jim are one of those couples who dropped out of corporate life to take up innkeeping, and they seem to have taken to it with great gusto. They are very friendly, hospitable people and make their guests at home, introducing them by name over the complimentary wine and cheese offered in the afternoon.

The strains of a Beethoven quartet greeted me as I walked through the beveled-glass front door, and Joyce mentioned that they are lucky to receive the Ohio State University FM station, with fine musical offerings. The living room is a very comfortable, pleasant room with sofas, rocking chairs, a nice brick fireplace, paintings, flowers, and a small game table.

Meals are served at common tables in the Inn's dining room. Dinner is prix fixe with entrées such as beef Wellington, turkey Gallantine with currant wine sauce, or cider-braised pork loin. Joyce serves a hearty breakfast of French toast (made from her own homemade bread) with sausage, and there are fresh fruit and freshly baked pastries.

A candlelight dinner can be arranged in front of the fire in the White Oak guest room for an intimate tête-à-tête or a special occasion.

The guest room doors have grapevine wreaths with plaid bows, and the rooms are decorated with fresh flowers, starchy ruffled curtains, and high, firm beds with hand-sewn quilts, some made by the Amish and others bought from antiques dealers.

Jim mentioned that the inn's special weekends—such as the Country Inn Cookery Weekend, the Naturalist Weekend, and the Wine Tastings weekend—have become very popular.

This is a homey kind of place where you can pull up a chair in the kitchen and have a good old-fashioned chat with Joyce, or you can just sit on one of the oak swings or rockers on the spacious front porch and smell the fragrant viburnum.

THE WHITE OAK INN, 29683 Walhonding Rd., Danville, OH 43014; 614-599-6107. A 10-guestroom (private baths) 1915 farmhouse-inn and a 3 room guest house on 16 acres of farmland and woods in the scenic Kokosing River valley, 15 mi. east of Mt. Vernon in north central Ohio. Queen and double beds. Three rooms have fireplaces. Complimentary breakfast; dinner served to house guests by 2-day advance reservation. Closed Thanksgiving and Christmas. Board games, 2 porch swings, antique rockers, nature walks, bird-watching on grounds. Inquire about the special weekends. Roscoe Village, a restored canal town, 25 mi., largest Amish population in U.S., 30 mi. No smoking. CCs: Visa, MC. Joyce and Jim Acton, owners/hosts.

DIRECTIONS: From I-71 take U.S. Rte. 36, or S.R. 13 to Mt. Vernon, then 11 mi. to S.R. 715; from I 77 take U.S. Rte. 36 to S.R. 715. The Inn is located on the north side of S.R. 715 3 miles from the west end of S.R. 715 or 9 miles from the east end of S.R. 715.

Wisconsin

OLD RITTENHOUSE INN
Bayfield, Wisconsin

"Jerry was still working on his music degree at the University of Wisconsin, and I had just gotten a teaching job. We came to Bayfield on our honeymoon in 1969, and as soon as we saw this lovely old house we fell in love with it."

The Old Rittenhouse Inn is a Queen Anne-style mansion with an unusually wide veranda, decorated with hanging flowers and wicker furniture.

The Phillipses then bought and restored the Mansion (now called Le Château Boutin). A third house, called Grey Oak, is also a part of the Old Rittenhouse Inn.

These two musician-innkeepers have refused from the very start to accept the idea that Bayfield was simply a summertime resort area. They began by staging Christmas and Valentine's Day dinner concerts at the inn, and these developed into many more activities. The success of their programs made it necessary to expand, and so today the original five guest rooms have been augmented by another seventeen, and Mary finally has a full and proper kitchen.

Antiques being one of Jerry's sidelines, each of the guest rooms has been handsomely outfitted with antique furniture, and all but one of them have their own fireplace.

It may be that Jerry and Mary are best known for their dinners. Jerry, resplendent in a Victorian tailcoat, describes the menu to his dinner guests, and it is also given in detail by the waitress later on. The fixed-price dinners start with several soups and a variety of entrées, including Lake Superior trout cooked in champagne, lamb, seafood crêpes, scallops, or chicken Cordon Bleu. The breads and preserves are all homemade. Their gourmet foods are also on sale at the inn and through a mail-order business that includes jams, jellies, marmalades, candies, fruit cakes, and many other delicious gifts.

The Phillipses have prepared a splendid new brochure entitled "The Old Rittenhouse Inn: An Innside Outlook." My copy lists every special event, seminar, festival, workshop, concert, and island adventure that can be enjoyed in Bayfield or on nearby Madeline Island throughout the year. Just to give you a quick idea, there's the Blossom Festival in June, the Christmas Dinner Concerts in December, ski touring under the auspices of the Audubon Society, and summer-day sails galore. The brochure continues with two cooking workshops, Valentine Sweetheart specials, two Murder-at-the-Mansion Mystery Weekends, a Bed and Breakfast Workshop in February, and, of course, the famous Apple Festival in October. The Phillipses will be glad to send you your copy.

It has certainly been a pleasure for me to visit and revisit the Old Rittenhouse Inn and enjoy good fun, good eating, and wonderful hospitality.

OLD RITTENHOUSE INN, Box 584, 301 Rittenhouse Ave., Bayfield, WI 54814; 715-779-5765. A 21-guestroom (private baths) and fireplaces Victorian inn in an area of historic and natural beauty, 80 mi. east of Duluth, Minn., on the shore of Lake Superior. King, queen, and double beds. European plan. Breakfast, lunch, and dinner served to travelers. Open May to November; weekends through the winter. Advance reservations most desirable. Extensive recreational activity of all kinds available throughout the year, including tours, hiking, and cycling on the nearby Apostle and Madeline Islands. No pets. CCs: Visa, MC. Jerry and Mary Phillips, owners/hosts.

DIRECTIONS: From the Duluth Airport, follow Rte. 53-S through the city of Duluth over the bridge to Superior, Wis. Turn east on Rte. 2 near Ashland (1-1/2 hrs.), turn north on 13-N to Bayfield.

THE WHITE GULL INN

Fish Creek, Wisconsin

By the time you reach the front door of the White Gull Inn on Wisconsin's famous Door Peninsula, you have long left behind the more familiar rolling Wisconsin landscape. As highway 42 winds its way northward up the rugged Peninsula or "thumb" of the state, dairy farms and corn fields are gradually replaced by apple and cherry orchards, interspersed with cedar forests and tiny bayside villages.

Eventually, the highway dips and curves down a rocky bluff and delivers you into the coastal town of Fish Creek, where, at the end of Main street sits the White Gull Inn, looking much like it did nearly a century ago. The inn and the little village of barely 100 occupants retain much of their turn-of-the-century flavor. Innkeepers Andy and Jan Coulson have presided over the White Gull since 1972, and have lovingly maintained, redecorated and improved the main lodge (a white clapboard three-story building with an air of informality) and surrounding cottages. Many of the antiques decorating the freshly-painted and wallpapered rooms date from the original owner. Comfort, however, is definitely up-to-date, with firm mattresses, air-conditioning, modern plumbing and little touches that make a guest feel right at home.

The White Gull has long been famous for its Door County fish boil, where guests stand around a blazing wood fire built behind the inn, watching their dinner of freshly caught Lake Michigan whitefish cooked before their eyes. The traditional meal, originated by Scandinavian settlers of the peninsula, is served with boiled potatoes, melted butter, fresh coleslaw, Swedish limpa bread, and Door County cherry pie for dessert. Materboiler Russ Ostrand, who has been at the inn for almost 30 years, entertains the dining guests with his old-fashioned button accordion. In recent years, the inn has become equally well-known for its quiet candlelight dinners, served on the nights when there is no fish boil, and for the bountiful breakfasts and hearty lunches, equally poplular with vacationers and the locals.

The Colulsons became the proud owners of another magnificent property in 1985, which has now been restored and renamed the Whistling Swan. Located one block from the White Gull, the Whistling Swan has seven bedrooms and suites.

There are back roads to explore and islands and lighthouses to visit. Antique stores and galleries featuring the many local artists can be found around every bend. Within a few minutes of the inns are numerous recreatonal activities, from cross-country skiing to wind surfing, from hiking to charter fishing. Fish Creek is also a center for the performing arts, and is the home of the Peninsula Players, America's oldest professional summer stock theatre, and the Peninsula Music Festival, now performing in a recently completed auditorium.

THE WHITE GULL INN, Fish Creek, WI 54212; 414-868-3517. A 13-guestroom inn with 5 cottages (14 private baths) and additional guestrooms in the Whistling Swan in a most scenic area in Door County, 23 mi. north of Sturgeon Bay. Queen, double, and twin beds. (Bookings for the Whistling Swan: P.O. Box 193; 414-868-3442.) Open year-round. European plan. Breakfast, lunch, and dinner except Thanksgiving and Christmas. Fish Boils: Wednesday, Friday, Saturday, Sunday nights May–October; Wednesday and Saturday nights November–April. All meals open to travelers; reservations requested. Wheelchair access to restaurant. Considerable outdoor and cultural attractions; golf, tennis, swimming, fishing, biking, sailing, xc skiing, and other summer and winter sports nearby. Excellent for children of all ages. No pets. CCs: Visa, MC, AE. Andy and Jan Coulson, owners/hosts.

DIRECTIONS: From Chicago: take I-94 to Milwaukee. Follow Rte. I-43 from Milwaukee to Manitowoc; Rte. 42 from Manitowoc to Fish Creek. Turn left at stop sign at the bottom of the hill, go 2-1/2 blocks to inn. From Green Bay; take Rte. 57 to Sturgeon Bay; Rte. 42 to Fish Creek.

WHITE LACE INN
Sturgeon Bay, Wisconsin

The first time I visited Dennis and Bonnie Statz at the White Lace Inn they were nowhere to be found. I quickly determined that they were

out walking the precincts to make sure the city would not increase the
occupancy tax. The powers that be wanted more money in the city
coffers. But they hadn't considered the energy of this bright and lovely
couple.

The next day, after celebrating their hard-earned victory, Dennis
was working on the Garden House in the rear of the Main House, and
we had a long talk about his garden area.

The Garden House has fireplaces in the six guest rooms, and living
up to its name, there are flowers everywhere.

So now, with the Garden House and another more recent addition,
the luxurious Washburn House, the White Lace Inn offers fifteen guest
rooms in three historic Victorian houses. Each room has period wall-
coverings, floral print fabrics in roses, peaches, and earth tones, polished hardwood floors, and many antiques. There are thick towels,
good linens, warm comforters, extra pillows, good lighting, and many
other things I like to find in country inns. Both the main house and
the Washburn House boast double whirlpool bathtubs, too. And the
focal point between the two is a beautiful white gazebo in the back
yard.

I was curious about the name White Lace. I suggested that perhaps
it was just a nice, pleasant, evocative term, but Bonnie assured me that
indeed there was "something of white lace in every one of the guest
rooms." It's kind of fun to find the white lace in each room. In one
room it's the hand-knotted lace canopy on the bed; in another it's the

Battenberg lace border on the cloth covering a table; in another, it's filmy lace curtains.

Bonnie and Dennis are both originally from Wisconsin. He had graduated from the Engineering School at the University of Wisconsin at Madison and she had studied interior design before they were married. They had moved to Connecticut, and when the "inn idea" got too strong to be ignored, they looked all over New England without success, until a friend suggested that they visit Door County in Wisconsin.

They found what they'd been looking for on a quiet street in the residential area of Sturgeon Bay, within five blocks of the bay and two blocks of the downtown National Historic District. Bonnie and Dennis put many hours of hard work into bringing the three nearly ruined houses back to life, and they have succeeded in creating a very special inn with a warm and intimate atmosphere.

A word or two about Door County, which is sometimes called one of the best-kept secrets in the country. I know of people who always look heavenward when extolling Door County's virtues. It's a good four-season resort area. Winter days can be spent cross-country skiing on the trails in the state parks or snowshoeing in the woods. After returning to the inn, it's fun to gather in front of the crackling fire and exchange information and enthusiasms with other guests. Of course, being on the lake, Door County in the summertime offers ever-expanding vacation delights, including sailing, windsurfing, fishing, and swimming.

I thought that it might be a bit quiet during the winter, but Bonnie assured me they have many full weekends between January and March, when people bring their cross-country skis and make a wonderful time of it.

Guests at the Garden House and the Washburn House enjoy continental breakfast at the Main House. Different kinds of home-baked muffins and breads and Scandinavian fruit soup are featured each day, as well as juice and plenty of aromatic hot coffee. The coffee pot is always on the stove at other times as well. "No one has ever left the table hungry at breakfast time here," Dennis said.

WHITE LACE INN, 16 N. Fifth Ave., Sturgeon Bay, WI 54235; 414-743-1105. A 15-guestroom (private baths) bed-and-breakfast inn in one of Wisconsin's attractive resort areas. Queen and double beds. Open year-round. Conveniently located near all of the cultural and recreational attractions in Door County. Special 3-, 4-, and 5-night packages available November–May. No pets. CCs: Visa, MC. Dennis and Bonnie Statz, owners/hosts.

DIRECTIONS: From the south take the Rte. 42–57 bypass across the new bridge, turn left on Michigan, and go right on Fifth Ave.

Southwest and Rocky Mountains

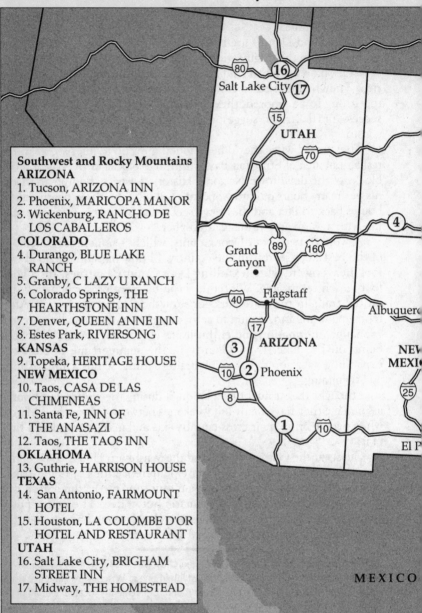

Southwest and Rocky Mountains
ARIZONA
1. Tucson, ARIZONA INN
2. Phoenix, MARICOPA MANOR
3. Wickenburg, RANCHO DE
   LOS CABALLEROS
COLORADO
4. Durango, BLUE LAKE
   RANCH
5. Granby, C LAZY U RANCH
6. Colorado Springs, THE
   HEARTHSTONE INN
7. Denver, QUEEN ANNE INN
8. Estes Park, RIVERSONG
KANSAS
9. Topeka, HERITAGE HOUSE
NEW MEXICO
10. Taos, CASA DE LAS
    CHIMENEAS
11. Santa Fe, INN OF
    THE ANASAZI
12. Taos, THE TAOS INN
OKLAHOMA
13. Guthrie, HARRISON HOUSE
TEXAS
14. San Antonio, FAIRMOUNT
    HOTEL
15. Houston, LA COLOMBE D'OR
    HOTEL AND RESTAURANT
UTAH
16. Salt Lake City, BRIGHAM
    STREET INN
17. Midway, THE HOMESTEAD

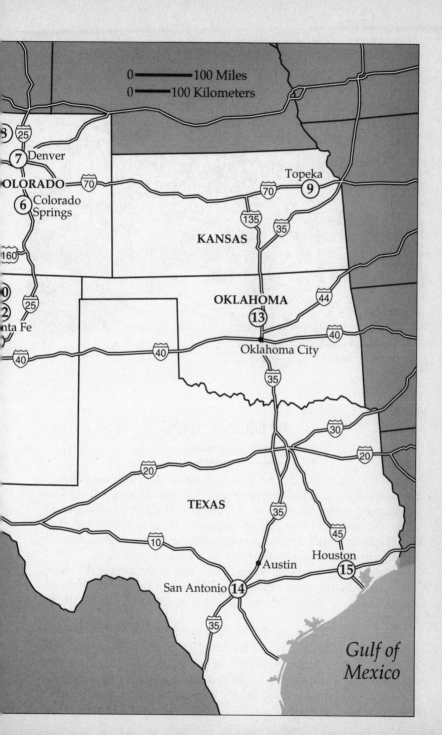

Arizona

ARIZONA INN
Tucson, Arizona

"When you walk into the Arizona Inn, you find a place that's significantly the same as it was 60 years ago," General Manager Patty Doar was quoted in the Tucson Inc. I found the Mediterranean/Spanish, adobe inn to be modern and up-to-date in its amenities. However, I quickly discovered what Patty, granddaughter to the original founder, was referring to...exceptional service to her guests.

"Our goal is to fulfill their needs," she states, speaking of the guests. There is no falling short of that goal. Although I could cite example after example of this, I suppose I had better familiarize you with the inn itself.

There was no question that we had arrived in the hot, Southwestern desert as we walked out of the airport terminal. As we pulled the rental car in front of the Arizona Inn, Louise, the gardener in my family, commented on the lush landscaping. Green lawns, drought tolerant shrubs, and trees surrounded the pink, adobe buildings that create the inn. Stone fountains, quite popular in this area, dotted the land-scape, with their ever-flowing geysers of water. I was amazed to later discover that this landscaping extends over 14 acres. Imagine...14 acres right in downtown Tucson!

Even though the inn has 80 rooms, we did not experience a lack of privacy. Our room had a double doors opening out to a patio, protected by trees, making it our own outdoor hideaway. The spacious room had thick-napped carpet, the color of wine, a sitting area, and connecting private bath. Its furnishing, as many throughout the inn, were origi-nals, and are upgraded and repaired as needed in a wood shop on the grounds. Our room also had a fireplace, obviously for the colder winter months, and a TV-radio combination.

The hotel attracts conventions, with its five conference and ban-quet rooms, and well-known celebrities, with it tenacity for safeguard-ing guest privacy. There is a formal policy forbidding staff discussion of VIP visitors that is strictly enforced. Within the thick walls, there is a library filled with classics, a sitting room, and a cocktail lounge, pro-viding piano music each evening.

The inn accommodated us with all our meals. We had the choice of being seated in the elegant, main dining room, a smaller, more pri-vate dining area, filled with lithographs by George Catlin, or enjoying the outdoor view from a terrace table. We opted for the main dining room that first night. I just had to try the appetizer of Roasted green chile, stuffed with goat cheese on tomato cullis. Even though the waiter tempted us with a chilled Kiwi Pineapple Bisque, we decided to move directed to the next course and share a Caesar Salad, prepared next to our table by the maitre'd. For an entrée, I chose the Filet Mignon, broiled with sauteed mushrooms from the traditional evening menu. Louise, a bit more daring, selected the broiled salmon with can-taloupe salsa (allowing me an occasional taste). I really didn't think I had room for dessert until observed apple pie ala mode being delivered to the next table. Once again, Louise offered a spoonful of her hot fudge sundae, crunchy with chopped nuts. We wandered back into the lounge to sip a glass of port and end a most enjoyable evening listening to music.

The following morning, I pulled on my hiking boots and set off to explore the magnificent Sabino Canyon, an early morning trek no one should miss. I left Louise eating her breakfast by the 60-foot pool, sur-rounding paths bordered with snapdragons, poppies, and anemones. The gardeners were at their work early, and sprinkler dampened the grass in preparation for the day's heat. On my way, I lingered briefly by the tennis courts, observing a couple of guests having their skills honed by the tennis pro on staff. Maybe that would improve my game, I thought, then proceeded on to catch the tour bus.

The sun was well overhead upon my return, and I was dusty and tired. We were planning to drive into Mexico, only an hour and a half away, to do some shopping and lunch on authentic Mexican food. I found Louise still pool side, visiting with some Danish guests who were waiting for reservations to be confirmed for a plane ride over the Grand Canyon. Staff members were scurrying to accommodate the short-notice arrangements, as the Danish folks were flying home the next day. No one should come to Arizona and not see the Grand Canyon. I applauded their spontaneity. Another attraction I highly recommend is the Desert Museum, an authentic replication of the desert and its inhabitants.

ARIZONA INN, 2200 East Elm St., Tucson, AZ. 85719; 602-325-1541; or 800-933-1093. 14 acres in the heart of Tucson. 80 private guest rooms including villas and casitas within this 1930 family owned Mediterranean/Spanish inn. Rooms may included private patios and fireplaces. Dining rooms offer varied menus for all meals. Cocktail lounge with nightly entertainment. Conference and banquet rooms for businesses or large groups. Pool and tennis courts, tennis pro available. Open year round, some seasonal specials offered. Nearby nature hikes through Sabino Canyon and state parks. Experience the "old-west" strolling through downtown Tucson. Ski the mountain slopes in the winter. Bring along your golf clubs when the sun shines. Car transportation available though the inn. Major credit cards accepted. Patty Doar/President & General Manager.

DIRECTIONS: From Interstate 10, take Kino Parkway north to Campbell Ave. Continue north taking a right turn onto East Elm. Look for the inn on the right side.

MARICOPA MANOR
Phoenix, Arizona

I have heard many stories of how people have come to own their inns, but this one was the most unusual.

Paul and Mary Ellen Kelley purchased this one-acre compound in 1970 because it was large enough to house their three children, eight foster children, and visiting exchange students, as well as Mary Ellen's mother and Aunt Jeannette (the latter still occupies one of the guest houses). As the last of the fledglings flew the nest, the Kelleys expanded their hospitality to the general public, opening Maricopa in February 1990.

The buildings, constructed in 1928 to display true Spanish Revival style, have been renovated and modernized. Red tile roofs and white stucco walls reflected the intense Arizona sunlight upon our arrival. In the courtyard, water trickled down the fountain. We could see the outdoor hot tub, centered in a lawn area and protected by a wooden lattice gazebo and palm trees reaching skyward.

The interior decoration is varied, as indicated by the names of guest rooms such as The Library Suite, The Victorian Suite, and The Palo Verde Suite, which is located in the main house. My wife and I stayed in the Library Suite with its convenient outside entrance to a private deck. A king-sized bed with white lace skirting and a brilliant blue canopy overhead is the centerpiece of the suite. Bookshelves filled with the Kelleys leather-bound collection climb up toward the redwood cathedral ceilings.

The guest cottage has two connecting suites, Reflections Past and Reflections Future, which can be rented separately or shared by larger parties. Reflections Past is warmly decorated with rich tapestry, a four-poster bed, walls of antique mirrors and an inviting fireplace. Reflections Future, exhibiting a contemporary black and white decor, offers a kitchen, a sizable living room, and a sun room. Both suites have private entrances.

White sofas and wing-backed chairs furnish the informal Gathering Room, which also serves as the breakfast room. A massive antique hutch with attached candelabra sits along one wall, accompanied by pastel prints. White carved columns herald the entrance into the Music Room, which holds a grand piano, an Irish harp, and other instruments. The dark hardwood floor is covered with a pale blue Oriental rug. The living room, with its fireplace and antique furniture, is even more elegant. The formal dining room is the perfect setting for business meetings, weddings, and receptions.

A complimentary "Breakfast in a Basket" filled with homemade breads, jams, fresh fruit, juices and gourmet coffees can be enjoyed in any of the common areas or in the privacy of your rooms. A seemingly endless supply of coffee, hot chocolate, and tea was always available in our suite.

My wife and I soon felt like one of the family under the wings of warm hospitality and care offered by the Kelleys.

MARICOPA MANOR, P.O. Box 7186, Phoenix, Arizona 85011-7186; 602-274-6302. Spanish-style B&B with five luxury suites. Continental breakfast included. Varied bed sizes. TV. Hot Tub. Smoking allowed in certain areas. Open all year. Five easy miles to shopping, restaurants, and entertainment in downtown Phoenix. Sky Harbor Airport only a 15-minute drive. No pets. Paul and Mary Ellen Kelley, owners/hosts.

DIRECTIONS: The inn is located at numbers 11 & 15 West Pasadena Avenue in North Central Phoenix.

RANCHO DE LOS CABALLEROS
Wickenburg, Arizona

Rancho de los Caballeros is a rather elegant ranch/inn. A continuous program of watering and irrigation makes it a green jewel in the desert. This is especially true of the 18-hole championship golf course. Many of the guest rooms and suites are built around a carefully planned cactus garden and oversized putting green and are decorated in Arizona desert colors with harmonizing hues of tan, yellow, and brown. Each accommodation, or *casita* as they are called in this part of the world, has a private patio, and many of them have fireplaces.

A program of planned activities for younger people is one of the reasons this ranch experience is so popular with families. "We feel that it is a good balance," says innkeeper Rusty Gant, "because children of all ages have several activities every morning, and in the afternoon they can join their parents for more trail riding or tennis or a swim in the pool. At dinner the children's counselor gathers them all together, and they even have their own dining room. They are kept occupied until bedtime. This has proven to be an excellent idea for both children and their parents alike.

"The idea of a winter vacation on a guest ranch in Arizona never occurred to us," said a letter I received from a Michigan reader. "Wickenburg seemed like such a long way and we weren't quite sure what kind of people would be there. We certainly weren't horseback riders and we thought we might feel out of place. However, we were reading your book about how much you enjoyed the noon buffet around the pool at Rancho de los Caballeros and getting some horseback riding tips from one of the wranglers, and we began to think that maybe we would enjoy it too.

"The trip from Detroit to Phoenix was quite short and the ranch car met us at the airport...We literally dragged our two early-teenage sons with us, and did their faces light up when almost as soon as we arrived they noticed other young people. I don't believe we saw them for the rest of the two weeks."

Rancho de los Caballeros..."the ranch of the gentlemen on horse-back." The name alone has an unusually romantic, melodic sound, and its location in the high country is equally romantic. As my correspondent from Michigan said later on in her letter, "The mountains and the desert literally grow on you."

I love to sit on the terrace at sunset and watch the changing colors and dimensions of the Bradshaw Mountains far across the valley.

RANCHO DE LOS CABALLEROS, Wickenburg, AZ 85358; 602-684-5484. A 74-gue-stroom (private baths) luxury ranch-resort, 60 mi. from Phoenix in the sunny, dry desert. Queen, double and twin beds available. American plan. Breakfast, lunch, dinner served to travelers daily. Open from mid–October to early May. Wheelchair access. Swimming pool, horseback riding, hiking, skeet shooting, putting green, tennis, and 18-hole championship golf course on grounds. Special children's program. No pets. No credit cards. Dallas C. Gant, Jr. and Mrs. Francis L. Hayman, owners.

DIRECTIONS: Rtes. 60, 89, and 93 lead to Wickenburg. Ranch is 2 mi. west of town on Rte. 60 and 2 mi. south on Vulture Mine Road.

Colorado

BLUE LAKE RANCH

Durango, Colorado

"No neighbors in sight, only one tiny light in the distance from a mine up in the mountains," David Alford, owner of Blue Lake Ranch, told me. That was exactly the reason my wife, Louise, and I had chosen Blue Lake. We were ready for some solitude, and this oasis in the high desert country of Colorado would provide it.

The ranch was homesteaded in the early 1900s by Swedish immigrants. It is surrounded by 100 acres that includes a lake filled with rainbow trout, and has a magnificent view of the La Plata mountains in the distance.

David purchased Blue Lake in 1982. Leaving behind a career in social work, he fulfilled a wish to work at home. He rolled up his sleeves and transformed the old farmhouse into a European country-style inn.

The main house has four guest rooms, filled with antiques and fresh flowers from the English gardens which surround the sturdy old structure. Among his many talents, David also exhibits a "green thumb," growing lavender for jelly and heirloom seeds. The vibrant colors of the magnificent gardens can be seen from every window of the inn and nearby cabin.

Louise and I stayed in the cabin, which overlooks the lake, enjoying the spaciousness of three bedrooms and two baths. It would be an ideal accommodation for a family. The window boxes were filled with geraniums, which spilled over onto the deck. This soon became our favorite place to enjoy afternoon tea. The living room, furnished in dark antiques, has a fireplace to temper the evening chill of the desert. Its warm, home-like environment made the large room a sanctuary for guests.

Breakfast is served European-style with warmed croissants, cheeses, cereals and a selection of fruit.

If the lack of people seems too overwhelming, Durango is only a 20-minute drive away. Mesa Verde National Park, with Indian caves carved into the mountains, is worth seeing. Louise and I explored several hiking trails in the San Juan Mountains. We put the inn's hot tub to use that evening, soothing our tired muscles in the warm circulating water.

Time passed too quickly, bringing an end to our stay. Yet we departed feeling a sense of peace and renewal from this desert oasis.

BLUE LAKE RANCH, 16919 Hwy.140, Durango, CO 81326; 303-385-4537. A 4-guestroom farmhouse with 3-bedroom cabin situated on 100 acres. European buffet breakfast included. TV & telephones in rooms. Afternoon tea. No smoking. Open May through October. Minimum stay in cabin. Trout-filled lake near inn. Short drive to Durango, Mesa Verde National Park, and San Juan Mountains. Fuzzy, the ranch cat, stays outdoors. No pets. David and Shirley Alford, owners/hosts.

DIRECTIONS: 12 mi. west on Hwy. 160. Turn right at Hwy. 140 at Hesperus. Travel 6.1 mi. south. Ranch on right side.

C LAZY U RANCH
Granby, Colorado

Through a friend, a former cowboy from Montana, I learned that even "pilgrims"—his term for city-slicker dudes like me—could have a great time and get the feel of a working ranch at Colorado's C Lazy U Ranch. Besides, after reading their brochure I knew that this was no ordinary ranch; I could always float in the luxury of the spring-fed heated swimming pool and soak in the whirlpool if I got saddle-sore.

While I don't have young children anymore, I must recommend the C Lazy U Ranch as a family vacation haven which also specializes in adult fun. Experienced counselors scoop up kids, to the kids' and parents' mutual delight, for adventures in horseback riding, fishing and hiking. The don't appear again until after the adult dinner hour. My wife brought me news from a Cincinnati mother whom she'd met at

the Ranch's pool. The family was back for their twenty-first year, "mostly because the kids love it."

Children eat lunch together and spend evenings sharing cooperative tasks. Paddle boats, and a game room which includes a ping-pong table and a mechanical soccer game (no video games here), supplement an all-you-can-eat ice cream bar.

Well, enough for the kids. What about the adults? I'm pleased to inform you that there is as much wonderful fun here for adults as there is for children.

"If you come in September after the kids are back in school, it gets really quiet here, and all our services are still available," manager John Fisher told me as we strolled to the racquetball courts. "And during our winter season the cross-country skiing is terrific."

Besides racquetball, swimming, fishing, riding, hot-tub soaks and an all-purpose activity room, adults are spoiled by spacious luxury guest rooms which include comfortable furnishings and extras down to a humidifier for dry weather and lip gloss to combat cracked lips. Special treats like fresh fruit, nuts and chocolates (replenished daily), and hefty terry-cloth robes are also provided.

The guest units surround the rambling native pine log lodge, where a cozy library, lounge, bar, card room and dining room are located. Inviting verandas offer spectacular views over Willow Creek to craggy Trail Peak.

The shake-roofed Patio House, directly across from the lodge, offers cookouts, staff talent shows, square dancing and, much to my wife's pleasure, lessons in Western Swing dancing.

All meals are included with your room rate—and don't expect jerky and beans. Breakfast is a buffet of fresh fruit, juices, cereals, eggs, pancakes, waffles, ham, sausage, bacon, and toast or rolls. Lunch and dinner are either served family-style or as a buffet, and a soup and salad bar is available during summer lunches.

The C Lazy U Ranch employees go out of their way to make you feel welcome. At the beginning of your stay you're matched with a horse suited to your skill level. This horse will be your equine companion for the week. But the best part is that you won't have to follow "head-to-tail" like most rental places require.

Oh, and just for my Montana friend's information, I now know the difference between a billet and a cinch, so I guess I'm no longer a "pilgrim"!

THE C LAZY U RANCH, P.O. Box 378, 3640 Colorado Hwy. 125, Granby, CO 80446; 303-887-3344. A 40-guestroom (private baths) modern ranch in Colorado's Peaceful Valley. Open June thru September, and mid–December–April 1. Weekly stay required thru Labor Day; 3-day min. in early June and September; 3-day min. in winter season. Modified American plan, including lunch. King and twin beds. Tennis, skiing, racquetball, swimming, fishing, horseback riding (lessons available), sauna, winter sports. Children welcome. No pets. Clark and Peg Murray, Owners-hosts; John H. Fisher, manager.

DIRECTIONS: Take I-70 west to Exit 232 (U.S. Hwy. 40). Take U.S. 40 to Granby. 3 mi. west of Granby turn right onto Hwy. 125. Go approx. 23-1/2 mi. then turn right at the C Lazy U gate.

THE HEARTHSTONE INN
Colorado Springs, Colorado

It was a most agreeable early August morning at the Hearthstone Inn. This time I was paying a visit in midsummer, when I could see the inn's beautiful lawn and flowers at their very best, and also sit on the front porch in one of the new handsome Tennessee country rockers.

I watched with amusement while a father, mother, and their four-year-old boy romped on the lawn, and then one of the staff came out and set up the croquet set. I had arrived just a few moments earlier, driving down from Denver and Boulder, and was immediately offered my choice of coffee or iced tea. "The coffee is on from early in the morning," explained Dot Williams, who with Ruth Williams (no relation), is the innkeeper at the Hearthstone.

Now I watched the few cars go by on Cascade Avenue, one of the

most impressive streets in Colorado Springs, and reflected on the many changes I have seen in the considerable number of years since the first night I landed in Denver. I had been picked up by Dot and Ruth and driven out to the Springs. These two women had opened up the first inn in Colorado Springs, overcoming many difficulties. At that time there was only one house; now there are two houses, cheek-by-jowl.

The most recent development is the completion of Sheltering Pines, a totally different type of accommodation in nearby Green Mountain Falls. I had visited it when it was just a bit more than a gleam in the innkeepers' eyes.

"It is slowly developing its own following," Dot said. "The cool of the mountain evenings and the clear air of our mountain days make this part of Colorado a real boon for those who suffer from heat or allergies. Family reunions or groups are enjoying the patio, barbecue grill, and the many trees. It's quite a bit higher than Colorado Springs."

Sheltering Pines is actually a duplex with two completely separate living areas. Each has a completely equipped kitchen with everything provided, including all of the bedding and towels. In the summer it is rented only by the week, but the rest of the year it's available for shorter stays with a two-night minimum.

The Hearthstone itself is well known from coast to coast as being one of the truly impressive Victorian restorations, and it is on the National Register of Historic Places. Every room has been furnished entirely with Victorian furniture and decorations, and the outside of this wonderful combination of two rambling houses has been finished in carefully researched Victorian colors. Visitors will be surprised, as was I, to see how gracefully they reflect the Mauve Decades.

I always look forward to breakfast at the Hearthstone, and there is a wide variety of hearty breakfast offerings, not just the usual. "We never serve the same guest the same breakfast twice," Ruth declared.

Dot and Ruth joined me on the front porch, and we watched the squirrels, Minnie the Moocher and Pearl the Squirrel, and their friend,

Jaws, eat themselves silly on sunflower seeds.

"I've always hoped that you would come out during Christmas some year," Ruth said. "Our guests all gather around for eggnog and the tradition of decorating the tree. Many guests bring a homemade ornament, and we tag each one with their name and the year, and it becomes a permanent part of each tree's decorations. Why don't you plan to come next year?"

I certainly would enjoy that experience very much!

THE HEARTHSTONE INN, 506 N. Cascade Ave., Colorado Springs, CO 80903; 719-473-4413. A 25-guestroom (23 private baths) bed-and-breakfast inn within sight of Pike's Peak, in the residential section of Colorado Springs. All-size beds. Complimentary full breakfast is the only meal served. Open every day all year. (Housekeeping units also available in Green Mountain Falls.) Convenient to spectacular Colorado mountain scenery as well as Air Force Academy, Garden of the Gods, Cave of the Winds, the McAllister House Museum, Fine Arts Center, and Broadmoor Resort. Golf, tennis, swimming, hiking, backroading, and Pikes Peak ski area nearby. Check innkeepers for pet policy. Dorothy Williams and Ruth Williams, innkeepers.

DIRECTIONS: From I-25 (the major north/south hwy.) use Exit 143 (Uintah St.); travel east (opposite direction from mountains) to third stoplight (Cascade Ave.). Turn right for 7 blocks. The inn will be on the right at the corner of St. Vrain and Cascade—a big Victorian house, tan with lilac trim.

QUEEN ANNE INN
Denver, Colorado

Charles and Anne Hillestad are a couple whose warmth and graciousness have made the Queen Anne Inn a restful haven in an active, cosmopolitan city. Charles, a transplanted Oregonian, moved to Denver to practice real estate law. He claims a particular interest in science fiction. Ann was raised on an Iowa farm where she developed her love for sewing, travel, music, and wildlife. The Hillestads' interests are apparent in the urbane ambience of their inn. Fine woods, stained-glass windows, original art, soft chamber music, fresh flowers, sherry, and a grand oak staircase attest to their appreciation for Victorian styling.

In the mid-1970s, Charles and Ann stepped in to help halt the demolition of homes on Denver's historic Tremont block. The Queen Anne Inn was one of these homes. The area is part of the oldest surviving residential neighborhood in Denver, which now borders on a fountain park and a buffer of open space.

Just four short blocks from the heart of Denver's central business district, the Queen Anne Inn offers a respite from the rigors of travel or the stress of everyday life. Listed as "one of the top ten places to spend a wedding night" by *Bridal Guide Magazine*, the inn appeals to

the romance in everyone. "If you can't win the heart of your significant other at the Queen Anne Inn, give up!" Charles told me.

Each guest room has its own character and style. For example, the Rooftop Room has French doors that open onto a private deck with a panoramic view of the city and mountains. While all the rooms boast original art, the Aspen Room *is* a work of art. Located in the turreted peak of the inn, the room has a wraparound and overhead mural of an alpine aspen grove in fall color. What a splendid scene to gaze upon the first thing in the morning! Some of the rooms highlight pillared canopy beds. Others have gleaming brass beds or carved wooden headboards. Although the beds are antiques, the mattresses are new and firm. Both queen and twin beds are available. All rooms have private modern baths.

The common rooms are light and airy, with high ceilings and tall windows. A peach-toned background and crisp white trim create warmth. The living room, dining room, kitchen, and private garden are all available for guest use. I enjoyed a complimentary glass of afternoon wine with Charles as we relaxed on the garden deck. Both the

Hillestads can recommend an impressive repertoire of attractions that are within walking distance from the inn: the Denver Chamber Orchestra and Symphony, the Center for the Performing Arts, the large Tivoli complex with movies, shops, restaurants, the Museum of Natural History, and the Denver Zoo. Galleries, clubs, and nearly fifty fine restaurants, many of which are five-star caliber, are close by. The Hallestads are pleased to help you design a day's itinerary.

Although lunch and dinner are not included in the room rate, Ann assured me that "anything from a picnic lunch to a three-course gourmet dinner" can be arranged with advance notice. A breakfast of fruits, breads, fresh-squeezed juice, homemade granola, yogurt, hard-boiled eggs, and special-blend coffee and teas is included in the tariff.

For a romantic evening, take a lovely tour in one of the Amish horse-drawn carriages that pulls up directly in front of the inn. Somehow the city atmosphere becomes distant and time stops, if only for one night.

QUEEN ANNE INN, 2147 Tremont Pl., Denver, CO 80205; 303-296-6666. A 10-guestroom (private baths) elegant Victorian within walking distance of downtown Denver, and only 1 hour from the Rocky Mountains. All size beds available. Open all year. Breakfast and afternoon refreshments included. Picnic lunch and gourmet dinner on advance request. Museums, shops, restaurants, and entertainment nearby. Smoking restricted. No pets. Children over 15. Charles and Ann Hillestad, owners/hosts.

DIRECTIONS: Take Exit 213 on I-25 to 23rd St., continuing to Tremont. Turn right for one block.

RIVER SONG
Estes Park, Colorado

The first time I walked through the door of RiverSong I knew that the owners of this small, intimate inn understand what it means to provide a place for guests to come together and exchange ideas and conversation.

In the middle of the living room a large crescent-shaped couch faces the floor-to-ceiling riverrock fireplace. Tall windows at the other end of the room beckon guests to enjoy the spectacular view of the Rockies' great peaks. Many books of all kinds indicate an active literary and intellectual curiosity on the part of innkeepers Sue and Gary Mansfield.

"Actually, we are an inn that basically appeals to outdoor-minded people," Gary told me. "Guests want to hike on the trails or ski or just spend time outside and smell the fresh air after a rain..." But when the weather is blustery, nothing beats a good read in front of the fire.

I meandered through RiverSong's grounds and noticed that the grass had been allowed to seek its own level, along with the wildflowers and flowering bushes. Ponds, pools and a gazebo accent the easy ambience of this inn. Through the trees I could see to the top of the great Continental Divide which, in August, was still snowcapped.

This view is even better from several of the inn's six guest rooms, all named after Rocky Mountain wildflowers. A rich heritage of family antiques graces each room. Handmade quilts, claw-foot bathtubs in the private baths, and spicy accents, like the suspended bed in one room and the scarlet Jacuzzi in the inn's large carriage house suite, provide every excuse for a romantic weekend.

My wife and I snuggled into the Chiming Bells suite. A fireplace, redwood shower, delightful sunken tub, and floral quilt-covered brass bed made for a cozy, welcoming room.

A new duplex cottage with two beautiful rooms overlooking the pond and stream and continental divide have a willow canopy bed and the other a waterfall shower. The meadow bright room has a stone fireplace that reaches the ceiling.

Over a breakfast of John Wayne's egg and chili casserole, fresh squeezed orange juice, and Sue's own crumbly corn meal muffins, Sue told me that almost all of the antiques in the inn have been handed down through her family. "It's nice to be able to share these things with other people who really appreciate them," she said. Fellow guests were happily digging into blueberry and rhubarb cobblers, Gary's tapioca parfait, and other early morning favorites.

Gourmet dinners are also served, built around seasonal ingredients. Besides a menu which includes meat entrées, a vegetarian dish is also available. Our Friday evening meal began with avocado RiverSong, a ripe avocado half heaped with fresh tomato, red onion, and tangy feta cheese drizzled with a vinegarette dressing. An unusual Oriental soup of shrimp and shiitake mushrooms preceded a succulent basil chicken breast slathered in a light cream sauce. Brown and wild rice pilaf sprinkled with almonds and a cumin-accented sauteed bok choi with shallots accompanied this dish. A velvety fudge walnut torte crowned the meal.

Gary is an avid hiker and aspiring naturalist who leads hiking jaunts. The inn's close proximity to Rocky Mountain National Park offers excellent terrain for both hiking and animal tracking.

As I explored the grounds one morning I wandered across a narrow little stone bridge into a tiny glade of evergreens, ending up at the edge of a pool where the wonderful music of splashing water can always be heard. I took a restful break here, and let the rigors of travel float away.

RIVERSONG, P.O. Box 1910, Estes Park, CO 80517; 303-586-4666. An 8-guestroom (private baths) mountain inn at the foot of the great Continental Divide, 70 mi. from Denver. Queen and double beds. Open all year. Full breakfast and afternoon tea included; gourmet dinners available. Hiking, guides for animal tracking, golf, tennis, antiquing. No pets. Smoking restricted. Sue and Gary Mansfield, owners/hosts.

DIRECTIONS: Take Hwy. 36 north of Denver to Boulder and then to Estes Park. At the 4th stoplight turn left. At the next light (Mary's Lake Rd.) turn left again. Go 1 blk. across bridge and turn right on gravel road—go to end.

Kansas

HERITAGE HOUSE
Topeka, Kansas

It isn't often that I have had the opportunity to stay in such a prestigious location as the Heritage House, the former residence of the historic Menninger Clinic. The turn-of-the-century white wood-frame house was originally purchased in 1925 by C.F. Menninger and two of his sons, Will and Karl. After modifications, the home opened its doors as the Menninger Clinic on May 5, 1925.

Almost sixty years later, in 1982, the clinic moved to a new location. Unfortunately, the farmhouse was left vacant and suffered damage due to vandalism. In 1988, it was chosen as the site of the Topeka Designers' Showhouse Home and underwent major renovation. In June of that year, Don and Betty Rich opened the Heritage House as a country inn.

The Riches have been in the hospitality industry for quite some time and appreciated the historical significance of the building. Their daughter, Sarah, had spent more than three years working in hotels and was a natural choice as the Heritage House's manager. She met me as I checked in and warmly discussed the history of the home and her dedication to her job: "Since I'm the daughter of the owners, I run Heritage House as they would, with total professionalism and the finest of quality."

Sarah took me on a tour of the inn's unusual living room and parlor. Both are hand-painted, using a marbleizing technique. Hardwood floors, Oriental rugs, and traditional-styled furnishings create a comfortable, inviting atmosphere. Multicolored floral patterns in shades of peach and jade green give a refreshing feeling. Once the setting of the Menninger Clinic's afternoon staff conferences, the rooms' real focal point is a fabulous green Italian fireplace located in the parlor.

One of the benefits of the inn's renovation is that the fifteen guest rooms have been individually decorated by Topeka designers. The most historically significant are Dr. Will and Dr. Karl Menninger's studies. Dr. Will's has the original knotty pine paneling and has been finished with a southwestern theme emphasizing earth tones. An original painting by Dr. Will's widow hangs on the wall. In contrast, Dr. Karl's paneled room is cool, decorated in shades of blue. An elegant mahogany four-poster bed and large picture window dominate the room.

Other rooms have a Kansas country decor, complete with pine furniture and ruffled curtains. The Magnolia Room features an exotic Oriental theme complete with a black lacquer four-poster bed and an elevated Jacuzzi tub. Most rooms have private baths with shower/tub combinations. All have telephones and color televisions.

The ambience of the inn is decidedly not stuffy, including the friendly house bar off the entry's living room where guests are encouraged to mix their own drinks on the honor system. Breakfast, lunch, and dinner are available, with a full breakfast included in the room tariff.

The dinner menu is à la carte and can be enjoyed on the inn's new wood deck during good weather. I ordered a rich crab cannelloni appetizer, then had a crisp house salad followed by a fresh piece of Pacific salmon with dill sauce. For dessert, I decided to splurge on calories and savored the white and dark chocolate buttercream gateau.

Topeka has a variety of special events to provide entertainment while you're visiting. Summer brings the Sunflower Music Festival and Fiesta Mexicana. In the fall you can have fun at Railroad Days, the Huff'n'Puff Balloon Rally, or Cider Days. The Heritage House is close to Gage Park, the State Capitol, and, of course, the Menninger Foundation. I know you'll enjoy the town, and the hospitality of the Heritage House.

HERITAGE HOUSE, 3535 S. W. 6th St., Topeka, KS 66606; 913-233-3800. A 15-guestroom (11 private baths) country inn located near downtown Topeka. Open all year. All bed sizes. Full breakfast included; lunch and dinner available by reservation. Smoking in common areas only. Seasonal events. No pets. Don and Betty Rich, owners; Sarah Rich, manager.

DIRECTIONS: From Kansas City, take I-70 west to Topeka. Take the East Turnpike exit to Gage Blvd. Go south on Gage to Sixth St. (first stop light) and turn left. Heritage House is on the right.

New Mexico

CASA DE LAS CHIMENEAS

Taos, New Mexico

Several years ago, innkeeper Susan Vernon's life became a romance story. Within five days of Valentine's Day, she had signed the closing papers for Casa de las Chimeneas and met Ron Rencher, her soon-to-be fiance. Nine weeks later they were engaged. "I couldn't believe two life dreams could actually come true, much less that they would both happen in the same week!" she said. Susan is a vibrant, energetic person who makes guests immediately feel welcome. Formerly in public relations, she came to Taos because it is "magical."

Chimeneas in Spanish means chimneys, and, true to its name, the inn has at least one kiva fireplace in each room. The beehive-shaped fireplaces based on centuries-old Pueblo Indian design have soft plaster corners and are embellished with hand-painted talavera tiles from across the border in Mexico. The spacious guest rooms have beamed ceilings, hand-carved furnishings, and luxurious touches like sheepskin mattress pads, lacy blanket covers and down pillows. Each guest room has its own private entrance off the terrace and a private bath with a brightly tiled vanity.

The light, airy common rooms are filled with plants and illuminated by skylights. A comfortable sitting area surrounds the living room fireplace. The white adobe walls throughout the house are hung with exceptional regional art, including work by innkeeper Ron, a successful artist.

"We have thought of other names for our inn that would be as appropriate and, perhaps, easier to pronounce," explains Susan. "Ron and I put so much energy into our gardens that we joke about changing the name to 'House of the Gardens' or 'Taos Oasis.'" Their efforts have, indeed, created an oasis in the heart of Taos. The front garden is formal, with a manicured lawn and seven-foot high wall that separates it from the street. Seventeen cottonwoods, several elms and a massive willow ring the nearly acre-sized property. Two fountains add the soothing sound of water and serve as playgrounds for neighborhood birds. Iris, tulips, daffodils, shasta daisies, pansies, columbine, lilies, hollyhocks, poppies, sweet william, wisteria and delphiniums form the backdrop for plantings of Susan and Ron's favorite annuals.

Behind the house, next to the outdoor hot tub that operates year-round, is yet another large garden space. Its radiating paths and trellises, all built by Ron, invite casual strolling. Here, herbs and vegetables grow alongside roses and painted daisies.

A full breakfast, featuring Southwestern specialties such as *huevos rancheros*, blue corn pancakes, breakfast enchiladas or New Mexico crêpes is served in the dining room, or outside on the back patio.

In the late afternoons guests enjoy Southwestern hors d'oeuvres—brownies, deviled eggs, feta cheese and tomatoes drizzled with garlic oil, cream cheese topped with spicy/sweet chile honey, vegetables with dip, and the house specialty: "moonshine cake," a rich yellow cake filled with fruit that has been steeped in liquor for 30 days—and soak in the outside hot tub.

CASA DE LAS CHIMENEAS, 405 Cordoba Rd., Box 5303, Taos, NM 87571; 505-758-4777. A 3-guestroom (private baths) luxurious adobe guest house in the heart of Taos. King, queen and twin beds. Outside hot tub. Open year-round. Breakfast and hor d'oeuvres included. No smoking or pets. Two cats in residence. CCs; Visa, MC. Susan Vernon and Ron Rencher, owners/hosts.

DIRECTIONS: From Santa Fe, go north on Paseo del Pueblo Sur, turn right on Los Pandos at traffic light. Go 2 blocks, turn right on Cordoba Rd.

INN OF THE ANASAZI
Santa Fe, New Mexico

"Honoring the spirit and the culture of the Anasazi or the ancient ones" is never forgotten in this inn, even by the staff. During my visit I was continually impressed with this ideal. Even before the architects were hired, visits were made to several of the Anasazi sites, including Chaco Canyon and Mesa Verde, and extensive research done through history books by the developers, RDZ/Washington Ave.Ltd. It is not very often, developers will make such efforts in their creations.

The Anasazi were Southwestern, cliff-dwelling Indians, with ori-

gins tracing back two thousand years. They disappeared around 1200 A.D., leaving behind pictographs and petroglyphs of their lives in the cliff walls, as well as pottery, baskets and textiles. Everything was studied intensely. Sifting through the information, it was decided that the interior design should reflect the power, purity, and simplicity of the Anasazi, while the exterior would reflect the Pueblo style. Once decided, this thread of honor extended into the 1991, when the inn opened its doors, with enlightened decisions to use natural foods and chemical free products to the hiring of staff members, who must understand the spiritual commitment of the inn and project that to receptive guests.

The inn has a certain peace and serenity, as if the "ancient ones" were nearby nodding their approval. Seated in the dining room, I admired the craftsmanship of the Vigas (beams) and interlaced Latillas (cross-beams) supporting the ceiling. Rough-hewn tables and bancos upholstered in handwoven Chimayo textile placed upon the wood floor emitted a certain earthiness. Not to mention the food, some contracted from the Pueblo, which is 70% organic, and, in my opinion, did not deter one bit from its tastefulness. I couldn't pass up one of my favorites for an appetizer, Navajo flat bread with fire roasted peppers. (I have a passion for any Indian bread). In keeping with tradition, I decided to sample the Pecan Grilled Range Chicken, spiced with garlic and sage, served up with corn pudding, as my entrée'. They are purchased direct from the Pueblo Reservation. I was not disappointed. Before I retiring to the Living Room, I requested a glass of wine from their private cellar and a copy of the menu, so I could investigate what selections were available for breakfast and lunch.

The Living Room is located just off the main lobby. A fire in the woodburning kiva fireplace had already taken the chill from the air. I could faintly hear the late fall desert wind outside heralding the approaching winter. Some guests had already claimed their space, but had graciously left a large arm chair of soft brown leather, not far from the fire, just for me. I settled back into a hand-woven pillow. The floor, comprised of irregular shaped flagstone, was brought to life by brightly colored rugs, with geometric designs. There was a pot of pink geraniums sitting on the coffee table, and a pottery tray holding an Indian rattle with a feather trailing from its handle. I was so taken with this atmosphere, that I never even looked at the menu I had brought along until I was back in my room.

The inn has fifty one guest rooms and eight suites. Again the beamed ceilings, kiva fireplaces, and hewned wood floors become a backdrop to four poster beds dressed with pure cotton sheets and spreads and a beautiful trastero, displaying a TV, VCR, coffee maker, and some drawers. A hint of cedar tinges the air of the bathroom from the locally made organic toiletries, and a cotton robe hung from a hook on the door. I was amazed by each detail that spoke so reverently to the environment. Massage and aromatherapy treatments are offered. And, if I wanted to keep physically fit, the staff would bring a stationary bicycle to my room. That idea prompted me to take a closer look at the menu I had retrieved from the dining room. A diverse selection existed for the daytime meals, but still leaned more towards Mexican flavor. I certainly wouldn't be forced outside this place for any meal, even though I was within walking distance of the Historic Plaza District and some local restaurants.

An archaeologist presented a lecture in the Inn's Library during my stay, which proved to be great preparation for some of the tours I went on. I had scheduled my visit to late for the Indian Market, taking place each August, which is the largest in the world. Oh well, another time!

INN OF THE ANASAZI, 113 Washington Ave., Santa Fe, New Mexico 87501; 505-988-3030. Centrally located near the Historic Plaza District, sits the Inn of the Anasazi, simple Pueblo exterior and environmentally conscious atmosphere. The fifty nine guestrooms and eight suites have kiva fireplaces, TV & VCR, a large selection of movies to enjoy, and four-poster or canopy beds. The restaurant features breakfast, lunch, and dinner. Private wine cellar. Library/Boardroom for business groups. Year round accommodations. Tour galleries, museums, and shops. Hike among the ancient Indian ruins of Chaco Canyon, Bandelier National Park, and Mesa Verde. Raft trips, hiking, fishing and skiing only a short drive away. No pets please. 113 Washington Avenue Limited Partnership, Owner/Robert D. Zimmer Group, Manager/Merry Stephenson, Managing Director.

DIRECTIONS: Adjacent to the Governor's Palace in the Historic Plaza District on 113 Washington Ave. Call Inn for more detailed directions from your location.

THE TAOS INN

Taos, New Mexico

As I stepped into the Taos Inn's two-story lobby, I thought I'd made a mistake and arrived during the wrong weekend. The lobby was buzzing with groups here and there in rapt conversation, and I didn't think there could possibly be enough room for all of us. Folks were standing on the interior balconies overlooking the decorative tiled fountain that I later learned had been the original town well. Others were viewing the exceptional artwork and brightly colored handwoven rugs that hung on the adobe walls. And quite a rousing discussion was taking place around the large sunken pueblo-style fireplace that dominates one corner of the room.

When I asked manager Kathleen Crislip if, in fact, I had arrived on the right date, she laughed and said, "Oh yes, certainly. It's always like this around here. Many of these people are local residents, most of them artists. We sometimes call our lobby 'the community living room.'" She went on to tell me that the inn had been a center of social activity in Taos for more than 300 years.

Just a short distance from the Taos Plaza, the inn has a remarkable history and is the only hotel in Taos on the National Register of Historic Places. Portions of the building date back to the late 1600s. With its rounded corners, slanted walls, curved archways, and soft light, the structure is a beautiful example of Spanish and Indian architecture that utilized local wood and adobe materials.

In 1895, Dr. T. Paul Martin, Taos's first physician, bought one of five 19th-century houses that surrounded a small plaza. Later, Dr. Martin and his wife, Helen, purchased the other four homes and rented them to local artists, creating a center for the Taos art community. After the doctor's death in 1935, Helen enclosed the patio, connecting the residences, and opened the Martin Hotel. In 1982, the inn was sold to present owner Scott Sanger and fellow investors, who proceeded to do extensive renovation and additions, including a Jacuzzi room and swimming pool.

The inn's 39 guest rooms feature pueblo-style fireplaces, antiques and handcrafted Southwestern furniture, hand-loomed Zapotec Indian bedspreads, and original art. The private baths are decorated with handpainted Mexican tile and each has a shower/tub combination.

Meals are available at the now-famous Doc Martin's Restaurant, established in the doctor's original clinic. Apparently many early Taos residents were born right in one of the intimate alcoves of the restaurant! The restaurant is popular with locals and visitors alike, so much so that reservations are recommended. The menu features made-from-scratch New American cuisine and original and traditional New Mexican specialties. Tender blue-corn pancakes, *carne adovada*, fresh fruit, and fantastic stuffed *sopaipillas* are just some of the breakfast choices available. The restaurant wine list has been granted an Award of Excellence by the prestigious *Wine Spectator* and also serves a fine selection of aperitifs and beers. For a more casual meal you might like to stroll across the street to the colorful Adobe Bar for more inexpensive Mexican food, shrimp, oysters, and terrific margaritas.

Taos offers a wide variety of entertainment and activities. People-watching alone can provide a full day of fun. Art galleries, boutiques, fascinating architecture, and the 900-year-old Taos Pueblo are within walking distance. The inn hosts a twice-yearly Meet the Artist series where guests can discuss the creative process with well-known Taos artists, and you might just come away having discovered your artist within.

THE TAOS INN, 125 Paseo del Pueblo Norte, Taos, NM 87571; 505-758-2233 or 800-TAOS-INN. A 39-guestroom (private baths) authentic historic adobe just steps from the Taos Plaza. Open year-round. All-size beds. Breakfast, lunch, dinner, and Sunday brunch available, but not included. Close to galleries, the Taos Pueblo, shopping, skiing, musical performances, theater, and art festivals. No pets. Handicap accessible. Betty and Scott Sanger, owners-hosts; Kathleen Crislip, manager.

DIRECTIONS: From Albuquerque, take I-25 north to Santa Fe. Take Exit 282 and follow signs to Taos and Espanola, picking up US 84–285 north. From Espanola take Rte. 68N to Taos. The inn is just north of the Taos Plaza on the right.

Oklahoma

HARRISON HOUSE
Guthrie, Oklahoma

I was greatly inspired by the pioneering spirit of community in Guthrie, originally the capital of the Oklahoma Territory and later the state. The whole town is on the National Register of Historic Places.

The Harrison House is a perfect example of that spirit. Phyllis Murray was a volunteer in the restoration of one of the buildings in the downtown historic district. Her husband Ron, a bank executive, was one of the local investors in the project to develop an inn in what had been a handsome bank and office building. They needed someone to furnish and decorate the rooms, and Phyllis took on the job.

Little did she realize how involved she would become. Today she is the innkeeper, and she loves it. "I wanted this inn to be special," she told me, "and I have always been partial to the Victorian period, so the idea of decorating it really appealed to me." And this is where the feeling of community comes in. Phyllis found everything she has used in the inn within the immediate area. This includes every piece of antique furniture, all of the fabrics and wallpapers, even the mattresses, made by a local company to fit the various-sized old beds.

"I felt that it was really important to have furnishings and the feeling of what Guthrie was like at the turn of the century, and also I wanted this restoration to benefit the local economy," Phyllis declared. "It has been wonderful to see the interest that people in town have taken in this project."

By the time she had finished her splendid job of decorating, she decided to stay on as its innkeeper. Phyllis is a warm and hospitable lady who seems to make her guests feel very much at home.

The Harrison House is a handsome red brick and sandstone building with an impressive arched entrance at the corner. The lobby is elegantly decorated with marble-topped tables, velvet upholstered chairs, deep green carpeting, and plum-colored draperies, and has a fine gift shop.

Upstairs is a parlor and dining area where a continental breakfast is served at tables set with old china and silver plate. "None of our china or silver matches," Phyllis laughed, "which makes it more fun—like being at Aunt Susie's or Grandma Murray's."

The guest rooms are all decorated differently with original antique beds and other interesting pieces, and they all have their own bathrooms. I noticed one room was named for Tom Mix, who had once lived here and worked just down the street.

The Murrays have recently purchased the Victor Building across the street to add 14 more guest rooms rooms to the Inn, with a restaurant on the top floor. All together they now have six retail spaces, and a 400 capacity conference room

I had a brief chat with Ron, a slow-talking, soft-spoken gentleman who now runs the Guthrie Job Corp. during the day. He told me how the town had accomplished the restoration of the Pollard Theatre, right next door to the inn. In fact, some of the guest rooms extend over the theater. "It's the only full-time professional repertory theater in Oklahoma," he said. "It opened with *Guys and Dolls*, and there will be ten musicals and plays presented throughout the year.

"We have a lot of history right here in Guthrie," he added. "You know, this town was established during the famous 'Run of '89,' when the Oklahoma Territory was opened to settlers."

And be sure not to miss the Cowboy Hall of Fame in Oklahoma City. I was amazed at the many outstanding paintings by famous artists.

HARRISON HOUSE, 124 W. Harrison St., P.O. Box 1555, Guthrie, OK 73044; 405-282-1000. A 35-guestroom (private baths) in-town bed-and-breakfast inn in the historic district of a bustling southwestern town, about 20 mi. north of Oklahoma City. King and double beds. Continental breakfast included in room rate. Open year-round.

Golf, fishing, bicycles, paddle boating, horseback riding, museums, theater, concerts, rodeos, territorial home tours, special events nearby. No pets. All major CCs. Phyllis and Ron Murray, owners/hosts.

DIRECTIONS: Guthrie is located on I-35, about 20 mi. north of Oklahoma City. The inn is at the corner of West Harrison and First Sts.

Texas

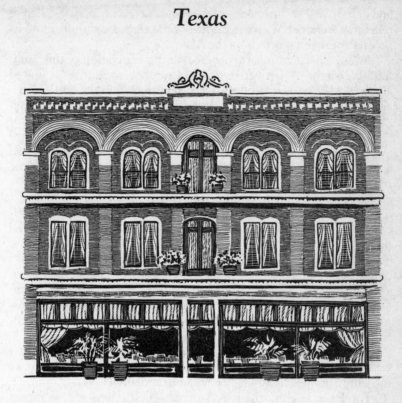

FAIRMOUNT HOTEL
San Antonio, Texas

In keeping with the Texas tradition of "doin' it bigger 'n' better," San Antonio become the home of the largest building ever moved—the turn-of-the-century Fairmount Hotel. The event was even noted in the *Guinness Book of World Records*.

The San Antonio Conservation Society rescued this spectacular example of Italianate Victorian architecture in 1980, and spent the next five years planning for its renovation. The first obstacle seemed insurmountable; the entire three-story structure had to be moved down the street and across a bridge to a new site near San Antonio's historic Riverwalk.

Using thirty-six dollies with pneumatic tires, the Fairmount was gingerly inched through San Antonio's streets and across the bridge (which had to be reinforced) to its new home. The move took six days and cost $650,000. I can only imagine the enormous collective sigh of relief that went out when the Fairmount was tipped and shifted into its new location, just blocks from the Alamo.

An unexpected find also occured during excavation of the building's basement. A University of Texas archaeological team sniffed around and discovered artifacts that had been used in the Battle of the Alamo: bayonets, cannon balls, and muskets revealed the preparation site of Santa Ana's army.

Luckily the hotel had been vacant for some time prior to its move so nothing of the original character had been tampered with. "We had a wonderful opportunity to see what a hotel built in this area at the turn of the century was like," architect Irby Hightower told me.

The renovation remained true to the elegance of its classical design features. Ten new rooms and a porte cochere were added, but so artistically that you will notice little, if any, difference between the old and the new.

Meticulous attention was paid to detail, including the restoration of porches at the rear of the hotel and verandahs at the front. Materials indigenous to the area, like textured throw rugs with Indian motifs and Mexican marble flooring, were paired with stone lamps, bleached wood floors, and warm desert colors to create a relaxed Southwestern ambience.

The soft peach of the walls, enhanced by contemporary abstract artwork, and the plush seating arrangements in the airy lobby, make the Fairmount feel like a small, charming residential hotel.

The lobby leads to the hotel's twenty guest rooms and seventeen suites. While the rooms are small, the feeling is intimate and personal. Lofted ceilings, walls that subtly become lighter in hue as they climb, and great expanses of windows create a sense of freshness and space. All the rooms have luxurious private baths and most have balconies.

Downstairs, oversized French doors lead to a pleasant inner courtyard where breakfast and lunch are served. Dinner in Polo's restaurant is a soul-satisfying experience. Small tables are organized around a cheerful wood-burning stove and antiques enhance the "at-home" feeling of this room.

Chef Michael Bomberg can whip out a Texas T-bone steak, or call upon his continental experience to create dishes from Africa, Asia, the Middle East, or Europe. Our dinner began with my appetizer of Texas quail, and my wife's choice of Gull crab and corn flan spiked with Jicama relish. A fresh salad of fried oysters and crisp greens was followed by a crisp pizza flavored with spicy lamb sausage.

Our entrée was shared: a plater of Gull prawns that had been coated with a pineapple-rum salsa, then grilled. Tender avacado fritters added a variety of texture and flavor.

After dinner we strolled the Riverwalk, just a hop-skip-and-jump from the Fairmount. Excursions to the River Center, the Alamo, the Governor's Palace, King William's Historical area, and the HemisFair Plaza and Convention Center are all close to the hotel.

FAIRMOUNT HOTEL, 401 S. Alamo, San Antonio, TX 78204; 512-224-8800, 1-800-642-3363 A distinctively renovated Italiante Victorian with 36 guestooms (private baths) and the ambience of an intimate residential hotel. Open all year. European plan. Close to Riverwalk, the Alamo, and shopping. No pets. Fairmont Hotel Company, owners.

DIRECTIONS: Contact the hotel for specific directions.

LA COLOMBE D'OR HOTEL AND RESTAURANT
Houston, Texas

Everything in Texas is vast. Expansive ranches, more cattle than you can count as you speed by on superhighways, oil fields with their every-pumping grasshopper like drills, and the somewhat surprisingly spectacular cosmopolitan cities. I had always expected to find cities more "western" in flavor here. That is why I was pleasantly amazed to find the European-inspired La Colombe d'Or in the heart of Houston.

Nestled on a city block surrounded by a residential area in the midst of Houston's art mueseums, La Colombe d'Or doesn't, thankfully, fit the Texas mold of big. With only six spectacular suites the ambience is one of an intimate private home where guests are treated with personal service. Stephen Zimmerman, La Colombe's owner, quickly complimented his staff when we first met and discussed his hotel. "You know, one of the wonderful things about La Colombe d'Or is the personable service we try to give all our guests," he confided. "In fact, we still have employees who have been with us since our opening."

Opening for La Colombe d'Oro took place in 1979 after Stephen saw the possiblities the rather run-down, yet splendid, old house offered. The home was originally built in 1923 and still had the fashionable qualities of architecture of the time. Stephen's skills as a lawyer and real estate developer certainly aided in the upgrading of the house, which he initially felt was in such disarray that it needed to be razed.

Already a successful proprietor of a local wine bar, Stephen was drawn to the challenge, and captured by the idea of opening an intimate restaurant and hotel like the ones he had been enchanted by during his summers on wine buying trips in the south of France.

The inn reflects Stephen's love of fine food, wine, and magnificent art. The six suites are all named for Impressionist painters, and each includes a private dining room where guests may entertain friends for dinner, or enjoy an intimate dinner for two. The rooms are elegant and tasteful. Four are decorated with Victorian antiques, one is more contemporary in style, and the sixth suite (the entire top floor) has its own Jacuzzi and a spacious view over the trees. Striking artwork, high ceilings, and polished hardwood floors covered by Oriental rugs adorn all the rooms.

The private baths are almost as large as the rooms and are studies in luxury. Scented English soap and almond shampoo are tucked near the tub, and snuggly terry cloth robes are conveniently hanging within your reach as you step from the bath.

The common areas of the hotel include the lovely four-room restaurant, the wood-paneled library with inviting wing backed chairs and tile framed fireplace, and the English-style pub. The pub is intimate, dark, and very lively, especially during weekends, when it draws on the surrounding art crowd.

While a continental breakfast is only available to guests, lunch and dinner are open to the public. Such fabulous specials as sauteed Gulf red snapper in an airy potato shell, laced with shiitaki mushrooms, are the norm (fresh fish arrives daily from the Gulf). Other choices may be a salad of breast of smoked squab on Texas field greens over a bed of sauteed wild mushrooms, or roast duck breast served with cinnamon-flavored seasonal fruit.

Whatever your choice, the freshest of ingredients are used, including herbs (more than 18 varieties) and restaurant-smoked meats and sausages. The hotel offers an extensive wine and cognac selection. An aperitif and port list is also available.

This is a charming hotel in the European tradition. In Stephen's words, "It has the casual elegance of the French Riviera."

LA COLOMBE D'OR HOTEL AND RESTAURANT, 3410 Montrose Blvd., Houston, TX 77006; 713-524-7999. An elegant 6-guestroom (private baths) European-style hotel in the museum area of Houston. Open all year. King beds. Continental breakfast included; lunch and dinner available. Walk to galleries, museums, Hermann Park, Astrodome. No pets. Smoking restricted. All major CCs. Stephen Zimmerman, owner/host.

DIRECTIONS: Just 5 minutes from Houston's central business district. Contact hotel for directions.

Utah

BRIGHAM STREET INN
Salt Lake City, Utah

The restoration and redecoration of this beautiful Victorian mansion, located on the street where Mormon leader Brigham Young had lived, makes an unusual story. What started as a fund-raising designers' showcase, with each room designed and decorated by a different interior designer, ended up being the Brigham Street Inn with award-winning designer rooms.

The fact that owners John and Nancy Pace had close ties with the architectural and interior design community helped. John heads an architectural firm and Nancy has been on the board of the Utah Heritage Foundation, and their purchase of what was a dilapidated but charming old home coalesced with the idea of a designer's showcase to benefit the Heritage Foundation. After an extremely successful show in 1982 with many awards and citations, the Paces purchased all of the furnishings and opened the inn.

There are eight working fireplaces, some with the original tile facings, and there are warm woods everywhere. Golden oak wainscotting highlights the entry, and bird's-eye maple is used in the parlor for the fireplace and a custom-made coffee table, while a cherrywood facade conceals a steel support in a third-floor guest room. In the dining room, with its shuttered windows and large table where guests enjoy a continental breakfast, a 17th-century Tibetan tapestry graces one wall. Local pianists sometimes come in the evening to play the grand piano in the sophisticated living room.

The innkeepers, however, do not rest on the laurels derived from their beautiful surroundings; they provide such special touches as turn-down service, clock radios, private telephones, concealed color TVs, morning newspapers, fresh flowers, and a host of additional helpful services, all aimed at their guests' comfort and enjoyment.

BRIGHAM STREET INN, 1135 East South Temple, Salt Lake City, UT 84102; 801-364-4461. A 9-guestroom (private baths) elegant B&B in a restored and revitalized neighborhood in the heart of Salt Lake City. Queen and twin beds. Complimentary continental breakfast and afternoon coffee or tea. Open all year. Air conditioning, telephones, color TV. Ski areas, University of Utah nearby and sightseeing in Utah's capital city. No pets. CCs: Visa, MC, AE. John and Nancy Pace, owners/hosts.

DIRECTIONS: From Temple Square in Salt Lake City, drive east on South Temple St. to 1135 E. South Temple.

THE HOMESTEAD
Midway, Utah

I felt exhilarated as I gazed far out across the plains and lush meadows to the magnificent snowcapped Mt. Timpanagos and Uinta ranges. I had no idea that Utah looked so much like Switzerland.

I was headed for the Homestead in the Heber Valley of north-central Utah; I'd been hearing good things about it. When I turned into the wide drive bordered by white fences and saw a cluster of buildings, dominated by the white manor house, amid the spacious grounds, I thought it looked very good, indeed.

Carole and Jerry Sanders are a young, enterprising, and enthusiastic couple who brought the Homestead back from the brink of disaster in the space of two years. Although they are dedicated to historic preservation, the remodeling and restoration of the buildings were only part of their plans, Jerry told me over an excellent dinner. "When Carole and I first saw this valley we were taken by its naturalness and beauty. Then I saw my two boys, ages seven and ten, chasing butterflies across the lawn, and I suddenly knew that's what I wanted the Homestead to be—a place where people could take the time to smell the roses and chase butterflies."

"Wasn't this originally a mineral hot springs resort?" I inquired.

"Yes," Carole replied. "Simon Schneitter started the Schneitter

House Hotel in 1886—it was later renamed the Virginia House. He was one of the many Swiss who settled in this valley, and who still retain their ethnic traditions, with special festivities on Labor Day weekend."

Other diners who were busily engaged with their dinners and their companions all seemed relaxed and happy. We were sitting in the large dining room (there are several others), with a piano and fireplace, many windows, a cart with flowers, and a number of antique pieces. The tables were nicely set with tablecloths and china. The whole aspect was most pleasant and inviting.

"We have a wonderful chef," Carole said. "He can really do anything, but we prefer to offer good country-type food, such as prime ribs and steaks. Our country-fried chicken has become quite famous." I was enjoying that country-fried chicken even as she spoke.

"Besides chasing butterflies," I asked, "what other sorts of things do your guests do?"

Jerry hastened to assure me that there is literally no end of activities available. "Our indoor pool has the mineral hot springs, and there are the outdoor pool and hot tub, along with all the usual resort activities, including children's activities. We have some special programs in the planning stages, one of which is a dude-ranch week, with riding lessons, breakfast rides, and overnight pack trips. We are also planning a health and fitness retreat."

The next morning, after a continental breakfast in my very attractive room in the Virginia House, which is run as a B&B and has a lovely little solarium and a hot tub, I was given a tour around the inn and the grounds. The guest rooms in each of the several buildings are decorated in a different motif. They are all most inviting and absolutely spotless.

There are little walks threading through the lawns and gardens, and there are sixty acres of fields, streams, and meadows. And there are lots of butterflies.

———————

THE HOMESTEAD, 700 No. Homestead Dr., Midway, UT 84049; 801-654-1102. (Outside Utah: 800-327-7220.) A 92-guestroom (private baths) historic country resort-inn nestled in Heber Valley, one of America's most beautiful alpine valleys, 50 mi. southeast of Salt Lake City. Breakfast, lunch, and dinner served daily. European plan. (Virginia House and Milk House include continental breakfast.) Open year-round. Indoor mineral and outdoor pools, hot tub, tennis, bicycles, horseback riding, snow-mobiling, xc skiing, buggy and sleigh rides, fishing, nature walks, shuffleboard, and volleyball on grounds. Golf, 4 major ski areas, Heber Valley railroad, hunting, and fishing nearby. No pets. Gerald and Carole Sanders, owners; Britt Mathwich, manager.

DIRECTIONS: From Salt Lake City, take I-80 east to Silver Creek Junction. Turn south on Hwy. 40/189 and in Heber City, turn west at Midway Lane (Rte. 113). Continue 5 mi. to Homestead Dr.

Pacific Coast and

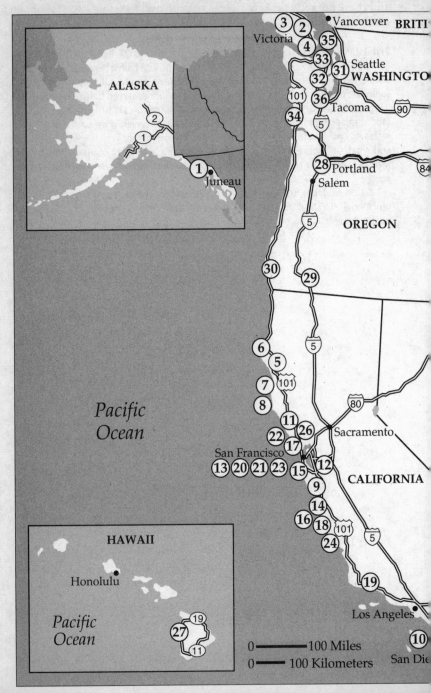

Victoria

Vancouver **BRITI**

Seattle **WASHINGTO**

Tacoma

Portland

Salem

OREGON

Sacramento

San Francisco

CALIFORNIA

Pacific Ocean

ALASKA

Juneau

HAWAII

Honolulu

Pacific Ocean

Los Angeles

San Die

| 0 | 100 Miles |
| 0 | 100 Kilometers |

British Columbia

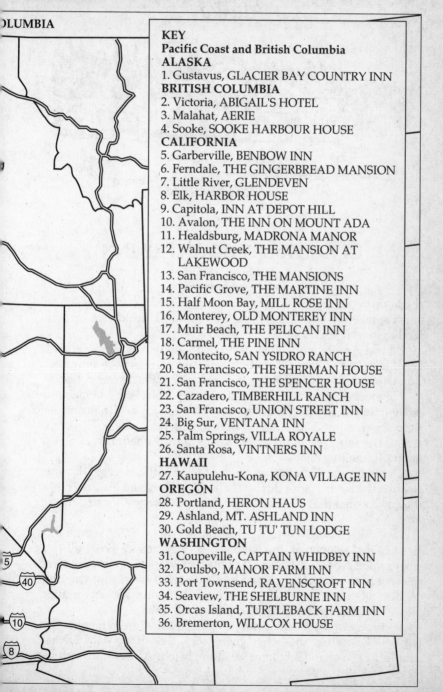

OLUMBIA

KEY
Pacific Coast and British Columbia
ALASKA
1. Gustavus, GLACIER BAY COUNTRY INN
BRITISH COLUMBIA
2. Victoria, ABIGAIL'S HOTEL
3. Malahat, AERIE
4. Sooke, SOOKE HARBOUR HOUSE
CALIFORNIA
5. Garberville, BENBOW INN
6. Ferndale, THE GINGERBREAD MANSION
7. Little River, GLENDEVEN
8. Elk, HARBOR HOUSE
9. Capitola, INN AT DEPOT HILL
10. Avalon, THE INN ON MOUNT ADA
11. Healdsburg, MADRONA MANOR
12. Walnut Creek, THE MANSION AT
    LAKEWOOD
13. San Francisco, THE MANSIONS
14. Pacific Grove, THE MARTINE INN
15. Half Moon Bay, MILL ROSE INN
16. Monterey, OLD MONTEREY INN
17. Muir Beach, THE PELICAN INN
18. Carmel, THE PINE INN
19. Montecito, SAN YSIDRO RANCH
20. San Francisco, THE SHERMAN HOUSE
21. San Francisco, THE SPENCER HOUSE
22. Cazadero, TIMBERHILL RANCH
23. San Francisco, UNION STREET INN
24. Big Sur, VENTANA INN
25. Palm Springs, VILLA ROYALE
26. Santa Rosa, VINTNERS INN
HAWAII
27. Kaupulehu-Kona, KONA VILLAGE INN
OREGON
28. Portland, HERON HAUS
29. Ashland, MT. ASHLAND INN
30. Gold Beach, TU TU' TUN LODGE
WASHINGTON
31. Coupeville, CAPTAIN WHIDBEY INN
32. Poulsbo, MANOR FARM INN
33. Port Townsend, RAVENSCROFT INN
34. Seaview, THE SHELBURNE INN
35. Orcas Island, TURTLEBACK FARM INN
36. Bremerton, WILLCOX HOUSE

Alaska

GLACIER BAY COUNTRY INN

Gustavus, Alaska

If you've ever thought of homesteading in Alaska's wilderness, you, and Glacier Bay's innkeepers Al and Annie Unrein, are made of hardier stuff than I.

Al and Annie's rustic lodge is nestled in Gustavus, a spectacularly beautiful spot on Glacier Bay which can only be reached by air or boat. The Unreins won the right to homestead their 160-acre site in 1979.

"There were only five parcels of land available," Al told me as we drove from the airport toward the inn. "With many applicants, names were drawn at random—and we were among the lucky five!" At the end of the inn's gravel drive the woods fanned open, revealing the impressive multi-gabled lodge.

Originally the Unreins had planned to farm the acreage. But after clearing the land, digging ditches, building bridges, and planting crops, they discovered that the market for their produce was located too far away.

"So, since Glacier Bay is a prime tourist attraction," Al continued, "we decided to open an inn. Besides, it's a great way to use all that great garden produce." The result of their six-year effort (three of those years with no electricity!) is a uniquely designed rustic inn with nine comfortable guest rooms, two lounges, and an intimate conversation pit with seating around an antique pot-bellied stove.

Annie greeted us at the dining room doorway. "Just in time! Lunch is on." We joined the other guests and, over a bowl of creamy cauliflower soup and a halibut salad sandwich, Al went on with his story. "We used the spruce, hemlock, and pine from right here on the property, and milled it ourselves," he said with pride.

Floor-to-ceiling windows gave me a northward view of hayfields, rainforests and mountains. The room is cozy and warm, kept toasty during winter months and chilly evenings by a large wood stove.

A warm, friendly woman, Annie has decorated the inn in an eclectic style with special attention paid to comfort. Cushy sofas and easy chairs, rockers, and Alaskan art and artifacts, including Annie's own cross-stitch pieces, create an informal country-casual atmosphere.

Since I was visiting on my own this trip, Annie suggested that I might like to stay in The Nest. Intrigued, I agreed. What fun! I had to climb a handcrafted log and rope spiral staircase through the library to reach this tiny, unusual room. Windows on three sides opened out to fantastic views (a feature shared by most of the rooms). Tucked away up there, snuggled between flannel sheets, I've never slept more soundly.

All three meals are included with the room rate. Breakfast includes a variety of choice tidbits. I particularly enjoyed the scrambled eggs with fresh garden herbs, crisp bacon, and fresh nectarine buckle, and there was plenty of rich coffee.

Local fishermen supplied a real treat for dinner—fresh Dungeness crab. The steamed crab was served with melted butter for dipping, homemade rolls, a crisp salad, sauteed new potatoes, and tender-crunchy stir-fried snow peas. Heaven!

Glacier Bay offers a multitude of outdoor activities: whale watching, fishing for giant halibut or coho and king salmon, and camera-stalking the local wildlife, including bears and great bald eagles. The Unreins are happy to help you make plans and can arrange a boat tour into Glacier Bay or a flightseeing tour. I got adventurous and explored by kayak, sharing the waters with some curious seals.

You may come away from your stay at Glacier Bay Country Inn with a renewed desire to follow the Unreins' lead and homestead in the serenity of Alaska. Me? I think I'll just come and visit Al and Annie.

GLACIER BAY COUNTRY INN, P.O. Box 5, Gustavus, AK 99826; 907-697-2288. From October to April, P.O. Box 2557, St. George, UT 84771, 801-673-8480, Fax: 801-673-8481. A warm, 9-guestroom (7 private baths) owner-built rustic country inn nestled on 160 acres of Alaskan wilderness. Open all year. Queen and twin beds. American plan. Sport fishing, kayaking, hiking, boat tours, flight tours, biking, and beach-walking. Pack warm, waterproof clothing. No pets. Smoking restricted. Annie and Al Unrein, owners/hosts.

DIRECTIONS: Contact inn to make arrangements.

ABIGAIL'S HOTEL

Victoria, B.C., Canada

"Fanciful. Feminine. Timeless." one magazine stated. "Romantic, European inn," described another. "The halls smell of good coffee and beautiful women," quoted one more. I eagerly anticipated my stay at Abigail's Hotel and I was not disappointed upon my arrival.

It fit all descriptions and exceeded my expectations, as did the friendly owner, Bill McKechnie, who has received nearly as much press as the hotels he creates. The builder/lawyer/architect/innkeeper has a knack for ferreting out the beauty of dilapidated, heritage homes and reworking them into masterpieces. His vision for Abigail's was inspired from a Rodin sculpture of a young woman with flowers in her hat. (A copy rests on a table at near the front door.)

Charming was the first word that came to mind as I approached the hotel, located in a residential cul-de-sac only a few blocks from downtown Victoria. Vibrant petunias, marigold, and pansies, along with evergreen shrubs surround the four story English Tudor, built in 1930.

Forest green and burnt orange trim set off the exterior stucco. Curved concrete hand railing arched up the stairway to the front door.

Catherine Wollner, Bill's choice of innkeeper for Abigail's, was on hand to welcome me, offering a quick tour of the first floor. Tones of soft peach, rose, teal, and ivory are sharpened by steep angled archways and high vaulted ceilings. The library, the social center of the inn, has comfortable, burgundy couches strategically placed to enjoy the warmth from the dark, granite fireplace. This became my favorite spot in the evenings to chat with other guests over port and hors d'oeuvre. Catherine introduced me to the inn's cook, attending to clean-up details from the morning's breakfast. Such a homey room.. lace curtains draped across the windows, light oak tables, and a brick fireplace along one wall. The dining area extends over a counter into the kitchen allowing for banter between guests and employees as well as delicious aromas to waft throughout the room. I caught a hint of baked coffee cake in the air even now.

"Just wait till you taste the baked eggs with smoked salmon and fresh asparagus tomorrow morning," Catherine said enticingly. As we made our way back to the front door to reclaim my luggage, Catherine informed me a wicker basket lunch was mine for the asking so long as I placed the request the evening before.

With Catherine in the lead, I climbed the stairs to my room. I knew this was a place I could spend some time in as soon as the door opened. I could just envision myself sprawled across the fluffy goose down comforter on the bed, an intriguing novel in hand, and a fire cracking and popping in the fireplace. The crystal chandelier sending beams of light to all corners of the room. Or I just might recover from an afternoon of sight-seeing and shopping by relaxing in the bubbling, warm waters of the Jacuzzi tub in the adjacent bath, with its glistening tile floors and brass fixtures. Hmmm...I might even be tempted to extend my stay!!

ABIGAIL'S HOTEL, 906 McClure St., Victoria, British Columbia, Canada V8V 3E7; 604-388-5363. A hint of Europe in this Tudor style hotel having sixteen guestrooms, some with fireplaces and Jacuzzi tubs. Open year round. Full breakfast included. A short walk brings you to antique shops, art galleries, gift stores, restaurants and pubs. (celebrate the English spirit with a home brewed ale) For history buffs, drive to the Lt. Governor's mansion, Craigcarroch Castle or the 106 year old Rithet Building, now a gallery. The hotel cannot accommodate pets. Welcomes CCs: MC, V. Bill McKechnie, owner/Catherine Wollner, host.

DIRECTIONS: From the Inner Harbour go north on Government St. Take a right onto Humboldt St. and continue four blks. to Vancouver St. Left on Vancouver St. four and one-half blks. then left onto McClure St. Abigail's is at the end of the cul-de-sac.

THE AERIE

Malahat, B.C., Canada

As I walked into the dining room, I didn't know where to look first...the panoramic view spanning from the gulf inlets below out to the Olympic Mountains or upwards to 23-carat gold leafed ceiling of the dining room. Both nearly more than my eyes could behold. There is very little about The Aerie that is not unique and unusual including its origination.

Leo and Maria Schuster, creators of The Aerie were living in the Bahamas, where Leo was executive chef of the Trump Hotels. Already seeking a cooler climate and a retirement form of life, when a friend suggested they explore Victoria, Leo and Maria planned a four-week vacation there.

As Leo explains it, "As soon as I set foot on the Malahat, I knew this was the place I wanted to retire." Maria's version is a bit more detailed.

"Having travelled the main and back road of the Malahat, determined to find property, we spotted a man leaning against a backhoe. We stopped and asked him if he knew of any property that was for sale. He responded that he owned 100 acres we were on, and although it wasn't for sale he would be happy to show it to us. Leo and I, dressed in our Bahama whites, climbed into the bucket of the backhoe for a tour of the mountain. I'll never forget when we met up with his wife. He said, 'Come over here, I've found two bloody tourists!'" Maria and Leo were both chuckling, as Maria continued her story, "That ride was the beginning of a friendship, and the eventual purchase of 15 acres above the look-out on the Malahat."

Leo took over from here, "Our original plan was to build a small bed and breakfast to support us into our retirement. But the people here are so friendly and enthusiastic!! Everyone just kept encouraging us to expand our vision and so we did."

The culmination of the vision was an expansive European style guesthouse tucked in the forest near the top of the mountain. Breathtaking views of the Pacific, Gulf Islands and Inlets, and beyond to the mountain range are just a part of the every day scenery. No automobile noises, just the whistle of wind through the trees and birds calling to one another. The inn is closed to the public during the day, ensuring even more privacy of guests occupying the twelve rooms and suites.

Each of the guest rooms presents its own special features. It include a private Jacuzzi, a fireplace, cozy sitting area, or spectacular views from a private balcony. Just so no one feels deprived, there is also a sauna, large hot tub, and sun deck made available to all the guests. My room also had handcarved furniture and a canopy bed.

Each night at 6:00, the doors open for public dining. Leo's expertise is well known to the local folks, and the restaurant fills to capacity quickly. The menu changes nightly testing Leo's creative talents. He never seems to fail. I began with a seafood bisque seasoned with cilantro, followed by a heaping plate of spring greens coated with a balsamic vinaigrette. I studied the entrée selection in detail and finally settled on Black Tiger Prawns with Herbs de Provence. The inn does not have a freezer, insuring that all the food prepared is fresh. The prawns had such flavor, as I sipped a glass of wine, chosen from their well stocked cellar, between bites. Freshly brewed Kona coffee accompanied my dessert choice of chilled cheese souffle with raspberry coulis. As I sat in the dining room, china and crystal place settings before me, gold ceiling above, and the beautiful view out picture windows, I felt a bit like the royalty Leo has served in his colorful past. The waiter reminded me that breakfast would be served bright and early to all the guests, although it was a little hard to think about another meal just then!

A helpful member of the staff arranged for a rental car and I took the 25 minute ride to Victoria to spend the day. By the end of the day I was longing to return to the peaceful solitude of that mountain retreat named The Aerie.

―――――

THE AERIE, P.O. Box 108, Malahat, B.C. V0R 2L0, Canada; 604-743-4055 or 604-743-7115. Escape to this adult-oriented European Guesthouse mountain retreat with only 12 guestrooms, including spacious suites. Some in- room Jacuzzis, fireplaces, and private balconies. Conference facilities offered. Sun deck, sauna, and large hot tub for guest use. Breakfast included. Dining room open to the public with menu changes each evening. Spectacular views to the Pacific, inlets, all the way to the mountain ranges. Open all year. Reservations suggested. If you can pull yourself away from the peace and quiet, it is only a 25 minute drive to Victoria. No pets, please. Leo and Maria Schuster, owners-hosts.

DIRECTIONS: From Victoria take the Trans-Canada Highway north to the Spectacle Lake Provincial Park turnoff. Take the first park turnoff and follow the sign to The Aerie.

SOOKE HARBOUR HOUSE
Sooke, B.C., Canada

Standing on the bluff at the top of the steps leading down to the shore, I looked out across the Strait of Juan de Fuca to the Olympic Mountain Peninsula and off to the east to East Sooke Park. Across the way was a very beautiful farm, toward which Sinclair Philip waved an arm. "Do you realize that farm is inhabited by a family of cougars? Seventy percent of the world's cougar population lives on Vancouver Island." I was amazed to hear that. Sinclair, a handsome, dark-haired young man with a neatly clipped beard, continued, "You can see deer on that farm and on our property, too. Harbor seals, sea lions, and otters are out there, and we frequently see gray and killer whales as well."

I had to admit this was a remarkable location for an inn, and Sinclair was certainly a walking encyclopedia on the infinite variety of animal and plant life that flourishes here on sea and land. I was looking down at a beautiful rock garden that terraced the slope, and many other gardens laced with little gravel paths surround the white clapboard inn buildings. They boast masses of vegetables, herbs, fruits, and edible flowers. Some garden chairs were grouped on the terrace facing the water.

This is a very informal, contemporary place with an emphasis on the natural surroundings. There are lots of plants and flowers, magazines and books, and modern paintings and wall hangings. One of the two dining rooms is arranged as a sort of living/dining room with a comfortable sofa and rocking chairs grouped around a fireplace, and on the other side of the room the dining area is lined with windows overlooking the water.

Sinclair and his wife, Fredrica, with the help of friends and others, who are variously architects, artisans, and craftspeople, have created an environment that is aesthetically pleasing in every way. Many of the guest rooms have their own private gardens and porches, with double whirlpool baths placed to afford spectacular views of the ocean.

Every room has a special theme that is carried out in the decor; for

instance, the Herb Garden Room is filled with herbs, and the hand-painted ceramic tiles in the bathroom depict various herbs. This is a split-level room with a fireplace and a private porch with a hot tub for two. (All of the rooms have fireplaces.) Stained-glass windows made with real underwater objects decorate the Underwater Garden Room.

Sinclair was telling me about the Indian Room. "This is the largest and most spectacular room we have, with a balcony extending the entire length of the room. There is a bathtub for two in front of the two-sided fireplace with a view of the ocean. It has multiple skylights, a vaulted ceiling, and is full of Indian artifacts and masks. Victor Newman, a very well-known Kwakiutl carver, helped decorate it."

Fredrica was born and raised in France, and she and Sinclair met in Nice on the Riviera. This unusual and talented couple found Sooke Harbour House in 1979, and in the intervening years they have established an international reputation for their imaginative and creative cuisine. With the abundance of the sea just outside their kitchen door, the daily changing menu features such unusual items as sea urchin, octopus, sea cucumbers, abalone, and limpets. Their chefs concoct delicacies that have aroused the admiration of food writers from around the world. The restaurant has been rated as one of the top ten in Canada for several years, and one year as *the* best restaurant in Canada. Besides their incredibly fresh fish and seafood specialties, they draw from their vast gardens and obtain local organically-raised meats like lamb, duck, suckling kid, squab, and young rabbit to round out the menu.

Watching the sun set over the ocean, I tried to think of someone who wouldn't love to stay here. I couldn't think of a soul.

———

SOOKE HARBOUR HOUSE, 1528 Whiffen Spit Rd., R.R. #4, Sooke, B.C., Canada V0S 1N0; 604-642-3421. A 13-guestroom (private baths) disarmingly informal country inn with sophisticated cuisine on the west coast of Vancouver Island, 23 mi. west of Victoria. King and queen beds. Full breakfast and light lunch included in room rate. Open year-round. Wheelchair access. Bicycles available on premises. Beachcombing, birdwatching, nature walks, Botanical Beach, kayaking, windsurfing, scuba diving, hiking in Pacific Rim park, and excellent fishing for winter Chinook and Tyee salmon nearby. Children welcome. Well-behaved pets welcome. Two dogs in residence. Smoking restricted in several rooms. Fredrica and Sinclair Philip, owners/hosts.

DIRECTIONS: From Victoria, take Hwy. 1 west to Hwy. 14. Continue on Hwy. 14 to Sooke. Turn left at Whiffen Spit Rd. (approx. 1 mi. past traffic light) and continue to inn.

California

BENBOW INN
Garberville, California

The owners-innkeepers of the Benbow are Patsy and Chuck Watts, whom I have known for many years. The one outstanding quality that each of them has in such marvelous abundance is enthusiasm, and all of the improvements and additions to this truly unusual northern California inn have been undertaken by them with great joy and love.

"Ever since Day One," said Chuck, "we have been very happy and have had a really tremendous time. It's a continuing challenge and we've gotten a great deal accomplished, but I like the idea that the future is big with plans."

"We feel that we are a destination resort-inn, able to accommodate and provide amusement and diversion for all our guests of any age," chimed in Patsy. "We have acquired some fabulous antique pieces, most particularly a magnificent carved buffet for the dining room. We have added a beautiful carved mantel for the fireplace in the lobby and have installed an antique mantel and a fireplace in the lounge.

"We will be having our wine tasting in November, and this has now become a semiannual affair, with many of the California boutique wineries represented."

I first visited the Benbow Inn in 1973 and was immediately intrigued not only with its location in the glorious redwood country of northern California, but also with its design, which shows definite influences of the Art Deco style of the early 1920s. There are also some touches of an English Tudor manor house found in the half-timbers, carved dark wood paneling, solid oak furniture, bookcases, hardwood floors, handsome Oriental rugs, and truly massive fireplace in the main living room.

Some guest rooms are on the terrace and garden levels with private patios. With four-poster beds, antiques, and country fabrics, their decor is most attractive. Three of them have fireplaces and VCRs. Other guest rooms in the main inn had also been handsomely redecorated, and my own room, Number 313, was on the top floor and looked out over the gardens and a wonderful changing panorama of clouds. For those who like to sleep with their windows open you will hear the traffic on Rte. 101.

The Benbow is, indeed, a destination resort-inn—in addition to swimming, it offers tennis on two tennis courts nearby, a good golf course within walking distance, hiking, and magnificent backroading. By the way, it's very accessible by public transportation since the Route 101 buses stop almost at the front door.

At Christmastime there's a twelve-foot tree with teddy bears playing drums hanging from every branch. Under the tree there are Patsy's very special antique, oversized toys. An antique sleigh is on the front porch filled with presents and wreaths. Holly and masses of decorations are all over the inn.

On Christmas Day there is a special two-seatings Christmas dinner and everyone has a wonderful time.

Incidentally, in the fall and all through the holidays, English tea and scones are served in the lobby. Chuck's mother, Marie, is the tea lady.

The Benbow also has a film library with over 300 classic films. These are shown every evening. On one of my visits I cheered and wept a little at James Cagney's great portrayal of George M. Cohan in *Yankee Doodle Dandy*.

Patsy, Chuck, and Truffles (their new Afghan hound, the most photographed canine in northern California) are having a wonderful time greeting guests, sharing their enthusiasm, and providing their own bubbling brand of warmth and hospitality. In short, they're model innkeepers. I'm glad they and the Benbow Inn found each other.

BENBOW INN, 445 Lake Benbow Dr., Garberville, CA 95440; 707-923-2124. A 55-guestroom (private baths) English Tudor inn in the redwood country of northern California. King, queen, and twin beds available. Air conditioning. On Rte. 101. European plan. Breakfast, lunch, and dinner served to travelers daily. Open mid–April to November 28; re-open December 17 for holiday season. Swimming on grounds; golf, tennis adjacent. Hiking and magnificent backroading. Chuck, Patsy, and Truffles Watts, owners/hosts.

DIRECTIONS: From San Francisco follow Rte. 101 north 200 mi. and exit at Benbow.

THE GINGERBREAD MANSION
Ferndale, California

What a fun place this is! From the moment innkeeper Ken Torbert showed me to the Fountain Suite with its fabulous fireplace, chaise lounge, and two old-fashioned Victorian clawfoot tubs, I knew I was in the lap of luxury. In fact, my wife and I couldn't wait to slide into his-and-her firelight-illuminated bubble baths after a hard day of touring.

If the Fountain Suite is occupied, there are eight other spacious rooms to inhabit here, including the deluxe Gingerbread Suite with its "toesy-to-toesy" tubs, or the romantic Rose Suite or Lilac Room. Each is unique and elegantly furnished with antiques. The rooms are spacious and papered in delicate patterns. Attention to detail is obvious. "We're sticklers for all the little things that make our guests comfortable," Ken confided to me. The hand-dipped chocolates waiting on our pillows were two of those little details.

Ken has created a showplace with his inn. The small village of Ferndale, often called the Victorian Village, is something of a marvel in

itself. Many examples of Victoriana still exist here, harking back to the late 1880s when Scandinavian, Swiss-Italian, and Portuguese dairy farmers prospered and built splendid homes known as "Butterfat Palaces" in the Eastlake, Carpenter Gothic, and Queen Anne styles. Ferndale has, in fact, been designated a State Historic Landmark.

None of these homes is more of a standout than the Gingerbread Mansion. The spectacular peach and yellow showplace is a combination of the Queen Anne and Eastlake architectural styles accented by elaborate woodwork around turrets, gables and porches. Three-story fuchsias, boxwood topiaries, and a fountain with two camellia trees add to the inn's English garden.

Originally built as a doctor's residence in 1899, the home was later enlarged and used as a hospital. Its checkered past also includes stints as a rest home, an American Legion Hall, and an apartment building. Ken rescued the structure in 1983, enventually expanding it to nine rooms and suites with private baths, plus four parlors.

The furnishings are Victorian, yet comfortable. A number of fireplaces offer cozy spots for relaxing. Afternoon tea and cakes are served in the parlors, where there are books, magazines, and a mind-boggling thousand-piece jigsaw puzzle of the inn.

Ken takes exceptional care in running the inn. His continental-plus breakfasts are served family style in the formal dining room overlooking the marvelous garden and fountain. Two large lace-covered tables are set with green depression glass. Home-baked goodies, including his special Lemony Lemon Bread, local cheeses, cakes, breads, hard-boiled eggs, fruit, fresh-squeezed orange juice, and rich brewed coffee are the fare.

Dinner suggestions are freely given and include recommendations to local restaurants. Leave for dinner early to explore the village. I found all sorts of interesting shops, including businesses that have been in operation since the 1880s: the pharmacy, the local newspaper, a wonderful old mercantile store, as well as a shop full of old and rare books, a candy factory, a blacksmith, and many crafts shops and galleries.

THE GINGERBREAD MANSION, 400 Berding St., Ferndale, CA 95536; 707-786-4000. A 9-guestroom (private baths) Victorian mansion in a historic landmark Victorian village in northern Calif., 5 mi. from the Pacific Coast. Queen beds; rooms with queen and twin beds available. Breakfast and afternoon tea included. Recommendations and reservations made for restaurants within walking distance. Open year-round. Garden, games, puzzles, and bicycles on premises. Unique village for sightseeing, shopping, antiquing, visiting crafts shops, art galleries, museum, repertory theater, coastal drives, Avenue of the Giants (redwoods), river activities, festivals, and many other events nearby. No pets. No smoking. CCs: Visa, MC. Ken Torbert, owner/host.

DIRECTIONS: From Hwy. 101, take Fernbridge exit and continue 5 mi. to Ferndale.

GLENDEVEN
Little River, California

This section of northern California on Highway 1 is rapidly becoming a weekend and midweek vacation area for residents of the Bay area. The drive up the coast with its tremendous cliffs and headlands is most spectacular. Glendeven is actually in Little River, just a mile and a half south of the historic coastal town of Mendocino, with its interesting shops, galleries and restaurants.

Innkeepers Jan and Janet de Vries told me that the original farmhouse, barn, and watertower were built by Isaiah Stevens in 1867. I must say that he picked a very gracious location and today this Victorian house is a cheerful bed-and-breakfast inn.

The center of activity is in the main farmhouse living room, with a fireplace, a baby grand piano, and windows facing south affording an extraordinary view of the well-tended garden and the bay. Both Jan and Janet de Vries are designers and are involved in contemporary arts and crafts, as evidenced by the ceramics, the paintings, and the numerous gallery notices.

The guest rooms have quite unusual furnishings with a generous number of antiques as well as contemporary decorations. The Stevenscroft rooms and Eastlin suite have their own fireplaces and decks. All guest rooms have views of the bay or the gardens. A refurbished barn has been converted into a two-story suite, perfect for four.

The continental breakfast is generous, including fresh orange juice, fresh fruit or baked apple, muffins, morning cakes, coffee, tea, and baskets of brown hard-boiled eggs.

GLENDEVEN, 8221 North Highway One, Little River. CA 95456; 707-937-0083. A 11-guestroom (9 private baths) bed-and-breakfast elegant farmhouse/inn on a headland meadow overlooking Little River Bay. Queen, double and twin beds. Open year-round. Most convenient for enjoyable excursions to the northern California coastal towns and many nearby parks and beaches. No pets. CCs: Visa, MC. Jan and Janet de Vries, owners/hosts.

DIRECTIONS: Either follow coastal Hwy. 1 all the way from San Francisco, skirting the shores of the Pacific, or follow Rte. 101 to Cloverdale; Rte. 128 to Hwy. 1, and then proceed north to Little River.

HARBOR HOUSE
Elk, California

This is another good place to greet spring, because spring comes lustily and vigorously in this part of the world, and the sea in its many moods washes ashore gently or raucously, but the rhythm never ceases. I awaken in the morning to look through the trees to the great rock formations that seem to have been thrown almost helter-skelter from the end of the headlands. Helen and Dean Turner, the innkeepers, had thoughtfully provided a very comfortable chair in the window, with a perfect view of the sea stacks and tunnels, which, along with the arches, caves, and small islands, provide an unusual view from the inn.

This particular group of rock formations was at one time a staging area for the loading and the unloading of lumber schooners. Fortunately, the story of this community has been graphically presented in the unusual brochure of the inn, with dramatic photographs showing just the scenes that I have described.

The subtitle for Harbor House on the rustic sign on Route 1 is "By the Sea." Fewer words are more apt than these. Although the main entrance is on the highway, the immediate focus of all the attention is in the rear of the inn, which looks out over the Pacific, and almost every guest room has this view.

The main building of the inn was built in 1916 as an executive's residence. The construction is entirely of virgin redwood from the nearby Albion Forest. In fact, it is an enlarged version of the "Home of Redwood" exhibit building of the 1915 Panama-Pacific International Exposition in San Francisco.

Guest rooms in the main building and adjacent cottages are individually heated and have private baths. Fireplaces and parlor stoves are stocked with wood, and some of the accommodations have sun decks.

I reflected that were it not for the dominance of the sea, the view from the *other* side of the house across the meadows and into the low coastal hills could be thought of as very beautiful.

Because Helen and Dean Turner have always had a great deal of involvement and interest in the arts, from time to time Harbor House presents programs by soloists and chamber music players. The living room with its wood paneling provides an ideal atmosphere. As Helen says, "So many artists live on the coast and an intimate concert in the living room is a wonderful way to hear them." Also, Helen tells me, "Sometimes these concerts are spontaneous and informal, as a talented guest sits down at the Steinway or picks up the guitar."

Our dinner was the nice, slow, mellow kind I love and get so rarely. It was such pleasant, unhurried service. We were free to be alone together or speak to others if we wished, a wonderful blend of solitude and society.

We got wonderful pictures of all the colorful flowers and scenery. Beautiful as the pictures are, they do not capture what it was like to be there, or explain why I felt homesick when I had to leave.

HARBOR HOUSE, 5600 S. Hwy. #1, Box 369, Elk, CA 95432; 707-877-3203. A 6-guestroom, 4-cottage (private baths) seaside inn, 16 mi. south of Mendocino, overlooking the Pacific. King and queen beds available. Fireplaces in four cottages. Breakfast and dinner served daily to house guests. Open year-round. Private beach, ocean wading, abalone and shell hunting, fishing, and hiking on grounds. Golf, biking, boating, ocean white-water tours, deep-sea fishing, and canoeing nearby. No pets. Three cats in residence. No credit cards. Dean and Helen Turner, innkeepers.

DIRECTIONS: Elk is approx. 3 hrs. from Golden Gate Bridge. Take Hwy. 101 to Cloverdale, then Hwy. 128 west to Hwy. 1. Continue on Hwy. 1 south 6 mi. to Harbor House.

INN AT DEPOT HILL

Capitola-by-the-Sea, California

Imagine you are aboard a train: the clank-clank of metal wheels on the tracks, the scenery a slow moving picture past your window, the constant gentle rocking motion lulling you into a dreamy state.

"Next stop...The Inn At Depot Hill!" calls the conductor of imagination. "All those getting off at Sissinghurst, Paris, Delft, Portofino! Next stop!" The hooting whistle heralds your approach into the station.

My dream state ends, replaced by the reality of my approach by car to the newly refurbished Inn at Depot Hill, on the bluffs above the Monterey Bay. Trains still pass by the Southern Pacific Depot several times a week. They do not stop, however, for the Depot was transformed into Capitola's first bed and breakfast in 1990 by Suzie Lankes, a onetime insurance adjuster, and Dan Floyd, a Silicon Valley entrepreneur. Suzie's great-grandfather was an architect for Southern Pacific Railroad, leaving her no stranger to depot blueprints. The inn became her inspiration.

The simple design of the old depot station, dating back to 1901, still retains much of its original style. Doric columns, some original

and some hand-milled to match, sturdily support the eaves which surround the tan and white structure. A wrought iron entrance gate opens
to a red brick courtyard and front porch. Around back is a garden
patio, bricks laid in a herringbone pattern, that overflows with climbing roses, trumpet vines, and azaleas, all flourishing in the cool ocean
climate. Patio tables neatly covered with starched white cloths make
this a perfect place to enjoy an afternoon glass of champagne.

Dan and Suzie enlisted the expertise of Dan's sister-in-law, Linda
Floyd, an interior designer from San Francisco, to complete the room
renovations. The dining room has a semi-circular bay window that
originally served as the ticket window. There are no tickets sold, however, for the delicious breakfasts—consisting of homemade muffins,
pastries, and hot entrées such as Quiche St. Germain, Fritatta Hicoise,
or Tynde Pandekager, served each morning on the unique three-
legged, lion-and-paw dining room table—are available only to guests.
Suzie told me that the unusual antique table came from the Philip-
pines, and was just one of the many pieces Linda had scouted out of
antique shops in England and France.

The parlor has a three-sided brocade pouffe, hot pink in color and
bordered with lively fringe. An Oriental rug partially covers the dark
sheen of the hardwood floor, and a gilded Venetian glass chandelier
hangs overhead. In addition to the baby grand piano, built-in bookshelves filled with reading material, and a cozy fireplace, an abundance
of railroad memorabilia captures the era.

"The guest rooms are named and fashioned after different parts of
the world, as if you are taking a railway journey and stopping off at different destinations," Suzie explained as I checked in. "All have fireplaces and feather beds, and some have hot tubs. We think Linda did
wonders in combining classic European design with a theme from each
location."

Leading the way, she informed me I would be staying in the Delft
Room, which displays a Dutch influence. The fireplace, already flam-
ing behind glass doors, is faced with blue and white tiles imported from
Holland. Varied shades of blue make the room a place of tranquility.
Bouquets of orange and red tulips added a hint of brightness. The room
has its own private garden and outdoor Jacuzzi, as well as a large marble shower in the adjoining bath.

Each morning I enjoyed a brisk walk along Capitola Beach, only a
block from the inn. One evening I heard an outdoor concert at the
beach, which are offered weekly towards the end of summer. The town
of Capitola offers plenty of shopping and restaurants. For a wider variety, Santa Cruz with its famous Boardwalk is only a short drive away,
and less than an hour behind the wheel took me into the Carmel-
Monterey area. But shopping was last on my list of things to do, for I

became quickly enchanted with the inn and its endless supply of memorabilia on local railroad history.

INN AT DEPOT HILL, 250 Monterey Ave., Capitola-by-the-Sea, CA 95010; 408-462-3376. Circa 1900 railroad depot converted into a handsome 8-guestroom B&B, each room with fireplaces and unique in design. Overlooking the village of Capitola and Monterey Bay. Breakfast included. Afternoon hors d'oeuvres, wines, and tea, plus late evening dessert treats. Mostly queen beds. Some hot tubs. Open all year. Two-night minimum with Saturday. Restricted smoking areas. Santa Cruz, a short drive away, offers fun at the Boardwalk and great shopping. Monterey and Carmel are less than an hour's drive. No pets welcome. CCs: Visa, MC, AE. Suzie Hanks and Dan Floyd, owners/hosts.

DIRECTIONS: Connect from Hwy. 1, 101, or 280 South to Hwy. 17/880 toward Santa Cruz. Take the Watsonville/Monterey/Hwy.#1 South turnoff. Pass the Soquel/Capitola exit, and take the Park Ave., New Brighton Beach exit, going right onto Park Ave. Proceed 1 mi. to T-intersection of Monterey Ave. Turn left. Driveway of inn is next left on corner of Park and Monterey Aves.

THE INN ON MOUNT ADA
Avalon, California

In 1921, when chewing gum magnate/philanthropist William Wrigley, Jr. stood back and, in his mind's eye, saw a vision of a summer home, he pulled out all the stops. Located on 5.5 acres of the lovely island of Santa Catalina, high atop hills overlooking Avalon Harbor, the compound covers nearly 7,000 square feet, which includes a main house ornamented with elaborate columns, arches, panel work, and handmade moldings. The den, sun room, living room, card lounge, dining rooms, and butler's pantry complete the first level. Six bedrooms fill the second floor.

Eventually the property was donated to the University of Southern California for use as a marine institute. The university funded rehabilitation to meet electrical and plumbing codes, as the building had been vacant for more than twenty-five years prior to the university's possession.

In February 1985, a thirty-year lease was signed by USC and the Mt. Ada Inn Corporation, composed of island residents Susie and Wayne Griffin, Marlene McAdam, and ex-residents Suzie and Scott Wauben, and the property was transformed into a B&B inn.

With backgrounds in home economics, restaurant management, computer bookkeeping services, interior design, and civic affairs, the partnership had the necessary combination of business experience to operate such an undertaking. "Everyone in Avalon has chosen to live here as an alternative life-style to the mainland," explained Susie Griffin, the assistant innkeeper and conference center coordinator.

The Georgian home, listed on the National Register of Historic Places, offers the stately architecture of detailed French doors, and paneled insets and dentil molding. Thought to commemorate the Bay of the Seven Moons, the L-shaped terrace is composed of seven configurations of local terra-cotta tile.

The common rooms are classical, restful, and custom-designed by the best in the business. Views to the ocean are commonplace, and sumptuous couches and rattan furniture invite conversation. Crafts indigenous to the area are found in the form of rare Catalina pottery, an art practiced by island craftsmen in the 1920s.

The six guest rooms are detailed with old-world antiques. Chandeliers, carpeting, drapery fabrics, bedding are thoughtfully created and coordinated by specialty designers. The installation of acoustical insulation to provide adequate privacy was one aspect of upgrading that took place when the rooms were prepared for guests. Most rooms have queen-size beds and all have private baths.

A hearty breakfast is included with the room tariff, and may offer bran muffins, freshly squeezed orange juice, poached pears with strawberry glaze, a mushroom, onion, jack and cheddar cheese omelet, bacon, and bagels. Hot and cold appetizers, freshly baked cookies, a coffee and tea tray, soft drinks, fresh fruit, and mixed nuts are available at all times. Late-afternoon relaxation is accompanied by red and white wines, sherry, port, beer, and champagne.

The owners call their style of food "simple." They've found that the rich foods they once served were too much for guests who stayed more than one night, so they listened to their repeat guests and simplified the cooking. I had a lovely salad with creamy vinaigrette, a roasted leg of lamb served with roasted new potatoes Provencale, sauteed cabbage and baked poppy seed rolls. The dessert was a blackberry custard tart.

The Inn on Mount Ada is a five-minute drive from town, by golf cart only, if you please. The island only allows travel by such unintrusive means. In fact, I had one of the most serene mornings of my life as I stood on my balcony at 5 a.m. watching a spectacular sunrise, with the sounds of small birds and the sea to keep me company.

THE INN ON MOUNT ADA, 398 Wrigley Rd., P.O. Box 2560, Avalon, CA 90704; 213-510-2030. A 6-guestroom (private baths) elegant Georgian Colonial on the fabled island of Santa Catalina. Queen and double beds..Open all year, except Christmas. Breakfast, lunch and dinner. No pets. CCs: Visa, MC, AE. Susie Griffin and Marlene McAdam, owners/hosts.

DIRECTIONS: Boat or helicopter from mainland.

MADRONA MANOR
Healdsburg, California

Many Easterners visiting northern California for the first time are struck with the unusual number of Victorian homes and buildings. I was reminded of this once again during a short drive around downtown Healdsburg on my way to Madrona Manor. I turned in at the impressive archway, flanked by a rainbow mass of flowers, and drove up the long winding drive to the three-story mansion. From the rambling front porch, I turned to look over the grounds and noticed that Madrona Manor sits on top of a knoll with flower gardens, sculptured hedges, numerous varieties of trees and bushes, and acres and acres of lawn.

I heard a step behind me and realized that the couple coming out the front door were the innkeepers of Madrona Manor, John and Carol Muir. "Oh, I see you are enjoying our view," John said.

Madrona Manor is furnished with beautiful Victorian antiques. There is a 100-year-old square piano in the music room, and throughout the house are massive pieces of carved walnut and mahogany furniture and Oriental carpets. "Five of our rooms have the antique furniture of the original owner, John Paxton, who was a San Francisco financier," Carol told me. "He built this house and also the Carriage House in 1881."

One of the guest rooms has a ten-foot-high canopied bed and a

huge armoire. The others have carved headboards, chaise longues, dressing tables with beveled mirrors, original light fixtures, and period wallpapers. There are fourteen-foot-high ceilings and many fireplaces with brightly painted tiles.

"I love fireplaces," I told John. "How many of your guest rooms have them?" He thought for a moment. "We have eighteen rooms with fireplaces, including the four we added in the third-floor rooms, which were originally servants' quarters. These rooms have antique-reproduction furniture.

John, a former engineer, converted the Carriage House into more guest rooms, and has used vast amounts of carved rosewood for lamps and tables, as well as door trim and paneling. My favorite suite is in this house as one can sit in a Jacuzzi and watch the fire in the fireplace. There is also a Garden Suite surrounded by lawn and flowers and another building with a very private country bedroom and suite. Madrona Manor is listed on the National Register of Historic Places as a historic district.

However, I think the big story at Madrona Manor is the food. Their big, efficient kitchen is a delight to behold, and includes a wood-burning oven, a mesquite grill, and a separate smokehouse. The Muir's son, Todd, is in command. The Muirs are obviously very proud of his talents as chef. "Todd's cooking has attracted the attention of *Gourmet* magazine, and we have guests who drive all the way from San Francisco just for dinner," John told me. I'd certainly be happy to make the trip for the dinner I had, which included a wonderful crusty goat-cheese soufflé seasoned with rosemary and garlic, a perfect green salad, and mesquite-grilled monkfish that was absolutely delicious. I couldn't resist trying the Mexican flan with rose petals (delightful). There is a prix-fixe menu and an à la carte menu. Everything is given special and interesting treatment and served with great aplomb.

Later that night, as I stood on the balcony of my room, looking out over the beautiful view, with Mount Saint Helena to the east, I thought a stay here in the Sonoma wine country at this beautiful inn is a very special experience.

MADRONA MANOR, 1001 Westside Rd., Box 818, Healdsburg, CA 95448; 707-433-4231; 1-800-258-4003; Fax: 707-433-0703. An 18-guestroom, 3-suite (private baths) Victorian mansion in the heart of Sonoma County wine country, 65 mi. north of San Francisco. All-size beds. Breakfast included in room rate. Dinner served daily; reservations recommended. Open year-round. Wheelchair access. Swimming pool on grounds. Golf, tennis, hiking, canoeing, fishing, winery tours nearby. Children and pets welcome by prearrangement. CCs: All major cards. John and Carol Muir, owners/hosts.

DIRECTIONS: From San Francisco, follow Rte. 101 north to the central Healdsburg exit. Continue north and turn left at Mill St. (first stoplight), which becomes Westside Rd.

THE MANSION AT LAKEWOOD
Walnut Creek, California

As I walked through the classic white wrought-iron gates of the Mansion at Lakewood, I entered a world of sweeping verandas and lush lawns skirted by colorful displays of flowers; three acres of nature only a quarter mile from downtown Walnut Creek and just ten miles from crowded Oakland. A heritage hickory nut tree, hundred-year-old oaks, magnolias, redwoods, and an ancient cactus garden separated me from the hurried world that existed just outside.

Mike and Sharyn McCoy also felt the tranquil charm of the Mansion when they toured the estate in 1986. After two years of hearings, their application for a B&B was approved, and major renovation began. Originally, the 1861 rambling two-story Victorian was part of a Mexican land grant. Sporting the rustic siding and raised verandas of the period, the 8,000-square-foot building still has its glass-etched transom with thirty-four stars to commemorate the year Kansas became the thirty-fourth state.

The Mansion has two parlors, a majestic library with redwood bookshelves and a black marble fireplace, and an elegant dining room. The large drawing room is decorated with wallpaper in shades of teal,

mauve, and burgundy. You may notice Sharyn's collection of toy bunnies peeking around corners throughout the inn.

All seven guest rooms are decorated with fine antiques and fabrics to create a feeling of country-fresh charm. The summerhouse is most unusual, with hand-painted floors, an original vault now used as a closet, and a clawfoot tub on the enclosed porch. All rooms have private baths and some suites include fireplaces. One suite has a black marble bath with a double Jacuzzi.

After a wonderful breakfast of homebaked croissants, crêpes, or quiche, step onto one of the lovely manicured lawns for a game of croquet. Or take a relaxing stroll on a nature path and catch the glint of Koi as they slide among the water lilies. Whatever your mood, the McCoys have created a gracious environment of tasteful elegance where you will feel pampered and completely relaxed.

THE MANSION AT LAKEWOOD, 1056 Hacienda Dr., Walnut Creek, CA 94598; 415-946-9075. A 7-guestroom (private baths) secluded country Victorian. Breakfast included. Open all year. 1/4 mi. to downtown Walnut Creek, 2 mi. to Mt. Diablo State Park. No smoking, pets, or alcohol. CCs: Visa, MC, D, AE. Michael and Sharyn McCoy, owners/hosts.

DIRECTIONS: Where Hwy. 24 and 680 cross in Walnut Creek, take Ygnacio Valley Rd. to Homestead Ave., turn right. First left after stop sign is Hacienda.

THE MANSIONS

San Francisco, California

Unique, elegant, and certainly out of the ordinary, The Mansions offer guests a visit they will long remember. Settled in a prestigious neighborhood that includes a number of San Francisco's most splendid homes, the hotel—an artistic joining of two adjacent houses—is only a short walk from the reburbished Fillmore district and Union Street, where some of the city's most unusual and fashionable boutiques, restaurants, and clubs are located.

From the moment you arrive and step into the grand foyer of the original hotel, welcomed by the soft tinkle of crystal chandeliers, there is an aura of excitement. To the strains of Bach's "Invention in C-Major," a large multicolored macaw screeches "hello" from his perch. Inventive murals tell the life story of the original Mansion. Tapestries, artifacts, great paintings, and sculptures surround you—treasures of times past.

The main parlor is an impressive example of Art Nouveau and is dominated by a 9-foot turquoise jardiniere. "Sotheby's wanted it shipped to New York," The Mansions' owner, Bob Pritikin, told me. Built in 1887 by Senator Chambers, the twin-turreted Queen Anne Victorian is one of San Francisco's original Grandes Dames and a designated city landmark. In 1990, the Greek Revival home next door—complete with its own parlor, nine guest rooms, and a lovely breakfast nook—became part of the hotel.

An author, advertising agency owner, and entertainer, Bob hosts a nightly Victorian Cabaret Theater that includes a fabulous magic show and a ghostly concert on the grand piano by the Mansions' resident ghost, Claudia. Claudia performs requests until the evening's end, when she completes her concert with a Scott Joplin rag, accompanied by guests who have been supplied with a multitude of rhythm instruments. Billed as America's Foremost Concert Saw Player, Bob often treats guests to a performance of "Moonlight Saw-nata." "I just love to step up to my saw and warble," he laughed. "You know, I've played with Liberace and Johnny Cash!"

The common rooms display more than a million dollars' worth of art and antiques, including works by Turner, Reynolds, and the famed sculptor Benjamin Buffano. The Mansions' dining room features a breathtaking stained-glass mural, one of the world's largest. The turn-of-the-century masterpiece stretches 32 continuous feet. "I'm not sure if I'm staying in a hotel or an art museum," said fellow guest Mildred Salway.

Murals are a theme throughout the hotel, even in many of the guest rooms. The rooms are furnished with valued antiques and decorated with whimsy and drama. Most rooms have king or queen beds, and all have additional sofa beds and private baths. Special gifts of candy and silk roses await guests, as do fresh flowers.

The full breakfast, which is included with the room rate, is opulent. Eggs any style, fresh-squeezed juice, jumbo "banger" sausages, hot cheese potatoes in mini-crocks, toasted crumpets, cereal, and fresh ground coffee are served in the cheerful West Wing breakfast room. Or, on request, you may have breakfast in bed!

The Mansions offers elegant evening dining. The restaurant is restricted to the pleasures of its guests and may include a menu of fennel soup, filet of elk, or roast grouse. A list of fine California and French wines is available, along with a full beer selection, including San Francisco's rare steam beer.

Packing my bags just prior to checkout, I couldn't help but wonder how Claudia had met her demise. When asked, Bob just smiled and glanced toward the soft tinkle of the chandelier. I guess I really don't want to know. The magic and elegance of the Mansions should remain a mystery.

THE MANSIONS, 2220 Sacramento St., San Francisco, CA 94115; 415-929-9444, 800-826-9398. A 29-guestroom (private baths) Queen Anne Victorian and Greek Revival mansion located in one of San Francisco's most lovely neighborhoods. Open all year. King, queen and double beds. Within walking distance to shops, restaurants, and clubs. City bus and taxi curbside; cable car 4 blocks away. Full breakfast included; dinner Monday–Saturday, by reservation. Telephones in rooms. Children and pets welcome. Bob Pritikin, owner-host; Tracy Pritikin-Pore, manager; Mark Evans, assistant manager.

DIRECTIONS: From Golden Gate Bridge drive to Marina and take a right on Webster St. to Sacramento. From Bay Bridge or from Peninsula take Van Ness Ave. and turn left on Sacramento St.

THE MARTINE INN

Pacific Grove, California

The Martine Inn is a grand old home overlooking the spectacular coastline of Pacific Grove on Monterey Bay. The epitome of elegance and luxury, the 10,750-square-foot "palace" was built in 1897 for James and Laura Parke, of Parke Davis Pharmaceuticals.

Purchased in 1972 by Marion and Don Martine, the structure underwent major renovation while keeping the authentic, turn-of-the-century features that make it unique. While the inn's exterior is now that of a rose-colored Mediterranean home, careful attention was paid to restoring the Victorian interior detail. Marion and Don opened the Inn in 1984. Although larger than most bed and breakfasts, the Martines have maintained an atmosphere of intimacy.

Each of the nineteen guest rooms is distinctive. A three pice 1850's American Walnut Bedroom Suite with massive carbed busts at Jenny Lynn dominate one room. Another is furnished with costume designer Edith Head's bedroom suite. Thirteen rooms are in the main house, some with fireplaces and views of the bay, while the carriage house has six rooms which overlook the courtyard pond and Oriental fountain.

All rooms are furnished in elegant museum-quality antiques and have private baths. One has an unusual 1920s shower with seven shower heads! An 1890s oak pool table and modern Jacuzzi are also available for guests.

Breakfast and afternoon wine and hors d'oeuvres are served in the family-style dining room. Marion uses the finest Victorian china, crystal, and old Sheffield silver pieces—daily. Champagne is served to honeymooners in 1850s Tiffany goblets. Newlyweds are also treated to a tour in Don's 1929 MG, one of his collection of 15 autos that he drives in vintage races.

The views of Monterey Bay from the dining room and two sitting rooms can bring surprises. Binoculars are placed along the window ledges so guests may scan the water. Watch carefully and you'll be treated to a show by the clown of the sea, the fuzzy brown sea otter. Through the open windows, listen over the crash of the waves and you may even hear the barking of sea lions as they sun their ungainly-looking bodies on the craggy rocks, or see whales, otters, dolphins, and pelicans

---

THE MARTINE INN, 255 Oceanview Boulevard, Pacific Grove, CA 93950; 408-373-3388. A 19-guestroom (private baths) mansion on the cliffs of Pacific Grove overlooking Monterey Bay. King, queen and double beds. Breakfast included. Open all year. Four blocks from the Monterey Bay Aquarium and Cannery Row. No pets. Smoking restricted. CCs: Visa, MC. Marion and Don Martine, owners/hosts.

DIRECTIONS: Hwy. 1, exit Monterey. Follow signs to Cannery Row. Continue to lighthouse, inn on left.

MILL ROSE INN
Half Moon Bay, California

Tucked away just off the road and two blocks from Half Moon Bay's Main Street is Mill Rose Inn, an intimate country retreat with a garden that could compete with any of the loveliest gardens in the English countryside. Bursting with beautiful color all year around, this oasis is the creation of Terry Baldwin, innkeeper, owner, and landscape designer. He has tastefully planted hundreds of perennials, annuals, and over 200 roses! Inside the inn there is also an abundance of flowers with a fresh-cut bouquet and a bowl of dried flower petals in each guest room.

Mill Rose Inn has six elegant, spacious, and comfortable rooms, all decorated by Terry's wife, Eve, who has an obvious flair for rich colors and soft lighting. The accommodations feature such special amenities as European feather beds, wood-burning fireplaces with hand-painted

mantles, bay-window seating, European antiques, claw foot tubs, small refrigerators, VCRs and in room movies, complimentary wine and sherry, and coffee makers—and each guest will find a Japanese dressing robe in the armoire.

Eve and Terry extend a warm welcome to guests when they arrive by treating them to complimentary refreshments in each room. And in the morning, a full country breakfast with champagne is presented either in one's room or in the dining room.

Another treat for the guests at Mill Rose is the spa, which is tucked inside an enclosed garden gazebo. Here there's room for seven people or it can be reserved for a private escape. Once again the theme of Mill Rose—tranquility and romance—are evident in the lovely surroundings in the spa area, tropical blooms, a charming brick courtyard, fragrant vines, and a cascading fountain.

MILL ROSE INN, 615 Mill St., Half Moon Bay, CA 94019; 415-726-9794. A 6-guestroom (private baths) Victorian inn within walking distance of the ocean and center of town. King, queen and double beds. Open year-round. Advance reservations necessary. Many diversions nearby: sandy beaches, wineries, jazz and classical concerts, historic sites, fishing, golf, riding, and sailing. Pets are not permitted. One cat and dog in residence. Smoking on decks and garden areas only. CCs: Visa, MC, AE. Eve and Terry Baldwin, owners/hosts.

DIRECTIONS: From San Francisco, travel south on Hwys. 101 or 280 and go west on Hwy. 92 to Half Moon Bay. Turn left on Main St. and right to Mill St.

No rooms on Friday or So

Monterey, California

Built in 1929, this three-story, half-timbered English Tudor-style home was converted into an inn 14 years ago and continues to be one of the very best. The proprietors, Gene and Ann Swett, have lived here for more than a decade.

Located in the heart of the city of Monterey, in a quiet residential neighborhood, the acre-plus grounds are studded with old oak, pine, and redwood trees, thick ivy, and even a running stream. Secluded out-door sitting areas invite guests to relax and enjoy the gardens filled with fuchsias, begonias, rhododendrons, and a formal rose garden.

In the inn itself, a blend of beautiful antiques and contemporary furnishings reflects an air of casual elegance. Most guest rooms have wood-burning fireplaces, while others have skylights, and stained-glass windows. Each room has a view of the peaceful gardens. There are canopied beds (either queen or king), European goose-down com-forters and pillows, and visually beautiful color schemes. Outside one guest room is a flower-filled Mexican fountain; in another is an antique chaise longue, and a couple have rocking chairs. A breakfast that might include Belgian waffles, quiche, French toast, homemade muffins, or crêpes, among other things, may be enjoyed in bed or downstairs in front of a fire, where early evening wine and cheese is also served.

OLD MONTEREY INN, 500 Martin St., Monterey, CA 93940; 408-375-8284. A 10-guestroom (private baths) English country house B&B on a hillside in a residential section of Monterey. King, queen and twin beds. Full breakfast and refreshments included. Open year-round. Minimum stay of 2 nights on weekends. Many golf courses, 17-Mile Drive, seal and whale watching, beaches, Cannery Row with aquarium, Carmel and Monterey shopping nearby. No pets. One dog in residence. No CCs. Smoking outside only. Ann and Gene Swett, owners/hosts.

DIRECTIONS: From Hwy. 1, take Munras Ave. exit heading toward the ocean. Turn left on Soledad Dr., then right on Pacific St. Martin St. is 6/10 mi. on your left.

THE PELICAN INN
Muir Beach, California

The Pelican is about as close to being an English West Country inn as one could find. I could well imagine that I was seated in the Lobster Pot in Mousehole in Cornwall. The Pelican has an Inglenook fireplace with the inscription, "Fear knocked at the door, Faith answered; No one was there." There's a resemblance to the Royal Oak Inn in Yattendon, the place where I like to stay on the nights before my departures from England.

Susan and Ed were good friends with the original owner of the inn, Charles Felix, an Englishman. Charles designed the inn, with its Tudor half-timbers and white exterior, and ran it most successfully for quite a few years. When he and his wife, Brenda, decided to go back to England, Susan and Ed were ecstatic at the prospect of becoming the new owners of the Pelican.

"Charles, of course, is a very hard act to follow," said Susan, "but I'm happy to say that one of our best moves was to make Barry Stock the manager of the inn. He's from Devonshire, England, where he ran some establishments. It was in Exeter that he met his late wife, Pamela, an American lady from Newport Beach, California. She lured him out here, and in the course of time they visited the Pelican and were smitten immediately. He was Charles right-hand man and managed the inn while he was away."

Almost on cue, Barry walked in and I had the pleasure of being introduced. He proved to have a very attractive English accent and soon all of us were enthusiastically conversing.

"Over the past few years we have really done a masterful job of freshening up the inn," he said. "We painted, we repaired, we

exchanged furniture that wasn't authentic to the period. We have several new Asian rugs with a 16th-century design, and we uncovered some beautiful wood floors, as you can see. I'm happy to say that we've received many compliments from guests who have been coming here for years, and this includes various members of Charles's family."

Our stroll took us abovestairs to the guest rooms, which have half-tester beds. The Hogarth prints, which I admired on my first visit a number of years ago, were still in place.

"We now have a proper 'snug,' which is really an English term for a living room," Barry explained. "It's been furnished in 17th- and 18th-century English antiques and has a library and a fireplace. When we're not having a special party here, inn guests use it, and it is a popular place for them to curl up and read or to mingle with other guests."

Barry and I returned to the dining room, which was taking on a festive dinner air. The candle flames were reflected on the many carved chairs, beautiful old tables, and massive sideboards.

Eating dinner was extremely romantic, however the last time I was there the food was not up to what I had experienced in past occasions.

THE PELICAN INN, 10 Pacific Way, Muir Beach, CA 94965; 415-383-6000 (for reservations, call between 9:30 and 4:30). A 7-guestroom (private baths) English inn on the northern California coast, 8 mi. from the Golden Gate Bridge. Queen-size beds available. Breakfast included in tariff. Lunch and dinner open to the public. Closed Christmas day. Limited wheelchair access to dining room. Swimming, beachcombing, backroading, walking, and all San Francisco attractions nearby. Ed and Susan Cunningham, owners; Barry Stock, manager.

DIRECTIONS: From Golden Gate Bridge follow Hwy. 101 north to Hwy. 1/Stinson Beach exit. Turn left at traffic lights and follow Hwy. 1/Stinson Beach Rd. 5 mi. to Muir Beach. (Do not go to Muir Woods.)

THE PINE INN
Carmel, California

I found it hard to believe that I was sitting in the oldest commercial building in Carmel as the domed glass ceiling of the Pine Inn's gazebo rolled back to reveal a vibrant blue sky. I also found it difficult to imagine that the original hotel had been rolled on pine logs right down Ocean Avenue to its present location. Yet, it was true. This lovely, authentic Victorian inn, with its subtle updating, has lost none of the classic elegance that has charmed guests for over three generations.

Located in the center of Carmel, within walking distance to the beach, The Pine Inn was originally built in 1890 as the Hotel Carmelo. After the precarious log-rolling move, the hotel opened in 1904 to an overbooking of guests who were finally accommodated in tents pitched on adjoining lots.

Such a whirlwind opening made way for what has become quite a tradition. "See you at the Pine Inn," became an oft-used phrase as the town of Carmel expanded around the inn. From the very beginning, celebrities frequented the guest register. "We can't lay claim to George Washington," manager Hoby J. Hooker told me. "But at least the actor who played him on television slept here." While that actor's name pales against our first president's, the list of celebrated guests is noteworthy: Bing Crosby, Frank Sinatra, Howard Duff, Red Skelton, Ernie Ford, Mel Ferrer, and Tarzan himself, Johnny Weissmuller.

Those who are not quite as well known receive the same special treatment as celebrities. Each guest room is decorated with Chinese-style Victorian decor. Pierre Deuz fabrics, authentic period furnishings, and lovely artworks created a mood of old-fashioned comfort and charm. Of course, I always feel the height of pampering is excellent room service, an area where the Pine Inn excels. All rooms have private baths and all-size beds are available.

Since World War II, the inn's Red Parlor has been one of *the* places to imbibe. More than a local watering hole, the cozy decor and friendly atmosphere have established it as a traditional meeting place. Subtle lighting and rosy stained glass set an intimate mood. All sorts of rumors abound concerning the clientele. Apparently author John Steinbeck met his second wife here while dipping olives into extra-dry martinis. W.C. Fields is also said to have warmed a bar stool now and then. Sandwiches and evening pub fare are available.

The outdoor patio was converted to a gazebo in 1972 with the addition of the opening dome. Breakfast, lunch, and dinner are served here and in the Garden Room. Seafood from the Monterey Bay, fresh local vegetables, and the best in California wines make dining a pleasure. The Friday-night buffet and Sunday brunch are more than any epicure could hope for.

After brunch, step just outside the inn's main lobby to the patio complex of Pine Inn Shops. Known as Little Carmel, due to the diversity of unique boutiques, you will find original fashions, men's clothing, antiques, and jewelry.

The picturesque town of Carmel can be covered easily on foot. Some of the best art galleries on the West Coast are located in the area, and for those interested in a day "on the links," seventeen world-class golf courses are within driving distance. Other points of interest include Fisherman's Wharf, the Seventeen-Mile Drive, and the incomparable Monterey Bay Aquarium.

THE PINE INN, Ocean Ave. at Lincoln, Box 250, Carmel, CA 93921; 408-624-3851. A 49-guestroom (private baths) historic Victorian inn located in beautiful Carmel-by-the-Sea. All-size beds. Open all year. Breakfast, lunch, and dinner available. Restaurants, boutiques, galleries, and beaches within walking distance. Exceptional golf, Monterey Bay Aquarium, and Fisherman's Wharf nearby. No pets. Richard Gunner, owner; Hoby J. Hooker, manager.

DIRECTIONS: From Coast Hwy. 1, take Ocean Ave. west to Lincoln St.

SAN YSIDRO RANCH
Montecito, California

Waiting to check in at San Ysidro Ranch's reception desk, I was certain that I had seen famous chef Julia Child stroll through the cozy Hacienda Lounge. Michael Ullman, the Ranch's general manager, confirmed my suspicion. "Oh, yes, she's one of our guests. A large number of celebrities have considered the Ranch a second home since it opened in 1893," he said. I was impressed with the list, which included honeymooners John and Jacqueline Kennedy, Paul Newman and Joanne Woodward, Bruce Springsteen, and Barbra Streisand. Writer Somerset Maugham used the haven of the Geranium House to complete some of his finest works. Sinclair Lewis wrote in the closet of the Oak Cottage, away from the spectacular but distracting ocean views. Sir Laurence Olivier and Vivien Leigh plighted their troth in the old-fashioned wedding garden.

It's easy to see why San Ysidro Ranch attracts romantic couples and those who just want to retreat to the rustic residential atmosphere. Nestled at the foot of the Santa Ynez Mountains, forty-three cottages are tucked into the 540-acre grounds, of which the main grounds and garden remain virtually unchanged since the original land grant adobe was built in 1825. Hundred-year-old trees and wide terraces of pungent citrus, flowers, and herbs surround the lawns. Hedges heavy with flowering jasmine and honeysuckle perfume the air.

Each cottage has its own personality. California-country charm is enhanced by polished antiques, cozy upholstered pieces in soft yellows and blues, fluffy pillows and coverlets, and cushioned wall-to-wall carpeting. Ten bungalows have private outdoor Jacuzzis, and all have wood-burning fireplaces and wide sun decks for lounging. King and twin beds are available, and all cottages have full baths with tub/shower combos. A special touch: Your name is engraved on a wooden sign outside your cottage to make you feel at home.

Complimentary morning coffee, newspapers, and an Honor Bar, where guests mix their own drinks, are located in the Hacienda Lounge. Here also are the Ranch's only television, and videos, should you decide to come out of hiding.

I had difficulty choosing among the outdoor entertainment possibilities. Tennis at one of three courts, golf, hiking, swimming in the sunny Ranch pool, or horseback riding? I chose to mount up and explore the resort's 500 acres of canyon wilderness trails that wind through forests, bubbling creeks, and chaparral. I felt gloriously invigorated by the unspoiled beauty that surrounded me.

After a soak in my private Jacuzzi, I dressed for what I knew would be a special dining experience. Formerly the Plow and Angel, the Ranch restaurant took on a new name with the arrival of French chef Marc Ehrler. Now known as the Stonehouse, Ehrler characterizes the restaurant's cuisine as "fresh." The fixed menu is adapted every three months to make maximum use of fresh ingredients in the Ranch garden. "It makes it interesting and motivates me to try new things," Ehrler told me. Ehler has his own herb garden, and cures the restaurant's meat and fish in a smoker. Breakfast and lunch are also available, and all meals can be served in your cottage.

San Ysidro Ranch is just five minutes from downtown Montecito and Santa Barbara. Few inns can provide such privacy, comfort, calmness and personalized service so close to the hustle and bustle of civilization.

SAN YSIDRO RANCH, 900 San Ysidro Lane, Montecito, CA 93108;805-969-5046. A 43-guest cottage (private baths) California-country retreat at the foot of the Santa Ynez Mountains. King and twin beds available. Open year-round; 2-night minimum. Very private. European plan. Breakfast, lunch, and dinner available. Tennis, swimming, golf, horseback riding, hiking. Five min. from Santa Barbara. Pets allowed with deposit. Claude Rouas and Bob Harmon, owners; Michael Ullman, general manager; Jan Martin Winn, manager.

DIRECTIONS: Take the San Ysidro exit off Hwy. 101; head toward the hills. Follow San Ysidro Rd. to San Ysidro Lane, which ends at the Ranch.

THE SHERMAN HOUSE

San Francisco, California

"Luxury, elegance, and tasteful comfort" is the way The Sherman House is described in its brochure. I would add impeccable service and graciousness. I requested a ride from the airport and knew my stay would be a special one when I was promptly met by the hotel's chauffeur in a vintage car. As I settled into the comfort of the leather seats, I readied myself for a visit that would take me back to a time when travelers were treated as if they were guests in a private home.

The Sherman House is chiefly Italiante in style. The magnificent, asymmetrical white-frame three-story structure is located in the prestigious Pacific Heights area of San Francisco, near famed Union Street with its unique boutiques.

In January 1981, Manouchehr Mobedshahi, an Iranian-born San Franciscan entrepreneur, purchased the Sherman House and began major restoration work. Both the main house and the original Carriage House were lifted so new concrete basements and foundations could be poured. Additionally, new steel beam supports were added to bring the buildings up to seismic code.

Since the home is a Designated Historical Landmark, no torch or chemicals could be used to remove the peeling exterior and interior paint, so it had to be painstakingly stripped by hand. Restoring the Sherman House to its original condition was quite a feat, but the results are spectacular, right down to the recreated plaster ornamentation and entrance posts and handrails. Besides the home's magnificently refinished hardwood floors, the solarium was refloored in black and white marble, and the bathrooms were done in black South American granite.

Both the public and individual rooms have been sumptuously decorated in French Second Empire, Austrian Biedermeier, and English Jacobean motifs and antiques. I was escorted to my room by the concierge as there is no traditional check-in. If requested, your luggage will be unpacked by the attentive staff, only one of the many services available, including tailoring, securing of opera and symphony tickets, and personalized shopping. If you must work while you travel, special arrangements can be made for stenographic, word-processing, translation, telegram, and telex services.

The elegant bedrooms have marble wood-burning fireplaces, draped canopy beds, and feather-down comforters. Modern features include wet bars, wall safes, televisions (even in the bathrooms!), and whirlpool baths. There are spectacular views of the Palace of Fine Arts, the Golden Gate, San Francisco Bay, and the hills of Marin.

I particularly enjoyed spending time in the hotel's large west wing, which consists of a three-story music and reception room, containing a platform for musicians, and a ceiling glowing with an ornate, leaded-glass skylight. The blue finch in the room's birdcage may cheerfully perform for you as you sit.

The furnished gallery is also the spot to meet before a lavish dinner. Guests are served appetizers as the maitre d' discusses the evening's menu, which may include such specialties as duck breast with cognac and truffles. Prices are not given unless requested, and can run from $35 to $80 per person. Swiss chef Neal Langermann shops daily for fresh ingredients and will prepare special menus for guests. Following appetizers, guests are seated in the dining room where their previously ordered first course is served.

Just before leaving, I spent a few quiet moments in the replicated Victorian greenhouse to steep in the wonderful service and luxury I had experienced.

———

THE SHERMAN HOUSE, 2160 Green St., San Francisco, CA 94123; 415-563-3600. A 15-guestroom (private baths) intimate, restored Victorian in San Francisco's elegant Pacific Heights district. Open all year. Queen and twin beds. European plan. Near shops, restaurants, theater, and most sightseeing areas. Full concierge services. Limited smoking. No pets. Manou and Vesta Mobedshahi, owners; Michael Levy, manager.

DIRECTIONS: From San Francisco Airport, go north on Hwy. 101. Follow signs to Golden Gate Bridge and exit on Franklin St. Bear left up the hill and continue for 18 blocks to Green St. Turn left on Green St. Sherman House is 5-1/2 blocks down on the right.

THE SPENCER HOUSE
San Francisco, California

There is an old saying: "Buy land—they aren't making it anymore."
Well, by the same token, be sure to visit the Spencer House, because
they aren't making homes like this anymore. Built in 1887, the Queen
Anne-style mansion features a prominent polygonal tower, Palladian
windows, marble staircase entry, triple-arched main entry porch, ten
stained-glass windows with faceted crystals, and extraordinary exterior
Victorian ornamentation. Numerous gables crown the graceful roof.
Barbara and Jack Chambers, fortunate owners of the Spencer House,
purchased the mansion in 1984 and opened it as a B&B in 1985.

Barbara and Jack worked diligently to restore the home to its original interior and exterior elegance. Barbara even traveled to England
for furnishings, linens, and housewares.

Vaulted ceilings, upholstered walls, gilded Lyncrist wallpaper, and
bay windows and alcoves are featured in the grand salon and formal
dining room on the lower floor. The large front parlor is cozily elegant,
with down-filled couches, Persian rugs, and antiques.

A grand staircase of hand-carved oak leads to the six upper-floor
guest rooms. Heavy, oversized solid wood doors open into enormous,
airy rooms with huge bay windows. All the beds have feather mattresses and down comforters and are furnished with antiques. Each

room has a glorious view of the park, the gardens, or Golden Gate Bridge.

The Chambers' cocker spaniels, Percy and Perry, roused from their nap spot in the sunny breakfast room when I entered, kept me company as I enjoyed a breakfast of poached pears, eggs Benedict, and homebaked muffins. The bay window framed the view of the lovely east garden.

The Spencer House is centrally located to all San Francisco attractions. It offers a unique opportunity to live, for a moment, in a style that showed the reverence for and mastery of craftsmanship, a style that "they're just not making anymore."

THE SPENCER HOUSE, 1080 Haight St., San Francisco, CA 94117; 415-626-9205. Fax: 626-9208. A 6-guestroom (private baths) Victorian landmark mansion in a quiet residential neighborhood. All size beds. Open all year. Breakfast included. No pets. Two dogs in residence. Near Golden Gate Park and cultural attractions. No CCs. Barbara and Jack Chambers, owners/hosts.

DIRECTIONS: From 101, take all signs that say Golden Gate Brdg. Exit on Fell/Laguna. Take Fell to Baker, turn left. Inn on left at corner of Haight and Baker.

TIMBERHILL RANCH
Cazadero, California

Standing in a clearing beneath spicy-scented, majestic redwoods, a thousand feet above the Pacific Ocean's coastal fog and wind, I could see why, in the 1800s, the Pomo Indians had chosen this sheltered bit of Northern California coast for their winter home. The serenity is a balm. Apparently the owners of Timberhill Ranch, Barbara Farrell, Tarran McDaid, and Michael Riordan, felt the same way when they left hectic corporate positions in San Francisco and purchased Timberhill.

Formerly a working ranch, and then the location of an alternative school, the main ranch house and ten cottages sit on 10 secluded acres. The ranch's other 70 acres are covered by meadows peppered with wild iris, bluebells, and forget-me-nots. Groves of blood red madrone and oak and fir neighbor stately redwoods. The ranch is surrounded by the 317-acre Kruse Rhododendron Reserve and the 6,000-acre Salt Point State Park. Miles of hiking trails traverse the park and meander to the sea.

As I hefted my bags, the shadow of a red-tailed hawk crossed over me. Watching this graceful bird ride an updraft, I hoped my grandfather had been right when he told me that it was a good omen.

The shake cedar exterior of the main ranch house may look rustic,

but the interior will immediately dispel any worries about "roughing it." A cozy, cushion-strewn sofa beckons guests to sink in front of the large stone fireplace. Smaller grouped seating areas encourage conversation. And books, magazines, puzzles, cards, and games offer entertainment after the last bit of daylight steals the spectacular views.

Fresh flowers appear in abundance in the cottages as well as the main lodge. The cottages are also rustic cedar, and are comfortable and romantic. Each has a wood-burning fireplace, with wood already cut and stacked, mini-bar, coffee maker, reading lamps and armchairs, and luxury amenities like fluffy robes and hair dryers. Colorful quilts, handmade by local artisans, adorn the beds. Private decks look onto views of the surrounding natural landscape, not on other cottages or the two world-class tennis courts or heated swimming pool and hot tub.

Should you choose to become somewhat of a hermit, you can easily stay at your cottage until dinner, since breakfast is delivered to your door. Lunch can be arranged and the staff will make up a picnic basket if you decide to do some hiking.

At dinnertime, a wonderful six-course meal is served in the intimate candlelit dining room. The meal begins with a selection of appetizers, and progresses leisurely through soup, salad, a palate-cleansing sorbet, an entrée and dessert. The menu changes nightly as the chef uses only the freshest of ingredients, and can include such specialties as roast Petaluma duckling with sun-dried figs, or grilled Pacific salmon with tomatillo coulis. All breads, pastries, and desserts are homemade, and a good selection of California wines is available.

On Sunday afternoon I decided that my hedonistic behavior needed to be tempered, so I grabbed my tennis racket for a bit of lobbing on the courts. Just as I bounced my first ball, two of the ranch's ducks, Mutt and Jeff, hurriedly waddled down, hoping to beg a treat. After greeting them, I turned back to my bucket of balls and, again, was crossed by the shadow of the redtail. This time I knew my grandfather had been right. It was a good omen. My stay at Timberhill Ranch had been nothing less than exceptional.

TIMBERHILL RANCH, 35755 Hauser Bridge Rd., Cazadero, CA 95421; 707-847-3258. A 10-cottage (private baths) secluded ranch resort on the spectacular northern Sonoma County coast. Open all year. Queen-size beds; twins available. Modified American plan. Handicapped and non-smoking cottages provided. Tennis courts, heated pool, and hiking trails on property. Close to beaches, whale watching, golf, and art galleries. One Australian shepherd in residence. Barbara Farrell, Tarran McDaid, and Michael Riordan, owners/hosts.

DIRECTIONS: Take Hwy. 101 north from San Francisco to the Washington St. exit in Petaluma. Go west through Bodega Bay and continue north on Hwy. 1; 5 mi. past Jenner, turn right on Meyers Grade Rd. Stay on paved road for 13.6 mi. The inn is on the right.

UNION STREET INN

San Francisco, California

"We are Edwardian, not Victorian."

Helen Stewart and I were having breakfast, seated in the sunny garden at the rear of the Union Street Inn. The fragrance of lilacs, camellias, and violets filled the air, and an occasional hummingbird darted from blossom to blossom. Some guests were enjoying breakfast on the spacious deck overlooking the garden, and there was the unmistakable aroma of fresh coffee and croissants. In this quiet retreat it was difficult to realize that we were in the heart of one of San Francisco's most attractive shopping and entertainment areas. "I say Edwardian," Helen continued, "because we're rather proud of the fact that in a city that has so much Victorian, we are a bit different. The Edwardians, already into the 20th century, were less ostentatious than their elders. Their ornamentation was tempered by a new conservatism, and we like to feel that many of our decorations and furnishings are understatements."

Helen is a former San Francisco schoolteacher, who found herself involved in a mid-life career change. She restored and remodeled this

handsome turn-of-the-century building, using tones and textures that are not only in the period, but also increase the feeling of hospitality.

The bedrooms have such intriguing names as Wildrose, Holly, Golden Gate, and English Garden.

Two of the bedrooms have queen-sized beds with canopies, two have gleaming brass beds; all have really impressive, carefully chosen antiques. The brochure of the inn explains the different color schemes for each room. "If reservations are made sufficiently in advance, and the guests can anticipate a mood, these can all be coordinated." Helen made this comment with the faint suggestion of a twinkle.

My room had one of the queen-sized beds with very pleasant dark green wallpaper and matching draperies, which were most helpful in keeping the sun from intruding too early. The walls were adorned with two of the well-known Degas prints of ballet dancers. I thought they were quite appropriate, remembering King Edward's fondness for pretty women.

One end of the room had been turned into an alcove containing a rather elegantly decorated washbasin with mirrors and generous, fluffy towels. A very handsome antique mahogany dressing table had a three-way oval mirror. This is typical of the appointments of the other bedrooms, and I found many welcome living plants in all of the bedrooms.

Helen has converted the old carriage house at the bottom of the garden into a very fetching accommodation, with a large bay window overlooking the garden and its own Jacuzzi. The garden has been remodeled, and a Victorian-looking curved fence with a lovely old-fashioned gate has been added. It truly does resemble an English garden.

A glance at the comments from the guest book told me the story: "Happiness is staying here!" "What a refreshing change from typical hotel stays." "Like returning to visit an old 'friend.'" "We'll be back for a second honeymoon."

Very fine restaurants are within walking distance.

UNION STREET INN, 2229 Union St., San Francisco, CA 94123; 415-346-0424. A 6-guestroom (private baths) bed-and-breakfast inn. King and queen beds available. Convenient to all of the San Francisco attractions. Breakfast only meal served. Open every day except Christmas and New Year's. No pets. Two dogs in residence. CCs: Visa, MC, AE. Helen Stewart, owner-host.

DIRECTIONS: Take the Van Ness exit from Rte. 101 to Union St., turn left. The inn is between Fillmore and Steiner on the left side of the street.

VENTANA INN
Big Sur, California

As impressed as I had been with the spectacular coastal views on my winding trip to the small community of Big Sur, nothing quite prepared me for the panorama from the restaurant deck at Ventana Inn. Ventana sits on 243 acres overlooking the Pacific, backed by rolling hills covered with oaks, redwoods and bay laurels. Its sixteen buildings built of natural cedar blend well with nature. It has undergone some renovation and additions since its construction in 1975.

As vice president and general manager Bob Bussinger states in the inn's brochure, "We listened carefully to guest comments over the years, and concentrated our effort in the expansion on maintaining the intimate feeling in spite of the increased capacity of the inn."

I saw these changes first-hand as I entered the remodeled and enlarged lobby. There was a fire crackling in the large stone fireplace, with a supply of wood sitting in a basket on the hearth. Two guests seated on the red print couch were enjoying its warmth. The many windows looked out over the natural landscape. Guests were wandering in to share glasses of wine and samplings of fruits and cheeses in the expanded reception area. I decided to deposit my bags in my room and come back to join them.

My room, with a warm cedar interior, was decorated in soft shades of pink and mauve, contrasted by the deep green of several house-

plants. It had its own bubbling hot tub and a large private deck. A fire had been laid in the fireplace, and two natural wicker chairs sat nearby. I quickly unpacked and returned to the lobby. As I sipped a delicious Chardonnay, I overhead a young couple describing the two spa areas with swimming pools, a sauna, and communal Japanese hot tubs. Protected sundecks were nearby, some with clothing-optional areas.

Intrigued, I finished my wine and set out to do some exploring. I discovered a library with an ocean view, which also serves as an additional breakfast room, and a more secluded reading room decorated to complement its rustic wooden walls. I returned to my room to pick up my bathing suit and head for the spas. The young couple had been accurate in their description. I was to enjoy this spot for the next several days.

Evening found me seated in the romantic restaurant at a table made with three-inch sections of redwood from trees taken off the land. The floors were a shiny tile of dark red. My dinner choice was a light California meal of fresh oysters followed by grilled salmon topped with fennel, pasilla chile, and roasted eggplant. I ended the evening with a liqueur in the adjoining bar, another recent addition.

The following morning I returned to the lobby after a brisk walk along the bluffs to the smell of fresh croissants, strudel, cinnamon rolls, and muffins baked in the in-house bakery. I poured myself a cup of coffee and grabbed a plate. Striking up a conversation with one of the guests, I learned that she had discovered some wonderful hiking in nearby Andrew Molera State Park at the north end of Big Sur, just eight miles away. She was planning to go into Big Sur to do some shop-hopping. I decided to spend the morning in the Japanese tubs, and ventured into Big Sur after a lunch of Mexican food on the restaurant terrace.

I completed my short stay at peace with the world once again, but feeling a bit sorry that Louise had not accompanied me. Ventana is a place for lovers, young and old.

VENTANA INN, Big Sur, CA 93920; 408-667-2331. A 62-guestroom (some suites) seaside retreat of rustic elegance. King and queen beds. Many rooms with hot tubs, TVs, VCRs and stereos. Continental breakfast included. Complimentary wine & cheese in the afternoon. Lunches and dinner available in restaurant, jackets required for gentlemen. Spa area with pools, sauna, Japanese tubs, and sundecks. Open all year. Restricted smoking areas. Walk to beaches. Shopping and state parks nearby at Big Sur. Gift shop at inn. No pets. Major credit cards accepted. Ventana Inn, Inc., owners; R.E. Bussinger, general manager.

DIRECTIONS: 28 mi. south of Carmel on Hwy. 1 at Big Sur.

VILLA ROYALE
Palm Springs, California

The sights, sounds, and scents of summer were all around me—the tinkling plash of a fountain, the deeper splash of a diver plunging into the swimming pool, the twitter of birds, the hum of an occasional bee, and everywhere the color and fragrance of flowers. I was leaning back in a chaise lounge in a little hideaway garden corner with a tinkling fountain and a Schubert serenade floating on the air. This was early in March, when there was still snow at the top of Mount San Jacinto, towering 8,500 feet above the desert floor, where lively, tony Palm Springs forms a green and glamorous oasis.

Earlier that March day I had found Villa Royale at the east end of town, sheltered from the wind blowing off the desert, and within its cluster of low, hacienda-style adobe buildings, red-tile roofs, and lush garden courtyards, I sensed a European ambience.

"We have architecturally altered each guest room to represent a different country." Chuck Murawski was taking me on the grand tour, after our initial meeting in the lobby. It was clear from the outset that gardens and flowers are an important part of the decor here. The lobby, with its Spanish tile floor, fireplace, many windows, and French doors

brings the outside in, and that means cascades of bougainvillea, frothy hibiscus, roses, petunias, and flowering shrubs and trees of all kinds.

Chuck and I threaded our way over winding, tree-shaded, flower-lined brick paths and around little private gardens and patios as we looked in on one fabulous room after another. He and his partner, Bob Lee, have roamed the world over, and the vast booty they have collected now adorns the rooms of this very special inn.

There's an elegant Monte Carlo suite reflecting colors and motifs from the south of France with tiled floors, stucco walls, a king-sized bed, canopied and curtained in a homespun fabric; the Greek Room is decorated with things Greek, even to the olive tree on the patio. Every room evokes the style and atmosphere of the country it represents, not only in its furniture but in the wall treatments, fixtures, pictures, and artifacts. Among those countries represented are Spain, Morocco, Germany, Italy, and England.

"This is our outdoor living room," Chuck said, as we strolled through a covered patio with a fireplace and tables and wicker chairs. "Sometimes there are three or four languages going on at the same time."

Over a delicious glass of iced tea, seated in the delightful little breakfast arcade with its series of arched French doors looking out on the courtyard and one of the two swimming pools, Chuck told me that they have carried their international theme into their dining room.

"We serve a different cuisine from a different country each night;

it's called the Europa Dinner. We also offer other á la carte choices, such as chicken with lemon and capers, Oriental chicken with hoisan sauce, steak au poivre, a pasta dish, and fish, along with appetizers, soup, salad, sourdough rolls, and some wonderful desserts."

The dining room is very romantic with little alcoves, an indoor-outdoor patio, a fireplace, and classical music.

If there was an ocean nearby, I'd think I was on the Riviera.

VILLA ROYALE, 1620 Indian Trail, Palm Springs, CA 92264; 619-327-2314. A 34-guestroom (private baths) luxurious but informal desert inn, 80 mi. from Los Angeles. King, queen, and twin beds available. Some suites with kitchens. Air conditioners; some fireplaces and private spas. Complimentary continental breakfast. Dinner by reservation. Open year-round; 2-day minimum stay on weekends; 3 days on holidays. Wheelchair access. Bicycles and 2 swimming pools on grounds. Tennis, golf, celebrity tours, fashionable shops and restaurants, horseback riding, museums, art galleries, national parks, Indian canyons and waterfalls, balloon rides nearby. No pets. CCs: Visa, MC, AE. Charles Murawski and Bob Lee, owners/hosts.

DIRECTIONS: Palm Springs has an international airport. By car from L.A., take the San Bernardino Freeway (Rte. 10) to Rte. 111, which becomes Palm Canyon in Palm Springs. Continue thru downtown (about 4 mi.) to Indian Trail.

VINTNERS INN
Santa Rosa, California

At the hub of the northern California wine country, Vintners Inn offers the ambience of a village in the south of France, right down to its house wine made from grapes grown on the property. Owners John and Francisca Duffy set out to recreate the French Mediterranean feeling when they began thinking about a design for their inn. The Duffys traveled to Europe and searched the regions surrounding Provence, photographing historical buildings and hamlets to garner information and inspiration.

John, an ex-nuclear physicist, and Francisca, a former Pan Am flight attendant, met during a tennis game. Neither will tell who won, but the match led to marriage and their shared vision for the Vintners Inn.

A native of Belgium, Francisca supervised the decoration of the inn's forty-four red-tile-roofed units. The units are joined by matching tiled walkways and surround a central plaza with a tranquil fountain. Arched windows, wrought-iron railings, and patios create a relaxed atmosphere. Antique European pine furnishings have been restored and refinished to complement the charming country-print fabrics and floral-patterned wall-papers. The rooms offer beamed ceilings, wood-burning fireplaces, wet bars, and views of the lush 45 acres of Pinot

Blanc, French Colombard, and Sauvignon Blanc vineyards. All rooms have private baths with luxurious oversized oval bathtubs.

The lobby sports an enormous wine basket, and along with old antique farm equipment decorating the walls, creates an old-world feeling. Plan to enjoy a glass of 1985 gold medal Sauvignon Blanc as you relax in the outdoor sundeck Jacuzzi and watch the colorful hot-air balloons as they drift overhead. There is also a VCR with a good movie library available for guests.

Breakfast is served in the sunlit dining room overlooking the court-yard. You'll enjoy a sumptuous buffet of fresh fruit and juices, cereals, homemade breads, and croissants along with teas and rich fresh-ground coffee. A luscious Belgian waffle (and Francisca knows how to make a *real* Belgian waffle), slathered with whipped cream and sea-sonal berries, can be made to order. For a romantic morning, you may choose to take your breakfast to your room.

When the Duffys designed their inn, they also provided a building to house the acclaimed restaurant John Ash & Company. Owner-chef John Ash focuses on local foods. He carefully selects produce from nearby farms, oysters from the Tomales Bay, chicken and game birds grown on Sonoma ranches, and the county's famous cheeses. The freshest of seafood is purchased from northern California and Oregon.

I had a wonderful dinner that began with a salad of fresh Oregon scallops sprinkled with coriander. A flaky California sea bass, grilled with fresh herbs and served on a bed of flavorful eggplant came next, followed by a palate-cleansing sorbet of mandarin oranges. My entrée of boned quail stuffed with a forcemeat of veal, walnuts, and leeks, served on top of fresh spinach, was done to perfection.

To finish, I sampled local goat cheeses, with baby greens and roasted walnuts. Elegant desserts will certainly tempt you, but I just couldn't eat another bite. The restaurant's wine list is excellent and has been given the Sweepstakes Award for 1985, 1986, and 1987 by the Sonoma County Harvest Fair.

John and Francisca are happy to help you plan tours of the area and will make recommendations on wineries, restaurants, points of interest, and picnic areas. Guest privileges can be arranged at nearby clubs for tennis, swimming, golf, and racquetball.

The Sonoma County wine country is in one of the most beautiful valleys in northern California. As I stood on my balcony overlooking the lovely manicured vineyards, I could see why John and Francisca chose this very special spot for their inn.

VINTNERS INN, 4350 Barnes Rd., Santa Rosa, CA 95403; 707-575-7350 or 800-421-2584. A 44-guestroom (private baths) inn complex nestled in the center of a vineyard in the heart of the Sonoma Valley in northern California. Open year-round. Queen beds. Breakfast included. Dinner at John Ash & Co. Accommodations for handicapped guests. Children welcome. Pets by arrangement. CCs: All major cards. John and Francisca Duffy, owners/hosts; Cindy Young, manager.

DIRECTIONS: From Hwy. 101 about 3 mi. north of Santa Rosa, take River Rd. turnoff west. First left turn is Barnes Rd.

Hawaii

KONA VILLAGE RESORT
Kaupulehu-Kona, Hawaii

Wet sand softly crunched beneath my bare feet as I walked along the beach, enjoying nature's artwork in the dawning skies. Waves lapped upon the shore, then receded to repeat the cycle. Only the sounds of nature filled the air at Kona Village this time of day.

The individual grass hut guest cottages (locally called hales) came into view as I made my way back to the resort. Although there are 125 hales at the resort, I was impressed by the seclusion each offered, screened by trees and foliage with trails leading to each doorway. My wife, Louise, was waiting for me on our private lanai. Our spacious hale was decorated in bold Polynesian prints and rattan furnishings. The fragrance of fresh flowers wafted through the air. A refrigerator stocked with juices and soft drinks sat along one wall, and a coffee maker that ground fresh Kona beans supplied us with our first morning cup. Notably absent from the cottage was a telephone, a radio, and a TV, but they were not missed. "Do Not Disturb" signs were replaced by the resort's tradition of exhibiting a coconut outside one's door to insure privacy.

Breakfast is served in the Hale Moana dining room, fronting on the ocean. We enjoyed fresh pineapple and macadamia nut pancakes floating in coconut syrup. The mid-day buffet lunch is outstanding. Served on outdoor tables, overflowing with fresh seafood, fruits, vegetables and several entrées, it is an impressive affair that compares to none. Evening dining, in the Hale Somoa as well as in the Hale Moana, offers seven nightly menus. One evening, we sampled an appetizer of Lobster Alexandra followed by cream of potato and Maui onion soup. Louise chose the house salad with fresh vegetables and Chilean Bay shrimp over a trio of greens called Salad Moana. I had my favorite, Caesar salad. Entrées are a combination of American, European, and Hawaiian cuisine. We chose from the large selection of fresh island fish which could be broiled, baked, or sautéed as we desired. I tried the local favorite, uku, sautéed in meuniere and capers. Louise had ono, broiled in a saffron and orange butter. Lamb chops, beef brochette, and baked quail, as well as a chicken and an angel hair pasta dish balanced the menu choices. We shared a wedge of macadamia nut pie for dessert and, of course, steaming cups of Kona coffee.

In true Polynesian tradition, there was a Friday night Luau at the Hale Ho'okipa (Hospitality House), which is located along a beautiful lagoon surrounded by lush gardens. The Paniolo Steakfry also takes place here every Wednesday evening. The Steakfry and the Luau are just two of the numerous activities available, which range from learning the art of lei making, hula dance lessons (put to good use when you attend the luau), and outrigger canoeing to guided walks at botanical sites or beaches. Tennis clinics are available on a daily basis. Kona also presents a "Keikis (Kids) in Paradise" program with supervised, fun-filled activities to entertain kids of all ages. Young guests are also treated to their own early dinner followed by a movie. Fred Duerr, General Manager, told me many of the children who visit with their parents will, years later, bring their own children back to be "keikis" at Kona. A chartered helicopter ride is a wonderful way to experience from above breathtaking waterfalls, valleys, and, from a distance, Kilauea, an active reminder of Mother Nature's volcanic power. Abundant sea life can be observed at the tidal pools, by underwater snorkeling or scuba diving, or in the comfort of the glass bottom excursion boat.

But I personally enjoyed lying on the clean, white beaches soaking in the warmth of tropical sun's rays while reading a good book in this private, romantic paradise.

KONA VILLAGE RESORT, P.O. BOX 1299, Kaupulehu-Kona, Hawaii 96745; 808-325-5555, 800-367-5290. Coastal tropical resort with 125 thatched-roof cottages. Mostly king-sized beds. Closed December 6–14 each year. Some minimum stays. All meals included in rates. Liquor available at bars or during meals. No phones, TVs, or A/C in rooms. Smoking allowed in most areas. Too many activities and sights to list within the resort. Nearest shopping centers 15 miles away. Mac, a rainbow macaw and Manu and Keo, two blue macaws plus mallards, peacocks, and black Australian swans in residence. No pets allowed. All major CCs. Kona Village Associates, owners; Fred Duerr, manager.

DIRECTIONS: From Keahole Airport, drive north 5 miles on Hwy. #19 to the thatched roof gatehouse entrance.

Oregon

HERON HAUS
Portland, Oregon

Julie Keppeler's many years in Hawaii are reflected not only in the overall feeling of airiness and light in this spacious three-story home but also in the names of the guest rooms: Kanui, Kulia, Ko, Manu, Maluhia, and Makua. Julie will translate for you.

She was drawn back to the Northwest, where her grandfather was one of the earliest settlers and her family has distinguished itself in the study of the area. Heron Haus, built in 1904, was in dire need of attention when Julie bought it in 1986, but she recognized its inherent quality and she couldn't resist the expansive views of mountains and city, the fruit trees in the lower garden, the old ballast stones from sailing ships, the leaded glass windows and intricate ceiling moldings, the servants' quarters on the third floor, or the cedar storage closet. And I can imagine her delight when she pulled up old carpeting to discover parquet flooring in mint condition.

Guests can certainly enjoy the ultimate in luxurious quarters here. The rooms, decorated in blues, lavenders, and rose, are spacious, with large, comfortable beds, sitting areas, and wonderful views. But it was the bathrooms that caught my eye. One has a raised spa with a view of the city, and another has a seven-nozzle shower with the original 1904 plumbing.

When I first drove up into the hills above Portland and turned into the curved drive to the house, I was smitten with the view of the Cascade Mountains to the east. As we toured the main floor, Julie pointed out the view of Mt. St. Helens from the living room and the book-filled mahogany library. There is still another view of the city from the very pleasant enclosed sun room, which overlooks the pool.

The plants, flowers, paintings, and books complete the feeling of hospitality and gracious living that Julie has created here.

HERON HAUS, 2545 N.W. Westover Rd., Portland, OR 97210. 503-274-1846. A 5-guestroom (private bath) gracious bed-and-breakfast home in the hills above Portland, 1 mi. from downtown. King and queen beds. Continental breakfast. Air conditioning in two rooms. Cable outlets, telephones. Open year-round. Swimming pool on grounds. Macintosh computer available by reservation. Restaurants, shopping, and all the attractions of Portland nearby. Public transportation, 1 block. No pets. No smoking. CCs: Visa, MC. Julie Keppeler, owner/host.

DIRECTIONS: From I-405 take Everett St. exit. Turn onto Glisan (one way). Turn right on 24th; 3 blocks to Johnson; left 1 block to Westover Rd. Proceed up incline to address on rock wall one-half block. Continue up driveway to parking by front door.

MT. ASHLAND INN
Ashland, Oregon

Jerry and Elaine Shanafelt are modern-day pioneers. Sixteen years ago they packed up their two Alaskan Huskie sled dogs and moved west to Ashland, Oregon, from Boston. They had a dream of owning mountain land and making a living from that land.

The 160 acres the Shanafelts purchased in 1975 is on the famous Pacific Crest trail, a trail that can be traveled from Canada to Mexico. One such traveler, an old man on a horse, leading a mule with pots and pans clanking, passed the inn as I was standing on the deck.

The two-story, 4,200-square foot inn is a unique log structure designed and built by the Shanafelts, using cedar logs cut from the surrounding property. Jerry's background is in designing and building, while Elaine worked as a director of nurses and nurse practitioners prior to their new life as owners of Mt. Ashland Inn.

Building the inn offered the perfect outlet for several of the couple's hobbies, such as Jerry's stained-glass work, woodcarving, and furniture-making and Elaine's interest in antiques and American needle-craft.

The inn's main room is dominated by a large, welcoming stone fireplace, where guests can congregate around game tables. Antiques, Oriental rugs, and large overstuffed furniture provide a comfortable atmo-

sphere for relaxing after a day of hiking or skiing.

The four guest rooms are located on the second floor to take advantage of the views. Each room has a private bath, a queen-sized bed, and an individually controlled thermostat. The Shanafelts' collection of Western furnishings and handmade quilts adorn each room.

To satisfy the appetites of active guests, a hearty breakfast is prepared. Apple-walnut whole-wheat pancakes, orange French toast, and shrimp quiche are a few of the specialties. Complimentary beverages are available throughout the day.

"We've put a lot of ourselves into this," said Elaine. "We consider ourselves quite privileged to be able to live where we do, and we built the Inn as a way to share this area with others."

MT. ASHLAND INN, P.O. Box 944, 550 Mt. Ashland Rd., Ashland, OR 97520; 503-482-8707. A 5-guestroom (private baths) 2-room, 3-suite mountain inn, 2 miles from the Mt. Ashland summit, 25 minutes from Ashland. King and queen beds. Open year-round. Cross country and downhill skiing; closest lodging to Mt. Ashland slopes. Warm clothing any season. No pets. Smoking permitted on deck. CCs: Visa, MC. Jerry and Elaine Shanafelt, owners/hosts.

DIRECTIONS: Take I-5 north. Get off at Mt. Ashland Exit. Follow signs for 6 miles. Elevation of Inn is 5,500 feet. 25 minutes from Ashland.

TU TU' TUN LODGE
Gold Beach, Oregon

Tu Tu' Tun (pronounced to-TOOT'n) is right on the Rogue River, just seven miles from the ocean. The name comes from an Indian tribe that once occupied this river bluff; a rough translation is "people close to the river."

My first impression as we drove into the grounds was of two rambling, weathered wood buildings with lots of glass, surrounded by beautiful plantings of native shrubs, bright blooms, and a manicured apple orchard.

True to their reputation as gracious hosts, Laurie and Dirk Van Zante greeted us and invited us into the main lodge, where a fire crackled in the massive stone fireplace.

Since it had been necessary for me to visit Tu Tu' Tun in April, during its off season, I asked Dirk about some of their customs. "Well," this handsome young man replied, "as the sun sets on the western hills, guests listen for the ringing of the big brass bell, summoning them to join us for hors d'oeuvres, one of which on occasion has a mysterious ingredient. The guests have a lot of fun guessing, and Laurie enjoys mixing a concoction to reward the winner!"

As I understand it, during this gathering time Dirk and Laurie have a chance to mingle with the guests and tell tales of the Rogue. Guests love to share their stories for their day fishing or wild river boating.

Birds, bear, beaver, and otter vie for the first place with the biggest catch of the day, although children may vote for how many deer they have fed in the orchard that afternoon.

As dinner begins, Dirk welcomes people into the dining room, where Lazy Susan tables are decorated with fresh flowers. Dirk seats the guests by name, another of the many ways people are made to feel special at Tu Tu' Tun. "We have a four-course set daily menu," Laurie told me, "including such items as fresh chinook salmon baked with lemon butter and served with caper sauce, or marinated rolled chicken breast in a light shallot Parmesan sauce. Creamy zucchini soup, salad made from locally grown greens, freshly baked rolls, and raspberry sorbet are among the many family recipes."

The madrona wood fires lit on the terrace during dinner provide a dramatic view for diners, as well as a gathering place after dinner where conversations continue. "I tend the fires," Dirk explained, "and I'll tell everyone when I see the salmon jumping or a bald eagle soaring overhead."

Furnishings are attractive, comfortable, and contemporary, and everything is immaculate. There are two suites in the main building and sixteen guest rooms in a motel-style building, where each room is decorated with logging, fishing, or mining artifacts. "Rooms are named after riffles in the river, and many returning guests request 'their' room, which might be 'Lobster Riffle,' 'Bear Riffle,' or 'Hog Eddy.' They have their favorite view and can enjoy reminiscing over what they wrote in the log book last season." Every room has a private balcony or porch overlooking the river, and there are always fresh flowers and plants.

This is experiencing the wilderness in a most civilized manner with two charming innkeepers.

TU TU' TUN LODGE, 96550 North Bank Rogue, Gold Beach, OR 97444; 503-247-6664. A 16-guestroom, 2-suite (private baths) contemporary lodge on the Rogue River, in a wilderness setting, 7 mi. from the Pacific Ocean in southern Oregon. King, queen and twin beds. European plan. Lunch served daily to registered guests only. Breakfast and dinner served to travelers by reservation. Breakfast and lunch baskets available. Open April 29–November 1. Heated pool, pitch-and-putt course, antique pool table, antique player piano, horseshoes, private dock and hiking trails on premises. Guides for steelhead and salmon fishing, whitewater excursions, hiking, scenic drives and flights, beachcombing, golf, horseback riding nearby. Pets welcome. Dirk and Laurie Van Zante, owners/hosts.

DIRECTIONS: From Rte. 101 follow signs for 7 mi. up north side of river to the lodge.

Washington

THE CAPTAIN WHIDBEY INN
Coupeville, Washington

There isn't a Captain Whidbey anymore, but there is a Captain John Colby Stone, who is also the innkeeper. With his Master's License from the Coast Guard, he is able to take passengers for a special cruise in his classic sloop, *Aeolus*, on the peaceful waters of Penn Cove. Gliding past the lush pastures and forests of Whidbey, guests who take this excursion might catch a glimpse of a majestic bald eagle, a great blue heron, porpoises, dolphins, or even an Orca whale.

The Captain Whidbey Inn, built in 1907 of distinctly regional peeled madrona logs, has been included in the Ebey's Landing National Historic Reserve, established by Congress. It is a romantic and rustic hideaway by the sea, on the shore of Penn Cove, with the feeling of an old-fashioned New England inn.

The natural center of the inn is the living room, with a very big fireplace made of round stones. Here, everybody—house guests and dinner guests alike—sits around talking and leafing through the dozens of magazines.

Some of the guest rooms are upstairs in the main house and an additional number of rustic lodges, called Lagoon Rooms, overlooking their own private lake, were built in the woods across the road from the main house a few years ago, and they have recently been remodeled and soundproofed. The guest rooms are tastefully furnished with antiques, and those in the main house have down comforters and featherbeds. A nice area for general relaxing has been set aside for house guests on the second floor with floor-to-ceiling bookshelves jam-packed with books.

The gazebo by the lagoon has a two-level dining deck with a grill overlooking the Cove. It's a great place to dine on the famous Penn Cove mussels, clam chowder, grilled Northwest salmon and halibut, along with other seafoods and local fruits and vegetables. All this and warm sun, gentle breezes, and spectacular vistas, with boats and sea-planes and the fluttering burgees of West Coast yacht clubs. The Cascade Range in the east is dominated by Mount Baker, over 10,000 feet high, and Mount Olympus in the west, at almost 8,000 feet.

Penn Cove mussels are a big story here, and an annual mussel festival is held by the inn during January. There's a mussel-eating contest, a seven-course mussel dinner cooked by the fine kitchen staff, a "Mussel Beach" party, and a mussel recipe contest.

THE CAPTAIN WHIDBEY INN, 2072 W. Captain Whidbey Inn Rd., Coupeville, WA 98239; 206-678-4097. A 31-guestroom (4 cottages; 20 private baths) country inn, on protected Penn Cove off Puget Sound, 50 mi. north of Seattle, 3 mi. north of Coupeville. All bed sizes. Breakfast, lunch, and dinner served daily to travelers. Open year-round. Boating and fishing on grounds. Golf nearby. Pets allowed in cottages only. Capt. John Colby Stone, owner/host.

DIRECTIONS: Whidbey Island is reached year-round from the south by the Columbia Beach-Mukilteo Ferry, and during the summer and on weekends by the Port Townsend-Keystone Ferry. From the north (Vancouver, BC and Bellingham), take the Deception Pass Bridge to Whidbey Island.

MANOR FARM INN
Poulsbo, Washington

As I wandered about the 30-acre farm, its lush pastures spreading across a picturesque valley tucked between the green hills of Kitsap County, I felt myself unwind. There's something about strolling across a meadow and watching a flock of sheep graze and pausing beside a quiet pond that instantly sets the mind and body at ease.

Later, at an outdoor table, I sipped a glass of wine with Manor Farm owners Robin and Jill Hughes, and asked about their concept of an inn combined with a farm. In his decidedly British accent, Robin said,

"The farm does provide fresh quality produce for the kitchen, but out main purpose is to help our guests enjoy simple, pastoral pleasures, apart from the frantic world—to give people a chance to truly relax."

With his ruddy face aglow and his voice full of vitality, he continued, "Here they can pet the animals, help gather eggs, pick apples from the trees, or they can simply lie on the grass and stare at the sky—whatever suits their needs."

Robin moved from England to Australia when he was 20. Before establishing the Manor Farm Inn in 1983, he had designed and developed over 35 "old-English type inns and restaurants" all the way from Australia through Canada and along the Pacific Coast. Yet he found time to practice veterinary medicine, which accounts for his love of the animals on his farm, their excellent condition, their variety, and their number. Within tidy white fences that surround large pastures are grazing horses, a young herd of Jerseys, and a flock of black-faced Suffolk and white Coopworth sheep. The pen is full of chickens, and the pond full of trout.

"Robin has a wonderful creative ability," said his wife, Jill, "and I operate the business end of the inn."

A section of the white clapboard farmhouse dates back to 1886, but the new wing, where most of the guest rooms are located, has been built in such a manner that it appears to be part of the original. Inside are high vaulted ceilings, exposed beams and trusses, and antique unpainted pine furniture. The total effect is something like an old French country farmhouse. Especially interesting architecturally is the long covered porch that leads from the drawing room to the dining room; in a corner, raincoats hang on hooks, waterproof boots rest on the floor beneath, and fishing rods stand nearby, ready for anyone's use.

In the morning, a knock on the door signals the arrival of a basket of hot scones, homemade jam, and fresh orange juice. Later, there will be a full farm breakfast in the dining room. Maybe this morning you will go fishing in the trout pond; this afternoon, horseback riding or hiking; this evening, an unforgettable dinner in the inn's restaurant, offering such delicacies as cream of wild asparagus soup and truffled chicken in champagne or grilled red snapper with lavage leaves. Then, after relaxing around the fire in the drawing room, let the crickets and frogs sing you to sleep.

MANOR FARM INN, 26069 Big Valley Road N.E., Poulsbo, WA 98370; 206-779-4628; fax 206-779-4876. A 6-guestroom (2 with fireplaces; private baths), French farm-style inn located in a beautiful rural valley. Also: 2 additional bedrooms with a shared bath in the old section, a 2-bedroom farm cottage across the street, and a 3-bedroom, 2-bath beach house nearby. Vegatable and flower gardens; farm animals; trout pond; hot tub. Guests are encouraged to hike about, participate in farm activities, and go pond fishing and boating. Horseback riding available. 10 minutes from the colorful Scandinavian town of Poulsbo and scenic Bainbridge Island; an hour from Olympic National Park. Full breakfast included. Smoking outside only. No pets. Closed on Thanksgiving and Christmas Days. Robin and Jill Hughes, owners/hosts.

DIRECTIONS: From Seattle, take Winslow Ferry at Coloman Dock and follow signs to Hood Canal Bridge. 4 mi. after turning right onto Hwy. 3, turn right onto Big Valley Road. The Manor Farm Inn is approximately 1 mi. further, located on right.

RAVENSCROFT INN

Port Townsend, Washington

Ravenscroft Inn is a replica of a Charleston single house, a long clapboard building with covered porches that extend full length on two levels. They give magnificent views of the Sound.

The spacious interior of the inn relfects the warmth of the owners: vibrant color combinations, European chintz, fresh flowers, and, on guest room doors, unique wreaths created by a local artist. All rooms are attractive; each one's decor is entirely unique, with interesting combinations of prints on chairs and spreads. Two guest rooms have fireplaces. The most opulent room has an elegant four-poster queen bed and French doors opening onto the piazza.

In the friendly living/dining area, or great room as it is traditionally called, there is a 12-foot-high ceiling and a massive Rumford fireplace.

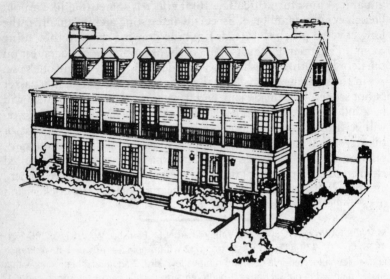

Here guests gather for breakfast to enjoy such delicacies as Cointreau French toast—puffed to perfection—and apricot-glazed sausages, while host John Rammey plays classical music on the grand piano. It's an experience to savor.

"For ten years we hunted for the right inn," said Leah Hammer, who, with John and her father, Papa Sam, own Ravenscroft. "We love Port Townsend; it's magical. I remember standing on the vacant lot where Ravenscroft is today and saying, 'We must come back.'"

The original owners built the inn and named it Ravenscroft. Leah, John, and Papa Sam could hardly believe their good fortune when they returned to the Northwest and found the inn for sale. What made it even more meaningful was their personal identification with the inn's name. John, a classical musician and concert pianist, had heard of a Ravenscroft who, in the 17th century, collected keyboard music; Leah, once a representative for crystal manufacturers, knew of a Ravenscroft, too—the first craftsman to use lead in glass-making. "We felt the inn was meant for us," she said.

That evening, still pondering Leah's story, I sat on the porch and sipped a glass of the inn's complimentary sherry. Mist hung over parts of the Sound, and from somewhere a gull cried. A ferryboat, ablaze with lights, slid like a jewel across the dark water. It was no wonder they had to come back.

RAVENSCROFT INN, 533 Quincy Street, Port Townsend, WA 98368; 206-385-2784; fax: 206-385-6724. An 8-guestroom (private baths) inn in the historic homes district overlooking the bay. Within walking distance of harbor, restaurants, and shops. 60 mi. from Seattle; less than an hour to Olympic National Park. Full breakfast included. No pets. Outside smoking only. Leah Hammer, John Ranney and Sam Turk, owners/hosts.

DIRECTIONS: From Seattle, take Winslow Ferry at Colman Dock. Follow signs to Hood Canal Bridge; cross bridge and continue until you see sign "To Port Townsend." In town, turn left on Kearney, right on Lawrence, then right on Quincy 1 block.

THE SHELBURNE INN

Seaview, Washington

"This little peninsula has the cleanest estuary in the country. We're kind of hidden away here, surrounded by waters and bays." David Campiche gestured out toward the wide expanse of sandy beach as he spoke. "There's an abundance of shellfish and oysters, salmon, sturgeon, and eight to ten varieties of whitefish. There are bird sanctuaries, state parks, big rock jetties with sea lions, and whale-watching, too." We had strolled out behind the inn and past some houses to the sand dunes bordering the beach. "This is one of the longest stretches of beach you'll find in the Pacific Northwest," he said. "It goes on for thirty miles."

I had driven down the coast in time for dinner in the Shoalwater Restaurant, which is actually part of the Shelburne Inn. I should explain that David Campiche and Laurie Anderson own the inn, and Tony and Ann Kischner lease the restaurant. We had a dinner there that I can only describe as exquisite, starting with a smoked fish mousse served with a variety of assorted smoked seafoods. Then there were local escargots served with Oregon hazelnuts and butter. After

that came a fillet of freshly caught sturgeon with a raspberry beurre blanc, followed by a green salad, which was followed by roast quail served with a marvelous sauce made from port wine, walnuts, and cream cheese. Among the dessert offerings was Ann's cranberry-swirl cheesecake with chocolate cranberry glaze, which placed first in a national contest. Tony Kischner is a most innovative restaurateur, and I'm not surprised that the restaurant has acquired national recognition.

Since the turn of the century there has been a Shelburne Inn in the tiny coastal town of Seaview. In those days Oregonians came by steamer and a narrow-gauge railway to spend their summers in the sleepy villages on Long Beach Peninsula, lazing on the pristine beach, fishing the bounteous waters, picking mushrooms, digging for clams, and clambering over the rocks around North Head Lighthouse, where the Columbia River empties into the Pacific Ocean.

In 1977, when David and Laurie found the Shelburne Inn, it was in a sad state. "There were cans in the rooms to collect the rainfall," David told me. He is a young, handsome fellow with a very relaxed, engaging manner. His bearded face is frequently wreathed in smiles. He speaks laughingly of the hard work of restoring and renovating an old building, but the etched and stained-glass windows, the tongue-and-groove wood paneling and open-beamed ceilings, brass chandeliers, and handsome antique-furnished rooms reveal how much thought and energy he and Laurie have lavished on the inn—and still lavish.

The inn is listed on the National Register of Historic Places. Many of their antiques were collected during their travels in Europe and England; in fact, several of their stained-glass windows were rescued from an old church in Morcambe, England.

Laurie, blond and blue-eyed, picked wallpapers and paint and lighting fixtures as well as the antique oak dressers and braided rugs and homespun quilts for the brass beds, and now she keeps the rooms bright with fresh flowers from their garden.

Some of their edible flowers adorned my breakfast plate the next morning, when I sat down at the big oval oak table in the pleasant lobby, where guests gather for breakfast and sociability. David and Laurie do great breakfasts.

A lovely old-fashioned inn, superb food, and friendly, hospitable hosts—I suggest you make your reservations now.

THE SHELBURNE INN, Pacific Hwy. 103 and 45th Pl., P.O. Box 250, Seaview, WA 98644; 206-642-2442. Fax # (206) 642 8904 A 16-guestroom (13 private baths) Victorian village hotel on Highway 103 on the Long Beach peninsula, 120 mi. northwest of Portland, Ore. Breakfast included in room rate. Queen, double and twin beds available. Shoalwater Restaurant open for lunch and dinner daily in the summer; check winter service. Reservations recommended. Gift shop and pub on premises. State parks, sandy beach, museums, fishing, and birdwatching nearby. No pets. David Campiche and Laurie Anderson, owners/hosts; Tony and Ann Kischner, restaurateurs.

DIRECTIONS: Take U.S. 101 to the Long Beach Peninsula. In Seaview, take Rte. 103 a short distance. Inn is on the left.

TURTLEBACK FARM INN

Orcas Island, Washington

Just getting to Turtleback Farm on Orcas Island is something of an adventure—first, leaving Anacortes on the ferry that plies the sparkling waters of Puget Sound through the San Juan archipelago, and then taking the road through beautiful Crow Valley, with its lush meadows, in the shadow of Turtleback Mountain. Driving over the dirt road that leads up to the unassuming green clapboard farmhouse is like coming back to grandmother's house.

Bill and Susan Fletcher found this old farmhouse when they were looking for a summer home in 1983. At first Bill was doubtful about starting a bed-and-breakfast business. But go into business they did, and they've made a most fetching little inn without changing the original character of the house. Renovating and expanding it, they created seven guest rooms with private baths, and all with marvelous views of meadows, orchards, duck ponds, trees, and garden.

A hearty breakfast to start the day is served in the dining room at tables set with fine bone china and linen or on the sun-washed deck. There are antique as well as contemporary furnishings in the common rooms and guest rooms.

Bill and Susan are raising sheep on the farm, some of which are Suffolks. They've been learning the hard way. "We delivered three of them," Susan told me. "We were down in the dark with the flashlight, reading the instructions on page 3!"

There's no end of recreational activities here, from golfing to kayaking, and the nearby town of Eastsound abounds with restaurants and shops. Guests are free to explore the eighty acres of farm and forest, but they are warned to be cautious of the ponds and the "rambunctious brown ram."

TURTLEBACK FARM INN, Crow Valley Rd., Rte. 1, Box 650, Eastsound, Orcas Island, WA 98245; 206-376-4914. A 7-guestroom (private baths) farmhouse B&B in beautiful Crow Valley on Orcas Island, 4 mi. from Eastsound. All bed sizes. Full breakfast. Open year-round. Nature walks and hiking trails in Moran State Park, summer swimming in Lake Cascade, picnicking, fishing, kayaking, sailing, charter boat rentals, bicycle rentals, mopeds, and golf nearby. No pets. Sheep, geese, chickens and dogs abound. Smoking outside only. CCs: Visa, MC. Bill and Susan Fletcher, owners/hosts.

DIRECTIONS: Reach Anacortes and San Juan Ferry Terminal via I-5 and Hwy. 20. From the ferry landing on Orcas Island, take Horseshoe Hwy. north approx. 3 mi. to first left turn and continue toward Deer Harbor. Turn right on Crow Valley Rd. and continue 3 mi. to Turtleback Farm.

WILLCOX HOUSE
Bremerton, Washington

I drove down a narrow winding road past glades of old-growth trees, their mossy trunks surrounded by sword ferns, huckleberry bushes, and rhododendrons, then, under the impressive moon gate. Ahead, nestled among plantings on a bluff overlooking an alpine scene, was a large red building with a copper roof.

Phillip Hughes, one of the owners, ushered me through double entry doors, whose glass inserts had a cut design of dolphins, into a decidedly art deco foyer: a large mirror with flower-shaped lamps graced a wall covered in white silk, the high ceiling painted metallic blue.

This 10,000-square-foot three-story mansion was designed and built in 1937 by noted Seattle architect Lionel Pries, and according to historical accounts the home became "the grand entertainment capital of the canal region". Clark Gable once stayed in the guest room with the balcony; the room is named after him, and his photograph is on the dresser.

In 1988 Phillip Hughes, a business administrator, and Cecilia Hughes, a fashion designer, purchased the mansion and embarked on a

program of complete renovation, adding modern conveniences for the sake of comfort but retaining an emphasis on its period look. The acres of grounds have numerous trails, spring-fed ponds, weeping willows and four Japanese lace-leaf maples that are 80 years old.

For dinner I had the Mayan port tenderloin with unusual spices from the Yucatan Peninsula, served with a special mango salsa. After dinner I won a game at darts in the game room, then in the library I curled up in a burgundy leather wing back chair with a mystery novel in front of a cheery blaze (one of five fireplaces in the house). Before retiring, I enjoyed a nightcap in the Colonel's Pub with its 13-foot-long mahogany bar. The decor is nautical. (And no, you haven't drunk too much—clock built into the back bar mirror does run backwards.

As you ascend the red-carpeted stairway to your spacious room, an oversized bed, mounds of pillows, down comforters, bathrobes, towel warmers, clothes steamer and panoramic views of Hood Canal and the Olympic Mountains await you.

WILLCOX HOUSE, 2390 Tekiu, Bremerton, WA 98312; 206-830-4492. A 5-guestroom (private baths) inn within a mansion of the art deco period. Extensive grounds with hiking trails, wildlife, mountain and water views, swimming pool, fishing, boating. 1/2 hour to town (antiques, shopping, restaurants); 3 golf courses nearby. Full breakfast and afternoon wine and cheese included. Lunch and dinner available to room guests; open all year. No pets. Smoking outside only. CCs: Visa, MC. Cecilia and Phillip Hughes, owners/hosts.

DIRECTIONS: From Seattle, take Bremerton Ferry at Colman Dock; drive west on 6th St. which becomes Kitsap Way; continue under the overpass 1.2 mi.; fork left onto Northlake Way for l.l mi.; fork left onto Sebeck Hwy 2.9 mi.; left on Holly Road 4.9 mi.; left onto Seabeck Holly Rd. 5.2 mi.; right on Old Holly Rd. then right at mailboxes onto Tekiu Rd, turning left at cabin and through gatehouse.

INDEX

RATES

Space limitations preclude any more than a general range of rates for each inn, and these should not be considered firm quotations. All inns serve full breakfasts unless noted as CB which is a continental breakfast, AP which is American Plan (must purchases your meals separately) and MAP which is modified American plan (Breakfast & Dinner included in rate for two.)

Please check with the inns for their various rates and special packages. It should be noted that many small inns do not have night staffs, and innkeepers will appreciate it if calls are made before 8:00 p.m.

CANADA

British Columbia

Malahat, AERIE	$150–290 (Canadian)
Sooke, SOOKE HARBOUR HOUSE	$123–275 B&L
Victoria, ABIGAIL'S HOTEL	$100–196 (Canadian) B

Ontario

Jackson's Point, BRIARS, THE	$176–304 (Canadian) AP

Quebec

North Hatley, HOVEY MANOR, THE	$175–330 (Canadian), MAP

UNITED STATES

Alaska

Gustavus, GLACIER BAY COUNTRY INN	$208 AP

Arizona

Phoenix, MARICOPA MANOR	$69–99 B
Tucson, ARIZONA INN	$82–145
Wickenburg, RANCHO DE LOS CABALLEROS	$115–190 AP

Arkansas

Eureka Springs, DAIRY HOLLOW HOUSE	$115–165 B

California

Avalon, INN ON MOUNT ADA, THE	$190–580 AP
Big Sur, VENTANA INN	$155–775 CB
Capitola, INN AT DEPOT HILL	$155–250

Carmel, PINE INN, THE $95–195
Cazadero, TIMBERHILL RANCH $266–298 MAP
Elk, HARBOR HOUSE $135–245 MAP
Ferndale, GINGERBREAD MANSION, THE $105–175 CB
Garberville, BENBOW INN $88–260
Half Moon Bay, MILL ROSE INN $150–275 B
Healdsburg, MADRONA MANOR $135–200 CB
Little River, GLENDEVEN $75–150 B
Montecito, SAN YSIDRO RANCH $185–540
Monterey, OLD MONTEREY INN $160–220 B
Muir Beach, PELICAN INN, THE $135–150 B
Pacific Grove, MARTINE INN, THE $115–225 B
Palm Springs, VILLA ROYALE $65–225 CB
San Francisco, MANSIONS, THE $89–350 B
San Francisco, SHERMAN HOUSE, THE $190–650
San Francisco, SPENCER HOUSE, THE $95–155 B
San Francisco, UNION STREET INN $115–225 CB
Santa Rosa, VINTNERS INN $108–185
Walnut Creek, MANSION AT LAKEWOOD, THE $85–225 B

Colorado

Colorado Springs, HEARTHSTONE INN, THE $78–120
Denver, QUEEN ANNE INN $79–131 CB
Durango, BLUE LAKE RANCH $85–195 B
Estes Park, RIVERSONG $85–160 B
Granby, C LAZY U RANCH $270–450 AP

Connecticut

Deep River, RIVERWIND INN $85–145 B
Greenwich, HOMESTEAD INN, THE $127–167 CB
New Preston, BOULDERS INN $145–225 MAP
Norfolk, MANOR HOUSE $65–155 B
Old Lyme, OLD LYME INN $90–110 CB
Ridgefield, WEST LANE INN $95–165 CB
Salisbury, UNDER MOUNTAIN INN $150–180 MAP

District of Columbia

Washington, HENLEY PARK HOTEL $85–225

Florida

Apalachicola, GIBSON INN $50–100 B
Key West, MARQUESA HOTEL, THE $105–275
Little Torch Key, LITTLE PALM ISLAND $335–750 AP (includes gratuity)
                                                  EP and MAP available
Orange Park, CLUB CONTINENTAL $55–65 B

Georgia

Savannah, GASTONIAN, THE $98–235 B
Senoia, VERANDA, THE $80–100

Hawaii

Kaupulehu-Kona, KONA VILLAGE INN $360–640 AP

Illinois

Elsah, MAPLE LEAF COTTAGE INN $75 B

Indiana

Goshen, CHECKERBERRY INN, THE $96–120 CB

Kansas

Topeka, HERITAGE HOUSE $55–80 B

Kentucky

Harrodsburg, BEAUMONT INN $70–85 B

Maine

Bar Harbor, INN AT CANOE POINT $75–195
Blue Hill, BLUE HILL INN $110–165 MAP
Blue Hill, JOHN PETERS INN $85–135 B
Camden, WINDWARD HOUSE BED AND BREAKFAST $65–125 B
Castine, PENTAGOET INN, THE $149–169 MAP
Deer Isle, PILGRIM'S INN, THE $120 B, $180 MAP
East Waterford, WATERFORD INNE, THE $55–90
Hancock Point, CROCKER HOUSE COUNTRY INN, THE $60–70 B
Kennebunkport, CAPTAIN LORD MANSION, THE $125–185 B
Kennebunkport, INN AT HARBOR HEAD, THE $95–175 B
Kennebunkport, WHITE BARN $125–300 CB
Newcastle, NEWCASTLE INN, THE $60–120 B, $115–176 MAP
Rangeley, COUNTRY CLUB INN, THE $87–97 B, $133–151 MAP
Rangeley, RANGELEY INN $65–100
Westport Island, SQUIRE TARBOX INN, THE $62–132, $120–190 MAP
York, DOCKSIDE GUEST QUARTERS $55–129

Maryland

Baltimore, ADMIRAL FELL INN $98–155 CB
Buckeystown, INN AT BUCKEYSTOWN, THE $167–272 MAP
Oxford, ROBERT MORRIS INN $80–180

Massachusetts

Auburn, CAPTAIN SAMUEL EDDY HOUSE COUNTRY INN $69–95 B
Barnstable, ASHLEY MANOR $100–155 B

Boston, LENOX HOTEL, THE $84–190
Chatham, CAPTAIN'S HOUSE INN OF CHATHAM $99–195 B
Deerfield, DEERFIELD INN $97–130 B, $115–155 MAP
Edgartown, CHARLOTTE INN $85–295 CB
Lenox, BLANTYRE $150–525 CB
Lenox, VILLAGE INN, THE $50–155 BB, $110–215 MAP
Nantucket, WAUWINET, THE $220–620
South Egremont, WEATHERVANE INN, THE $110–160 MAP
South Lee, MERRELL TAVERN INN $65–125 B
South Sudbury, LONGFELLOW'S WAYSIDE INN $75
Stockbridge, INN AT STOCKBRIDGE, THE $75–225 B
Vineyard Haven, THORNCROFT INN $99–299 B

Michigan

Coldwater, CHICAGO PIKE INN $75–130 B
Lakeside, PEBBLE HOUSE, THE $90–130 B
Mackinac Island, HOTEL IROQUOIS $65–310
Marshall, MCCARTHY'S BEAR CREEK INN $49–85 B
Petoskey, STAFFORD'S BAY VIEW INN $94–128 B
Saginaw, MONTAGUE INN $55–125 CB

Minnesota

Lanesboro, MRS. B'S HISTORIC LANESBORO INN $53–95 B
New Prague, SCHUMACHER'S NEW PRAGUE HOTEL $104–150

Missouri

Springfield, WALNUT STREET INN $65–95 B

New Hampshire

Conway, DARBY FIELD INN, THE $60–140 B, $110–180 MAP
Etna, MOOSE MOUNTAIN LODGE $100 B, $156 MAP
Francestown, INN AT CROTCHED MOUNTAIN, THE $60–70 B,
                                                $100–120 MAP
Hart's Location, NOTCHLAND INN, THE $13610–166 MAP
Henniker, MEETING HOUSE INN, THE $65–93 B
Jackson, CHRISTMAS FARM INN $136–164 MAP
Jackson, INN AT THORN HILL $110–180 MAP
New London, NEW LONDON INN $70–95 B
North Sutton, FOLLANSBEE INN $70–90 B
Snowville, SNOWVILLAGE INN $70–150 B, $110–190 MAP
Sugar Hill, SUGAR HILL INN $90–105 B, $140–175 MAP
Sunapee, DEXTER'S INN AND TENNIS CLUB $100–140, $125–175 MAP
Temple, BIRCHWOOD INN, THE $55–70 B
West Chesterfield, CHESTERFIELD INN $99–169 B

New Jersey

Cape May, MAINSTAY INN & COTTAGE, THE	$90–175

New Mexico

Santa Fe, INN OF THE ANASAZI	$165–395
Taos, CASA DE LAS CHIMENEAS	$130–150 B
Taos, TAOS INN	$80–125

New York

Amenia, MARSHFIELD	$95–150 B
Blue Mountain Lake, HEDGES, THE	$116–140 MAP
Cazenovia, LINCKLAEN HOUSE	$70–130 CB
Clarence, ASA RANSOM HOUSE	$85–135
Dover Plains, OLD DROVERS INN	$90–170 CB or B
Fredonia, WHITE INN, THE	$59–159 B
Ithaca, ROSE INN, THE	$100–230 B
Millerton, SIMMONS' WAY VILLAGE INN	$115–150 CB, 110–125 MAP
Mumford, GENESEE COUNTRY INN, THE	$80–120 B
Pittsford, OLIVER LOUD'S INN	$115–145 CB
Rhinebeck, BEEKMAN ARMS	$75–99
Saratoga Springs, ADELPHI HOTEL	$65–250 CB

North Carolina

Ashville, RICHMOND HILL INN	$115–275 B
Black Mountain, RED ROCKER INN	$40–65 B
Bryson City, HEMLOCK INN	$110–150 MAP
Chapel Hill, FEARRINGTON HOUSE, THE	$125–215 CB
Clyde, WINDSONG: A MOUNTAIN INN	$80–85 B
Edenton, GRANVILLE QUEEN INN	$85–95 B
Highlands, HIGHLANDS INN-THE OLD EDWARDS INN	$65–100 CB
Pilot Mountain, PILOT KNOB INN	$85–105 B
Saluda, ORCHARD INN, THE	$75–125 B
Valle Crucis, INN AT THE TAYLOR HOUSE, THE	$95–135 B
Valle Crucis, MAST FARM INN	$90–155 MAP

Ohio

Danville, WHITE OAK INN, THE	$60–130 B
Millersburg, INN AT HONEY RUN, THE	$75–150 CB
West Union, MURPHIN RIDGE INN	$75–85

Oklahoma

Guthrie, HARRISON HOUSE	$55–95 CB

Oregon

Ashland, MT. ASHLAND INN	$80–125 B

Gold Beach, TU TU' TUN LODGE $168–200 MAP
Portland, HERON HAUS $95–250 B

Pennsylvania

Ephrata, SMITHTON INN $65–170 B
Fogelsville, GLASBERN $95–200 B, $185–200 MAP
Mercersburg, MERCERSBURG INN, THE $105–175 CB
Orrtanna, HICKORY BRIDGE FARM $75–85 B
Starlight, INN AT STARLIGHT LAKE, THE $85–100 B, $89–154 MAP

Rhode Island

Newport, MELVILLE HOUSE, THE $40–100 B
Newport, WAYSIDE $95–100 B
Wakefield, LARCHWOOD INN $40–90

South Carolina

Beaufort, RHETT HOUSE INN, THE $80–120 B

Texas

Houston, LA COLOMBE D'OR HOTEL AND RESTAURANT $195–250 CB
San Antonio, FAIRMOUNT HOTEL $125–165

Utah

Midway, HOMESTEAD, THE $59–165 CB
Salt Lake City, BRIGHAM STREET INN $75–150 CB

Vermont

Arlington, WEST MOUNTAIN INN $140 MAP
Bridgewater Corners, OCTOBER COUNTRY INN $70–85 B, $105–145 MAP
Chester, INN AT LONG LAST, THE $160 MAP
Chittenden, TULIP TREE INN $120–210 MAP
Dorset, BARROWS HOUSE, THE $160–210 MAP
Dorset, CORNUCOPIA OF DORSET $85–190 B
Fair Haven, VERMONT MARBLE INN $160–190 MAP
Goshen, BLUEBERRY HILL $156–220 MAP
Jamaica, THREE MOUNTAIN INN $100–190 MAP
Lower Waterford, RABBIT HILL INN $88–159 B, $130–190 MAP
Ludlow, GOVERNOR'S INN, THE $180 MAP
Manchester Village, 1811 HOUSE $110–180 B
Manchester, BIRCH HILL INN $100–120 MAP
Newfane, FOUR COLUMNS INN, THE $95–170 B, $195–270 MAP
Pittsfield, INN AT PITTSFIELD, THE $95–130 MAP
Simonsville, ROWELL'S INN $70–90 B, $140–160 MAP
South Newfane, INN AT SOUTH NEWFANE, THE $170–190 MAP
Waitsfield, INN AT THE ROUND BARN FARM, THE $90–130 B

West Dover, INN AT SAWMILL FARM $260–310 MAP
West Townshend, WINDHAM HILL INN $160–180 MAP

Virginia

Alexandria, MORRISON HOUSE $120–230 B
Christianburg, OAKS, THE $65–85 B
Fairfax, BAILIWICK INN $105–225 B
Millboro, FORT LEWIS LODGE $120–MAP
Nellysford, TRILLIUM HOUSE $80–100 B
Orange, HIDDEN INN $79–159 B
Scotsville, HIGH MEADOWS INN $85–165 CB
Staunton, BELLE GRAE INN $55–90 B
Trevilians, PROSPECT HILL $120–160 B, $180–260 MAP
Vesuvius, IRISH GAP INNS $68–98 B
White Post, L'AUBERGE PROVENÇALE $115–165 B

Washington

Bremerton, WILLCOX HOUSE $110–165 B
Coupeville, CAPTAIN WHIDBEY INN, THE $75–175 B
Orcas Island, TURTLEBACK FARM INN $70–150 B
Port Townsend, RAVENSCROFT INN $65–150 B
Poulsbo, MANOR FARM INN $90–125 B
Seaview, SHELBURNE INN, THE $69–100 B

West Virgina

Berkeley Springs, COUNTRY INN, THE $35–145
Charles Town, HILLBROOK INN $120–225 B

Wisconsin

Bayfield, OLD RITTENHOUSE INN $79–179 CB
Fish Creek, WHITE GULL INN, THE $62–126
Sturgeon Bay, WHITE LACE INN $64–145 CB

AP-American Plan
MAP-Modified American Plan
B-Full Breakfast
CB-Continental Breakfast.

et Me Hear From You ...

lease use this page to let me know about your reactions—
ive and negative—to your stay at any of the inns recom-
ded in *Country Inns and Back Roads: North America,* and to
e about the inns you've enjoyed that I may have overlooked.
tear out this page and send your comments to me at the
ess below.

Thanks for your ..., and happy traveling!

Jerry Levitin
1565 Partrick Road
Napa, CA 94558